TOWN AND COUNTRY IN EUROPE, 1300–1800

Edited by

S. R. Epstein

London School of Economics and Political Science

CAMBRIDGE
UNIVERSITY PRESS

PUBLISHED BY THE PRESS SYNDICATE OF THE UNIVERSITY OF CAMBRIDGE
The Pitt Building, Trumpington Street, Cambridge, United Kingdom

CAMBRIDGE UNIVERSITY PRESS
The Edinburgh Building, Cambridge CB2 2RU, UK
40 West 20th Street, New York NY 10011–4211, USA
477 Williamstown Road, Port Melbourne, VIC 3207, Australia
Ruiz de Alarcón 13, 28014 Madrid, Spain
Dock House, The Waterfront, Cape Town 8001, South Africa

http://www.cambridge.org

First published 2001
Reprinted 2003
First paperback edition 2003

Typeset in Plantin 10/12pt   System 3b2   [CE]

A catalogue record for this book is available from the British Library

ISBN 0 521 63341 9 hardback
ISBN 0 521 54804 7 paperback

Contents

Figures

Tables

Notes on the contributors

CARLO MARCO BELFANTI is Associate Professor of Economic History at the University of Brescia. He has published extensively on craft guilds, rural proto-industry and technical change in early modern Italy.

THOMAS BRENNAN is Professor of Early Modern European History at the United States Naval Academy. He is the author of *Public drinking and popular culture in eighteenth-century Paris* (Princeton, 1988) and *Burgundy to Champagne. The wine trade in early modern France* (Baltimore, 1997), which won the Pinkney Prize from the Society for French Historical Studies.

MARKUS CERMAN lectures in Economic and Social History at the University of Vienna. He has edited (with S. C. Ogilvie) *European proto-industrialization* (Cambridge, 1996; German-language edition Vienna, 1994).

S. R. EPSTEIN is Reader in Economic History at the London School of Economics and Political Science. His recent publications include (with G. Haupt, C. Poni and H. Soly), *Guilds, economy and society* (Madrid, 1998) and *Freedom and growth: the rise of states and markets in Europe, 1300–1750* (London, 2000).

JAMES A. GALLOWAY is a researcher at the Centre for Metropolitan History, Institute of Historical Research, University of London. He is currently principal investigator on the project 'Metropolitan market networks *c*.1300–1600', and has published on various aspects of London's regional and national impact in the later middle ages.

PAUL GLENNIE is Senior Lecturer in Human Geography at the University of Bristol. His research interests lie in agrarian change and productivity, urban economies, and histories of consumption, with current work on geographies of early modern wages, and the provision and uses of clock time in medieval and early modern towns and villages.

PETER C. M. HOPPENBROUWERS is Reader in Medieval History at the University of Leiden. His doctoral thesis, published in 1992, examined medieval village communities in the Dutch central river area. He has published extensively on various aspects of the rural history of the Netherlands.

ANDRZEJ JANECZEK is Fellow and Deputy Director of the Institute of Archaeology and Ethnology (formerly Institute of the History of Material Culture), Polish Academy of Sciences, Warsaw. He is the author of a monograph on the Polish–Ruthenian borderland and has published widely on settlement, urbanisation and ethnic relations in the late medieval Polish Commonwealth.

HERBERT KNITTLER is Professor of Economic and Social History at the University of Vienna. His recent publications include *Nutzen, Renten, Erträge* (Vienna, 1989) and *Die europäische Stadt in der frühen Neuzeit. Institutionen, Strukturen, Entwicklungen* (Vienna, 2000).

MARTIN KÖRNER is Professor of Swiss History at the University of Berne; he is currently Vice-President of the Swiss Research Council. His recent publications include (with S. Guex and A. Tanner) *Staatsfinanzierung und Sozialkonflikte (14.–20.Jh.)* (Zurich, 1994) and *Destruction and reconstruction of towns* 3 vols. (Berne, 1999–2000).

BRIGITTE MARIN teaches early modern history at the University of Provence. Formerly of the Ecole Normale Supérieure de Saint-Cloud and member of the Ecole française de Rome, she is the author (with C. Vallat and G. Biondi) of *Naples. Démythifier la ville* (Paris, 1998) and of several articles on the urban and medical history of early modern Naples.

PABLO SÁNCHEZ LEÓN researches on early modern and modern history at the Universidad Autónoma of Madrid. He is the author of *Absolutismo y comunidad. Los orígenes sociales de la guerra de los comuneros de Castilla* (Madrid, 1998).

ROBERT SANDBERG is Assistant Professor in History at the University College of South Stockholm. He is the author of *I slottets skugga. Stockholm och kronan 1599–1620 (In the shadow of the castle. Stockholm and the crown 1599–1620*, Stockholm, 1991) and of articles on the medieval and early modern history of Sweden and the Baltic.

TOM SCOTT is Reader in History at the University of Liverpool. His recent publications include *Regional identity and economic change: the Upper Rhine 1450–1600* (Oxford, 1997), *The peasantries of Europe from the fourteenth to the eighteenth centuries* (London/New York, 1998), and (with P. Ainsworth) *Regions and landscapes: reality and imagination in late medieval and early modern northern Europe* (Berne, 2000).

MARJOLEIN 'T HART is Senior Lecturer in Economic and Social History at the University of Amsterdam. She is the author of *The making of a bourgeois state. War, politics and finance during the Dutch Revolt* (Manchester, 1993) and editor (with J. Jonker and J. L. van Zanden) of *A financial history of the Netherlands* (Cambridge, 1997).

1 Introduction. Town and country in Europe, 1300–1800

S. R. Epstein

'Town and country' is among the most abiding metaphors of economic and social development in the past. Relations between town and country are central to several of the most significant 'grand narratives' in economic history, including the extension of markets, the rise of capitalism, and the growth of modern manufacture. The metaphor's success is partly dependent on its deceptively simple dichotomy, which is apparent in the very etymology of the term 'country': originating in the late Latin *contrata*, meaning 'that which lies opposite', the term subsequently took on in opposition to 'town' the meaning of 'those parts of a region distant from cities or courts'.[1] From its very origin, country came to signify what 'townness' was not – a residual meaning, so to speak, which raises the fundamental problem of defining what a town is.

The considerable geographical and historical variation between towns in terms of size, function (industrial, commercial, administrative and cultural), and political and institutional features, makes clear and unambiguous definitions hard to come by. Most historians have chosen either a demographic or a functional definition depending on the questions they wished to answer. The approach pioneered by E. A. Wrigley, Jan de Vries and Paul Bairoch defines urbanity in strictly demographic terms as centres with more than 5,000 or 10,000 inhabitants.[2] This method uses urban ratios (the proportion of the total population living in towns over a specified threshold) to estimate changes in agricultural productivity, in functional specialisation and in market integration across space and over long stretches of time. It is therefore particularly suited for comparative surveys and first-order generalisations; but what the method gains in consistency and comparability it loses in precision, because a very significant proportion of pre-

[1] See *Oxford English dictionary*, 1st edn, s.v. Town.
[2] E. A. Wrigley, 'Urban growth and agricultural change: England and the Continent in the early modern period', in E. A. Wrigley, *People, cities and wealth: the transformation of traditional society* (Oxford, 1987), pp. 157–93; J. de Vries, *European urbanisation 1500–1800* (London, 1984); P. Bairoch, J. Batou and P. Chèvre, *La Population des villes européennes 800–1850* (Geneva, 1988).

1

modern European towns fell below what are unavoidably arbitrary demographic thresholds.

'The small town was a constant and quintessential feature of the European landscape', it has been said, so much so that in pre-modern Europe 'small towns' accounted for five or more times as many settlements as all other urban centres put together.[3] This was particularly true in the less urbanised European regions north of the Alps and the Pyrenees; but even in countries with more concentrated urban settlements like Castile, Italy and the Low Countries, a large proportion of the population lived in settlements too small to be caught in the mesh of mainstream urban studies. Moreover, far from disappearing after the mid-seventeenth-century crises, the economic and political significance of small towns increased, thanks to their greater adaptability and dynamism compared to larger, better established peers. As Paul Glennie reminds us below, no more than 100 of the 700 or so urban places in England exceeded 5,000 inhabitants as late as 1801. When the evolving character of town–country relations is being addressed, the small towns in closest contact with the rural world cannot therefore be ignored. For this reason, contributors to this volume reject strictly demographic definitions of urbanity and emphasise instead the commercial, manufacturing and administrative functions of settlements with regard to their hinterland and to regional and national urban hierarchies. Any loss in terms of precision – particularly at the lower end of the urban hierarchy where it is notoriously difficult to distinguish small towns from villages – is more than made up for by the number and variety of towns and by the breadth of institutional, political, cultural and economic factors such an approach is able to take into account.

The functional approach privileged in this volume has two further advantages. In the first place, it more accurately represents the extent of the medieval and early modern division of labour between rural and agricultural activities and the manufacturing and service sectors, which were mostly concentrated in towns. Several contributors to this volume deploy this fact to make a positive re-evaluation of the size and contribution of urban industries and services to European economy and society after the Black Death. Thus, the inclusion of functionally urban communities as small as a few hundred inhabitants in England (James Galloway), Switzerland (Martin Körner), and the Austrian–Czech lands (Markus Cerman and Herbert Knittler) raises the estimate of urban levels in these countries from less than 10 per cent to 15–20 per cent;

[3] P. Clark (ed.), *Small towns in early modern Europe* (Cambridge, 1995), p. 1. 'Pre-modern' is defined here somewhat arbitrarily as *c*.1300–1800; reasons for viewing the period in chronological unity are discussed below.

equally, a large proportion of the astonishing 40 per cent urban ratio of late medieval Holland includes the population of small towns at the lower end of the urban hierarchy (Peter Hoppenbrouwers). In chapters 12 and 14, Pablo Sánchez León and Brigitte Marin discuss the implications of similar revisions for regions traditionally viewed as under-urbanised and underdeveloped like Castile, the kingdom of Naples and Sicily where in fact, in the fifteenth and sixteenth centuries, between 20 and 40 per cent of the population lived in centres with urban functions.[4]

These new estimates of average urban levels indicate that by the early fourteenth century the more peripheral European economies were far more commercialised and specialised than previously assumed, and therefore give support to recent, more optimistic assessments of pre-modern economic growth.[5] However, the substantial increase in estimated *absolute* urban ratios in less urbanised regions does not significantly alter the latter's *relative* standing with respect to more urbanised regions; if one includes 'small towns' of a few hundred inhabitants in current urban estimates for Flanders and the more developed regions of Italy, France and southern Germany, their urban ratio rises from 30–40 per cent (estimated using 'traditional' urban thresholds of several thousand inhabitants) to 50–60 per cent or more.

The second advantage of a functional definition is that it raises important comparative questions of both substance and method. Most continental historians, represented in this volume by the chapters on Sweden, Holland, Poland, Austrian–Czech and German lands, Switzerland, Castile and north-central Italy, adopt a legal definition of towns as centres which were granted an official charter of rights and privileges. This appears to make the distinction between town and country (or village) very sharp. English historians instead tend to downplay the significance of legal rights for urban growth, and contrast the more liberal conditions applying in England with those of the rest of Europe. While there is undoubtedly some truth in this distinction, particularly as far as smaller towns are concerned, the contrast is also a consequence of different historiographical traditions. Thus, English historians downplay the fact that English towns continued to seek and defend urban corporate privilege far into the eighteenth century, while Italian historians, as noted by Brigitte Marin, have long neglected southern Italian towns because they lacked the political and institutional privileges of north Italian communes, which the national historiography identified as the

---

[4] For Naples and Sicily, see S. R. Epstein, *Freedom and growth. The rise of states and markets in Europe 1300–1750* (London, 2000), ch. 5.
[5] Ibid., chs. 1–2.

siue qua non of urbanity.[6] Equally, while continental historians may have sometimes exaggerated the ability of more 'coercive' urban systems to enforce political privilege, an older English historiographical tradition also emphasised the intensity of governmental intervention and of corporate and institutional rent-seeking in and by towns up at least to the mid-seventeenth century.[7] The interaction between coercive and market forces was evidently more complex and multi-layered than a simple institutional dichotomy between England and continental Europe implies.

Given these premises, contributors to the present volume were asked to consider in particular the nature of the institutionalised power of town over country and its regional differences. In doing so, they also address relations between towns and the state in a period when the states' fiscal and political demands were increasing, their administrative reach was growing, and their regulatory pretensions were becoming more burdensome, while at the same time they were challenging ancient privileges and sources of rent-seeking. The focus throughout this volume is on the evolving structural constraints within pre-modern political economies, not only because that is where the greater part of past and current debates has been concentrated but also because it is where institutional differences between states were felt most keenly. Several contributions are explicitly comparative, and all adopt a long-term perspective, which frequently straddles the traditional chronological demarcation between medieval and early modern eras, and emphasises the similarities and structural continuities between the two. The purpose of this introduction is to facilitate such a comparative exercise by briefly retracing the historiographical background, spelling out the regional and national analogies and contrasts, and suggesting future avenues of research.

The division of labour between town and country

Ever since the mid-eighteenth century, when the French Physiocrats developed a model of growth centred on agricultural primacy, and

---

[6] For England, see P. Clark, 'Changes in the pattern of English small towns in the early modern period', in A. Maczak and C. Smout (eds.), *Gründung und Bedeutung kleinerer Städte in nördlichen Europa der frühen Neuzeit* (Wiesbaden, 1991), pp. 67–84; for a recent restatement of the north Italian viewpoint, see M. Berengo, *L'Europa delle città. Il volto della società urbana europea tra Medioevo ed età moderna* (Turin, 1999).

[7] See e.g. E. Lipson, *The economic history of England*, 3 vols. (London, 1945–8); recently H. Swanson, *Medieval British towns* (Houndmills and New York, 1999), chs. 3–4, has once again underlined the significance of political and institutional influences on urban economies; there is, however, still a dearth of modern studies of local and state intervention and regulation of trade (J. Chartres, *Internal trade in England 1500–1700* (London and Basingstoke, 1977), ch. 5).

Adam Smith developed the alternative view that towns were the major sources of institutional innovation in traditional societies, debates on town and country in the pre-modern economy have revolved around two questions. First, what were the 'prime movers' of economic growth? Second, what was the balance in the growth process between market competition and political coercion? The two questions can be summed up as one: could peasants generate markets autonomously, or did they need to be pushed, that is, coerced through asymmetrical power relations, or pulled into trade through price incentives? To this question historians have offered three answers, defined by Langton and Hoppe some years ago as the town-based model, the country-based model, and the specialisation model.[8]

The classical or town-based model which held sway until recent years identified towns and urban industry and commerce unequivocally with urbanity, civilisation and economic and social progress. It was adhered to by the fathers of modern social science and by many of the most influential economic historians of the past century. Thus, Adam Smith wrote how 'the silent and insensible operation of foreign commerce and manufactures gradually' effected the dissolution of feudal mores and institutions;[9] Marx, while declaring robustly that 'the foundation of every division of labour . . . is the separation of town from country',[10] went on to dismiss the peasantry as 'a vast mass . . . almost self-sufficient . . . [which] directly produces the major part of its consumption and thus acquires its means of life more through exchange with nature than in intercourse with society . . . much as potatoes in a sack form a sack of potatoes';[11] while Max Weber saw the medieval European city as 'inseparably linked as one of the crucial factors' to the rise of modern capitalism and the modern state.[12] Following in their footsteps, Henri Pirenne and Fernand Braudel elevated the figure of the urban-

---

[8] J. Langton and G. Hoppe, *Town and country in the development of early modern western Europe* (Norwich, 1983).

[9] A. Smith, *An inquiry into the nature and causes of the wealth of nations*, ed. E. Cannan (Chicago, 1976), p. 437. On Smith's discussion of 'town and country', see M. Berg, 'Political economy and the principles of manufacture 1700–1800', in M. Berg, P. Hudson and M. Sonenscher (eds.), *Manufacture in town and country before the factory* (Cambridge, 1983), pp. 33–60.

[10] K. Marx, *Capital*, transl. B. Fowkes, 3 vols. (Harmondsworth, 1976–81), vol. I, pp. xii, 4; see also K. Marx and F. Engels, *The German ideology*, in *Collected works* (London, 1973), vol. V, pp. 19–20: 'the greatest division of mental and material labour is the separation of town and country'.

[11] K. Marx, *The Eighteenth Brumaire of Louis Napoleon*, in *Collected works* (London, 1979), vol. XI, p. 187.

[12] M. Weber, *Economy and society*, ed. G. Roth and C. Wittich, 2 vols. (Berkeley, Los Angeles and London, 1978), vol. II, p. 1323.

based, international merchant to the role of avatar and midwife of modern capitalism.[13]

The economic model underlying these descriptions is dualistic. Towns, which are generally identified with their commercial elites, are defined as the 'advanced' sector relaying capital, information, technological and institutional innovation to a 'backward' or 'traditional' countryside dominated by a quasi-natural peasant economy. The commercial influence of towns acts as a 'solvent' of rural self-sufficiency, idiocy and inertia. By destroying feudal property rights in the countryside, urban trade created the landless proletariat needed for urban manufacture, invigorated agricultural productivity and reduced the costs of food and raw materials; as M. M. Postan famously put it, medieval towns were 'non-feudal islands in a feudal sea'.[14] The 1950s debate on the 'transition from feudalism to capitalism' between Paul Sweezy and Maurice Dobb centred on Sweezy's similar assumption – based upon Pirenne's influential work – that towns and commerce were 'external' to the feudal economy and that they brought about its capitalist transformation.[15] Braudel's understanding of the role of towns was similarly coloured, although he also recognised that towns could sometimes act more ambiguously.[16]

During the 1970s the dominant town-based dualism came under attack from two new 'meta-theories' of the capitalist transition, Robert Brenner's theory of agrarian capitalism and Franklin Mendels's theory of proto-industrialisation.[17] Both harked back to the Physiocratic claim that the most salient economic development was to be found in the countryside, and depicted towns as parasitical consumers of 'feudal

---

[13] H. Pirenne, *Economic and social history of medieval Europe*, transl. I. E. Clegg (London, 1947); F. Braudel, *Civilisation and capitalism*, vol. II: *The wheels of commerce*, transl. S. Roberts (London, 1982).

[14] M. M. Postan, *The medieval economy and society* (Harmondsworth, 1975), p. 212.

[15] R. H. Hilton (ed.), *The transition from feudalism to capitalism* (London, 1976). The 'centre–periphery' metaphor at the heart of Immanuel Wallerstein's world systems theory describes a similar 'dual economy' in which commercially and industrially advanced 'towns' control and exploit backward and agrarian 'countries' (I. M. Wallerstein, *The modern world-system*, vol. I: *Capitalist agriculture and the origins of the world-economy in the sixteenth century* (New York, 1974)).

[16] F. Braudel, *Civilisation and capitalism*, vol. I: *The structures of everyday life: the limits of the possible*, transl. M. Kochan and S. Roberts (London, 1982), ch. 1.

[17] R. Brenner, 'Agrarian class structure and economic development in pre-industrial Europe', *Past and Present* 70 (1976), 30–75, restated (with some change in emphasis) in R. Brenner, 'The agrarian roots of European capitalism', *Past and Present* 97 (1982), 16–113; F. Mendels, 'Proto-industrialisation: the first phase of the industrialisation process?', *Journal of Economic History* 32 (1972), 241–61. The 1970s witnessed a proliferation of theories of pre-modern growth, including Wallerstein's 'world system theory' (see note 15) and Douglass North's property rights approach (D. C. North and R. P. Thomas, *The rise of the western world* (Cambridge, 1973)).

surplus' which offered no positive stimulus, and as rent-seekers which protected their traditional industrial monopolies against unfettered rural competition. However, at this point Brenner and Mendels parted ways. Brenner, who followed the town-based model and argued that peasants were *not* the avatars of capitalism because peasant agricultural supply was inelastic, at the same time ignored the role of urban manufacture and rural proto-industry in tune with his dismissal of the industrial and service sector's contributions to pre-modern economic growth.[18] Not surprisingly, Brenner's work concentrated on poorly urbanised countries like England, France and east-central Europe and had little to say about the economically more dynamic, highly urbanised regions of Holland, Flanders, southern Germany and north-central Italy.

The contribution of Mendels' and his successors' proto-industrial theory to town–country debates was more positive. First, the theory helped mitigate the singularly optimistic views of urban-centred models of development by focusing attention on the negative and coercive aspects of urban policy – particularly but not solely guild-inspired – towards upstart proto-industrial manufacture in the countryside. This had the further effect of highlighting the considerable institutional variation in town–country relations and opened the way for more rigorous cross-regional comparisons. The insight, derived from proto-industrial theory, that town–country relations were shaped differently between regions and over time is a central tenet of the present volume. Secondly, the strong emphasis on the regional dimensions of proto-industry contributed to a change in focus from the interaction between individual towns and their hinterland, to the broader context of regional and national urban systems. This change in focus constitutes one of the major methodological advances for the analysis of town–country relations over the past three decades, and underlies the increased use by social and economic historians of the tools of urban and historical geographers who focus by training on spatial interaction. Sensitive usage of concepts like central places, urban hierarchies and networks and von Thünen rings – the latter particularly in evidence in the chapters on England by Galloway and Glennie – reveals patterns in resource allocation for which more direct evidence is unavailable, and offers answers to several central questions raised by the present volume, about the overall impact of proto-industrial activities on the urban sector, about the

---

[18] The influential proto-industrial theory of Peter Kriedte, Hans Medick and Jürgen Schlumbohm similarly stated that peasants took up proto-industrial activities only if they owned insufficient land to achieve self-sufficiency (P. Kriedte, H. Medick and J. Schlumbohm, *Industrialisation before industrialisation: rural industry in the genesis of capitalism*, transl. B. Schempp, with contributions from H. Kisch and F. L. Mendels (Cambridge, 1981)).

development of markets and market integration, and about the distributional consequences of the rise of capital cities.

Despite their differences, both the older town-based approach and proto-industrial theory presented models of unbalanced growth in which the advanced urban or rural sector develops at a disproportionate rate to pull the more backward sector to a higher growth path. Both approaches focused on towns as the main source of dynamism or inertia, but stressed only one term of the antinomy and ignored the positive, dynamic aspects of the division of labour between town and country. Both took the existence, character and co-ordination of pre-modern markets for granted, and did not question how markets emerged in the first place or how different institutional constellations might lead to different economic outcomes. Both models also assumed that peasants had to be coerced into regular production for the market, despite considerable evidence that commercial farming and rural manufacture were standard peasant activities since at least the later middle ages (as discussed by this volume's contributions on England, Holland, Germany and the Austro-Czech lands).

Dissatisfaction with models that could not easily explain urban–rural interaction led, during the 1980s, to a new emphasis on towns as co-ordinating centres for rural trade and as concentrated sources of demand that stimulated agrarian specialisation.[19] The shift in focus was first apparent in England, where economic historians grappling with the first industrial transition have often been more sensitive to developmental and dynamic models, and where the influence of historical geography has been felt more keenly. The new interest in towns as centres of demand and commercial distribution within a regional or national framework, foreshadowed by work on proto-industrialisation, also reflected a broader historiographical shift away from the neo-Ricardian and neo-Malthusian, pessimistic interpretations of the pre-modern economy that had dominated post-war historiography, towards models of Smithian growth which placed more emphasis on slow, incremental change through functional specialisation and the division of labour within growing markets. Thus, in an influential essay, E. A. Wrigley argued that the huge growth of early modern London created a source of concentrated demand for rural produce that was 'probably the most important single factor in engendering agricultural improvement' before the Industrial Revolution and which stimulated the rise of an integrated national market.[20]

[19] Langton and Hoppe, *Town and country*, p. 36.
[20] E. A. Wrigley, 'A simple model of London's importance in changing English society and economy, 1650–1750', in Wrigley, *People, cities and wealth*, pp. 133–55.

Elsewhere, Wrigley noted that in a closed market with insignificant agricultural imports, both the level and the rate of change of urban populations depend on the size of the agricultural surplus available to the non-agrarian sector, and proceeded to use this insight to estimate agricultural and industrial productivity over time and across countries.[21] Wrigley recognised that urban levels did not precisely reflect the division of labour between town and country because of the presence of proto-industrial and service activities in the countryside; however, his model of town–country specialisation assumed that the size of the urban population reflected the level of agricultural productivity, and that it would respond quite smoothly to changes in agrarian output. However, this use of pre-industrial rates of urbanisation to infer the technological capacity to feed urban populations has recently been questioned. Drawing on research on ancien regime France, George Grantham has suggested that the technology available to peasants was capable of producing a large enough surplus to carry an urban ratio of about 60 per cent, twice to three times the levels actually achieved in eighteenth-century France. Since the agricultural technology available at that time did not differ significantly from that documented for several European regions during the thirteenth century, Grantham concludes that low agricultural productivity could not be held responsible for the low rates of urbanisation in Europe between 1300 and the Industrial Revolution.[22]

An explanation of European patterns of urbanisation and of the division of labour between town and country before the Industrial Revolution must be set against the available evidence summarised in Table 1.1, which lists urban ratios above an urban threshold of 5,000 in the period from 1500 to 1750 according to modern national boundaries. Although national aggregates disguise significant regional differences and must therefore be treated with caution, they nevertheless offer a credible long-run measure of *relative* national performance (as noted previously, the exclusion of small towns only affects absolute measures of urbanisation).

The data plausibly indicate four broad conclusions. First, the only country ever to come close to achieving its full urban potential of 60 per

[21] Wrigley, 'Urban growth'; E. A. Wrigley, 'Parasite or stimulus: the town in a pre-industrial economy', in P. Abrams and E. A. Wrigley (eds.), *Towns in societies. Essays in economic history and historical sociology* (Cambridge, 1978), pp. 295–309.

[22] G. W. Grantham, 'Divisions of labour: agricultural productivity and occupational specialisation in pre-industrial France', *Economic History Review*, 2nd ser., 46 (1993), 478–502; G. W. Grantham, 'Espaces privilégiés. Productivité agraire et zones d'approvisionnement des villes dans l'Europe préindustrielle', *Annales HSS* 52 (1997), 695–725; G. W. Grantham, 'Contra Ricardo: on the macroeconomics of pre-industrial economies', *European Review of Economic History* 3 (1999), 199–232.

Table 1.1. *Rates of urbanisation in Western Europe, 1500–1750 (percentages)*

	1500	1600	1700	1750
Austria–Hungary–Czechoslovakia	4.8	4.9	4.9	7.3
Belgium	28.0	29.3	22.2	22.2
England and Wales	7.9	10.8	16.9	27.7
France	8.8	10.8	12.3	12.7
Germany	8.2	8.5	7.7	8.8
Italy	22.1	22.6	22.6	22.5
Netherlands	29.5	34.7	38.9	36.3
Portugal	15.0	16.7	18.5	17.5
Scandinavia (other)	1.5	6.9	6.5	8.6
Scotland	7.4	7.9	7.1	10.2
Spain	18.4	21.3	20.3	21.4
Sweden	1.7	1.2	3.8	4.6
Switzerland	6.8	5.5	5.9	7.7
Mean	12.3	14.6	15.1	16.2
Coefficient of variation (%)	76.7	73.4	70.0	59.6

Source: Bairoch, Batou and Chèvre, *Population.*

cent as defined by Grantham was the Dutch Republic; even England was still seriously under-urbanised in 1750, despite its remarkable spurt of growth after 1600. Second, between 1500 and 1750 only Sweden, France, and England and Wales experienced uninterrupted urban growth, while elsewhere towns either stagnated, as in Portugal, Spain, Italy, Switzerland and Germany, or declined, as in the southern Low Countries (modern Belgium). Third, cross-country rankings and absolute levels of urbanisation were extremely stable over time and the rate of dispersion around the mean remained a high 73–76 per cent until 1700, suggesting that there was little pressure for international convergence. Although urbanisation began to converge quite rapidly after 1700, the rate of dispersion in 1750 was still close to 60 per cent and the only significant change was England's rise to the top rankings.[23] The evidence therefore appears to contradict the common hypothesis that more urbanised societies will grow faster thanks to economies of scale and higher concentrations of human capital;[24] however, barring the important

[23] If the United Kingdom is excluded, the coefficient of variation of urban ratios was 0.64, 0.65, 0.65 and 0.56 respectively in 1500, 1600, 1700 and 1750. The process of convergence between 1700 and 1750 was thus broadly European.

[24] See W. C. Wheaton and H. Shishido, 'Urban concentration, agglomeration economies, and the level of economic development', *Economic Development and Cultural Change* 30 (1981–2), 1, 17–30; P. Krugman, *Geography and trade* (Cambridge, MA, 1991); E. L. Glaeser, H. D. Kallal, J. A. Scheinkman and A. Shleifer, 'Growth in cities', *Journal of Political Economy* 100 (1992), 6, 1126–52; J. Mokyr, 'Urbanization, technological progress, and economic history', in H. Giersch (ed.), *Urban agglomeration and economic growth* (Berlin and New York, 1995), pp. 3–34.

exception of the Dutch Republic, it also seems to contravene the alternative view that less developed countries tend to catch up with the economic leaders as a result of market integration and technological diffusion. Fourth, since none of the important changes in national economic performance during the period – notably the relative decline of Italy and the southern Netherlands, the rise followed by the decline of Spain, and the ascent from peripheral to core status of England – is adequately reflected in the urban data, we are forced to conclude that urbanisation is a remarkably poor index and predictor of economic development at this time. For example, in the early sixteenth century the urban ratio was four times higher in Spain than in England and Spain continued to be more urbanised in 1750 despite the intervening changes in economic performance in the two countries; conversely, in 1700 countries with very different economic performances like Castile and the southern Netherlands had nearly identical urban ratios.

The lack of correlation between a country's urban ratio and its long-run economic performance confirms Philip Hoffman's recent demonstration that in early modern France urban size bore little relation to agricultural productivity.[25] Grantham has argued that the main constraint on urban size lay in the structure of agricultural labour markets, in particular in the efficiency with which they met surges in demand for wage labour during the grain and wine harvests. In principle, seasonal labourers could have lived in towns for much of the year and could have migrated to the countryside temporarily at harvest time, but in practice they were held back by high information and transport costs; to earn high harvesting wages, they had to reside permanently in the countryside where, during the rest of the year, they could engage in proto-industrial activities. While less productive than urban manufacture, rural proto-industry persisted because inefficient agricultural labour markets raised migration costs for peasants who might have wished to move to the towns.[26]

To attribute the discrepancies between actual and potential levels of urbanisation, the degree of regional variation, and the lack of inter-

[25] P. Hoffman, *Growth in a traditional society. The French countryside, 1450–1815* (Princeton, 1996), pp. 170–84; see also Mokyr, 'Urbanization', p. 11.

[26] See above, n. 22. For discussions about the effects of labour markets on urbanisation, see also J. L. van Zanden, *The rise and decline of Holland's economy. Merchant capitalism and the labour market* (Manchester, 1993), pp. 19–43; S. R. Epstein, 'The peasantries of Italy 1350–1750', in T. Scott (ed.), *The peasantries of Europe from the fourteenth to the eighteenth century* (London, 1998), pp. 97–8, 108. The reasons for persistence of dispersed proto-industry are explained along Grantham's lines by K. L. Sokoloff and D. Dollar, 'Agricultural seasonality and the organization of manufacturing in early industrial economies: the contrast between England and the United States', *Journal of Economic History* 57 (1997), 288–321.

national convergence simply to high transport and information costs is nevertheless implausible. The remarkable stability of urban ratios over a period of nearly three centuries and their weak correlation with economic performance suggest that urbanisation in most countries was trapped in low-level institutional equilibria determined by non-market forces. If so, this conclusion requires taking a closer look at the institutional factors that determined the towns' role as central places, about which the specialisation model of town–country relations has little to say.

The specialisation model assumes that urban demand generates its own agricultural supply, along the lines set out by the nineteenth-century German economist Johann Heinrich von Thünen and utilised in this volume by James Galloway, Tom Scott and Marco Belfanti. Thünen suggested that the main variable influencing agricultural supply will be the producer's transport costs to the urban market. Transport costs determine the producer price; at each price, the producer selects the crop and method of production which offer the highest return. For heuristic purposes Thünen presumed the existence of a central urban market, disregarded all transaction costs except the cost of transport to the market, and postulated that peasants would trade willingly and spontaneously on the urban market.[27] Thünen's deliberate abstraction is, however, inappropriate for medieval and early modern societies in which search, information, co-ordination and enforcement costs were extremely high and tariffs and politically sanctioned market power were ubiquitous.

The high transaction costs typical of pre-modern societies meant that many markets were too 'thin' for prices to signal supply and demand unambiguously.[28] Asymmetric information and poor co-ordination between producers and consumers created mismatches and reduced the scope of markets and trade. The resulting low-level economic equilibria could only be broken by external agents who were in a position to enforce new, more efficient 'rules of the game'.[29] One such agent was

[27] J. H. von Thünen, *Von Thünen's isolated state*, ed. P. Hall, transl. C. M. Wartenberg (Oxford, 1966), includes only Part I of Thünen's *magnum opus*, which has yet to be fully translated into English. See M. Nerlove, 'Von Thünen's model of the dual economy', in A. Maunder and A. Valdés (eds.), *Agriculture and governments in an interdependent world* (Aldershot and Brookfield, 1989), pp. 96–109.

[28] Grantham, 'Contra Ricardo'. For applications of Thünen's model to pre-modern agrarian economies, see also C. Reinicke, *Agrarkonjunktur und technisch-organisatorisch Innovationen auf dem Agrarsektor im Spiegel niederrheinischer Pachtverträge 1200–1600* (Cologne and Vienna, 1989); J. Bieleman, 'Dutch agriculture in the Golden Age, 1570–1660', *Economic and Social History in the Netherlands* 4 (1992), 159–84.

[29] The consequences of co-ordination failures in pre-modern economies are discussed in Epstein, *Freedom and growth*. An equilibrium occurs when no individual agent stands to

the pre-modern town, which offered economies of scale in production and lower transport costs by concentrating production, services and demand. The town's development as a market co-ordinator, however, was restricted by both physical and institutional factors that are central to arguments in this book. Urban co-ordination could be hampered by high distances and low population densities, as in Poland (Andrzej Janeczek) and Sweden (Robert Sandberg); it could be limited by intense political and institutional fragmentation which raised barriers to trade and made inter-urban agreements more costly, as in Switzerland (Körner), Germany (Scott) and the Austro-Czech lands (Cerman and Knittler); or it could be restricted by hostile territorial monarchies or feudal lords, as occurred nearly everywhere in Europe including England, as both Galloway and Glennie remark.

The pattern of urbanisation in peripheral countries like early modern Sweden and the Polish Commonwealth described by Sandberg and Janeczek follows a political model that had been established several centuries earlier in the western European core. Medieval and early modern European towns did not emerge spontaneously from the natural operations of the market, but were the product of deliberate acts of political, legal and economic coercion. They were established (or in the case of Roman foundations, renewed) by monarchs and feudal lords; they gained economic, administrative, or political centrality by exercising chartered rights over a rural territory; and they became collective lords in their own right through the conscious usurpation of feudal power, what Max Weber termed 'non-legitimate domination'.

The evidence presented in this book suggests that the major factor determining a country's level of urbanisation between the fifteenth century and the Industrial Revolution was the extent of urban jurisdictional coercion and territorial influence established during the previous three centuries. However, because patterns of urban coercion were shaped by the strength of countervailing monarchical and feudal powers, they were also regionally very diverse. Thus towns in the Low Countries, northern Italy and central and southern Castile, where the process of the Reconquista gave cities strong rural prerogatives, displayed considerable administrative and economic independence and were therefore very large (or could rapidly increase in size when economic circumstances changed in their favour, as in Holland during the fifteenth century). By contrast, towns in northern Spain, England, Habsburg east-central Europe, the Polish Commonwealth and Sweden,

gain by defecting if the other agents stick to their actions, and is therefore self-enforcing.

which had to contend with strong monarchs or powerful feudal estates, were on average rather small.[30]

Regional comparisons of this kind must grapple not only with the complexity of local circumstances but with the fact that in most of the 'core' European regions, and in some notable 'peripheral' ones like England, most of the basic institutions framing town–country relations were already established around 1300. Nevertheless, the most plausible reason why territorial coercion by towns showed positive returns to scale seems to be that it gave urban elites the security and financial incentives to invest in the physical infrastructure (roads and military safety) and in the institutional framework (law courts, unified measurements, and co-ordinated tariffs) which were needed to lower the costs of town–country trade and to establish the town's role as a service and manufacturing hub. Coercion provided peasants with stable markets and reduced urban supply costs, lowered the risks of investment in craft training and manufacture by giving artisans a secure outlet in the countryside, and raised the benefits of urban immigration. The strong positive correlation between urban institutional power and economic development in Italy and Flanders before the Black Death shows that urban-based coercion was at that time more capable of mobilising resources and stimulating agrarian development than its institutional alternatives.[31] However, the comparatively poor economic performance of 'urban coercive' regions like Italy and Flanders after 1500, and of Castile and the German-speaking lands after 1600, suggests that coercive modes of growth had reached their limits and were beginning to run into diminishing returns, as the benefits of market interventionism were outweighed by rent-seeking opportunities.[32] The northern Netherlands, examined here by Hoppenbrouwers and 't Hart, offer the only qualified exception to this rule: there, the towns' attempts to develop into coercive city-states during the late middle ages were frustrated by an institutional frame-work that promoted inter-urban and urban–rural competition.

[30] South-eastern England could, however, benefit from proximity to the 'urban-coercive' conurbation stretching from the old Burgundian lands of Flanders, Holland and northern France into the German Rhineland. See B. M. S. Campbell, 'The sources of tradable surpluses: English agricultural exports 1250–1350', in N. Hybel and A. Landen (eds.), *The emergence of large-scale trade in northern Europe 1150–1400* (Toronto, 2000).

[31] J. R. Hicks, *A theory of economic history* (Oxford, 1969); H. Spruyt, *The sovereign state and its competitors. An analysis of systems change* (Princeton, 1994); S. R. Epstein, 'The rise and fall of Italian city-states', in M. H. Hansen (ed.), *City-state cultures in world history* (Copenhagen, 2000).

[32] For a recent discussion of Flemish towns and urbanisation, see P. Stabel, *Dwarfs among giants. The Flemish urban network in the late middle ages* (Leuven and Apeldoorn, 1997).

Towns and the rise of the modern state

Twentieth-century debates and controversies on the interaction between town and country have therefore tended to underscore one or the other term in a dialectical relation between coercion and freedom in markets. Political coercion was necessary to establish markets in the first place and to fix the 'rules of the game' that overcame incomplete information and free riding and established commercial security. Once the rudiments of markets were established, however, the laws of demand and supply had to be allowed into play; if legal privilege and rent-seeking were allowed free rein, the result was simply market fragmentation, inefficient resource allocation, and dead-weight costs.

Under the fragmented political conditions prevailing in the high middle ages, coercion could be exercised equally by territorial monarchs, local feudal lords, or towns. Towns, however, seem to have provided the most effective solution because their elites had the strongest incentives and the best economic, administrative and political skills to co-ordinate reciprocally beneficial trading relations with the countryside. Where power was more centralised, as in medieval and early modern England and Sweden, the monarchs' fear of turning towns into rival power bases led them to set strict limits to urban prerogatives. On the other hand, political centralisation benefited towns by establishing shared commercial rules and legal parameters for town–country relations across the whole country.

In England, however, where political centralisation was achieved several centuries before Sweden, a fully unified institutional framework could be taken largely for granted already by the fourteenth century and thereafter became – at least for modern historians – largely invisible. Where, by contrast, political authority remained parcellised and towns could not achieve independence, as in early modern Castile, Poland and in part in the Austro-Czech lands, towns benefited neither from coercion nor from an institutionally integrated market. Habsburg Castile and the Polish Commonwealth were in many ways at the opposite ends of the institutional spectrum, epitomising 'absolutist' centralisation and 'federal' autonomy respectively; nevertheless, town–state relations in the two countries during the sixteenth and seventeenth centuries followed a similar trajectory typified by vast numbers of new town foundations. Despite the fact that town settlements in Castile were promoted largely by the crown, whereas they were generally initiated by feudal lords in the Polish lands, Janeczek and Sánchez León's descriptions of their effects are analogous. In both countries, urban fortunes were defined more by political than by market success: extensive economic privileges protected new towns from market competition, created incentives for rent-seeking, and caused institutional and commercial fragmentation.

Even where the town exercised state power itself, as in late medieval Tuscany and the early modern Venetian state discussed by Belfanti, political and institutional interaction between towns and state power set the balance between coercion and markets. Most early modern states were composed of a patchwork of overlapping, competing or ranked jurisdictions, rights and 'liberties' which rulers had to come to terms and bargain with. Many of those rights and liberties were vested in towns, and many of them defined the towns' relations with their rural hinterland. The process of negotiating and redefining such rights, and the rebellions and unrest triggered by a breakdown in negotiations when the state's demands were deemed too intrusive, are an integral part of the history of early modern states and markets. They figure prominently in the chapters on the Dutch Republic, Castile and the Italian Mezzogiorno.

Underlying these discussions is an important debate led by Charles Tilly, Wim Blockmans and others on the role of pre-modern towns in European state formation. According to them, different trajectories of European state formation resulted from a fundamental conflict of interests between urban 'capitalists', who benefited from open travel and communication and wished to remain politically unencumbered, and 'coercive' monarchs, who milked the capital-rich towns for taxes to achieve full sovereignty within clear political boundaries. Urban capitalism could therefore only flourish beyond the reach of the more powerful monarchies where towns were strong and states weak.[33]

Tilly and Blockmans recognise that relations between states and towns also rested upon a bargaining process based upon the late medieval principle of 'no taxation without representation'; yet the dichotomy they draw hides more than it reveals. It appears to be contradicted by the evidence that strong political autonomy *hindered* urban growth in early modern Italy, Castile, Flanders and Germany; it also underestimates the complex articulation between the economic functions of pre-modern towns and their political and institutional powers. Urban economies relied to varying degrees on forms of rural coercion and on their roles as political, administrative or religious centres within

---

[33] C. Tilly and W. P. Blockmans (eds.), *Cities and the rise of states in Europe, A.D. 1000 to 1800* (Boulder, CO, 1994). Following Max Weber, *Economy and society*, and Otto Hintze, *The historical essays of Otto Hintze*, ed. F. Gilbert (New York, 1975), Perry Anderson in *Lineages of the absolutist state* (London, 1974) similarly argues that the 'parcellisation of sovereignty' and 'free towns' were preconditions for European capitalism.

urban hierarchies framed and articulated by the state. Early modern towns frequently benefited from state growth, be it directly, as in peripheral and under-urbanised countries like Sweden (Sandberg), the Polish Commonwealth (Janeczek) or Habsburg Castile (Sánchez León), where rulers actively supported old towns and founded new ones, or indirectly, and perhaps more significantly, through state influence over the political geography of trade and markets – in Holland (Hoppenbrouwers, 't Hart), where actions by the provincial government to limit individual towns' pretensions may have hurt individual towns in the short term, but benefited the entire urban sector over the longer run; in Austria (Cerman and Knittler), where the monarchy protected royal towns against feudal offensives; in Germany (Scott), where territorial princes mediated between urban manufactures and proto-industries at the regional level; in Switzerland (Körner), where the urban republics and their allied regions got payments from Swiss mercenary forces to pay off their debts; or in England (Galloway, Glennie), where a highly centralised monarchy dispensed justice and political stability to all.

While states did not hesitate to punish towns for political insubordination – witness the penalties meted out to the rebellious Flemish cities during the regency of Maximilian I of Austria (1482–94) and to Castilian cities after the revolt of the Comuneros (1520–1)[34] – for most towns the hypothetical city-state alternative to monarchical rule was not necessarily much better. For example, despite the fact that towns paid lower taxes than the countryside under virtually all constitutional regimes including monarchies, the chapters on Castile, Italy, southern Germany and Holland suggest that city-states with the authority to tax exploited the small and medium-sized towns under their control far more ruthlessly than monarchs. Nor did towns left to their own devices work particularly well together. Failure to co-operate effectively and durably ultimately led to the collapse of urban federations like the north European Hansa and of territorial republics like Florentine Tuscany; the lack of urban co-ordination caused the failure of several concerted revolts during the later middle ages and of the Neapolitan revolution of 1647;[35] while deep-seated and justified suspicion of their peers explains

[34] See M. Boone, 'Destroying and reconstructing the city. The inculcation and arrogation of princely power in the Burgundian–Habsburg Netherlands (14th–16th centuries)', in M. Gosman, A. Vanderjagt and J. Veenstra (eds.), *The propagation of power in the medieval West* (Groningen, 1997), pp. 1–33; S. Haliczer, *The Comuneros of Castile. The forging of a revolution 1475–1521* (Madison, 1981).

[35] For urban failure to co-operate, see Spruyt, *The sovereign state*; Epstein, 'The rise and fall'. For failed urban rebellions, see above, note 34; G. Chittolini, *Città, comunità e feudi negli stati dell'Italia centro-settentrionale (XIV–XVI secolo)* (Milan, 1996), ch. 9; R. Villari, *La rivolta antispagnola a Napoli. Le origini (1585–1647)* (Bari, 1976).

why the Dutch cities chose a town with no political or commercial powers like The Hague as the Republic's capital, and why their underlying conflicts of interest could turn into a debilitating institutional deadlock after the end of the wars with Spain.[36] Underlying these political failures was the towns' ingrained hostility towards voluntary co-ordination.

In counterpoise to one of this book's central themes, that of the rise and consolidation of more complex and integrated urban hierarchies and networks which reflected the growth of market integration and functional specialisation, can be found the description of the many institutional obstacles to market integration and specialisation arising from the towns themselves. Not least among such obstacles were urban jurisdictional claims over trade and manufacture in the countryside. Thus, towns in Holland, Castile, Habsburg central Europe and elsewhere systematically opposed the creation of new rural markets and fairs after the Black Death; Italian, German, Swiss, Dutch and French towns protected their supplies of grain and raw materials by setting up staples and elaborate commercial regulations; and virtually everywhere, towns resisted concessions of jurisdictional prerogatives to 'new towns' which challenged their traditional primacy. In some regions, most notably in Holland but also in parts of north and central Germany, urban pretensions were neutralised by a competitive institutional framework; but in the many regions where towns could exercise their claims with near impunity, or where their claims were matched by equally strong counter-claims by rent-seeking feudal lords as in the Austrian, Polish and Castilian lands, the long-term economic damage could be severe.

Institutional and market particularism took many forms. In Castile, the towns' strong jurisdictional rights enhanced their centrality in the context of their rural hinterlands and sustained a period of strong urban growth during the 'long' sixteenth century; as Sánchez León demonstrates, however, each town could act as a local monopolist and had few incentives to co-operate with its neighbours, a fact which hindered regional integration and urban specialisation. The Castilian monarchy, unable to challenge the cities' prerogatives, exacerbated the problem by negotiating directly with individual towns (which undermined urban collaboration and solidarity at the regional and national levels), and by creating new chartered towns out of existing urban territories (which further fragmented regional and national markets).[37] In the Polish

---

[36] In addition to chapter 4 below, see M. 't Hart, 'Intercity rivalry and the making of the Dutch state', in Tilly and Blockmans, *Cities and the rise of states*, pp. 196–217.

[37] For the debate on Castilian urbanisation and the role of Madrid, see also I. del Val Valdivieso, 'Urban growth and royal interventionism in late medieval Castile', *Urban History* 24 (1997), 129–40; J. E. Gelabert, 'Il declino della rete urbana nella Castiglia dei secoli XVI–XVIII', *Cheiron* 6 (1989–90), 9–45; P. Sánchez León, 'El campo en la

Commonwealth and the Austro-Czech lands, towns and monarchy were politically weaker and the initiative to found competing market centres and 'demesne towns' came directly from the feudal aristocracy; the institutional effects on market integration were, however, analogous. Similar tensions or conflicts between towns and markets under royal and feudal authority existed in the kingdom of Naples.[38] In Germany, the shifting balance of power between emperor, territorial princes, the feudal aristocracy, and imperial, feudal and independent cities, gave rise to endless permutations of the same underlying theme of jurisdictional fragmentation and failure of market co-ordination.[39]

It was previously remarked that the propensity for towns to exert jurisdictional coercion over the hinterland also created opportunities for political and economic rent-seeking, and that jurisdictionally powerful towns consequently opposed actions that challenged their customary rights and hastened territorial integration. The essays in this book make clear that late medieval and early modern states did not come into conflict with towns primarily over rights to free trade – which in most cases was in fact supported by central states – and over capital mobility, as argued by Tilly and Blockmans, but over claims to exercise legal, political and economic prerogatives which gave rise to market power and fiscal revenue. Blockmans's recent demonstration that the persistence of major discrepancies in the fiscal burden between town and countryside and across provinces in the Burgundian and Habsburg Low Countries was caused by urban and feudal opposition to fiscal and institutional integration, provides a good example of the difficulties that pre-modern European states faced in overcoming politically legitimate vested interests.[40] Similar co-ordination failures also arose in poorly urbanised countries like the Polish Commonwealth, the Austro-Czech lands, and the kingdom of Naples, where local aristocracies used their fiscal and political rights to divert trade from existing towns to their own markets. There, as in Castile and Germany, quasi-monopolistic competition between market towns stimulated rural commercialisation and small-town urbanisation during the long sixteenth-century expansion, but led to the near collapse of domestic trading systems during the demographic,

ciudad y la ciudad en el campo: urbanización e instituciones en Castilla durante la Edad Moderna', *Hispania* 58 (1998), 439-70; D. R. Ringrose, 'Historia urbana y urbanización en la España moderna', *Hispania* 58 (1998), 489-512.

[38] S. R. Epstein, *An island for itself. Economic development and social change in late medieval Sicily* (Cambridge, 1992), ch. 8.

[39] Developmental impasse in the early modern Rhineland caused by territorial fragmentation and market failure is examined by T. Scott, *Regional identity and economic change. The upper Rhine, 1450-1600* (Oxford, 1997).

[40] W. P. Blockmans, 'The Low Countries in the middle ages', in R. Bonney (ed.), *The rise of the fiscal state in Europe c.1200-1815* (Oxford, 1999), pp. 281-308.

military and economic disruptions of the seventeenth century, when individual towns and lords took refuge behind their privileges and moved towards commercial autarchy.

Successful integration required strong – that is, weakly contested – states, be they the English variety whose relations with towns were by and large consolidated by the late middle ages,[41] or the Swedish variant which overcame the co-ordination problems arising from its thinly scattered population by establishing urban hierarchies, a town–country division of labour, regional specialisation and inter-regional trade networks through a combination of formal legislation and outright coercion, but then refrained from further intervention.[42] The state's role in overcoming jurisdictional deadlock is apparent also where towns and feudal lords were able to put up stronger opposition, as in Lombardy and the Venetian Terraferma, late seventeenth-century France, and eighteenth-century Austria, where the Habsburgs' attack on urban and feudal privilege led to rapid economic expansion after 1720. The major exception to this rule, the Dutch Republic, managed to survive the centrifugal pressures of urban rivalry in part because of the significant powers assigned to the rural villages and the aristocracy arising from the complex mixture of provincial and 'national' institutions inherited from the Habsburgs, and in part because of the glue provided by the war of independence against Spain (1578–1648). As 't Hart has argued elsewhere, however, once the external threat dissolved, the absence of an authoritative centre allowed the country's elites to backslide into traditional forms of urban rent-seeking.[43] Despite being bound together by a similarly complex mixture of transalpine trade, Habsburg and French threats, and institutional compromise between city- and peasant states described here by Körner and Scott, the Swiss Confederation never achieved the same degree of integration because it never faced the same kind of concerted external military aggression.

[41] D. Palliser, 'Towns and the English state, 1066–1500', in D. M. Palliser and J. R. Maddicott (eds.), The medieval state. Essays presented to James Campbell (London and Rio Grande, 2000), pp. 127–45.

[42] In other words, state coercion raised the returns to specialisation in Sweden, which in turn increased the optimal size of the urban population.

[43] Above, note 36; M. 't Hart, The making of a bourgeois state: war, politics and finance during the Dutch Revolt (Manchester, 1993). For disagreement between towns in Holland before the end of the war with Spain, see also J. Israel, 'The Holland towns and the Dutch–Spanish conflict, 1621–1648', Bijdragen en mededelinen betreffenden geschiedenis der Nederlanden 94 (1979), 41–69. For rent-seeking, see J. de Vries and A. W. van der Woude, The first modern economy. Success, failure, and perseverance of the Dutch economy, 1500–1815 (Cambridge, 1997); van Zanden, Rise and decline.

Towns and proto-industrialisation

Hoppenbrouwers, Galloway, Glennie, Cerman and Knittler, Scott, Sánchez León and Belfanti identify two major watersheds in urban and market integration during the late medieval and seventeenth-century 'distribution crises', when the needs of the fiscal and administrative state became unusually pressing and governments became more disposed to challenge the traditional rights and privileges of their subjects.[44] An important characteristic of both phases was the growth of proto-industrial activities in the countryside. Early arguments that proto-industrialisation was peculiar to the late seventeenth and eighteenth centuries were used to justify the claim that proto-industry was a necessary lead-up to industrialisation. However, it is now recognised that Europe experienced a very similar phase of industrial expansion between the Black Death and the mid-sixteenth century. Early modern proto-industrialisation was more an extension of a process of rural diversification and specialisation that stretched back to the later middle ages than a revolutionary break with the past; many successful rural industries of the late seventeenth and eighteenth centuries were located in areas that had experienced strong manufacturing growth in the later middle ages.[45] Pre-modern proto-industrialisation was more than a purely cyclical recurrence of rural manufacture driven by changes in population and patterns of demand;[46] it was, however, also a kind of activity that did not require or necessarily provoke fundamental changes in social and productive relations in the countryside.

Galloway, Scott, Cerman and Knittler, and Tom Brennan also agree that the original view that proto-industries arose in competition with the technological conservatism and high operating costs of craft-based urban manufacture was based on an excessively simplistic model of pre-industrial manufacture. Urban and rural industries were generally not players in a zero-sum game in which gains for the one produced losses for the other; conditions in Castile described in such terms by Sánchez

---

[44] For an interpretation of the late medieval crisis as an 'integration crisis', see Epstein, *Freedom and growth*, ch. 3; for the seventeenth century, see N. Steensgard, 'The seventeenth-century crisis', in G. Parker and L. M. Smith (eds.), *The general crisis of the seventeenth century* (London, 1978), pp. 26–56, followed in the regional case study by S. C. Ogilvie, 'Germany and the seventeenth-century crisis', *Historical Journal* 35 (1992), 417–41.

[45] See also Epstein, *Freedom and growth*, chs. 3 and 7 for further references.

[46] As suggested by H. Kellenbenz, 'Rural industries in the West from the end of the middle ages to the 18th century', in P. Earle (ed.), *Essays in European economic history 1500–1800* (Oxford, 1974), pp. 45–88, and P. M. Hohenberg and L. H. Lees, *The making of urban Europe, 1000–1950* (Cambridge, MA, and London, 1985), pp. 113–20.

León appear to have been highly unusual. In most regions, dispersed proto-industrial and urban manufacture were distinctive modes of production with distinctive organisational and technological characteristics. Proto-industrial activities had to adapt to the seasonal requirements for agricultural labour and were heavily concentrated in the metalwork and textile industries that had access to cheap raw materials and could utilise traditional peasant skills learned through the normal process of socialisation. The peasantry's lack of training, on the other hand, also restricted it to the production of a narrow and technically unsophisticated range of goods. Urban manufacture, by contrast, employed full-time, skilled labour, largely trained and organised by craft guilds, whose main purpose was to uphold the standards of apprenticeship and workmanship and the commercial reputation that gave town manufactures their major comparative advantage.[47]

The technological and organisational differences between urban and dispersed rural manufacture explain two well-attested puzzles of proto-industrialisation. The first puzzle is the tendency for successful proto-industries to cluster in densely urbanised areas, despite the towns' notorious hostility towards rural competitors. The second puzzle is that successful proto-industries tended to urbanise over time and frequently became organised into formal craft guilds.[48] The transformation of 'industrial villages' into industrial towns or cities, which was typical of north-western England from the late seventeenth century, was also a characteristic, albeit more muted, feature of urbanisation across the rest of Europe in both the late medieval and the early modern phases of proto-industrial growth. The essays on Sweden, England, the German-speaking lands, the Netherlands and northern Italy describe how the difficulties faced by many 'traditional' small towns during the late medieval and seventeenth-century crises, although partly a consequence of proto-industrial competition, were more than matched by the successful transformation of proto-industrial settlements into small towns. Proto-industry's propensity to urbanise was a constant source of rejuvenation for Europe's urban system and was one of the most important sources of urban dynamism before the Industrial Revolution. Successful

[47] For a model analysis of urban–rural industrial interaction, see J. K. J. Thomson, 'Variations in industrial structure in pre-industrial Languedoc', in Berg, Hudson and Sonenscher, *Manufacture in town and country*, pp. 61–91; for the technological role of guilds, see S. R. Epstein, G. Haupt, C. Poni and H. Soly (eds.), *Guilds, economy and society* (Madrid, 1998); W. Reininghaus (ed.), *Zunftlandschaften in Deutschland und den Niederlanden im Vergleich* (Münster, 1999); S. R. Epstein, 'Craft guilds, apprenticeship, and technological change in pre-industrial Europe', *Journal of Economic History* 53 (1998), 684–713.

[48] S. C. Ogilvie, 'Social institutions and proto-industrialization', in S. C. Ogilvie and M. Cerman (eds.), *European proto-industrialization* (Cambridge, 1996), pp. 23–37.

proto-industries tended to become more, rather than less, urban over time.[49]

Industrial clustering and the urbanisation and corporatisation of proto-industrial activities responded to commercial and technological demands that traditional, dispersed proto-industries alone could not meet. Towns supplied capital, raw materials and commercial and management skills, and co-ordinated access to international markets; their craftsmen put the finishing touches to proto-industrial cloth and metalware before export abroad; and their craft guilds provided the skilled workforce to help upgrade low-quality proto-industries to higher quality industry. Relations between urban and proto-industrial manufacture were therefore both complementary and competitive. They were complementary in that they covered different stages of the production cycle and supplied different product markets; they were competitive in that they drew on the same markets for raw materials, capital and labour, and insofar as those proto-industries which moved up the product scale and adopted traditional urban structures forced town crafts to upgrade their own production systems and output or else be competed away.

In addition to technological 'spillovers' from neighbouring towns which helped proto-industries to lock in competitive advantage, proto-industrial continuity or path-dependence was the outcome of long-lasting institutional factors which defined the opportunity costs of rural production, including the legal right for a rural manufacture to be established. Urban manufacturers – frequently dominated by merchants rather than craft guilds, which in late medieval and early modern Castile, Switzerland, England and many parts of France were weak or non-existent – were invariably hostile towards rural competition and did their utmost to quash it. The jurisdictional powers of towns over the countryside were thus of particular importance for rural manufacturing activities, and jurisdictional segregation from the towns was a fundamental prerequisite for proto-industrial growth. Where urban jurisdiction was strong and territorially extensive, as in Tuscany and Castile, the towns were able to stop all but the most basic rural manufacturing activities in their tracks.[50] Towns in the Dutch Republic fought long and hard for a similar result, going so far as to obtain provisions in 1531 and 1540 that banned all 'urban' activities from the countryside; the only reason their efforts were largely neutralised was the presence of villages under feudal or ecclesiastical jurisdiction which could be insulated from urban supervision. In England, where towns were for the most part jurisdictionally weak, a more pressing institutional precondition – at least during the

[49] Clark, 'Introduction', pp. 11–18.
[50] For Tuscany, see Epstein, *Freedom and growth*, ch. 6.

later middle ages – may have been the absence of seigniorial controls.[51] As Stuart Pollard recently noted, the reason why proto-industrial activities were so frequently situated in geographically peripheral regions was less the poverty of the local inhabitants or the availability of cheap raw materials, than the areas' traditional freedom from urban and seigniorial rule.[52]

Despite the fact that craft guilds and merchants made the most of urban and corporate privileges to subvert the development of independent proto-industries in the countryside (as the chapters on Holland, the Swiss-Austro-Germanic lands, northern Italy and Castile remind us), the widespread fragmentation of rural jurisdiction between chartered rural communities and urban, feudal and ecclesiastical lords created political interstices which rural industries could exploit. Areas of jurisdictional autonomy or 'freedoms' underpinned the rise of successful and long-lived proto-industrial districts in densely urbanised regions such as the Netherlands, Flanders, Saxony, Swabia, southern Germany, Lombardy and Catalonia, where proto-industries could benefit from the technological and commercial externalities of strong urban networks. Sometimes the balance of power between urban and rural industry could even tilt in the latter's favour, as in parts of southern Germany where the rapid growth of late medieval proto-industries led to their reorganisation as 'regional' corporations under the aegis of the territorial prince.[53]

If the patterns and distribution of rural industry were shaped by the relative costs of setting up new economic institutions, particularly by the presence of institutional enclaves protecting them from urban control, industrial location could easily become a matter of historical accident rather than strictly economic rationale. Proto-industries could develop in the 'wrong' – that is, the more costly – place, so to speak, simply because this happened to be outside the towns' jurisdiction. Similar caveats apply to the development of 'new towns' that challenged established urban hierarchies, which generally required an act of jurisdictional segregation and elevation. We noted previously that the growth of

[51] P. Hudson, 'Proto-industrialization in England', in Ogilvie and Cerman, *European proto-industrialization*, pp. 55–6.
[52] S. Pollard, *Marginal Europe. The contribution of the marginal lands since the middle ages* (Oxford, 1997). With the exception of mining activities which faced unavoidable locational constraints, however, proto-industrial activities far removed from urban networks were seldom economically successful for the reasons previously discussed.
[53] Stabel, *Dwarfs among giants*, ch. 7; S. C. Ogilvie, 'The beginnings of industrialisation', in S. C. Ogilvie (ed.), *Germany. A new social and economic history*, vol. II: *1630–1800* (London, 1996), pp. 263–308; J. K. J. Thomson, 'Proto-industrialization in Spain', in Ogilvie and Cerman, *European proto-industrialization*, pp. 85–101; Epstein, 'The peasantries of Italy', pp. 105–6.

new towns was not restricted to late seventeenth- and eighteenth-century England, where their rapid expansion underpinned the 'fundamental discontinuity' between the sixteenth- and the eighteenth-century economies described by Glennie. As in England, in continental Europe too the rise of small towns was often the consequence of proto-industrial success. However, outside England new towns were just as frequently founded with primarily fiscal and redistributive purposes through initiatives from above, by feudal lords in Poland, Habsburg Austria and the Czech lands, Castile and the Italian south, and by the monarchy in Sweden. This made their economic benefits consequently more muted.

The most remarkable aspect of late seventeenth- and eighteenth-century English urbanisation, therefore, appears not to be the rise of new small towns but the speed with which the urban and rural sectors were able to adapt to changes in patterns of production and specialisation. The absence of institutional restrictions on urban growth allowed England to increase its urbanisation in a comparatively short space of time. Perhaps also because the returns to urban rent-seeking were comparatively low, from the late seventeenth century 'old' corporate and guilded towns like Newcastle (which in addition to the coal trade had iron, glass and salt manufactures), Nottingham (hosiery), Bristol, Liverpool and Leeds were able to deploy their established skilled labour force successfully alongside the burgeoning economy of the 'new towns'.[54] High institutional barriers to urban renewal and high returns to urban rent-seeking explain, by contrast, the remarkable stability of continental urban ratios, and testify to the difficulty faced by most countries in raising urban levels significantly above what they inherited from the later middle ages.

Towns and country, states and markets in a European perspective

Although contributors to this volume were given a broad remit reflected in the range of approaches adopted and topics addressed, in its essence the volume focuses on the interaction between institutions and economic performance. The main institutions shaping town–country relations in the period between the Black Death and the Industrial Revolution were the bundle of jurisdictional rights over economic activities in the countryside, obtained for the most part by towns before 1500 and filtered through the prism of state and feudal power. Political and legal rights shaped patterns of urbanisation, proto-industrial activities, and the operation of rural markets.

[54] Langton and Hoppe, *Town and country*, p. 39.

Interactions between towns and state were central to town–country relations between 1300 and 1800. Territorial states offered a model of political rule and economic co-ordination that towns found hard to emulate. Towns needed to co-operate for commercial and military purposes, but the latter conflicted with the towns' aspirations to territorial lordship, and their inability to build durable coalitions undermined their attempts to establish a serious institutional alternative to the territorial state. Territorial states also increasingly determined the political framework for commercial and manufacturing activities and co-ordinated competing urban and rural corporate and status groups – both urban and rural craft guilds, urban merchants, feudal lords and chartered rural communities – in order to extend their sovereignty and enlarge their tax base; even overtly economic policies were primarily fiscal in intention and thus subject to short-termism and vacillation as financial requirements ebbed and flowed. Remarkably, the political and institutional parameters for negotiation established during the late middle ages seem to have exerted a powerful restraint on the levels both of urbanisation and of proto-industrial activities well into the eighteenth century. Only the Dutch Republic, England and Sweden managed to break free of the late medieval equilibrium and raise their urban levels significantly above those achieved in and around 1500 (Table 1.1).

While emphasising the importance of political factors in town–country relations, contributors to this volume also highlight the ambiguity and tension between coercive and market-led solutions to the requirements of exchange. High levels of coercion seem to have been strongly associated with a high degree of urban concentration, with stronger urban hierarchies, and, up to the fifteenth century at least, with higher levels of agricultural and urban specialisation; conversely, low levels of urban coercion were generally linked to less differentiated and hierarchical urban systems based around small towns. However, precisely how these systems of coercion emerged and were perpetuated, and how the benefits of a coercive system of urban growth could be outweighed over time by its costs, require more systematic comparative research. Among the topics for worthwhile comparison touched upon in this volume are the extent to which urban industrial monopolies constrained labour productivity in agriculture by making it harder to shift into rural industry; the effects of political fragmentation on economic co-ordination between towns and on proto-industrial activity; and the consequences of different urban supply policies on market efficiency and integration. The central underlying question, touched upon explicitly by Hoppenbrouwers, 't Hart, Sánchez León, Belfanti, and Cerman and Knittler, is whether the poor economic performance after 1500 of regions with jurisdictionally powerful towns can be explained by these towns' persistent political particularism.

Although contributors do not stray too far beyond the period they are most familiar with, they have responded to the editorial proposal to consider the period from the fourteenth to the eighteenth century as a structural unity by focusing on major institutional continuities and shifts, and by challenging in refreshingly heterodox ways the traditional chronological demarcations. The decision by several contributors to discuss the period between the Black Death and the late sixteenth or the early seventeenth century as an analytical whole follows naturally from the identification of the mid-fourteenth century as a more significant institutional and economic break-point than the late fifteenth. On the other hand, the authors also display some interpretative ambiguity towards the late medieval crisis, which they depict – not necessarily contradictorily – as a period when intense social and political upheaval stimulated extensive economic restructuring and market integration with positive long-term consequences (e.g. in England and Holland), and as a time when towns were able to consolidate political and commercial restrictions over the countryside (e.g. in north-central Italy and the Austro-Czech lands). The late medieval and seventeenth-century 'crises' also emerge from these essays – most explicitly in the chapter by Cerman and Knittler – as periods with several important similarities, when the prevailing institutional balance between town and country was challenged by the rise of small proto-industrial towns and by a proliferation of new town plantations. Both the political economic consequences of the late medieval crisis, and the similarities and differ-ences between the later fourteenth and fifteenth centuries and the seventeenth, deserve more systematic comparison and research.

Comparative research can also help us explore and question some of the unspoken assumptions of national historiography. Regional differ-ences in the institutionalised power of town over country may explain why many north European historians hold a more sanguine view of the economic role of towns than their central and southern European counterparts; but there is also a clear need for more rigorous compar-isons of the effects of coercive and market-led solutions to pre-modern economic predicaments, which neither take legislators' claims at face value nor dismiss the role of political institutions in shaping and constraining pre-modern markets. Although the institutionalised powers of town over country were never entirely resistant to market competition and their efficacy tended to decline over time – only Castile, Italy and Germano-Austrian Europe witnessed significant reactionary movements during the seventeenth-century crisis – most urban and territorial

administrations continued to expend considerable resources on market
regulation. One such highly sensitive sector mentioned by Brennan,
Scott, Glennie and Marin in the present volume was the grain trade,
which continued to be regulated in much of Europe up to the late
eighteenth century and beyond in the deep-rooted belief that administrative intervention helped mitigate the consequences of market failure.
Despite more than two centuries of debate on the matter, both the
political economy of intervention and its consequences for urban consumers and for agricultural producers are still open to widely divergent
interpretations. As with debates over proto-industry, future discussions
of grain market regulation will need to take account of the range of
institutional variation in pre-modern markets presented in this volume.

Another issue that still attracts strongly contrasting opinions is the
effect on town–country relations of the rapid rise of capital cities,
discussed in the chapters on England, Habsburg Austria, Castile and
Italy. Although it is generally agreed that the phenomenon reflects the
rapid growth in size and centralisation of state administration after the
mid-fifteenth century, interpretations of its consequences differ remarkably across countries. Whereas English historians, as we saw, portray
London as an engine of growth and play down any negative consequences of its national dominance, most Castilian and Italian historians
subscribe to the Physiocratic claim that the great early modern capitals
were 'parasitical' consumers of rural surpluses and contributed little to
agricultural progress. As Sánchez León and Marin note, however,
Physiocratic claims may both overestimate the consequences for the
national market of capital cities' demands for food, and underestimate
the commercial benefits for the capitals' agrarian hinterland. Whereas
high urban primacy in the modern world is strongly linked to commercial protectionism and authoritarian (non-market) systems of resource
allocation, it is still an open question whether pre-modern urban
primacy was a cause or a consequence of institutional coercion and
fragmented markets.[55] Some historians have interpreted the customary

[55] A. A. Ades and E. L. Glaeser, 'Trade and circuses: explaining urban giants', *Quarterly Journal of Economics* 110 (1995), 1, 195–227; P. Krugman and R. Livas Elizondo, 'Trade policy and the Third World metropolis', *Journal of Development Economics* 49 (1996), 137–50; C. A. Smith, 'Types of city-size distributions. A comparative analysis', in A. van der Woude, A. Hayami and J. de Vries (eds.), *Urbanisation in history. A process of dynamic interactions* (Oxford, 1990), pp. 20–42. For a range of opinions on the economic impact of capital cities, see E. Aerts and P. Clark (eds.), *Metropolitan cities and their hinterlands in early modern Europe* (Leuven, 1990) and P. Clark and B. Lepetit (eds.), *Capital cities and their hinterlands in early modern Europe* (Aldershot, 1996). Hoffman, *Growth*, pp. 170–84, finds that Paris had a measurable effect on agricultural productivity whereas other French towns did not. Two explanations for this seeming imbalance come to mind. As the residence of the political elites, Paris attracted higher

privileges of capital cities towards basic food supplies as evidence of rent-seeking and political authoritarianism. However, de Vries's suggestion that the early modern capitals' demand for grain was a strong source of market integration,[56] and the fact that two allegedly 'parasitical' cities, Madrid and Naples, stopped growing during the seventeenth century as their domestic markets disintegrated under the crosscurrents of urban and feudal protectionism, offer grounds for believing that the capitals' supply privileges served more to destroy than preserve barriers to trade in domestic grain markets. More conclusive answers about the causes and consequences of urban primacy in the pre-modern world require further systematic study open to a comparative European perspective.

To the degree that the simple dichotomies – backward/advanced, capitalist/coercive, regulated/unregulated, industrial/proto-industrial – which historians have used to model the economic and political roles of towns in the wider society are built around the idea that their characteristics and functions flowed from basic behavioural, economic or political essences, they are no longer of much explanatory use. 'Town and country' is a legitimate metaphor so long as the expression's metaphorical status is made clear; its epistemological benefits are more doubtful. Some years ago Langton and Hoppe suggested that the terms 'town' and 'country' described phenomena so diverse and inconsistent that attempts to generalise from them were pointless. The essays in this volume take the criticism forward by proposing an institutional approach to urban–rural interaction that allows for generalisation while also accounting for historical contingency and difference. The comparative questions they raise should also encourage further questioning of historiographical assumptions, including those underlying the narratives the essays themselves propose.

---

per caput investment in supply networks for food; the city could also lobby effectively against jurisdictional barriers to trade raised by smaller cities and feudal lords. Paris stimulated agriculture because it helped create more efficient markets.

[56] J. de Vries, 'Patterns of urbanisation in pre-industrial Europe, 1500–1800', in H. Schmal (ed.), *Patterns of European urbanisation since 1500* (London, 1981), pp. 79–109.

2   Town and country in Sweden, 1450–1650

Robert Sandberg

Urban size and networks

In the course of the seventeenth century Sweden became one of the great European powers. Among the reasons for the country's military success was the administrative efficiency of the Swedish state, led by king and nobility in unison. The government had previously aimed to modernise society, and among its targets had been the urban system, including not only the towns but also relations between towns and their hinterland. This chapter discusses the urban policy of the Swedish state and its effects on town–country relations from the fifteenth to the mid-seventeenth century. It examines the division of labour and interactions between town and country and the institutional framework in which relations took place, including the character and consequences of town policy. The discussion ends with the first half of the seventeenth century, when the urban system within the old Swedish territory was extensively transformed and the borders of the Swedish realm changed.

Sweden was one of the least urbanised countries in Europe until the end of the nineteenth century. As late as 1850, less than 10 per cent of the population lived in towns and half of the towns had fewer than 1,500 people.[1] While this implies *a fortiori* that early modern Sweden was a relatively backward country, it also reflects the country's vast size and high transport costs, which made it difficult to support a high level of urbanisation. Moreover, although the degree of urban specialisation and economic development was low compared to that of the more advanced European regions, standards of living among the Swedish peasantry were probably higher than in much of the Continent.

Sweden's territory today is very different from that of the period under consideration. Before the mid-seventeenth century, the southern part of modern Sweden, including the counties of Skåne, Halland and Blekinge, belonged to Denmark, as did the island of Gotland, while the

[1] The calculation is based on the statistics in L. Nilsson, *Historisk tätortsstatistik*, vol. I: *Folkmängden i administrativa tätorter 1800–1970* (Stockholm, 1992).

1 Stockholm	9 Växjö	16 Norrköping	23 Nykadeby	30 Filipstad
2 Åbo	10 Jönköping	17 Göteborg	24 Karlshamn	31 Sala
3 Gävle	11 Helsinki	18 Falun	25 Karlskrona	32 Nyköping
4 Kalmar	12 Viborg	19 Borås	26 Karlstad	33 Arboga
5 Uppsala	13 Askersund	20 Vasa	27 Nora	34 Nya Lödöse
6 Linköping	14 Köping	21 Gamlakarleby	28 Hudiksvall	35 Malmö
7 Strängnäs	15 Västerås	22 Uleåborg	29 Umeå	36 Reval (Tallinn)
8 Skara				

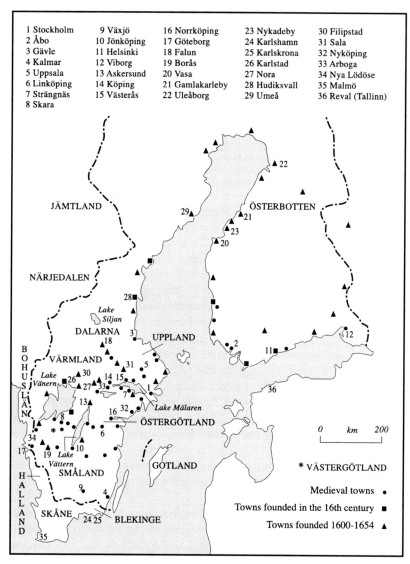

Figure 2.1   Swedish towns in 1654. The conquered provinces are not included.
Source: Sandberg, 'Urban landownership', p. 183 (see n. 51).

Table 2.1. *Urbanisation and urban growth in Sweden, 1550–1800*

| | No. of towns | Population[a] | | Rate of urbanisation | Growth rate (% p. a.) |
		Urban	Sweden		
1550	44	33	850	3.9	
1600	49	41	1,215	3.4	0.4
1650	80	100	1,586	6.3	(1.8)
1700[a]	101	164	1,790	9.2	1.0
1750[a]	102	186	2,222	8.4	0.3
1800[a]	106	290	3,180	9.1	0.9

Notes: [a] Population figures in thousands.
[b] Figures include the former Danish and Norwegian towns.
Source: Lilja, 'Tjuvehål och stolta städer' (n. 4), Table 9:1.

western counties of Bohuslän, Härjedalen and Jämtland were Norwegian. In the north, frontiers with Norway and Russia were unstable and often the object of military conflict. Sweden's only access to the sea was therefore by way of a narrow strip of land at the mouth of the river Göta älv in the west. On the other hand, Sweden included present-day Finland and the Gulf of Bothnia in the northern Baltic, and the country's central axis ran from Stockholm to Åbo (Turku).

Sweden's territorial expansion began in the 1560s, when the town of Reval (Tallinn), which in the late middle ages had belonged to the Teutonic Knights, surrendered itself voluntarily to the Swedish king to gain protection against the Russians. Thereafter Sweden became increasingly involved in the eastern Baltic area south of the Gulf of Finland, and over time Estonia, Latvia and northern Lithuania came under the Swedish crown. During the 1640s and 1650s Sweden also conquered the previously mentioned Danish and Norwegian counties, and with the Peace of Westphalia of 1648 the country obtained German-speaking territories on the south Baltic coast; most of the German and east Baltic provinces were lost after the Great Northern War of 1700–21.

Here discussion will be restricted to Sweden's territory prior to the 1560s, because the Danish and Norwegian towns came under Swedish control only at the end of the period being considered, and the east Baltic towns never became integrated into the Swedish urban system. The incorporation of Danish and Norwegian towns in any case hardly affected the shape of Sweden's urban system. Skåne and Halland were slightly more urbanised than the old Swedish realm, but town sizes were the same, and regional differences within Sweden were greater than those between Sweden and the newly annexed Nordic areas.

By the late middle ages, Sweden and Finland numbered about forty towns, mainly concentrated in the central zones of medieval Sweden, primarily in the Mälar valley and in the county of Östergötland.[2] Large parts of the country, such as Norrland and inner Finland, lacked towns altogether. In Sweden proper, Gävle (some 150 km north of Stockholm) was the northernmost town; the whole of Finland had only six towns, all of them situated on the coast. Two or three of Sweden's towns dated from the eleventh and twelfth centuries, but most of them were founded during the thirteenth century or later.[3] Of the forty chartered towns, perhaps five or six had more than 1,000 inhabitants, and only Stockholm had over 5,000. The entire urban population numbered about 30,000, which was less than 5 per cent of the country's total.[4]

Late medieval Swedish towns were mainly local marketplaces. A few had a royal castle, which headed a fiscal district that could extend far beyond the urban hinterland and which in some cases possessed considerable military importance up to the early sixteenth century, but neither fact conveyed any broader administrative functions to the towns.[5] Towns were not centres of a judicial district and had no jurisdiction over their hinterland, although in most cases they had their own court districts. Only Stockholm and Kalmar on the south-east coast near the Danish border had town walls. On the other hand, a number of the late medieval towns possessed significant ecclesiastical functions that could be of value to the hinterland. The few cathedral towns were of course the most important, but a clear majority of towns, whatever their size, had one or more abbeys or convents and nearly half also had a hospital.[6] Except for the cathedral towns, the towns' ecclesiastical functions came to an end with the Reformation, which also dealt a blow to the bishops' political power and led to the expropriation of church land. As a consequence cathedral towns like Uppsala, Linköping and Skara, which were not trading ports, lost ground to the coastal towns.

If we disregard the position of Stockholm, the urban system lacked a clear national hierarchy before the seventeenth century. Every town and

---

[2] For our purposes, a town is defined as a place granted town charters.

[3] H. Andersson, *Sjuttiosex medeltidsstäder – aspekter på stadsarkeologi och medeltida urbaniseringsprocess i Sverige och Finland* (Stockholm, 1990), pp. 63–7.

[4] S. Lilja, 'Swedish urbanisation *c.*1570–1800. Chronology, structure and causes', *Scandinavian Journal of History* 19 (1994), 281, cites a figure of 40,000, but he has recently revised this; see S. Lilja, *Tjuvehål och stolta städer. Urbaniseringens kronologi och geografi i Sverige (med Finland) ca 1570–tal till 1810–tal* (Stockholm, 2000).

[5] Most castles or royal houses that headed a tax district were not situated in towns. See B. Fritz, *Hus, land och län. Förvaltningen i Sverige 1250–1434*, 2 vols. (Stockholm, 1972), vol. I, pp. 64–9.

[6] Andersson, *Sjuttiosex medeltidsstäder*, pp. 72–4. The cathedral towns were Uppsala, Strängnäs and Västerås in the Mälar counties, Skara in Västergötland, Linköping in Östergötland, Växjö in Småland and Åbo in Finland.

its burghers had the right to actively ply foreign trade with their ships, but only coastal towns held the privilege of passive foreign trade, that is, of receiving foreign merchants. However, it is far from clear whether such privileges made any difference, since foreign trade tended in any case to concentrate in only a few towns and especially in Stockholm. In other respects urban functions were distributed fairly equally, no doubt in part because the great distances between the towns made it difficult to establish strong hierarchical relations. Swedish towns before the seventeenth century formed not one single central place system but rather several quasi-independent ones, the most important of which centred upon the Mälar valley. Above these urban systems one town, Stockholm, towered above all others in terms both of size and of trading importance. About two-thirds of Swedish foreign trade passed through Stockholm, and its merchants had extensive contacts with the Hanseatic towns in Germany. Stockholm was a 'gateway primate city' in an under-developed urban system, acting as the main trading connection between central Sweden, trading ports in the Baltic outside the Swedish realm, and the continental European urban network.[7] On the other hand, contacts between Stockholm and the Swedish towns south of the Mälar valley do not seem to have been particularly strong.[8]

Institutional framework

Legislation and charters

During the late middle ages and even more in the early modern period, Sweden was ruled by a comparatively uniform system of legislation and taxation based on two general law codes introduced in the mid-four-teenth century, one for the country and one for the towns. Many aspects of the codes were the same, but there were also some important differences related mainly to commercial and administrative matters. The codes stayed in force for almost four centuries, and not until the 1730s was there a single national legislation. Insofar, however, as the medieval legal system was unable to address the problems arising from

---

[7] The expression 'gateway primate city' is taken from R. J. Johnston, *City and society: an outline for urban geography* (Harmondsworth, 1980). See also P. M. Hohenberg and L. H. Lees, *The making of urban Europe 1000–1950* (Cambridge, MA, 1985), pp. 62–73. Stockholm acted as a transit port for the metal trade; transactions between producers and the exporters were settled in the mining districts or the Mälar towns. See B. Odén, *Kopparhandel och statsmonopol. Studier i svensk handelshistoria under senare 1500–talet* (Stockholm, 1960), pp. 161–2; R. Sandberg, *I slottets skugga. Stockholm och kronan 1599–1620* (Stockholm, 1991), p. 134.

[8] Å. Sandström, *Mellan Torneå och Amsterdam. En undersökning av Stockholms roll som förmedlare av varor i regional- och utrikeshandeln 1600–1650* (Stockholm, 1990), p. 299.

an increasingly complex society, particularly in towns, the laws were largely outdated long before they were repealed. Town law was therefore gradually supplemented by a body of royal ordinances, several of which touched also upon the relations between town and country.

Although the frequency of such ordinances increased significantly after 1500, the king lacked the right to legislate without his subjects' approval and could act arbitrarily or indeed enforce much legislation only under extraordinary circumstances. Most of the large body of royal ordinances and decrees issued during the sixteenth century therefore had rather little impact, but under Gustavus Adolphus (1611–32) and thereafter circumstances changed, on the basis of a procedure for the issuance of ordinances and their approval by the four estates that was put to the Riksdag (parliament) in 1617. The provision stated that, if the estates did not agree among themselves, the king could choose whichever opinion best suited his purposes. Since the aristocracy and clergy did not usually oppose royal requests regarding trade, the monarchy could in effect dictate most decisions.[9] This major change in the manner of enforcing government decisions was soon apparent in the area of town policy.

Royal ordinances were not the only legal supplement to town law. Individual towns also received specifically targeted charters, which established the centre's legal status as a town and therefore its right to abide by the urban law code, and its economic privileges.[10] The oldest known town charter in Sweden was granted to Jönköping in 1284, but their number and frequency increased over time.[11] By the fifteenth century at the latest it had become customary for each new king to issue new charters or to confirm the old ones, since in principle they decayed with the issuer's death. In practice, towns made use of any charters they were granted, even when for some reason they were not confirmed by successive monarchs.

During the sixteenth century it became more common for kings to modify old town charters. Gustav Vasa, the king who broke the late medieval union with Denmark and Norway, was particularly active in the matter, a clear indication of his autocratic leanings being his habit of

[9] The Riksdag ordinance is published in A. A. von Stiernman, *Alla Riksdagars och Mötens Besluth*, 3 vols. (Stockholm, 1728–33), vol. I. Note also N. Ahnlund, 'Ståndsriksdagens utdaning 1592–1672', in *Sveriges riksdag*, 17 vols. (Stockholm, 1933–8), vol. I:3, p. 145.
[10] Sandberg, *I slottets skugga*, pp. 59–61; Sandberg, 'Growth and transformation of an early modern capital city. Stockholm in the first half of the 17th century', *Scandinavian Journal of History* 17 (1992), 294–314.
[11] Swedish town charters granted up to 1632 are printed in *Privilegier, resolutioner och förordningar för Sveriges städer*, 6 vols. (Stockholm, 1927–85).

moving entire towns with their inhabitants to a new location. The reasons for doing so included improvements to defence and to trade, but also simply royal displeasure. More than a third of the forty or so Swedish towns were ordered by Gustav Vasa to move, either to another town or to a fresh site. Thus, when Helsinki was founded in 1550, the inhabitants of four Finnish towns were ordered to move to the new foundation. However, it is also an indication of the limits of sixteenth-century Swedish royal power that in most cases the orders were never carried out, or were only partially obeyed.[12]

Taxation

Few Swedish towns acted as administrative centres for the surrounding countryside. On the contrary, from the 1540s onwards a great many towns were integrated into a system of rural fiscal districts established by Gustav Vasa. Prior to this, both burghers and peasants had belonged to larger administrative districts under the jurisdiction of a royal castle or demesne, only some of which – Stockholm castle being the principal example – were situated in towns. Independently from the royal admin-istration of rural districts and castles, most towns had their own municipal administration led by the burgomaster and council, which also officiated over the town court. The countryside came under the remit of rural courts headed by a layman, usually a member of the gentry, with a jury of land-owning peasants. Conflicts between towns-people and countrymen could be prosecuted in either court depending on where the matter had first arisen, but perhaps because of the towns' role as marketplaces, cases seem to have been heard far more frequently in urban than in rural courts.[13] Finally in 1614 a single supreme court was established, to which cases from both urban and rural courts could be submitted.

The administrative reforms of the 1540s also changed the system of taxation in the countryside. Formerly taxes had often been assessed collectively, but from then on farms were taxed individually. The farms owned by the nobility, which at the time included just over 20 per cent of the total, were for the most part exempted from regular taxation, but their tenants still had to submit to frequent 'extraordinary' levies. By contrast, the yeoman farms (a good 50 per cent of the total) and the farms owned by the crown had to pay an annual tax in addition to the extraordinary taxes.

12 Å. Sandström, *Plöjande borgare och handlande bönder. Mötet mellan den europeiska urbana ekonomin och vasatidens Sverige* (Stockholm, 1996), pp. 97–104.
13 Ibid., pp. 82–92.

Peasants paid the greater part of their taxes in kind because of the country's low level of monetisation. By the seventeenth century the peasantry was required to pay a larger proportion of their taxes in money, but at the end of the century a new tax reform reverted to the arrangement established in the 1540s based on payments in kind. Taxes in kind were collected by the bailiff of the tax district, who was responsible for delivering the goods to a royal castle or farm or for disposing of them on the market. He was also charged with the payment in kind of royal officials and merchants who were creditors with the crown. Because such a small part of the tax revenues actually passed through the market, it is doubtful if they played a significant role in developing urban commercial functions.[14]

The towns were assessed separately from the countryside, on the basis of fixed annual collective levies in cash paid by the town burghers and occasionally of taxes on individuals, for which other town inhabitants (excluding the nobility) could also be assessed. Before the seventeenth century, urban returns were a small proportion of taxes raised on the peasantry;[15] but although the real value of the towns' regular annual taxes decreased through inflation, extraordinary levies could be high. On the other hand, although burghers had to pay municipal taxes and other local fees as well, they were also the sole beneficiaries of town privileges and liberties.

Customs and excises

During the first half of the seventeenth century indirect taxation became an increasingly important source of revenue. Previously Sweden's domestic excise taxes were rather low by comparison with the economically more developed regions in Europe, and during the sixteenth century even customs dues on foreign trade had been modest, with frequent exemptions and reductions being granted.[16]

From the 1620s onwards the government attempted to replace the traditional land tax with indirect taxes on trade. Although the strategy's efficacy is open to question, it can be seen as an attempt to compensate for the monarchy's contemporary policy of gifting and selling land and direct tax revenues to the nobility, which weakened the crown's permanent fiscal base. To implement this plan, it was thought necessary to force the country's trade into the towns where it could be better

[14] For the organisation of revenue collection, see B. Odén, *Rikets uppbörd och utgift. Statsfinanser och finansförvaltning under senare 1500-talet* (Lund, 1955).
[15] Sandberg, *I slottets skugga*, pp. 265–368.
[16] Ibid., p. 355; Sandström, *Mellan Torneå och Amsterdam*, pp. 65–8.

controlled.[17] In 1622, the government decided with the estates' consent to impose the first general custom on domestic trade, specifically a duty on all wares brought from the countryside into the towns that remained in force for two centuries. However, although foreign trade could to some extent be restricted to the coastal towns, domestic trade (which had previously been largely tax-exempt) was far harder to control, since domestic customs rates had previously not been uniform and customs places were few and far between.[18]

Town and country before the seventeenth century

Political theory

The theory underlying economic relations between farmers and burghers can be inferred from the urban and trade policies of the crown. As elsewhere in Europe, there existed in Sweden a belief that trade and manufacture should be primarily urban activities. Rural trade was frowned upon, with few exceptions. Peasants and the aristocracy had the right to sell their produce and to buy for personal consumption, but exchange had to occur in a town or in sanctioned marketplaces. Rural inhabitants could not by right trade with the person of their choice, and were absolutely forbidden any contact with foreign merchants.[19]

This official view of rural trade was already hinted at in town laws of the 1350s, although it was not mentioned in contemporary rural legislation. According to the urban law, town merchants could travel to a number of seasonal fairs to trade with rural inhabitants. If they visited a different town from their own outside the period of the fairs, they could only trade with that town's burghers. By contrast, the revised rural legislation of the 1440s merely stated that peasants could not travel and trade full time, but there was no outright ban on peasant trade.[20]

By the sixteenth century, however, royal ordinances and decrees and town charters regularly banned rural trade and manufacture. Gustav Vasa and his successors issued a stream of letters addressing commercial regulation; more than half of these communications dealt with urban

---

[17] From 1615 the export duty was about 15 per cent and the import duty 5–10 per cent, and they remained about this size at least up to the 1650s (Sandström, *Mellan Torneå och Amsterdam*, p. 96; Sandberg, *I slottets skugga*, p. 355).
[18] Sandberg, *I slottets skugga*, p. 342.
[19] Ibid., pp. 38ff., 98–101. See E. F. Heckscher, 'Den ekonomiska innebörden av 1500– och 1600–talens svenska stadsgrundningar', *Historisk tidskrift* 1923, pp. 309–50.
[20] Sandström, *Plöjande borgare*, pp. 29ff.

matters.[21] Many of the letters concerned rural trade, which the king wished to put an end to, but there were also grander strategic plans for regulating the entire country's trade. Perhaps Gustav Vasa's most grandiose and unrealistic scheme involved redirecting commercial flows from Viborg in eastern Finland to Askersund, an insignificant community near Lake Vättern in southern Sweden which was only granted a town charter in the 1640s.[22] As this example suggests, the sort of sweeping decree that sixteenth-century kings loved to issue seldom had much effect. The decrees did not have any clear legal force either, since they had to be approved in some way by the communities concerned and the latter preferred simply to ignore them.

By contrast, the town charters did have legal authority, and it was mostly there that the privileges of individual towns were set down. A large number of such liberties concerned trade, and among the most significant were those that defined the extent of a town's hinterland. The town burghers took it as a matter of fact that peasants in the immediate vicinity should trade only on the town market – but the immediate vicinity was usually not enough to satisfy them. Towns therefore strove to enlarge their legal hinterland as far as possible, and this brought them into conflict with their neighbours. Sometimes the king mistakenly granted charters with the same exclusive privileges to different towns, since a systematic rationalisation of concessions was not attempted before the seventeenth century.[23]

The definition of an urban hinterland applied only to urban trade; it had no relevance for the town's jurisdiction defined more broadly. Commercial privileges were seen as a source of protection against competition by other towns rather than being directed against the peasantry. If a merchant from another town intruded upon a privilege, the town concerned tried to prosecute the offender in its own court. When conflicts arose between rival town magistrates they turned to the king or parliament, since there was no higher court of appeal that could handle such disputes. Commercial conflicts of this kind were common across the country, although Stockholm merchants were probably more involved than others because their trading networks were more extensive.[24] The largest hinterland by a considerable margin belonged to Stockholm. A series of trade ordinances in the first half of the seventeenth century stated that all burghers and peasants of Norrland and

[21] E. F. Heckscher, *Sveriges ekonomiska historia*, 4 vols. (Stockholm, 1935–49), vol. I:1, pp. 15f.
[22] Sandström, *Plöjande borgare*, pp. 31ff.
[23] Ibid., pp. 123–9; Sandberg, *I slottets skugga*, p. 85.
[24] Examples in Sandberg, *I slottets skugga*, pp. 130–9.

Table 2.2. *Swedish exports, 1559–1721 (percentages)*

	1559	1576	1590	1613	1637	1645	1661	1685	1721	1724
Iron and steel	28.8	44.7	38.6	39.0	35.4	53.6	58.2	57.0	77.6	73.0
Copper and brass	5.5	14.8	20.1	43.6	27.3	29.8	24.3	23.5	9.3	10.0
Pitch and tar	1.1	0.8	1.7	2.0	7.9	6.5	6.0	8.1	2.7	7.0
Timber	11.6	0.4	3.0	1.1	4.1	3.2	4.1	2.4	6.3	6.1
Grain	4.0	4.8	1.8	4.6	16.0	1.4	1.0	0.1	–	–
Hides and furs	22.3	13.2	17.5	3.8	2.4	1.1	0.8	0.1	–	–
Butter and fat	24.7	20.0	15.5	5.1	–	–	–	–	–	–
Other goods	2.0	1.3	1.8	0.8	6.9	4.4	5.6	8.8	4.1	3.9
Total	100	100	100	100	100	100	100	100	100	100

Source: Heckscher, *Sveriges ekonomiska historia* (n. 21), vol. I:1, Appendix V.

Finland had to carry their goods to Stockholm or Åbo for sale. This provided Stockholm merchants with a gigantic hinterland and became known as the 'Bothnian trading constraint', which the capital's merchants defended tooth and nail far into the eighteenth century.[25]

Practice: trade

All this applied in legislative and political theory. But what actually happened on the ground? Although the overwhelming majority of Swedes were peasants, rural circumstances were far from homogeneous, and probably comparatively few peasants were simple farmers.[26] Rather, they were jacks-of-all-trades.[27] Pure arable land was rare in Sweden before the nineteenth century. Cereal yields were low, and the typical farmstead ran a mixed economy. Large parts of the country specialised in raising livestock, and elsewhere also pasture and meadowland were more significant than arable. Indeed, for most peasants butter was the main source of cash, not least because it was comparatively easy to transport. In the fifteenth and sixteenth centuries butter was one of Sweden's main exports (Table 2.2).[28]

Sweden and Finland's large number of lakes and extensive coasts and forests meant that woodlands and fishing were also resources of great importance. Forests were a source of iron ore, charcoal and pitch in addition to fuel, building materials, pasture, forage and game. Charcoal was necessary for the expanding iron industry, and during the seventeenth century pitch became an important export, above all from Finland. As with butter production, tar boiling was in the hands of the peasantry, and until the early seventeenth century the same could be said for iron. In Bergslagen many mines and foundries were owned collectively by peasants who spent part of their time producing iron.[29]

During the sixteenth century, there is increasing evidence that regional economies were becoming more specialised.[30] The most signifi-

---

[25] Ibid., p. 181.

[26] See C. J. Gadd, *Självhushållning eller arbetsdelning? Svenskt lant- och stadshantverk ca 1400–1860* (Göteborg, 1991), p. 22, who argues that probably more people were engaged in agriculture in Nordic countries than elsewhere in western Europe, but for a shorter part of the year.

[27] Sandström, *Plöjande borgare*, pp. 63ff.

[28] H. Yrwing, 'Smörhandel', *Kulturhistoriskt lexikon för nordisk medeltid*, 21 vols., 2nd edn (Copenhagen, 1982), vol. XVI, pp. 322–6; Heckscher, *Sveriges ekonomiska historia*, vol. I, pp. 125, 127ff.; N. Friberg, *Stockholm i bottniska farvatten. Stockholms bottniska handelsfält under senmedeltiden och Gustav Vasa* (Stockholm, 1983), pp. 349–51.

[29] L. Magnusson, *Sveriges ekonomiska historia* (Stockholm, 1996), pp. 132–5.

[30] J. Myrdal and J. Söderberg, *Kontinuitetens dynamik. Agrar ekonomi i 1500-talets Sverige* (Stockholm, 1991), pp. 517–19.

cant developments occurred in metal production and cattle-breeding. The growing importance of iron and copper production in the Swedish region of Bergslagen meant that food supplies had to be imported from other regions. Grain was brought from the neighbouring areas east and south of Bergslagen, while cattle came from the counties of Småland and Västergötland in southern Sweden. The Bergslagen supply networks created the most substantial domestic trade flows, which attracted merchants from Stockholm and peasants from other regions in addition to burghers from the towns north of Lake Mälaren. Because of the importance of supplying the iron-producing regions with food, the crown tolerated a greater diversity of trade than was customary. For instance, the markets in Bergslagen were granted the same legal status as town markets, which meant that peasants from other regions were allowed to sell their goods there.[31]

As elsewhere in Europe, the livestock trade gained in significance during the sixteenth and seventeenth centuries. However, in contrast with patterns elsewhere, trade was mainly between southern Sweden and Bergslagen rather than for export; owing to the country's size, however, the distances covered were comparable to export trade elsewhere. In the late middle ages livestock crossed the border into Denmark, but by the sixteenth century it was directed to Bergslagen and during the following century also to Stockholm. Some 5,000 to 10,000 oxen were driven annually over distances between 300 and 500 kilometres, which puts the Swedish livestock trade at a similar level of intensity to that in central and western Europe. Most trade was in the hands of merchants from the small towns of Småland and Västergötland, who bought up the oxen from the peasants and organised the droves to Bergslagen. There they were sold at the two great cattle fairs of Köping (on 29 July) and Västerås (on 8 September), two towns north of Mälaren that had the closest contacts with Bergslagen.[32]

In addition to the trade in iron, pitch, grain and livestock, peasants also gained valuable income from handicrafts and small-scale trade. Peasants seem to have preferred trading directly with consumers or with foreign merchants rather than relying on middlemen. Many people living along the coast or on the Danish border also exported their goods themselves, sometimes sailing across the Gulf of Bothnia or from Öland island off Kalmar in the south of Sweden to north German or east Baltic

[31] See K. Bodell, *Stad, bondebygd och bergslag vid mitten av 1600–talet* (Stockholm, 1970), pp. 48, 55, 60.
[32] Myrdal and Söderberg, *Kontinuitetens dynamik*, pp. 450–84.

ports, or taking their goods from Småland and Västergötland to the Danish towns across the border.[33]

Although the towns were not entirely independent of the countryside, many of them were nearly self-supporting. Most had large arable areas at their disposal, often a royal donation, which provided them with valuable foodstuffs. Most burghers probably also had small plots for vegetables and for tending cattle, pigs and goats, and in addition to this they fished. Thus, although contemporary ideology and economic logic suggested that townspeople be employed in trades and crafts, these were only a part of their total activities. Those merchants in Stockholm and some other coastal towns who practised their trade on a full-time basis were exceptions; the rule was that the volume of trade was simply too small to provide a livelihood for most people. The majority of burghers seem to have devoted far more time to farming, stock-breeding and fishing than to trades and crafts.[34]

Practice: crafts and manufacture

Handicraft production was naturally not entirely absent. The government intended Swedish urban artisans to be organised in guilds along the lines of the German crafts, but in fact before the seventeenth century guild organisations could be found only in Stockholm. Most other towns were simply too small to support a craft guild, although individual shoemakers, tailors, blacksmiths and tanners abounded. Outside Stockholm craft guilds appeared only in the larger towns in the seventeenth century, and in the middle ranking centres not until the eighteenth.[35] But the absence of guilds did not make practising a craft entirely free. To work as an urban artisan one had to belong to the burghership or town freedom and one was supervised by the local magistracy and the other town artisans. In Stockholm, the craft members of the freedom did their best to exclude unchartered artisans, particularly those employed by the crown and nobility who were not burghers and who were forbidden to work except for their principal employers. Despite this, in Stockholm the number of non-freemen artisans grew rapidly, especially during the seventeenth century.[36]

Most urban craft production took place in artisans' workshops. Before the seventeenth century we know of few other forms of produc-

[33] Sandström, *Plöjande borgare*, pp. 63–75.
[34] Ibid., pp. 42–63.
[35] Gadd, *Självhushållning*, p. 273; F. Lindberg, *Hantverkarna*, 2 vols. (Stockholm, 1947), vol. I, pp. 35, 40, 45, 62–6, 99.
[36] A. Jansson, *Bördor och bärkraft. Borgare och kronotjänare i Stockholm 1644–1672* (Stockholm, 1991), pp. 29ff., 67.

tion in Swedish towns; only in Stockholm and in a couple of other towns were there any larger work sites, mostly with a military orientation like shipyards and ropeyards. As Sweden built up a strong military force after the 1620s, naval production expanded somewhat in the capital, but it was still modest in scale. Outside Stockholm, Norrköping in Östergötland was the most notable industrial centre, with both small arms and textile factories founded there in the early seventeenth century. Norrköping later became the country's most important industrial town outside the capital.[37]

Textile, wood and metal crafts seem also to have been widely practised in the Swedish countryside in the late medieval period. Rural industries were concentrated in southern Västergötland, western and southwestern Småland, and in the region around Lake Siljan in Dalarna. Perhaps not coincidentally, none of these areas had any towns before the seventeenth century, although it must also be said that the presence of towns did not necessarily exclude rural manufacture. There are many instances long before the seventeenth century of peasants elsewhere taking metalwork or various kinds of carpentry to sell at town markets.[38]

Rural crafts lacked any formal organisation, and most rural craftsmen seem not to have had independent workshops either. The commonest among them, tailors, shoemakers and suchlike, travelled between farms and performed their jobs on the spot. The most likely to have permanent workshops were blacksmiths and millers.[39] Recent research suggests that rural crafts were advantaged by the fact that Swedish peasants had a large degree of control over their production, similarly to the regions in western Germany where *Grundherrschaft* was established in the late middle ages and where rural crafts were also well developed. On the other hand, Sweden's market for rural manufacture was neither broad nor deep. Before the seventeenth century the country lacked a powerful nobility to provide a demand, and before the eighteenth century the Swedish rural cottar or labourer class was fairly small. Rural manufacture therefore seems to have been practised mainly by comparatively well-off farmers selling to other farmers.[40]

Large-scale manufacture like the copper and arms industries was almost always situated outside the towns. Initially, iron production was organised on a very small scale and was highly decentralised, with

[37] B. Ericsson, 'The foundation and function of small towns in the early modern period', in A. Mączak and C. Smout (eds.), *Gründung und Bedeutung kleinerer Städte im nördlichen Europa der frühen Neuzeit* (Wiesbaden, 1991), pp. 114f.

[38] Gadd, *Självhushållning*, p. 57; Heckscher, *Sveriges ekonomiska historia*, vol. I:2, pp. 529–32; Magnusson, *Sveriges ekonomiska historia*, pp. 215–17.

[39] Gadd, *Självhushållning*, p. 28.

[40] Ibid., pp. 210ff.

Table 2.3. *The ten largest Swedish towns, 1530–1690*

	1530		1610		1690	
1	Stockholm	8,000	Stockholm	8,900	Stockholm	57,000
2	Åbo	2,000	Åbo	2,100	Åbo	5,800
3	Uppsala	1,700	Nyköping	1,900	Falun	5,800
4	Viborg	1,400	Norrköping	1,900	Malmö[a]	5,700
5	Kalmar	1,400	Uppsala	1,700	Göteborg	5,000
6	Nyköping	1,300	Gävle	1,500	Karlskrona[b]	4,000
7	Vadstena	1,000	Kalmar	1,400	Norrköping	3,700
8	Västerås	900	Viborg	1,400	Jönköping	2,700
9	Gävle	900	Arboga	1,400	Viborg	2,500
10	Arboga	900	Nya Lödöse	1,300	Uppsala	2,400

Notes:
Note that population figures for 1530 and to a lesser extent for 1610 are very uncertain.
[a] Malmö in Skåne became Swedish in 1658.
[b] Founded in 1680 as a naval base.
Sources: Lilja, *Historisk tätortsstatistik* (n. 42), Table 2; Lilja, *Tjuvehål och stolta städer* (n. 4), Table A:5.

foundries across Bergslagen from Värmland in the west to northern Uppland in the east, and in Östergötland and Småland in the south of the country. However, by the seventeenth century the size of newly established ironworks had increased. At first these ironworks were largely financed by Dutch capital, which began to reach the country in the 1610s, most famously through the entrepreneur Louis De Geer; De Geer also initiated the manufactures in Norrköping. Most foreign capital was either invested directly in an industry by immigrants like De Geer, who turned into a full-time manufacturer, or was advanced as credit to merchants in Stockholm and later Göteborg, who in turn acted as credit brokers for local manufacturers and mining peasants.[41]

The copper industry was more centralised. Sweden probably had Europe's most important copper mine in Falun in Dalarna, which was being exploited already in medieval times; by the late sixteenth and early seventeenth centuries copper had become the country's most valuable export together with iron and steel (Table 2.2). Both copper production and trade were strictly regulated. An urban settlement that arose in the neighbourhood of the Falun mine was granted a legal and administrative system reminiscent of a chartered town's. By 1641, when Falun received formal town charters, it had become one of the biggest urban communities in Sweden after Stockholm (Table 2.3).[42] The copper mine and

[41] Heckscher, *Sveriges ekonomiska historia,* vol. I:2, pp. 360–75, 565–70.
[42] Apart from Stockholm, perhaps only Åbo was bigger than Falun. See S. Lilja, *Historisk*

the neighbouring furnaces and forges were the largest industrial site in the country before the nineteenth century.[43]

The main reason why the ban against rural commerce was so ineffective was the country's vast distances and low demographic density. For many farmers the distances to the nearest town were huge, and besides, most towns were too small and poor to have much to offer in exchange. Peasants also regarded the merchants as unalloyed monopolists. High transport costs made trade a seasonal activity to be carried out in the dead periods of the agricultural year, mainly the winter, and rendered seasonal fairs particularly attractive. Almost every town had at least one fair, which was either a restricted market to which merchants from other towns had no access, or a free market open to all towns. Rural fairs could also be either restricted and linked to a specific town, or free; the latter were more attractive for the peasantry, partly because they drew more substantial merchants from the bigger towns. Fairs were also major social events, which the monarchy used until the early seventeenth century to table negotiations with the peasantry from a given region.[44]

Like small-scale craftwork, a large part of the trade in rural manufactures was based upon house-to-house peddling. Pedlars from the three main industrial regions travelled far and wide to sell their wares. In 1622, Borås was founded in the middle of the manufacturing area of Västergötland with the purpose of getting the rural merchants and pedlars to settle and become burghers. The experiment, however, had only limited success, and both rural production and trade continued to prosper around Borås as well as in the other two areas up to the nineteenth century.[45] However grand the government's plans, and however determined it was to concentrate trade within the towns, it was forced to face up to the towns' limitations. It has also been suggested that the monarchy displayed a pragmatic acceptance of rural exchange, particularly after 1610, and tacitly ignored the formal bans it had previously enacted.[46] Despite this, it was in precisely those years that the most far-reaching regulation of trade took place.

tätortsstatistik, vol. II: *Städernas folkmängd och tillväxt. Sverige (med Finland) ca 1570–tal till 1810–tal* (Stockholm, 1996).

[43] Ericsson, 'Foundation', p. 116.

[44] Sandström, *Plöjande borgare*, pp. 116–21; N. Staf, *Marknad och möte. Studier rörande politiska underhandlingar med folkmenigheter i Sverige och Finland intill Gustav II Adolfs tid* (Stockholm, 1935).

[45] Magnusson, *Sveriges ekonomiska historia*, pp. 215–17; Sandström, *Plöjande borgare*, pp. 125ff.

[46] Magnusson, *Sveriges ekonomiska historia*, pp. 77–82.

Town and country in the seventeenth century

New town foundations

During the seventeenth century town–country relations underwent major changes in response to the strengthening of the Swedish state. During the 1620s, Sweden became the strongest power in northern Europe through the systematic deployment of all available resources for military purposes. The two men behind these developments were Gustavus Adolphus, who came to the throne in 1611, and Axel Oxenstierna, the leader of the aristocracy who managed to secure a monopoly over the higher offices of the state and who, as chancellor and head of government from 1612 until his death in 1654, masterminded a remarkable transformation of the administration into perhaps the most modern and efficient bureaucracy of his time.

These developments hit the Swedish peasantry hard. Taxes rose to unprecedented levels. Conscription ballooned, as Gustavus Adolphus decided to rely on an army of enlisted peasants rather than primarily of mercenary soldiers. During the period of most intense conscription in the 1620s and '30s, almost every year every ten men over fifteen years of age had to supply one soldier. When Sweden entered the German war in 1630, the army consisted of 31,000 alien mercenaries and 41,000 Swedes and Finns; about 50,000 conscripts had already died in the wars of the 1620s. These losses hit a population numbering as little as 1.25 million.[47]

Sweden's transformation into a military state affected towns in three ways: first, through the rising burden of fiscal and other demands; second, through governmental reforms of local and regional administration, which also included the governance and autonomy of the towns; and third, through the transformation of the urban system in terms both of the total number of towns and of their functional roles. It is to this third effect that we now turn.

Between the 1580s and the 1650s about forty-five new towns were founded in Sweden; three more had been founded around the middle of the sixteenth century (Figure 2.1). With only a few exceptions the crown founded all the new towns, and all but nine were established during Axel Oxenstierna's chancellorship.[48] By the mid-seventeenth

[47] S. A. Nilsson, 'Imperial Sweden: nation-building, war and social changes', in A. Losman, M. Lundström and M. Revera (eds.), *The age of new Sweden* (Stockholm, 1988), pp. 7–39; Nilsson, *De stora krigens tid. Om Sverige som militärstat och bondesamhälle* (Uppsala, 1990), pp. 162, 283.
[48] See B. Ericsson, 'De anlagda städerna i Sverige ca. 1580–1800' and S. E. Åström 'Anlagda städer och centralortssystemet i Finland 1550–1785', both in *De anlagte steder på 1600–1700 tallet* (Oslo, 1977). The number depends on whether one counts all new

century the old parts of Sweden and Finland numbered some eighty-five chartered towns, to which must be added about twenty others situated in the newly conquered regions of Denmark and Norway.[49] The new towns were generally located in areas that lacked medieval towns, with the result that by the mid-seventeenth century Bergslagen and the coast of the Gulf of Bothnia had several towns, and even the Finnish interior got its first urban foundations. The new foundations increased the country's rate of urbanisation. Compared to *c.*4 per cent of the Swedish population living in towns in the early 1600s, 9–10 per cent were urbanised a century later, and this proportion stayed the same until the second part of the nineteenth century. Although about a third of the increase was due to the growth of Stockholm, the smaller towns also had their fair share.[50]

The fiscal purposes of the urban settlements were probably paramount: the government found it easier to tax trade that was concentrated rather than dispersed, and it is clear that almost all towns were meant to be commercial centres in one way or another. Not surprisingly, the state's fiscal objectives were fully compatible with the ideological justification for banning rural trade discussed previously, namely that trade was by its very nature a purely urban activity. Most new towns were situated in regions that were already served by some formal markets and fairs, or where the peasants were active traders and were used to sailing south to sell their products, but also where there was virtually no prior urban development. The initiative almost always came from the crown rather than from the peasantry, which appears to have been either uninterested or hostile. The lack of competing urban centres meant that the crown was free to choose the foundation's position so as to optimise land concessions to attract settlers. However, some towns never took off and were abandoned within a few years of being founded, while elsewhere it took a long time to attract a sufficient number of inhabitants.[51]

town foundations; for example, Taipale, Salmis, Sordavala and Kuopio in Finland languished almost immediately after they were established. See R. Ranta, 'Stadsväsendet under stormaktstiden', in *Stadsväsendets historia i Finland* (Helsingfors, 1987), pp. 44, 46.

[49] Two further towns (Karlshamn and Karlskrona) were founded in the late seventeenth century in the old Danish county of Blekinge. Karlskrona, founded as a naval base in 1680, became in a short time one of the largest towns in Sweden.

[50] S. Lilja, 'Small towns in the periphery: population and economy of small towns in Sweden and Finland during the early modern period', in P. Clark (ed.), *Small towns in early modern Europe* (Cambridge, 1995), pp. 54ff. Stockholm's share of the total urban population rose from about 12 to 26 per cent between the 1610s and the 1690s, thus contributing 32 per cent of total urban growth in the period. The estimate is based on figures in Lilja, *Tjuvehål och stolta städer*, Table 6:3.

[51] R. Sandberg, 'Urban landownership in early modern Sweden', in F. E. Eliassen and

The staple system

According to Axel Oxenstierna and other members of the government, however, new town foundations were not enough to increase trade significantly. It was also essential that the trade of existing towns be regulated and that the towns themselves be forced into a specific ranking. Urban order, it was believed, would be enough to make towns and trade develop and prosper and to increase crown revenues. Accordingly, Gustavus Adolphus and Axel Oxenstierna issued a statute in 1614 that regulated the functions of different towns and imposed a drastic division of trade between coastal and inland towns, the so-called 'uptowns'. The provision deprived inland towns of the right to practise foreign trade actively, that is, to sail their own ships to ports outside the kingdom of Sweden. By way of compensation it gave them exclusive rights to trade in Bergslagen, as well as a monopoly on trade with non-burgher groups at their own markets. Although the burghers of coastal towns were still allowed to visit the free markets of inland towns, they could only trade with the local burghers and not with the non-burghers, peasants and others.

These trade regulations were imposed upon the towns against their will. The coastal staple towns got a monopoly over foreign trade, but lost their ancient contacts with inland producers. The inland towns, both old and new, were granted the sole right to trade with the peasantry on their own restricted markets, but lost the right to engage actively in foreign trade, for which they now depended upon the staple towns. But the latter protested more loudly, so three years later the government issued a new ordinance that allowed the staple towns to trade directly with the peasants and miners under specified circumstances.

The trade ordinances, which were revised once again in 1636 for the benefit of Stockholm, helped to differentiate urban functions more clearly. On the one hand, they are unlikely to have had any impact on the volume of foreign trade or even on its dominance by foreign merchants, as the government had hoped. Although Swedish foreign trade expanded enormously during the seventeenth century – for example, iron exports rose fivefold – the main causes of domestic growth lay elsewhere.[52] On the other hand, as far as the inland towns were concerned the legislation effectively cut them off from foreign trade and gave the staple town merchants the chance to act as mid-

G. A. Ersland (eds.), *Power, profit and urban land. Landownership in medieval and early modern northern European towns* (Aldershot, 1996), pp. 79–93.
[52] Heckscher, *Sveriges ekonomiska historia*, vol. I:2, pp. 473ff., 556–61; Sandström, *Plöjande borgare*, pp. 170–8.

dlemen between inland towns and foreign traders. The same goes for
the new towns on the Gulf of Bothnia, which were not granted staple
rights and whose merchants were forced after 1636 to trade in either
Stockholm or Åbo. The authorities in the capital were granted the
power to enforce the ruling.[53] Stockholm benefited particularly from the
trade ordinances, which enabled it to defend its position as the main
trading hub for its huge rural hinterland. The new city of Göteborg
achieved a similar position on the western coast, where its hinterland
consisted of Västergötland and of the part of Bergslagen situated in the
county of Värmland.[54]

These interventions helped to give Sweden a radically different urban
hierarchy by the middle of the seventeenth century. The more complex
central place functions that developed were not restricted to trade.
Administrative functions were more diverse as well, as a consequence of
the reorganisation in the 1630s by Axel Oxenstierna of the regional
administration, which divided Sweden into fifteen provinces (*län*). A
governor, who resided with his small staff in one of the provincial towns,
headed each province. In addition to these provincial capitals, five of
them new foundations, some newly founded mining towns also assumed
stronger central place functions.[55]

To assess the consequences of the new urban system established by
Axel Oxenstierna for relations between town and country we need to
relate it to the attempt to force trade into towns for tax purposes.
Perhaps the most radical change to established practice took place in the
northern Gulf of Bothnia. Before the 1620s the region lacked towns,
and it was largely up to the peasantry itself to bring their goods south to
Stockholm. (To what extent they sailed all the way to foreign ports is
unknown.) Once the new coastal towns were founded, the old trading
patterns became illegal, as the new foundations were meant to act as
trading posts between the peasants and the capital city, and were therefore deliberately established in areas with the greatest number of rural
merchants. Although rural trade did not cease entirely after the 1620s,
its volume clearly decreased. Thus already by 1624, 70 per cent of
registered shiploads of pitch from Österbotten, a county on the Finnish
side of the Gulf that had always exported large quantities of pitch to
Stockholm, passed through the new towns of Vasa (Vaasa), Gamlakar-
leby (Kokkola), Uleåborg (Oulu) and Nykarleby (Uusikaarlepyy). By

[53] Sandberg, *I slottets skugga*, pp. 176–80; Sandström, *Mellan Torneå och Amsterdam*,
pp. 378ff.
[54] Sandström, *Plöjande borgare*, pp. 146ff.
[55] Ericsson, 'De anlagda städerna', pp. 109–19. The five newly founded provincial
capitals before the 1650s were Karlstad, Nora, Falun, Hudiksvall and Umeå. The new
mining towns were Filipstad, Falun and Sala.

the 1640s, the proportion had risen to more than 90 per cent. Unless the peasant traders were able to avoid the Stockholm customs, the figures suggest that a major shift in patterns of trade had occurred very rapidly indeed.[56]

In Finland, where distances between towns were even greater than in Sweden and competition was even more muted, the peasantry became closely bound to town merchants who provided them with credit and lodging when they visited the town for trading purposes. Merchant credit became especially important after the 1620s because of the increased level of taxation, which had to be paid in cash to a greater degree than in the past. In exchange for advancing the peasant's tax dues, the merchant established a right to the peasant's merchandise, which therefore never reached the market as it was supposed to do by law. Since the peasant was obliged to sell his goods to his creditor as long as he was in debt, the arrangement was one the debtor frequently found it hard to cut free from. Although this credit system was also practised elsewhere in the kingdom and was common among rural miners, for a long time it was most frequently found in southern Finland.[57]

Winners and losers

Those who gained most from the state's urban policy were in the first place the most important staple towns, headed by Stockholm, although the merchants of Stockholm themselves held a different view. They complained regularly that they were cut off from their former contacts among the peasants and miners and that they found it difficult to claim their debts because of the ban on travel around the countryside. But there is little doubt that in the long run the ordinances, particularly that of 1636, gave Stockholm a much tighter hold over its immense hinterland comprising the Mälar valley, Bergslagen and the entire region bordering on the Gulf of Bothnia.

The main innovation introduced by the ordinance of 1614 was the definitive submission of the towns of the Mälar valley to Stockholm's influence. Although never Stockholm's equals, they had formerly played a more independent role, based on the fact that the inland towns or 'uptowns' were meant to act as middlemen between the peasantry and the staple towns that monopolised the foreign trade. This principle was

[56] Sandström, *Plöjande borgare*, p. 67.
[57] Heckscher, *Sveriges ekonomiska historia*, vol. I:2, pp. 569ff.; Ranta, 'Stadsväsendet under stormaktstiden', p. 61; O. Nikula, 'Stadsväsendet i Finland 1721–1875', in *Stadsväsendets historia i Finland*, pp. 142–4.

overturned by the second ordinance of 1617, which granted staple town merchants the right to trade directly with peasants at uptown markets. By depriving the Mälar towns of their trading role, the ordinance also tied the mining region of Bergslagen closer to Stockholm, and allowed the penetration by capital from Stockholm and abroad of metal production there. One observes a similar development with the merchants of Göteborg, who were able to dominate a vast region in western Sweden.[58]

Although the extent of the uptowns' participation in foreign trade before the law of 1614 was very modest, amounting to only a few percentage points of total exports, one should not underestimate the competitive impact of this trade on the terms the uptowns could obtain from staple town merchants. On the other hand, the inland towns often lacked the capital to finance more extensive domestic trade and thus could not always supply the countryside, which was an essential government objective. Even during the seventeenth century many uptowns relied mainly on farming for their livelihood, and the peasantry had to supply itself with necessities, particularly grain, either directly from abroad or by way of the coastal towns.[59]

Rural crafts were also affected by the new urban policy. As with trade, manufacture was meant to be an urban occupation, and from the end of the sixteenth century a large number of decrees were issued on the matter. Between 1580 and the 1620s a number of towns were granted jurisdiction over 'craft districts' in their hinterlands where no rural artisan was allowed to practise. All rural craftsmen within such districts were told to move into the town. In practice, artisans – like rural merchants – remained in the countryside, but had to pay a fee to the town and to the guild where one existed. But even though rural craftsmen had an incentive to pay up because the towns could protect them and their sons against military conscription,[60] the vast majority of rural craftsmen were beyond the towns' reach.

Conclusion

Before the seventeenth century the peasantry had been virtually independent, supplementing what it produced itself with a small range of goods which it could mostly obtain without passing through the towns. The crown tried to stop rural trade, but before the seventeenth century

[58] Heckscher, *Sveriges ekonomiska historia*, vol. I:2, pp. 568ff.; Sandström, *Plöjande borgare*, pp. 146f.
[59] Sandström, *Plöjande borgare*, pp. 154f.
[60] Gadd, *Självhushållning*, pp. 232ff., 254; Lindberg, *Hantverkarna*, pp. 101–12.

the odds were against it, not only because the population was spread out so thinly, but because towns were too few and too small to provide the countryside with an adequate supply network.

During the seventeenth century conditions changed. The Swedish state created a large number of new towns and a staple system, both of which had significant effects on town–country relations. From the 1610s onwards the royal administration was reformed, while at the same time the country pursued a deliberate policy of militarisation. The state's attempt to develop and reorganise the urban system led to a doubling in the total number of chartered towns, to an increase in their functional complexity, and to the concentration of both foreign and domestic trade within town walls for tax purposes. By contrast, it is unclear whether the volume of trade itself was affected as the government hoped. The huge increase in Swedish trade during the seventeenth century probably had little to do with urban policy. Towns also appear to have done little to stimulate economic growth according to state plan.

The engine of the Swedish economy during the early modern period was more probably the mining, metals and arms industries, all of which were mostly rural phenomena. To a great extent they were also financed by foreign capital, even if some Stockholm merchants joined in. A further stimulus was provided by the state's fiscal demands, which forced peasants to raise more cash on the export markets and brought them into increased contact with the towns. Although the rate of urbanisation rose, most towns remained extremely small: by the end of the seventeenth century two-thirds had fewer than 1,000 inhabitants, and half of these numbered fewer than 500 people. Most of the gains were made by Stockholm, by a few other staple towns like Göteborg and Norrköping, and by the mining town of Falun.[61] But the towns were also too small to act parasitically on the countryside.[62] Like the countryside, the towns were to a large extent self-sufficient, and indeed the difference between the smaller Swedish towns and the countryside was not very great. Within this pattern it was Stockholm that stood out. Stockholm benefited from its dual status as the dominant staple town in foreign trade and as the capital of an expanding military state with great power ambitions.[63] Thus, the state influenced town–country relations to a greater degree indirectly than directly.

[61] Lilja, *Historisk tätortsstatistik*.
[62] For a somewhat different opinion, see Lilja, 'Small towns'.
[63] Sandberg, 'Growth and transformation', p. 314.

3   Town and country in Holland, 1300–1550[1]

Peter C. M. Hoppenbrouwers

Introduction

Although it is easy to see retrospectively that the foundations for the
state that came to be known as the Dutch Republic were laid during the
late middle ages, as late as 1550 no one could have imagined its coming
into being, let alone predicted its territorial composition and boundaries. Until the 1540s the driving force of state formation had been the
conscious assemblage of principalities in the area of the Low Countries
by the dukes of Burgundy and their successors, the Habsburg emperors
of Germany. The process began with Philip the Bold entering into
possession of the County of Flanders in 1384, and it ended with the
submission of the duchy of Guelders to Charles V in 1543. The County
of Holland that is the subject of this chapter was added to the Burgundian multiple state in 1428, when Duke Philip the Good successfully
intervened in the protracted civil war between Jacqueline and John of
Bavaria, the German house that had ruled Holland from 1349.

The focus on the County of Holland, which was only one of the seven
provinces later to constitute the Dutch Republic, suffers to some extent
from a retrospective bias. In the Republic's Golden Age, Holland's
demographic, economic and political preponderance was overwhelming.
In 1622 more than 40 per cent of the Republic's population lived in
Holland alone.[2] Regional patterns of urbanisation were even more
skewed. Yet Holland's dominance within the Republic demands a
historical explanation, which leads us inevitably back to the late middle
ages when towns in Holland showed themselves to be remarkably
successful in terms of demographic growth, economic development, and
the extension of political power.

The total size of Holland's population at the beginning of the

[1] I am grateful to Amanda Pipkin for correcting several of my English drafts, and staying
cheerful and encouraging all the time.
[2] J. de Vries and A. van der Woude, *The first modern economy. Success, failure, and
perseverance of the Dutch economy, 1500–1815* (Cambridge, 1997), pp. 51–3.

1 Terschelling
2 Medemblik
3 West-Friesland
4 Kennemerland
5 Zeevang
6 Waterland
7 Amstelland
8 Gooiland
9 Rijnland
10 Woerden
11 Delfland
12 Schieland
13 Land van Gouda
14 Zuidholland
15 Land van Arkel and Land van Leede
16 Oost-Voorne
17 West-Voorne
18 Land van Heusden
19 Zeeland Beoostenschelde
20 Zeeland Bewestenschelde
21 Putten and Strijen

North Sea

Figure 3.1   Holland and Zeeland in 1433

sixteenth century was probably similar to that towards 1340, somewhat over 250,000 people;[3] but during the same period the number of people living in towns doubled. On the basis of the so-called Informacie, an inquiry into the state of the region's towns and villages made in 1514 by the Habsburg authorities, 45 per cent of all Hollanders lived in thirty-five communities of urban status, which ranged in size from 400–500 to 13,500 inhabitants (Table 3.1).[4] The expansion of urban trade and industry during the second half of the fourteenth century laid the ground for Holland's subsequent 'forging ahead'.[5] Although the advance was not a sudden leap forward – the roots of the larger towns' success can be traced back to the second half of the thirteenth century[6] – growth after the mid-fourteenth century is nevertheless remarkable. During the century thereafter Hollanders began to export beer, cloth, herring and subsequently butter and cheese, cattle and peat, to the middle Rhineland around Cologne and to Brabant, Flanders and the Baltic area, where salted herring was in strong demand.[7] At the same

---

[3] D. E. H. de Boer, *Graaf en grafiek. Sociale en economische ontwikkelingen in het middeleeuwse 'Noordholland' tussen ca. 1345 en ca.1415* (Leiden, 1978), p. 45; W. Blockmans and W. Prevenier, *De Bourgondiërs. De Nederlanden op weg naar eenheid, 1384–1530* (Amsterdam–Leuven, 1997), p. 174 and n. 18.

[4] My definition of towns has followed contemporary usage, rather than modern demographic, spatial, economic, or social criteria, which can seldom be verified in the sources. Between twenty-five and thirty-five locations were considered to have urban status in the late medieval county of Holland, although contemporaries did not regard all towns as equal. By 1500 six 'capital' or 'large' towns, as they were called – Dordrecht, Haarlem, Leiden, Delft, Gouda, and Amsterdam – stood out from the rest (J. G. Smit, *Vorst en onderdaan. Studies over Holland en Zeeland in de late Middeleeuwen* (Leuven, 1995), p. 398). According to an estimate based on the measurement of intramural surfaces of towns as calculated from the detailed maps which the cartographer Jacob van Deventer drew around 1560, combined with known population figures, the present-day Netherlands counted 121 places with urban status in the mid-sixteenth century, 35 of which (29 per cent) were situated in Holland. Of the 35 towns with over 2,500 inhabitants, 15 (43 per cent) were in Holland (J. C. Visser, 'Dichtheid van de bevolking in de laat-middeleeuwse stad', *Historisch-Geografisch Tijdschrift* 3 (1985), 10–21). For population figures in 1514, see W. P. Blockmans et al., 'Tussen crisis en welvaart. Sociale veranderingen 1300–1500', in *Algemene Geschiedenis der Nederlanden* (Bussum, 1980), vol. IV, pp. 42–86, Table 1; Blockmans and Prevenier, *Bourgondiërs*, p. 174.

[5] H. P. H. Jansen, 'Holland's advance', *Acta Historiae Neerlandicae* 10 (1976), 1–19.

[6] D. E. H. de Boer, '"Op weg naar de volwassenheid". De ontwikkeling van productie en consumptie in de Hollandse en Zeeuwse steden in de dertiende eeuw', in *De Hollandse stad in de dertiende eeuw* (Zutphen, 1988), pp. 28–43; D. E. H. de Boer, 'Florerend vanuit de delta. De handelsbetrekkingen van Holland en Zeeland in de tweede helft van de dertiende eeuw', in D. E. H. de Boer, E. H. P. Cordfunke and H. Sarfatij (eds.), *Wi Florens . . . De Hollandse graaf Floris V in de samenleving van de dertiende eeuw* (Utrecht, 1996), pp. 126–52.

[7] J. L. van Zanden, 'Holland en de Zuidelijke Nederlanden in de periode 1500–1570: divergerende ontwikkelingen of voortgaande economische integratie?', in E. Aerts, B. Henau, P. Janssens and R. van Uytven (eds.), *Studia Historica Oeconomica. Liber amicorum Herman van der Wee* (Leuven, 1993), pp. 357–67.

Table 3.1. *Urban population in Holland, 1433–1560*

	1433[a]	1494[b]	1514[b]	c.1560[b]
Alkmaar	800	n/a	3,600–4,000	c.7,500
Amsterdam	3,000	7,700–8,600	10,100–11,400	30,000
Asperen	n/a	n/a	720–810	800
Beverwijk	500	800–900	800–900	1,400
Delft	3,500	13,100–14,700	10,500–11,800	15,000
Den Briel	n/a	n/a	n/a	2,500
Dordrecht	2,000	n/a	c.11,000	12,500
Edam	n/a	1,800–2,000	2,000–2,200	c.3,400
Enkhuizen	500	2,500–2,900	2,900–3,200	7,750
Geertruidenberg	n/a	n/a	1,500–1,700	n/a
Gorinchem	n/a	2,600–2,900	2,800–4,500	n/a
Gouda	2,000	6,600–7,400	6,800–7,600	9,000
's-Gravenhage[c]	700	5,400–6,100	4,800–5,400	6,000
's-Gravenzande	400	500–560	430–480	n/a
Haarlem	3,500	9,700–10,900	10,900–12,200	16,000
Heukelum	n/a	n/a	440–500	600
Heusden	600	1,000–1,100	1,000–1,100	1,600
Hoorn	2,000	3,400–3,900	4,500–5,000	8,000
Leerdam	n/a	n/a	n/a	c.500
Leiden	3,500	12,100–13,600	12,100–13,600	12,500
Nieuwpoort	n/a	380–430	n/a	n/a
Medemblik[d]	500	1,300–1,500	1,300–1,400	1,100
Monnickendam	600	1,200–1,400	1,900–2,200	2,200
Muiden	n/a	430–490	400–450	1,000
Naarden	n/a	1,200–1,400	2,000–2,300	1,700
Purmerend	165	n/a	850–950	1,700
Oudewater	500	1,200–1,300	1,300–1,500	c.2,200
Rotterdam	800	3,900–4,400	4,500–5,100	c.7,500
Schiedam	600	1,900–2,000	1,900–2,100	4,100
Schoonhoven	500	1,800–2,000	1,800–2,100	2,800
Vlaardingen	n/a	760–860	800–900	2,800
Weesp	n/a	800–900	400–500	1,700
Woerden	400	1,100–1,200	1,100–1,200	c.2,100

Notes: Towns include all places described as *steden* in the Informacie of 1514. Numbers of hearths were multiplied by 4 and 4.5 for 1494 and 1514 and by 4.25 for c.1560 to obtain population estimates.
[a] Tax assessment (assigned nos. of tax 'shields').
[b] Hearths.
[c] With adjacent villages.
[d] Inclusive of the adjacent villages of Oostwoude, Opperdoes and Wevershoeve.
Sources: The tax assessment of 1433 from J. A. M. Y. Bos-Rops, *Graven op zoek naar geld. De inkomsten van de graven van Holland en Zeeland, 1389–1433* (Hilversum, 1993), pp. 365–9; population data from P. Lourens and J. Lucassen, *Inwoneraantallen van Nederlandse steden ca. 1300–1800* (Amsterdam, 1997).

time Dutch freighters, which could rely on a steady demand for return loads of cereals, timber and salt for the home market, rose to dominate the overseas transport business on the Baltic–Atlantic axis.[8]

The second half of the fourteenth century also saw the towns move to the centre of the political stage. Already during the civil war that broke out in the aftermath of Count William IV's death against the Frisians in 1345, the towns had expanded their influence by backing the winner, William of Bavaria. Although once in power Count William V acted to reduce urban influence on his government,[9] the towns' ascendancy could not be arrested so long as the counts required financial support for their political and military ambitions. In return for ever more frequent taxes, the towns demanded economic privileges and a say on monetary matters and on the size of general subsidies or aids (*extraordinaris beden*). The new civil war between Jacqueline of Bavaria and her uncle John in 1417–25 marked a turning point in the rise to political dominance of the large towns of Holland.[10] Thereafter no major decision bearing on the county's general welfare – which included declarations of war and recruitment of armies, proclamations of embargoes, levying of general taxes, but also the financing of large dike projects and purely economic issues, in particular monetary matters – could be taken without consulting the towns' representatives.[11]

The extraordinary success of Holland's towns raises the question of its effects on relations between town and countryside. This chapter addresses the question under three headings. The first section discusses the actions of individuals and the influence of institutions on the operation of market forces. The second section addresses the political economy of urban–rural relations, in particular the protectionist interventions by town governments, and the third section is concerned with the political process, characterised by urban interference with administration, law-making and justice in the villages. In all instances the towns tightened their grip over the countryside in various ways. The final

[8] See W. Blockmans, 'The economic expansion of Holland and Zeeland in the fourteenth–sixteenth centuries', in *Studia Historica Oeconomica*, pp. 50–3.

[9] H. M. Brokken, *Het ontstaan van de Hoekse en Kabeljauwse twisten* (Zutphen, 1982), pp. 291–2; H. Kokken, *Steden en staten. Dagvaarten van steden en Staten van Holland onder Maria van Bourgondië en het eerste regentschap van Maximiliaan van Oostenrijk (1477–1494)* (The Hague, 1991), pp. 23–5.

[10] J. A. M. Y. Bos-Rops, *Graven op zoek naar geld. De inkomsten van de graven van Holland en Zeeland, 1389–1433* (Hilversum, 1993), pp. 182–3.

[11] The need to consult the towns on a more regular basis is reflected in a sharp increase in the number of *dagvaarten* – meetings of what gradually came to be seen as representatives of the Estates – from 12–13 per year during the government of Count Albrecht of Bavaria (1358–1404) and his son William VI (1404–17), to 31–33 per annum during the civil war and the subsequent rule of Philip of Burgundy (1417–67). See Bos-Rops, *Graven*, p. 252, Table 42.

section examines why, despite these successes, the largest and most powerful among Holland's towns did not succeed in turning themselves into autonomous city-states along the lines of the northern Italian communes.

Production and trade

Proto-industry in the countryside

According to Jan de Vries, the low level of occupational differentiation in the countryside outlined by the Informacie of 1514 and by a less complete survey of 1494 reflects the underdeveloped division of labour characteristic of the medieval rural economy. He therefore described early modern development in Holland's coastal regions as a departure from that pattern, in terms of growing commercialisation and specialisation. De Vries's inferences have been disputed, however, and the current synthesis proposed by van Zanden sees Holland's rural economy at the threshold of the early modern period as at the same time highly commercialised (Noordegraaf) and unspecialised (de Vries).[12] Towards 1500 the majority of the rural population combined small-scale agriculture with various forms of commercially oriented by-employment linked to urban demand. Activities of this sort were often performed as wage-work and included, besides the standard textile industries, linen bleaching, salt refining for the herring industry, ship-building, salt- and sweet-water fishing, reed cutting and peat digging, brick making, and the building and maintenance of dikes; labour-intensive, small-scale horticulture and cash crops like flax, rape seed, hemp and hops were also widespread. Although little is known about the organisation of these activities,[13] van Zanden describes them as

[12] J. L. van Zanden, 'Op zoek naar de "missing link"'. Hypothesen over de opkomst van Holland in de late middeleeuwen en de vroeg-moderne tijd', *Tijdschrift voor Sociale Geschiedenis* 14 (1988), 359–86; J. L. van Zanden, *The rise and decline of Holland's economy. Merchant capitalism and the labour market*, Engl. transl. (Manchester–New York, 1993), ch. 2; J. de Vries, *The Dutch rural economy in the Golden Age, 1500–1700* (New Haven–London, 1974), esp. ch. 2; L. Noordegraaf, 'Het platteland van Holland in de zestiende eeuw. Anachronismen, modelgebruik en traditionele bronnenkritiek', *Economisch- en Sociaalhistorisch Jaarboek* 48 (1985), 8–18. See also de Vries's recent reassessment, 'The transition to capitalism in a land without feudalism', supplementary to the conference 'The Brenner debate and the late medieval and early modern history of the Low Countries', Utrecht, 17–18 June 1994, forthcoming (cited hereafter as BDLC).

[13] Only sweet-water fisheries and the building and repairing of dikes, canals and sluices have been studied from this point of view; see P. van Dam, *Vissen in veenmeren. De sluisvisserij op aal tussen Haarlem en Amsterdam en de ecologische transformatie in Rijnland, 1440–1530* (Hilversum, 1998), ch. 5; D. E. H. de Boer, '"Roerende van der visscheryen". Enkele aspecten van de visvangst in Holland en Zeeland tot de Sint

'proto-industrial' and the rural population as 'proto-proletarian' rather than 'peasant'.[14]

The causes of these new arrangements must be sought in two directions. On the one hand, the growing problems faced by arable subsistence farming in the peat areas as a consequence of ground subsidence could lead to more extensive raising of cattle, horses or sheep, although this was not always possible. Approximately half the cultivated area in late medieval Holland seems to have been made up of small plots owned by the peasantry, who were unwilling to give up possession of their land; even though during most of the fifteenth century land was cheap to buy and lease, it was therefore not always easy to consolidate large farms for pasture. On the other hand, urban expansion generated strong demand for raw materials and semi-manufactured goods like dry turf and bricks. The effect of increased production for the market and rural diversification, however, was to enhance the smallholders' economic resilience and, paradoxically, to reinforce the lack of rural specialisation. This 'proto-industrial' structure only disappeared in Holland during the seventeenth century, when peasant smallholdings collapsed as the rising size of farms and growing demand by urban textile industries reduced the supply of part-time rural labour.[15]

Markets and urban hierarchies

Although we have only a limited understanding of urban developments in Holland during the thirteenth century, most towns probably functioned only as economic and administrative centres for the surrounding countryside. It is unlikely that at this early stage they played much of a

Elisabethsvloed van 1421', in *Holland en het water in de middeleeuwen. Strijd tegen het water en beheersing en gebruik van het water* (Hilversum, 1997), pp. 115–40; P. C. M. Hoppenbrouwers, *Een middeleeuwse samenleving. Het Land van Heusden, ca. 1360–ca. 1515* (Groningen–Wageningen, 1992), vol. I, pp. 268–70; P. van Dam, 'Gravers, ofzetters en berriedragers. Werkgelegenheid aan de Spaarndammerdijk omstreeks 1510', *Tijdschrift voor Sociale Geschiedenis* 18 (1992), 447–79. For references to the rural cloth industry in the early sixteenth century, see E. C. G. Brünner, *De Order op de Buitennering van 1531* (Utrecht, 1918), p. 65. It is unclear whether franchisees of regalian rights financed and organised the fishing farms, or simply leased them for short-term profit.
14 J. L. van Zanden, 'De prijs van de vooruitgang? Economische modernisering en sociale polarisatie op het Nederlandse platteland na 1500', *Economisch- en Sociaalhistorisch Jaarboek* 51 (1988), 82–3; van Zanden, *Rise and decline*, pp. 41–53.
15 J. de Vries, 'The labour market', in K. Davids and L. Noordegraaf (eds.), *The Dutch economy in the Golden Age. Nine studies* (Amsterdam, 1993), pp. 58–9, 65; van Zanden, *Rise and decline*, pp. 41–53; J. L. van Zanden, 'Proto-industrialisation and the moderate nature of the later medieval crisis in Flanders and in Holland, 1350–1550', in BDLC.

role in regional and supraregional markets, for the countryside was also as yet too underdeveloped. All of this changed during the late middle ages, when Holland's regional trading system expanded rapidly along its two pre-existing axes and more sharply defined market hierarchies began to emerge.[16]

By the first half of the thirteenth century, when the river Gouwe was made navigable for larger barges, Holland's regional trading system was shaped like an inverted 'T', with an east–west axis formed by the rivers Lek, Merwede and Meuse, and a north–south axis running from the Zuiderzee through the lakes north-east of Leiden and the rivers Gouwe and Hollandse IJssel down to the Rhine (Lek, Merwede)–Meuse delta near Rotterdam.[17] The east–west axis was, in fact, part of an international trading system dating back to Roman times that made the lower Rhine into the natural transit area between the upper Rhine and England. From the early eleventh century the system's centre of gravity began to move westwards under the impulse of the counts of Holland, who were establishing a complex toll system in the Rhine–Meuse–Schelde delta centred upon Dordrecht.[18] Dordrecht's position as a major port was further bolstered by a succession of staple rights granted by the counts between 1299 and 1355, which forced virtually all ships navigating the two arms of the Rhine, the Meuse and the Hollandse IJssel to offer their cargo for sale in the city.[19] Although by the end of the fourteenth century the towns of Holland and some villages were largely exempted from this staple, Dordrecht did not pay much attention to their rights; the ensuing animosity was aggravated by Dordrecht's fiscal privileges.[20] Nevertheless, the would-be 'Bruges-on-the-Meuse' failed to gain metropolitan status. Around 1500 Dordrecht was still a major commercial centre specialising in Rhine wine, timber and natural stone

---

[16] C. Lesger, *Hoorn als stedelijk knooppunt. Stedensystemen tijdens de late middeleeuwen en de vroegmoderne tijd* (Hilversum, 1990), ch. 3; C. Lesger, 'Intraregional trade and the port system in Holland, 1400–1700', in Davids and Noordegraaf, *The Dutch economy*, pp. 186–217.

[17] Smit, *Vorst*, pp. 437–44; B. Ibelings, 'De route "binnendunen". De scheepvaartroute langs de Goudse sluis en tol, de Wassenaerse Gouwesluis en de Spaarndammertol (13e to 16e eeuw)', in D. E. H. de Boer, J. W. Marsilje and J. G. Smit (eds.), *Vander Rekeninghe. Bijdragen aan het symposium over onderzoek en editieproblematiek van middeleeuws rekeningmateriaal* (The Hague, 1998), pp. 221–55, 323–39.

[18] C. L. Verkerk, 'Tollen en waterwegen in Holland en Zeeland tot de Sint Elisabethsvloed van 1421', in *Holland en het water*, pp. 97–114; J. G. Smit (ed.), *Bronnen voor de economische geschiedenis van het Beneden – Maasgebied, II. Rekeningen van de Hollandse tollen, 1422–1534* (The Hague, 1997), pp. ix–xl.

[19] *Geschiedenis van Dordrecht tot 1572* (Hilversum, 1996), pp. 79–84. The most comprehensive charter, granted by the countess Marguerite of Bavaria in 1351, is published in J. F. Niermeijer (ed.), *Bronnen voor de economische geschiedenis van het Beneden-Maasgebied. Eerste deel: 1104–1399* (The Hague, 1968), n. 383.

[20] For an overview, see *Geschiedenis Dordrecht*, p. 88.

and offering work to dozens of coopers, shipwrights and ship-masters, but by then its regional role was diminished. During the second half of the fourteenth century the alternative, north–south axis became increasingly important for international trade.[21] Gouda was initially the main commercial centre along this route, which gave it an important position in international shipping until the end of the fifteenth century.[22] Amsterdam, however, although never granted formal staple rights like Dordrecht, gradually supplanted Dordrecht and Gouda as the region's principal port, with the inland towns of Kennemerland (Haarlem and Alkmaar) and the Zuiderzee port towns of West-Friesland and Waterland (Hoorn, Enkhuizen, Medemblik and Edam) acting as secondary centres.[23]

Before the mid-fifteenth century, however, there was still no clear hierarchy among Dutch towns.[24] A turning point in market organisation occurred during the politically and militarily turbulent two decades that followed the death of Charles the Bold on a Swiss battlefield in 1477. The period witnessed a deep economic slump, and although it was followed by a twenty-year recovery, recession struck again in the 1520s.[25] A long-term effect of these problems was the gradual restructuring of the port system, as the smaller town ports lost their role as gateways and Dordrecht and Amsterdam reinforced their dominance over foreign trade. By 1514 the two main ports 'were the only towns with a large fleet of inland waterway vessels',[26] but Amsterdam was probably already pulling ahead. The rapid increase in traffic through the Gouda sluice documented shortly after 1540 suggests that Amsterdam was developing strong links with the Antwerp metropolis,[27] while a register of export dues from 1543–5 suggests that the total value of Amsterdam's exports may already have been more than ten times that of Dordrecht's.[28] At the same time Amsterdam went about strengthening its intermediary functions to the north, the most striking measure being the setting up in 1529 of a regular boat service between Amsterdam and

---

[21] de Boer, *Graaf*, pp. 320–6.

[22] Ibelings, 'De route', pp. 226–7.

[23] The standard work on the rise of Amsterdam is F. Ketner, *Handel en scheepvaart van Amsterdam in de vijftiende eeuw* (Leiden, 1946).

[24] Lesger, 'Intraregional trade', p. 194.

[25] L. Noordegraaf, *Hollands welvaren? Levensstandaard in Holland, 1450–1650* (Bergen, 1985), pp. 77–90, emphasises the negative consequences of warfare between 1475 and 1575.

[26] Lesger, 'Intraregional trade', pp. 191, 205. The size of the merchant and fishing fleet in the sixteenth century is discussed in M. van Tielhof, *De Hollandse graanhandel 1470–1570. Koren op de Amsterdamse molen* (The Hague, 1995), pp. 106–10.

[27] Ibelings, 'De route', pp. 223–5.

[28] Lesger, 'Intraregional trade', p. 209, Table 1.

Hoorn. With barges departing at fixed days and hours this was the first example of the so-called *beurtvaart*-system, which according to Sombart initiated a veritable transport revolution.[29] Although commercial concentration could in principle make it easier for smaller towns to gain access to supraregional markets, not every town was happy to support Amsterdam's rise to prominence. Alkmaar, for instance, tried to protect its markets both by forbidding the surrounding rural inhabitants from trading in Amsterdam, Haarlem and Hoorn and by improving the roads and waterways that connected its hinterland with the town.[30]

Such developments accentuated the hierarchical ordering of markets and particularly affected those on the lowest rung, the village markets. De Vries's dating of most village markets to the sixteenth century is clearly too late.[31] Among the three oldest marketplaces of any renown in the County of Holland – Vlaardingen, Voorschoten and Valkenburg – only Vlaardingen was a chartered town; other village markets are recorded before the sixteenth century in Rijsoord, Heerjansdam, Akersloot, Schoorl and Nieuwe Niedorp.[32] All these markets were so-called 'free markets' established by charter by the counts of Holland before and after the mid-fourteenth century,[33] but other lords also had the right to grant market privileges for which no records survive. There were also a certain number of villages that held markets or fairs without their lord's explicit permission and about which one sometimes hears by chance, one such being the important fish mart at Katwijk.[34] Lastly, several of the so-called 'urban villages' of West-Friesland, like Schagen, held markets during the fifteenth century. In sum, it is clear that village markets were common long before 1500 and that the late medieval rural economy was already highly commercialised. Villages both gained and lost from the development of denser and more complex market networks. They gained from lower transaction costs and improved opportunities to specialise, but they lost because commercial integration also increased the towns' reach into the economy of the countryside. From the towns' point of view, on the other hand, the proliferation of rural markets seemed in the short term to spell a net loss of commercial power, which explains why in Holland, as elsewhere in late medieval

[29] Ibid., p. 195.
[30] D. Aten, *'Als het gewelt comt . . .' Politiek en economie in Holland benoorden het IJ 1500–1800* (Hilversum, 1995), pp. 37–49, 62–3.
[31] Noordegraaf, 'Het platteland', pp. 13–16.
[32] Ibid., pp. 13–14; L. Noordegraaf, 'Internal trade and internal trade conflicts in the northern Netherlands: autonomy, centralism, and state formation in the pre-industrial era', in S. Groenveld and M. Wintle (eds.), *Government and the economy in Britain and the Netherlands since the middle ages* (Zutphen, 1992), pp. 14–15.
[33] Noordegraaf, 'Het platteland', p. 13.
[34] De Boer, 'Roerende', pp. 122–3.

Europe, towns did their utmost to hinder the development of autonomous markets in the countryside.[35]

Political economy

Buitenneringen *and regional staples*

Urban attempts to thwart commercial and industrial development in the
countryside followed a twin strategy based upon the prohibition of
village trades and industries (*buitenneringen*) and the imposition of staple
obligations (forced marketing). Urban policy was motivated as much by
fiscal objectives, since urban taxation relied heavily on excise, as by the
fear of rural competition; town governments were understandably concerned to stop consumers purchasing duty-free goods outside the city
walls and entrepreneurs from shifting cloth or beer production to the
countryside. But urban protectionism was also upheld, as elsewhere in
Europe, by a strong ideological argument favouring a clear-cut division
of labour between town and countryside: *neringen* had to take place in
towns, and fields had to be tilled, cattle grazed, and peat dug in the
countryside. This formed the basis of 'a long-lasting and consistently
maintained principle in the domestic policy of the towns' that was
economically protectionist and politically expansionist.[36] The latter
stance was reinforced by the fact that in Holland, unlike Flanders, the
textile industries were increasingly concentrated in the large towns after
the depression of *c.*1475–95.[37]

Conflicts over *buitenneringen*, which, besides craft production, included commercial food processing (corn milling, baking and brewing)
and retail trade, went back a long time. Leiden had already obtained a
privilege in 1351 that banned all competing textile industries within a
certain radius of its walls; Haarlem's oldest surviving local ordinances
(*keuren*) of *c.*1400 forbade the weaving and fulling of cloth outside the
town walls; and Amsterdam introduced its first measures against rural

---

[35] See S. R. Epstein, 'Regional fairs, institutional innovation, and economic growth in late
medieval Europe', *Economic History Review* 47 (1994), 459–82.
[36] Noordegraaf, 'Internal trade', pp. 13, 20. The larger Dutch towns appear also to have
developed a model of the 'natural' division of labour between towns, set out in
Dordrecht's defence of its staple rights in 1505, which presupposed the countryside's
exclusion from manufacturing and trade. Dordrecht argued that, just as Amsterdam
had its overseas trade, Haarlem its breweries, Leiden its cloth industry, Delft and
Gouda both brewing and cloth industries, and Rotterdam its herring fishery, Dordrecht
should be allowed the staple that was so vital for its survival (*Geschiedenis Dordrecht*,
pp. 79–80).
[37] H. Kaptein, *De Hollandse textielnijverheid 1350–1600. Conjunctuur en continuïteit*
(Hilversum, 1998), p. 94.

breweries in 1413.[38] But these concessions did not prevent industrial activities from spreading across the countryside. At the beginning of the sixteenth century we hear of rural woollen and linen industries, commercial breweries, bakeries, shipyards and tanneries.[39] The *buitenneringen*'s comparative advantage lay not so much in lower wages as in the lower prices of raw materials and in the lack of excise taxes. The latter was a particular advantage for the retail and service trades, like alehouses, which could set up in the vicinity of the towns and be assured of a regular clientele. Attempts to prevent burghers from drinking outside the town walls were to no avail. In 1498 the West-Frisian Hoorn proclaimed a 'beer league', a variant on the long-standing 'ban league' (French *banlieu*) that applied within a mile of the city walls, but four decades later the Hoorn magistrate was still attempting to enforce the rule against publicans who served ale inside the urban precinct. In the same period Alkmaar waged its own war against country ale-houses with such alluring names as De Naedorst (lit. 'the thirst after excessive drink') in nearby Heiloo.[40]

After Charles V's accession in 1515 the Dutch towns began to co-ordinate attempts to get *buitenneringen* banned by the sovereign. Repeated demands for taxes by the Habsburg government gave them the opportunity to request compensating legislation. During negotiations over a new subsidy in 1531 the towns finally succeeded in getting their concerns listened to. Councillor Joost Sasbout was ordered to hold an inquiry, which led on 11 October 1531 to the promulgation of the Order op de Buitennering. Although the ordinance achieved fame for appearing to mark the first successful attempt at co-ordinated action by the towns, the provisions only forbade new *buitenneringen* and left existing ones in business and thus did not fully meet the petitioners' concerns. A new tax led the emperor to proclaim a second Ordinance in 1540 which established that existing *neringen* could under certain circumstances be shut down. Although this law was also riddled with ambiguities and both ordinances were frequently honoured in the breach,[41] they established the legal basis for subsequent action by the towns.[42]

The *buitenneringen*'s success could only be halted through effective enforcement of the ordinances, which failed, however, to occur. Thanks to two inquiries held on Leiden's request in 1540 and 1541 we are

---

[38] Brünner, *Order*, p. 131; Kaptein, *Hollandse textielnijverheid*, pp. 151–2.
[39] Brünner, *Order*, pp. 64–7, 101–3, 106, 117.
[40] Aten, *Als het gewelt*, pp. 206–8.
[41] Ibid., pp. 281–2; Brünner, *Order*, pp. 122–7.
[42] Aten, *Als het gewelt*, p. 286.

unusually well informed about village *neringen* in the city's vicinity soon after the Ordinance of 1531.[43] In the village of Zoeterwoude alone, which according to the Informacie of 1514 had eighty hearths, there were twelve weavers working with cheap inland wool, eight shipwrights, a couple of potters, a glazier, a basket maker, a hooper, a butcher-cum-publican and a baker. Some of these were clearly full-time professionals, such as the couple who employed women and girls to spin and comb wool from Alkmaar; others were more probably part-timers, like the midwife who made some money on the side by spinning wool from Zealand.[44]

In 1543, the six large towns once again engaged in joint action against rural enterprise. In 1548 they supported Woerden's lawsuit against neighbouring villagers who had infringed the Ordinance of 1531, first before the High Court of Holland and later in appeal before the Grote Raad, the supreme court of the Burgundian–Habsburg Netherlands. The central government, however, seemed very reluctant to pursue these cases – possibly because elsewhere in the Netherlands, particularly in Brabant and Flanders, no such prohibitions applied. The Dutch towns thus had to wait until 1554 to get a favourable verdict from the Grote Raad and to launch a wave of prosecutions against infringements of the 1531 Ordinance. The latter led to renewed tensions in successful textile areas, such as in the linen-weaving region of Haarlem during the 1560s.[45]

The towns' second strategy to impede or control commercial developments in the countryside was to force villages to direct their surpluses to urban markets, as in the case of Alkmaar mentioned previously. The main reason for this policy was to ensure adequate supplies of food for towns. Dordrecht seems to have been especially concerned on this front, particularly after the disastrous flood of 1421, which isolated the town and brought a large area to its south under water. Dordrecht's administration secured food provisioning by establishing 'regional staple rights', which required about twenty-five villages within Dordrecht's self-defined district to use the town markets and allowed fifteen others to pay only excise.[46] Although the central government in 1515 described these trading obligations as illegitimate,

---

[43] The inquiry of 1540 is published in Brünner, *Order*, Annexe VI; the inquiry of 1541 is in N. W. Posthumus, 'Een zestiende-eeuwsche enquête naar de buitenneringen rondom de stad Leiden', *Bijdragen en Mededeelingen van het Historisch Genootschap* 33 (1912), 1–11.

[44] Brünner, *Order*, Annexe VI, pp. 231–9.

[45] Ibid., pp. 183–6, 190; Kaptein, *Hollandse textielnijverheid*, pp. 214–15.

[46] Brünner, *Order*, pp. 78–9; Noordegraaf, 'Internal trade', pp. 15–16 and n. 17.

the town government did not give in.[47] Five years later its policy was vindicated with the concession of the Groot Octrooi or Octrooi Serviel that remained in force until 1589, and in which Charles V renewed Dordrecht's regional staple, extended its right to tax beer from a radius of two miles beyond the city walls to the entire district of Zuidholland, and forced the peasantry of Zuidholland into compulsory labour services to dredge the town's harbour.[48] On this occasion Dordrecht took enforcement of its rights seriously, raising a special police force that compelled even the pettiest of traders to sell their goods on Dordrecht's market, and that led to appeals in the courts based upon the Scholastic doctrine of 'just price'.[49]

Urban landholdings and rural property rights

The application of commercial and manufacturing restrictions is only one aspect – albeit perhaps the most conspicuous one – of the unequal relations between town and countryside in late medieval Holland. A more insidious source of economic power came from the expansion of urban landownership in the countryside. For many Marxist historians, this caused the 'internal involution [of towns] towards rentier forms of wealth, the flight of urban capital into land, state bonds and tax-farming . . . which transformed the urban élite into a landed or rentier aristocracy, merged in turn with the absentee nobility itself'.[50] Paradoxically, however, the transfer of landed property from the peasantry to the urban bourgeoisie is also claimed to be a precondition for the transition from feudalism to the 'organisation of agriculture as an industry producing exchange-values', or, as Robert Brenner has put it, for the 'short-circuiting of the . . . predominance of small peasant property' through expropriation from the land.[51] To what extent did changing relations between town and country in late medieval Holland affect the extent of

---

[47] R. Fruin (ed.), *Informacie up den staet, faculteyt ende gelegentheyt van de steden ende dorpen van Hollant ende Vrieslant om daernae te reguleren de nyeuwe schiltaele, gedaen in den jaere MDXIV* (Leiden, 1866), p. xviii.

[48] Ibid., p. xxiii. Other examples of collective labour services in late medieval Holland: T. S. Jansma, *Tekst en uitleg* (The Hague, 1974), p. 42.

[49] The enforcement of the Octrooi Serviel has been studied by H. O. van Rees, 'Stad en land', unpublished mimeo, University of Amsterdam, n.d.; see also Noordegraaf, 'Internal trade', pp. 15–16.

[50] J. Merrington, 'Town and country in the transition to capitalism', in R. Hilton (ed.), *The transition from feudalism to capitalism* (London–New York, 1975), p. 183.

[51] Ibid., p. 189; R. P. Brenner, 'Agrarian class structure and economic development in pre-industrial Europe', in T. H. Aston and C. H. E. Philpin (eds.), *The Brenner debate. Agrarian class structure and economic development in pre-industrial Europe* (Cambridge, 1985), p. 30.

peasant property rights to land, and what effects did changes in ownership have?

On the basis of the Informacie of 1514, Brünner established that
peasant landownership was subject to intense local variation, ranging
from next to nothing to well over 75 per cent of the cultivated area.[52]
The reasons for such differences are not easy to fathom, and require
intimate knowledge of a range of ecological, economic and socio-
political factors at work at a local or subregional level over an extended
period of time. Even within a small region like the Land van Heusden in
the south-west, local variation in the extent of peasant land ownership
could be huge.[53] Nevertheless, Brünner's conclusion that by the early
sixteenth century peasant ownership in over two-thirds of Dutch villages
was restricted to less than half the cultivated area has been confirmed by
de Vries, who suggested that little more than 40 per cent of Holland's
arable land was in peasant ownership.[54] Since the Informacie frequently
understated the area under cultivation and it is likely that most of what
was left out was peasant property which was harder to assess, towards
the mid-sixteenth century total peasant ownership was in fact probably
closer to 50 per cent, with burghers owning 20–30 per cent, religious
and charitable institutions over 10 per cent, and the aristocracy the
remaining 5–15 per cent.[55]

Arguments about the economic consequences of property rights to
land rest essentially on the distribution of ownership between peasants
and townsmen. The latter were allegedly progressive elements who
viewed land as a profit-maximising investment to be leased to farmers
on short-term contracts, by contrast with the peasantry, which pursued
conservative or subsistence strategies. But whatever the case with the
peasantry, this view of urban landownership must be heavily qualified.
First, many urban landowners owned only small plots of land, which
they did not lease out but exploited directly.[56] How and to what purpose

---

[52] Brünner, *Order*, pp. 35–55, 71 (table), based on J. C. Naber, 'Een terugblik', *Bijdragen
van het Statistisch Instituut* 4 (1885), 41–4, Annexe XIV. Data on the social distribution
of landownership in the Informacie is frequently incomplete or too generic.

[53] Hoppenbrouwers, *Middeleeuwse samenleving*, pp. 375–80, 819–30 (Annexe C).

[54] Brünner, *Order*, p. 52; de Vries, *Dutch rural economy*, pp. 34–67. Naber, 'Terugblik',
p. 43, Annexe XIV, 'Verzamelstaat' gives 38 per cent.

[55] Thus, for example, the detailed land registers for the upper drainage board of Rijnland
in 1540–4 indicate that at least 60 per cent of the Rijnland was owned by peasants,
compared to about 30 per cent according to the Informacie. See de Vries, *Dutch rural
economy*, pp. 34–47, 50; Naber, 'Terugblik', pp. 42–3; H. F. K. van Nierop, *The
nobility of Holland: from knights to regents, 1500–1650*, Engl. transl. (Cambridge, 1993),
pp. 111–12. For a more detailed discussion, see P. C. M. Hoppenbrouwers, 'Mapping
an unexplored field. The Brenner debate and the late medieval and early modern
history of Holland', in BDLC.

[56] Brünner, *Order*, p. 53; Hoppenbrouwers, *Middeleeuwse samenleving*, pp. 376–7, 439.

they used their plots remains a mystery. Some may have grown grain, peas or vegetables for domestic use, others may have grazed a cow or a horse, and many plots will have been peat land supplying fuel. The larger owner-users may have held entire farms directly under a salaried overseer.[57] Secondly, land did not need to be bought to gain access to the rural economy. According to a register of tax-payers dated *c.*1465, as many as 139 shipmasters, merchants, carpenters and fishermen in the coastal town of Edam owned an average of two cows which they leased to neighbouring farmers.[58] In fact, a far more important form of investment than land was the purchase of annuities mortgaged on rural property, many of which probably arose from loans advanced to peasants wishing to buy land themselves. Many plots in peasant ownership were burdened by one and frequently two or more of these 'constituted rents', which until after the mid-fifteenth century were considered to be perpetual and non-redeemable.[59] This did not necessarily make them a burden on the rural economy, however, for – as Thoen has argued for the east Flemish countryside – peasants mortgaged their land not so much to buy land or to stave off economic distress as to invest in improvements of farm buildings and to purchase implements and animals.[60] Although there is insufficient evidence about this for Holland, the fact that median interest rates on constituted rents in the Land van Heusden during the fifteenth and early sixteenth centuries were 8 per cent suggests that the supply of capital was comparatively abundant.[61]

Politics

The state and political consultation

Village communities had by ancient tradition the right to participate in Holland's elaborate consultative customs. At his accession, the count

---

[57] For an example of the latter, see Hoppenbrouwers, 'Mapping'.

[58] J. Sparreboom, 'Twee fiscale bronnen uit het stadsarchief van Edam, circa 1462', *Holland. Regionaal-Historisch Tijdschrift* 13 (1981), 158.

[59] Hoppenbrouwers, *Middeleeuwse samenleving*, pp. 400–9.

[60] See Merrington, 'Town and country', pp. 184–5 for the pessimistic case; E. Thoen, *Landbouwekonomie en bevolking in Vlaanderen gedurende de late Middeleeuwen en het begin van de Moderne Tijden. Testregio: de kasselrijen van Oudenaarde en Aalst (eind 13de-eerste helft 16de eeuw)*, 2 vols. (Ghent, 1988), vol. II, pp. 929–40. P. Stabel, *Dwarfs among giants. The Flemish urban network in the late middle ages* (Leuven and Apeldoorn, 1997), p. 1, is also quite positive on this point with respect to Flanders.

[61] Hoppenbrouwers, *Middeleeuwse samenleving*, pp. 405–6, Table 20.2. Interest rates were, however, higher than in southern England in the same period; see G. Clark, 'The cost of capital and medieval agricultural technique', *Explorations in Economic History* 25 (1988), 273–4, Tables 3–4.

had to take a formal oath of allegiance from all his subjects, and he had
to obtain their consent for all general taxes he wished to impose. Both
procedures involved a tour of the county by the lord and his council.[62]
Villagers were also regularly consulted on other issues of general
concern such as defence and major dike or drainage schemes. All this
began to change in the course of the fifteenth century. The Burgundian
Empire was becoming too vast to allow the dukes to pay regular visits to
every province, and the dukes were also increasingly calling upon
representatives of the nobility and of the larger towns, which were
described as the Estates of Holland for the first time in 1428. The
summons brought two fundamental principles into conflict: the ancient
one that stipulated the prince's duty to meet all his subjects on certain
specified occasions; and the new one that limited active participation in
imperial policy to the estates. A statement by the Leiden town government concerning a new aid in 1469 clearly reveals this shift. There was
no need to consult 'the peasant (*de lantman*) . . . since there are only two
estates in Holland . . ., the nobility and the associated towns (*ridderscip
ende gemene steden*)', the burghers stated. They alone were required to
consent to general taxes; the countryside could be taxed on the basis of
the total levy decided by the two estates and in conformity with the
villages' financial capacities.[63] The writing was on the wall, and the
countryside was fully and duly consulted for the last time in 1469 and
1472. Following the death of Charles the Bold, the countryside still took
part in the public acclamation of the new countess, Maria, and her
husband Maximilian of Austria in 1478, but thereafter even that custom
fell everywhere into decay with the exception of the district of Zuidholland, which was, however, considered a virtual extension of Holland's
'first town', Dordrecht.[64]

Thereafter, the countryside was seldom summoned even for a *dag-
vaart*, the designation for any kind of meeting of representatives of
county society. Between 1477 and 1494 villagers were invited on only
16 out of 286 occasions,[65] the rare summons being directed either to
village communities or to the *baljuwen* (bailiffs or sheriffs), who desig-
nated representatives to their liking, usually two per village, invariably

[62] Smit, *Vorst*, Parts I and II.
[63] J. G. Smit (ed.), *Bronnen voor de geschiedenis der dagvaarten van de Staten en steden van Holland voor 1544*, vol. III: *1467–1477* (The Hague, 1998), n. 64. The government of Leiden did not consider the clergy a separate estate, although they consulted it on important matters from 1455 onwards (Kokken, *Steden*, p. 27).
[64] Smit, *Vorst*, pp. 399–400, esp. n. 6.
[65] The figure excludes nine summonses for The Hague alone, which I have considered to be a town; Kokken, *Steden*, pp. 113 (Table 5), 118.

described as the 'most able' (*bequaemste*) or as the 'most notable and wealthy' (*notabelste ende rijcxten*). By about 1500 the countryside was being represented at the Estates' meetings by members of the nobility (*ridderschap*) – again with the exception of Zuidholland, which remained attached to Dordrecht – and shortly thereafter the *ridderschap* began also to represent all the towns, with the exception of the six largest.[66]

Taxation

As the preceding discussion implies, the main source of friction between town and country was taxation. Starting in the early fifteenth century, the counts of Holland began to raise annual taxes in which the total levy was fixed in advance and then divided among liable communities after local negotiations. Whereas towns paid their quota largely out of excise raised on the urban market, the villages allocated their dues on the basis of individual wealth assessments; however, just as villages claimed freedom from urban excise, urban landlords refused to contribute to assessments in the villages where they held property. This would have caused no problems had rural tax allocations taken account of changing patterns of ownership, in particular of the reduction in the amount of land held by the villagers themselves; but tax rolls were seldom updated, the allocations set at the level fixed in the late 1420s being revised only in 1462, 1496 and 1518 and always after an official inquiry.[67]

Resistance to fiscal revisions came from the towns, who claimed that the peasantry had little to complain about since the burghers bore the heaviest part of the fiscal burden. This was superficially true. The six large towns alone claimed they paid up to a third of each aid despite having only about 23 per cent of the population, and if anything this underestimated their contribution. Between 1433 and 1496 the tax share paid by the large towns seems to have increased considerably, at least for the two quarters (districts) of Kennemerland (headed by Haarlem) and Rijnland (Leiden) for which data can be accurately compared; in the quarters of Delfland (Delft) and Amstelland (Amsterdam) the increase was not as sharp (Table 3.2). In 1518 the six large towns were assessed for 50 to 80 per cent of the tax burden of their quarter, according to the latter's size and to the number of villages it

---

[66] Ibid., pp. 118–20; Smit, *Vorst*, p. 413. On average about twenty noblemen were summoned to represent the *ridderschap*.

[67] Bos-Rops, *Graven*, pp. 365–9, surveys the allocation of the late 1420s. B. J. P. Ibelings has recently rediscovered the allocation of 1462 that was believed lost. For the allocations of 1496, 1515 and 1518, see Table 3.1, Sources.

Table 3.2. *Tax allocations between cities, towns and countryside in Holland,*
1433–1518 (percentages)

	1433[1]	1496	1515	1518
Quarter of Zuidholland				
Dordrecht	–	–	51	49
Small town (Geertruidenberg)	–	–	3	4
Villages	–	–	46	47
Quarter of Kennemerland				
Haarlem	37	53	46	48
Small town (Beverwijk)	5	1	1	1
Villages[2]	58	46	53	51
Quarter of West Friesland				
Small towns (n=4)	35	31	33	32
Villages[3]	65	69	67	68
Quarter of Amstelland[4]				
Amsterdam	38 (?)	45	53	50
Small towns (n=6)	[19][5]	28	20	23
Villages	[43][5]	27	26	27
Quarter of Rijnland				
Leiden	37	62	54	56
Small towns (n=2)	9	4	6	6
Villages	54	34	39	37
Quarter of Delfland				
Delft	67 (?)	69	58	63
Small towns (n=3)[6]	[21][7]	13	21	14
Villages	12 (?)	18	21	23
Quarter of Schieland				
Small towns (n=2)	100	78	78	76
Villages	–	22	22	24
Quarter of Gouda				
Gouda	80	78	84	79
Small town (Schoonhoven)	20	11	9	10
Villages	–	11	7	10

Notes:
[1] Data for 'Kennemerland' and the 'possessions of Marguerite of Burgundy' in 1433 are distributed across Kennemerland, West-Friesland (with adjacent villages), Rijnland and Delfland according to the listings of 1496–1518.
[2] Not including Egmond.
[3] Data for 1496, 1515 and 1518 include the Kennemergevolg region and the islands of Texel, Wieringen, Oge and Vlieland.
[4] 'Amstelland' includes Waterland, Zeevang and Gooiland.
[5] Small towns and villages cannot be distinguished.
[6] Includes 's-Gravenzande, which in 1433 was wrongly listed among the villages of Rijnland.
[7] Vlaardingen is not included because described as 'burnt down'.
Sources: For 1433, see Table 3.1. For 1496, 1515 and 1518, see R. Fruin, *Enqueste ende Informatie upt stuck van den reductie ende reformatie van de schildtaelen* (Leiden, 1876), Annexe 'Zettingen en omslagen van 1496, 1515 en 1518'.

contained, and their overall share in the subsidy of 60,000 lb. was 42 per cent.[68]

At face value the complaints of Holland's large towns therefore do not seem unreasonable, but there are reasons to believe that the real terms of the matter were rather different. Average wealth and income in the larger towns was clearly considerably greater than in the countryside,[69] and from the end of the fourteenth century at the latest towns were able to shift part of their tax burden onto the peasants by paying the greater part of their tax assessments with excises on basic foods and industrial products.[70] Indirect taxes were levied on all transactions by the peasantry within the town walls, and from about 1500 many towns managed to extend excise to their surrounding villages. By contrast, no bourgeois landholder was ever made to contribute to the countryside's share of tax.

Towns and rural administration

Urban interference in rural affairs went furthest when towns tried to gain control of the villages' administrative and jurisdictional activities. By and large such attempts took two forms. First, towns could force villagers to make use of town courts of justice, a strategy that sometimes ended in the imposition over villagers of town law – paradoxical as that may sound. Secondly, they could try to buy entire rights of lordship, in which case town governments became feudal lords themselves and gained full administrative and jurisdictional control. The first instances of this practice occurred in the first half of the sixteenth century, when the governments of Gouda, Amsterdam and Leiden bought seigniorial rights over a number of hamlets and small villages in their immediate vicinity.[71] However, the practice remained unusual; in the mid-seventeenth century when members of the upper bourgeoisie owned dozens of such village lordships, town governments held only fourteen, equivalent to 8 per cent.

Since the administrative and jurisdictional autonomy of local commu-

---

[68] In 1515 the towns collectively bore 58 per cent of the tax burden, but by 1550 the proportion had declined to 42 per cent, 'almost exactly the reverse of the assessment of 1515' (J. D. Tracy, *Holland under Habsburg rule, 1506–1566. The formation of a body politic* (Berkeley–Los Angeles, 1990), p. 142).

[69] In Florence in 1427, for instance, per caput wealth was twenty times that of the Tuscan countryside; see S. R. Epstein, 'Town and country: economy and institutions in late medieval Italy', *Economic History Review* 46 (1993), 454 n. 8.

[70] Another important source of revenue was the voluntary or compulsory sale of annuities; direct taxation of property was very unpopular in towns (J. W. Marsilje, 'Les modes d'imposition en Hollande, 1477–1515', *Publications du Centre Européen d'Etudes Bourguignonnes (XIVe–XVIe siècles)* 28 (1988), 159–71).

[71] de Vries, *Dutch rural economy*, p. 48.

nities was as firmly entrenched in the countryside as it was in towns, the latter could not easily intrude upon the authority of village courts. The ways in which town councils attempted to encroach upon rural liberties have been studied in some detail for the small town and villages of Land van Heusden, especially in comparison with conditions in the neighbouring Brabantine city of 's Hertogenbosch (Bois-le-Duc), which had extensive rights of jurisdiction over a large number of villages in its rural district, the Meierij.[72] The latter included the right for anyone sentenced in a village court of justice to lodge an appeal with the aldermen of Bois-le-Duc, and, conversely, extensive rights for the aldermen to intervene in civil and criminal cases originating in the countryside.

Probably with their powerful neighbours' example in their minds, the Heusden aldermen tried to get a similar grip over the village courts of Land van Heusden. Their existing authority, which they traced back to the thirteenth century, was restricted to so-called voluntary jurisdiction, whereby local courts acted as registrars for the sale and mortgaging of land and other activities of that kind; but even in that sphere the villagers tried to circumvent the town's jurisdiction. A useful lever for the aldermen's attempts to extend their jurisdiction in civil law was probably the *ingebod-recht*, which gave them the right to call upon villagers who might be in breach of a contract drawn up before the aldermen's bench. Their competences developed more slowly in the sphere of criminal law, probably because passing judgement on matters of high justice remained for a long time the prerogative of the aristocracy. However, at some point the same right was granted to Heusden's aldermen, who were as often as not of noble birth. But still the villagers claimed the right to refuse trial in the town, and demanded that their cases be heard in a rural court with rural noblemen sitting as judges.

The tug-of-war over jurisdictional rights that raged in Land van Heusden is well documented in a number of trials held around 1475 before the Hof van Holland (the high court of the counts of Holland) and the Grote Raad (the supreme court of the Burgundian Low Countries). In 1478, the local villages collectively filed a number of complaints against Heusden, denouncing unlawful urban excises levied in the villages and the use of blatantly discriminatory legal procedures in the town court, such as the possibility in some circumstances for townspeople to choose between declaring an oath of innocence and calling witnesses, unlike villagers, who had to produce witnesses at all times. The villages won their case, but that did not stop Heusden from continuing its policy of jurisdictional expansion, which culminated with

---

[72] Hoppenbrouwers, *Middeleeuwse samenleving*, pp. 609–15.

the first compilation of Heusden customary law in 1569. By then the village courts were reduced to annexes of the town aldermen's bench; the latter could interfere when and where they wanted. The villagers were in effect subjected to town law, something they did not perceive as an advantage. Elsewhere, the Rijnland village of Noordwijk was granted town law as a special privilege in 1398, but the grant was withdrawn soon afterwards because not all villagers approved of it.[73]

Whether comparable developments took place elsewhere in Holland has yet to be discovered. Dordrecht seems in many respects a case apart, standing midway between the two forms of political and jurisdictional domination just described. It was the only town in Holland that claimed an ancient right to consider the surrounding countryside its *districtus*, a fact mentioned incidentally in a charter of 1266 in which the Dordrechters promised to protect merchants from Hamburg within their entire 'district', described rather vaguely as the area both of the town proper and of the surrounding countryside.[74] A privilege of December 1270 that forbade the arrest of Dordrecht burghers and the seizure of their goods within the *baljuwschap* (bailiwick) of Zuidholland suggests that the Dordrecht district coincided with the *baljuwschap*. This would remain the case until at least the beginning of the sixteenth century.[75]

Dordrecht was also able from the early fifteenth century to interfere in regional water management by obtaining that all officials appointed to act on the count's behalf in Dordrecht or Zuidholland or on the high drainage board (*hoogheemraadschap*) of the Grote Waard be Dordrecht natives.[76] Other towns followed suit. Intrusion by town governments in the important Rijnland Drainage Board, which supervised an area of some 45,500 hectares towards the end of the government of Philip the Good, followed two paths. First, in the course of the sixteenth century the governments of Leiden and Haarlem managed to gain control over three out of seven seats in the highest administrative organ of the Rijnland drainage district. Secondly, right from the start the same two governments were permanently represented on the so-called 'board of main landowners', which gradually took form around the same time. The latter's main task was initially to exert financial control, but it soon extended its authority over drainage regimes and over the contracting out of dike and sluice works, at the expense of the financial and administrative autonomy of village officials.[77]

[73] Smit, *Vorst*, p. 144.
[74] D. E. H. de Boer, 'Florerend vanuit de delta. De handelsbetrekkingen van Holland en Zeeland in de tweede helft van de dertiende eeuw', in de Boer, Cordfunke and Sarfatij, *Wi Florens*, p. 133. See also *Geschiedenis Dordrecht*, p. 33.
[75] Tracy, *Holland*, p. 36.   [76] *Geschiedenis Dordrecht*, p. 107.
[77] M. H. V. van Amstel-Horák and R. W. G. Lombarts (eds.), *Regestenboek van het*

Why did Dutch towns not become city-states?

Given the economic and political power gained by Dutch towns during the fifteenth century, their firm grip over the countryside causes no surprise. It is perhaps more surprising that small towns like Edam or Heusden established legal and political hegemony more successfully than larger centres like Leiden, Haarlem or Dordrecht. The simplest, though undocumented, explanation would seem to be that the larger cities could not be bothered because the gains were too small. But other factors were clearly also at work: first, the strong resistance to urban intrusion by feudal possessors of village lordships; second, the lack of collaboration between the towns themselves; and third, the growth of princely power, which kept the towns' broader ambitions in check.

Time and again during the fifteenth and early sixteenth centuries, the support of village lords (*gerechtsheren*, lit. 'lords of justice') proved decisive for villages faced with an urban offensive, although the support was less a noble-minded protection of the common people than a defence of more ancient rights of exploitation. There were two sorts of *gerechtsheren*. Most, known as *ambachtsheren*, had only limited rights of jurisdiction which did not include rights of high justice that allowed corporal punishment or the death penalty. Only a few *gerechtsheren* held rights of high justice, and their lordships were virtually unassailable by the towns. By the fifteenth century all the lordships in the County of Holland were held in liege from the counts, but high lordships were frequently held as quasi-immunities. Their subjects contributed to general tax levies only when the lord gave his consent,[78] and they had no right of appeal to the county's high court of justice for criminal cases.[79] During the late middle ages the counts reacted to this quasi-independence by attempting to bring important high lordships under their control and granting them to close relatives or to trusted noblemen under more restrictive conditions. Thus in 1456 Philip the Good purchased the vast lordship of Putten and Strijen from Jakob of Gaasbeek and promptly turned it over to his son Charles, count of Charolais, later Duke Charles the Bold.[80]

hoogheemraadschap van Rijnland, april 1253–oktober 1814 (Leiden, 1992), pp. xi–xvi. For comparable developments in other major drainage districts, see C. Postma, *Het hoogheemraadschap Delfland in de middeleeuwen 1289–1589* (Hilversum, 1989), pp. 401–12.

[78] Bos-Rops, *Graven*, p. 216; J. A. M. Y. Bos-Rops, 'Van incidentele gunst tot jaarlijkse belasting: de bede in het vijftiende-eeuwse Holland', in J. Th. de Smidt et al. (eds.), *Fiscaliteit in Nederland* (Zutphen–Deventer, 1987), p. 27.

[79] In civil litigations they were allowed to lodge an appeal with the Supreme Court (Grote Raad) of the Burgundian Netherlands.

[80] Smit, *Vorst*, p. 210.

If the lord of Holland himself had only limited control over the *gerechtsheren*, town governments could hardly do better. Until the end of the sixteenth century the possessors of feudal lordships were mainly members of the nobility or *ridderschap*, who more often than not refused to identify with urban interests. Many conflicts between 'town' and 'country' undoubtedly arose from struggles between towns and the rural nobility rather than between towns and rural communities, as shown by the ban by a powerful town such as Leiden on building fortified stone houses within its *banlieu*.[81] Only over the course of the seventeenth century would this confrontation gradually decline. In 1585, 138 out of 171 lordships (81 per cent) were in the hands of noblemen compared with 104 out of 179 (58 per cent) in 1650. In the latter year, town governments held 14 village lordships or 8 per cent of the total, and most of the remaining 61 were privately owned by the upper bourgeoisie.[82] Although town representatives had their say in the meetings of the Estates, and a growing number of state officials and bureaucrats stemmed from the bourgeoisie, most councillors of the high and supreme courts of justice as well as of the important high drainage boards were still noblemen who tended to lend a more sympathetic ear to the voice of their peers. What town governments could do best of all, of course, was to buy *gerechtsheren* off: sometimes lords agreed to limit the number of *neringen* in their villages, and on rare occasions they sold their entire lordship to the towns.

The second explanation for the towns' relatively weak control over the countryside was their failure to act collectively for a common purpose. In many conflicts between towns and villages we see the former fighting each other. Economically motivated animosity could be intensified by party strife, which during the fifteenth century centred upon pro- and anti-Burgundian feelings that cut right across society. Dordrecht was a particular target of other towns because it insisted on being treated differently. Brandishing its old charters of liberty, it refused to pay its tax share and enforced its staple rights without demur. In their actions against Dordrecht the villages of Zuidholland could therefore always count on the support of neighbouring smaller towns like Rotterdam and Schoonhoven, which also suffered from Dordrecht's marketing rights.[83] On the other hand, there were aspects of the relationship between Dordrecht and its *districtus* that were to the villages' advantage. Just as

---

[81] Jansma, *Tekst en uitleg*, pp. 45–7.
[82] H. F. K. van Nierop, *Van ridders tot regenten* (Amsterdam, 1984), Appendices 5–6. Some grants included more than one lordship: in 1555 168 concessions were made of a total of 240 lordships. Some lordships were very small, covering less than 10 hectares.
[83] Brünner, *Order*, pp. 80–1, 192–3; Jansma, *Tekst en uitleg*, pp. 146–77; Tracy, *Holland*, pp. 54–5.

Dordrecht never paid its share of the general taxes, neither did the villages of Zuidholland which were perceived as Dordrecht's appendage; thus when in 1462 there was an attempt at last to collect Dordrecht's allotted tax share (one-ninth of the total) the collectors were faced with a rioting crowd that included both townsmen and villagers.[84]

Among the many examples of inter-urban conflicts, the commonest concerned freedom of transit on rivers and other navigable waterways.[85] One well-known case involved the struggle over the Leidsche dam which obstructed the river Vliet between Leiden and Delft.[86] Amsterdam, Haarlem and Leiden to the north wanted to replace the dam's two *overtomen* (slides and windlasses) with more modern locks, which would have turned the Vliet into a viable alternative route to the main artery across the Hollandse IJssel that avoided the town and toll of Gouda. Delft and the feudal owner of the Leidsche dam also supported the move, the former because the locks would have improved the quality of the water for Delft's major beer industry; the latter because the reforms were expected to increase transit revenues. The plan was of course opposed by Gouda and also by Dordrecht, which perceived a threat to its staple, together with the high drainage board of Rijnland and most of the surrounding villages, who probably feared that a higher average water level south of the Leidsche dam would endanger the inland dikes. When in 1491, after years of litigation, work on the first lock finally began, the governments of Gouda and Dordrecht had the new lock sealed up with military backing. This moved the issue to the high courts, which struck a compromise in 1506 that would provide Delft with good-quality fresh water and allow small barges to pass the dam without using the old *overtomen*, which were only replaced in 1648.

The third and final reason why the towns did not develop into city-states was strong princely power. Unlike many of their German peers, the counts of Holland could most of the time ensure the rural peace that was so vital to the towns' commercial interests.[87] There was thus no urgent need for towns themselves to provide for those ends, given also the expense of maintaining a complex military and jurisdictional apparatus; any temptations in that direction were in any case nipped in the

[84] Bos-Rops, 'Van incidentele gunst', pp. 27–9.

[85] Tracy, *Holland*, pp. 56–9.

[86] Smit, *Vorst*, pp. 448–58. For another case involving Rotterdam and Delft, see J. M. van Herwaarden, 'Stedelijke rivaliteit in de Middeleeuwen: Toscane, Vlaanderen, Holland', in P. B. M. Blaas and J. van Herwaarden (eds.), *Stedelijke naijver. De betekenis van interstedelijke conflicten in de geschiedenis. Enige beschouwingen en case-studies* (The Hague, 1986), pp. 76–7.

[87] See W. Rösener, 'Aspekte der Stadt–Land Beziehungen im spätmittelalterlichen Deutschland', in J.-M. Duvosquel and E. Thoen (eds.), *Peasants and townsmen. Studia in honorem Adriaan Verhulst* (Ghent, 1995), pp. 670–1; Jansma, *Tekst en uitleg*, p. 38.

bud by the Burgundian and Habsburg rulers. On the other hand, perhaps the most striking aspect of Dutch political developments in the sixteenth century was the victory of centrifugal urban forces over the centralising impulse of the Habsburg rulers.

In Holland – as indeed also in neighbouring Flanders – conflicts between town and countryside were overshadowed in the long run by the almost allegorical struggle between town and state that accompanied the process of state formation.[88] Rallying around the centralising forces led by the Habsburgs was the new state's 'super nobility', the governors, state councillors and elite professional officials, whose supraregional goals included territorial consolidation and enlargement, legal and jurisdictional centralisation, the establishment of a more uniform system of taxation and, subsequently, an uncompromising defence of the true Catholic Church against heretical attack. On the other side, under the banner of decentralisation, were to be found all regional and particular-istic interests, led as always by the towns which in both Holland and Flanders played a dominant role in the regional estates. Still in the mid-sixteenth century, few could have predicted that in only a few decades the centrifugal forces would be decisively beaten in Flanders, but emerge victorious in Holland.

The reasons for this have to be sought in the larger scheme of power politics. Habsburg princes were inclined to give more rein to urban particularism in Holland than they were prepared to do in Flanders, because the stakes in Holland were far lower. The military power of Leiden and Dordrecht was insignificant compared to that of Ghent, nor did Dordrecht or Amsterdam yet have the economic value of Bruges or later Antwerp. However, the space that was left in Holland for urban particularism in the fifteenth and early sixteenth centuries did not 'paralyse economic development and prospects for growth' as it had done at an earlier stage in Flanders. The costs of political and jurisdic-tional fragmentation were successfully countered by the growing poli-tical role of the States of Holland, which consistently promoted the collective economic interest of the large Holland towns.[89]

---

[88] W. P. Blockmans and J. van Herwaarden, 'De Nederlanden van 1493 tot 1555: binnenlandse en buitenlandse politiek', in *Algemene Geschiedenis der Nederlanden*, vol. V, pp. 443–91, esp. 446, 485–91.

[89] See Jonathan Israel's comment on P. Stabel, 'Economic development, urbanisation and political organisation in the late medieval southern Low Countries', in P. Bernholz, M. E. Streit and R. Vaubel (eds.), *Political competition, innovation and growth. A historical analysis* (Berlin, 1998), p. 207.

4   Town and country in the Dutch Republic, 1550–1800[1]

Marjolein 't Hart

Introduction

The sixteenth and the first half of the seventeenth century was a period of expansion for most Dutch towns. By 1650, approximately 42 per cent of the almost 2 million inhabitants of the northern Netherlands lived in towns numbering at least 2,500. Urban concentrations were strongest in the maritime western provinces; in the province of Holland alone, which included about two-fifths of the total Dutch population, the proportion living in towns came to 61 per cent. Although inland the population was less concentrated, the overall rate of urbanisation (taking 2,500 as the urban threshold) was still between 20 and 30 per cent.[2]

Most historians link seventeenth-century Dutch wealth and power to the simultaneous rise of trade and the political co-operation of Holland's urban elites. The countryside is seen as being carried along with the towns, with a similar display of rising commercialisation and specialisation and a general increase in labour productivity.[3] What this picture leaves out is the relation between town and country and, more specifically, the control exerted by Dutch towns over their surrounding countryside. Most urban histories treat the towns as if they were islands and leave out the surrounding hinterland, whereas agrarian historians generally evade the issue of urban control.[4] Both the dominance of urban elites in 'high politics' and the countryside's prosperity are taken for

---

[1] I wish to thank Leo Noordegraaf and Harm Hoogendoorn for their helpful comments.

[2] A. van der Woude, 'Demografische ontwikkeling van de Noordelijke Nederlanden', *Algemene Geschiedenis der Nederlanden* 5 (1980), 135.

[3] For recent introductions to the political history of the Dutch Republic, see J. L. Price, *Holland and the Dutch Republic in the seventeenth century. The politics of particularism* (Oxford, 1994) and J. Israel, *The Dutch Republic. Its rise, greatness, and fall 1477–1806* (Oxford, 1995).

[4] For example J. Bieleman, *Geschiedenis van de landbouw in Nederland 1500–1950* (Meppel, 1992) does not mention rural industries. J. de Vries and A. van der Woude, *The first modern economy. Success, failure, and perseverance of the Dutch economy, 1500–1815* (Cambridge, 1997), while conveying a wealth of economic information, disregard the socio-political aspects of town–country relations.

80

I	Dutch Brabant
II	Dutch Flanders
III	Limburg
IV	Walcheren
V	Twente
VI	Zaan/Zaanstreek
VII	Westerwolde
VIII	Oldambt
IX	Gorecht
X	Ommelanden

Figure 4.1   The Dutch Republic, c.1650

granted, even though the extensive privileges and political rights of the towns were often directed against rural trade and industry. Only a handful of studies on specific districts or industries convey some information about the socio-economic links between town and country.

This chapter brings together recent findings on town–country relations, concentrating in particular on the political and economic foundations of urban power and their effects on the countryside. It sets the scene by outlining the constitutional arrangements between town and country that began to emerge during the late middle ages and were consolidated during the first decades of the Dutch Revolt (1568–1648). It then examines attempts by towns to suppress rural industries and the protests against such urban incursions by the rural communities. It shows how the development of rural industry relied on the existence of self-sufficient peasant communities in the commercial periphery and on the unequal distribution of the tax burden across the Republic, which generated a significant difference in real wages between the western coastal districts and the inland territories. Finally, it discusses how control over polders and peateries constituted a further potential source of town–country conflict, and shows how political circumstances gave rise to significant differences in approach between towns.

In addressing these topics we will generally contrast the maritime west, which included the provinces of Holland, Zeeland, Utrecht and Friesland's coastal districts, with the inland regions, which comprised the provinces of Gelderland, Overijssel, Drenthe, Groningen, Friesland's inner district and the conquered areas of Brabant, Flanders and Limburg. During much of the seventeenth century, the former were prosperous and the latter stagnated. From about 1670, however, the economic vigour of the urbanised west of the country – which had previously stood out against a pattern of generalised European decline – began to suffer. By 1750 the economic balance had shifted decisively in favour of the rural and inland communities. In the end, as we shall see, even the oft-told tale of the rise and decline of Dutch political power can be related to the social and economic relations between town and country.

Constitutional arrangements

The constituency of the Seven United Provinces in the northern Netherlands, which arose in the 1570s and 1580s, strongly favoured the political domination of town over country. Of the forty-seven votes in the seven sovereign diets, thirty-three were reserved for the towns, thirteen for the nobility, gentry and other rural representatives, and one for the clergy. The distribution of power varied between provinces, but practically everywhere the towns prevailed, *de facto* if not *de jure*. Towns were particularly prevalent in the maritime west. In the province of Holland they mustered eighteen votes in the provincial assembly against one for the nobility; in neighbouring Zeeland six votes were reserved for the towns and only one for the nobility. In the provinces of Utrecht, Groningen, Overijssel and Gelderland urban and rural representatives were equally matched. Only in Friesland did rural representatives outvote urban ones by three to one. In turn, the provincial assemblies sent delegates to the States General in The Hague, where matters pertaining to the whole Union were decided according to a one province –one vote system (Drenthe, although a sovereign province, was too poor to send deputies). In the Council of State, which can be regarded as the executive body of the Republic, Holland was dominant. The areas of the Republic that were conquered subsequently – the so-called Generality Lands: Dutch Brabant, Dutch Flanders, parts of Limburg and Wester-wolde – were not granted sovereignty and came under the direct rule of the Council of State.

The towns' political predominance originated in the constitutional arrangements debated in the 1570s. At that juncture, the towns of Holland and Zeeland found themselves with a double advantage. The prevailing political culture, which emphasised past privileges, naturally favoured the constituent towns that had also traditionally provided the provinces with their major financial support.[5] The countryside, by contrast, was in dire economic straits. Besieging and marauding armies had plundered farmsteads, polders and fields had been inundated for defensive purposes, and country people had fled in large numbers to the towns.[6] Yet, despite these favourable circumstances, the towns of Holland and Zeeland did not obtain exclusive rights over the country-side. Even the most powerful town remained subordinate to the provin-cial government, where the votes of the nobility acted as a restraint. In Holland, where they cast only one vote against the eighteen of the towns, the nobility gained weight from the fact they were to vote first, a significant privilege in a political culture that valued consensus and unanimity very highly. Their secretaries therefore often became some of the most influential political leaders of the Republic.[7] In Zeeland also, the single vote of the nobility against six urban votes carried additional power from being officially reserved to the Prince of Orange.

Within the boundaries set by provincial governments, the village

[5] J. D. Tracy, A financial revolution in the Habsburg Netherlands: 'Renten' and 'renteniers' in the county of Holland, 1515–1566 (Berkeley, 1985). However, attempts by the Dutch towns to establish control over the countryside went back at least to the later middle ages; see L. Noordegraaf, 'Domestic trade and domestic trade conflicts in the Low Countries. Autonomy, centralism and state formation in the pre-industrial era', in S. Groenveld and M. Wintle (eds.), State and trade. Britain and the Netherlands 10 (Zutphen, 1993), pp. 14–16.

[6] H. C. E. M. Rottier, Stedelijke strukturen in historisch perspektief (Hulst, 1974), p. 71. For the flooding of polders for defensive purposes, see A. J. M. de Kraker, Landschap uit balans. De vier ambachten van het Land van Saeftinghe tussen 1488 en 1609 (Utrecht, 1997), p. 144.

[7] H. F. K. van Nierop, Van ridders tot regenten. De Hollandse adel in de zestiende en de eerste helft van de zeventiende eeuw (The Hague, 1984), p. 178.

administrations (organised in *ambachten*, where a single *ambacht* could include one or more villages) mustered a significant degree of autonomy. Like the towns, they cherished their 'ancient rights and privileges'.[8] Land purchases and the exploitation of former religious goods by towns and burghers affected local autonomy only indirectly. Urban infiltration was more profound when the town managed to buy the lordship of the village (*ambachtsheerlijkheid*). Whereas most *ambachten* were owned by nobles or the villages themselves, a minority were assigned as hereditary fiefs. Eventually some towns gained possession of these lordships, which included jurisdictional rights and powers of appointment of churchwardens and polder officials.[9] Amsterdam, for example, bought the lordship of Volewijk bordering it on the north in 1393; Amstelveen to the south was acquired in 1529; and finally, Diemen and Ouderkerk to the south-east were bought in 1731.[10] Likewise, the town of Groningen managed to gain Gorecht (to the south of the town) and Westerwolde (the district between Oldambt and East Frisia); the town also claimed the lordship over the Oldambt region located between Gorecht and Westerwolde. Above all, these lordships gave the towns a major say in running the drainage systems and in the exploitation of peateries.

Outside these hereditary lordships, however, the high density of towns meant that urban control over the countryside was strongly contested. Coercive moves by one town could always be hindered or mitigated by the actions of another. What is more, inter-urban rivalries involved several centres at the same time. For example, Delft's controversies with The Hague, Rotterdam and Gouda curbed its power over its surrounding lands. Likewise, Hoorn was involved in several disputes with Amsterdam, Alkmaar and Enkhuizen; Middelburg bickered with Veere, Vlissingen and Arnemuiden; Gouda was involved in disputes with Amsterdam, Rotterdam and Dordrecht; and Dordrecht feuded with almost every city that came in its way. Importantly, therefore, competition between towns tended to neutralise the power of individual centres over their hinterland.

Towns were nevertheless eager to control the surrounding lands.

[8] M. J. A. V. Kocken, *Van stads- en plattelandsbestuur naar gemeentebestuur. Proeve van een geschiedenis van ontstaan en ontwikkeling van het Nederlandse gemeentebestuur tot en met de Gemeentewet van 1851* (The Hague, 1973); A. Th. van Deursen, *Een dorp in de polder. Graft in de zeventiende eeuw* (Amsterdam, 1994), pp. 192–6.

[9] van Nierop, *Van ridders tot regenten*, pp. 212–14.

[10] P. H. J. van der Laan, 'Some aspects of the relations between Amsterdam and the countryside (14th–18th centuries)', *Storia della Città* 36 (1986), p. 39. On the protests from villages against the purchase of these lordships by constituent towns, see D. Aten, *Als het geweld comt . . . Politiek en economie in Holland benoorden het IJ 1500–1800* (Hilversum, 1995), p. 350.

There were frequent disputes over flooding levels, roads, canals and bridges. Towns tried to monopolise the marketable produce of local farmers; a diversion in trade routes resulting from a new canal, bridge or sluice frequently evoked protests from urban locations that were likely to be bypassed. However, urban marketplaces proved extremely vulnerable to concerted actions by villagers. For example, in a tax dispute in 1614 the Enkhuizen council was put under considerable pressure when the region's fishermen threatened to use another harbour, and in 1725–8, when the local dairy farmers decided to stop bringing cheese to the Purmerend market, neighbouring Edam and Volendam welcomed them with open arms.[11] Generally speaking, most rural communities with access to a dense network of canals and rivers – in particular in Holland, Zeeland, Utrecht and Friesland – could easily find alternative markets at similar cost.[12]

Political arrangements inland differed from those in the maritime west in that urban centres generally acted as capitals of counties, districts or provinces. More than in the coastal provinces, these centres wielded political and legal powers over their hinterlands. Inter-urban rivalries were often as strong as in the west, but the borders of the hinterlands were more strictly defined, a heritage of the late middle ages when these towns had performed crucial tasks in the continental trading networks. Under the Republic, the major centres in the east continued to maintain city-state aspirations, clinging to their individual privileges and acting as islands of jurisdictional power in a subject rural sea.[13] Some towns even operated an independent mint on the basis of their former status as imperial cities (*Rijkssteden*) of the Holy Roman Empire. Needless to say, craft corporations within these cities often maintained a particularly strong identity.[14]

In a sense, the Revolt and the ensuing war against Spain proved a turning point for urban centres in the east, as newly established political borders raised tariffs and commercial restraints and caused their trading hinterlands to contract. The diversion of trade routes from the Deventer

---

[11] Ibid., pp. 177, 356.

[12] D. J. Noordam, *Leven in Maasland. Een hoogontwikkelde plattelandssamenleving in de achttiende en het begin van de negentiende eeuw* (Hilversum, 1986), p. 18.

[13] P. Kooy, 'Peripheral cities and their regions in the Dutch urban system until 1900', *Journal of economic history* 48 (1988), 361; J. C. Streng, *Stemme in staat. De bestuurlijke elite in de stadsrepubliek Zwolle* (Hilversum, 1997), p. 75; J. C. G. M. Jansen, 'De relatie tussen stad en platteland rond Maastricht in de 18e eeuw. Een terreinverkenning', *Economisch- en sociaal-historisch jaarboek* 38 (1975), 78.

[14] W. Th.M. Frijhoff, 'Zutphen's geschiedenis, 1591–1814', in W. Th.M. Frijhoff (ed.), *Geschiedenis van Zutphen* (Zutphen, 1989), p. 112; P. G. Bos, *Het Groningsche gild- en stapelrecht tot de reductie in 1594* (Groningen, 1904), p. 367. In the maritime west, Dordrecht was the only town in which guilds held on to comparable political rights.

market provides a good example of these changes. In the sixteenth century, Deventer's fairs were famous far beyond the country's borders; Amsterdam merchants had long depended upon Deventer's middlemen. Between 1587 and 1591, however, the war cut off all contacts with traders from the German territories. Long-distance trade was increasingly carried out by sea rather than on the inland rivers; trade and agriculture in the area contracted.[15] At the same time, the neighbouring town of Zutphen tried to reorientate regional trade towards its own market. One of Zutphen's recurrent tactics was to destroy a bridge over the river Berkel which constituted Deventer's vital link to the German-speaking territories. Other centres in the east experienced similar difficulties. Zwolle tried to uphold its privilege as a regional staple for rye, only to find itself undermined by the dominant rye market in Amsterdam.[16]

City-state aspirations were also in greater evidence in the inland provincial diets. The far more explicit distinction drawn there between the urban and rural worlds resulted in town and gentry taking turns in offices and courts in the countryside.[17] In the provinces of Groningen, Overijssel and Gelderland in particular, the rural districts and the towns were far less politically integrated compared to the maritime west. The cities clung strongly to their staple rights and tax privileges. In Gelderland, the province lacked a capital throughout the republican period; no accounts of the province were received in The Hague, because all matters of 'high politics' were dealt with separately by the three counties and their respective capitals. Overijssel's government was paralysed for decades by a fierce struggle over former monastic properties; finally, a settlement in the 1660s stipulated that rural property was to go to the province, and urban property to the towns.

Groningen probably held the strongest urban prerogatives of all inland centres. From the early sixteenth century, it built up a powerful role based upon extensive staple rights for its 20,000 inhabitants. Following the Revolt, the urban government managed to retain most of its staple privileges, which included a ban on the export of all grain that had not been previously offered on the town's market. When Groningen joined the Union in the 1590s, the rift between town and country was so stark that right from the start the States General was named as the arbitrating high court. Up to the end of the eighteenth century, town

---

15 P. Holthuis, *Frontierstad bij het scheiden van de markt. Deventer: militair, demografisch, economisch, 1578–1648* (Houten, 1993), pp. 139–42.

16 A. H. Wertheim-Gijse Weenink, *Twee woelige jaren in Zutphen. De plooierijen van 1703 tot 1705* (Zutphen, 1977), p. 25; Streng, *Stemme in staat*, p. 76.

17 S. W. Verstegen, *Gegoede ingezetenen. Jonkers en geërfden op de Veluwe 1650–1830* (Zutphen, 1990), p. 48.

and country in this province could not decide upon common delegates to the States General, with the result that separate deputies arrived from the town of Groningen itself and from the Ommelanden, the surrounding countryside.[18]

Still, in clay-soil Groningen the countryside presented a socio-economic continuum with the town that was more similar to the coastal territories than the more sandy-soil inland provinces of Drenthe, Overijssel and Gelderland, where urban–rural distinctions regarding occupations and services were most pronounced. In the provinces of Holland, Zeeland, Friesland, Groningen and Utrecht the lack of sharp socio-economic distinctions between town and country was underlined by the similar wage levels that prevailed over large parts of the coast. There, small-scale enterprises dominated both farming and industrial production. Rural prices of crucial products such as bread and milk often followed trends in nearby towns.[19] The number of households on the coastal *platteland* engaged in agriculture was surprisingly low, frequently no more than 45–50 per cent, although this admittedly compared with only 5 to 10 per cent of the workforce engaged in dairy production or tilling in the towns. While farmers had no need to rely on townspeople for much of their trade, several highly specialised services, such as Latin schools, were located only in towns; on the other hand, some book-printers and highly specialised artisans chose to reside in the countryside.[20] Differences in consumption patterns were also small. Apparently typical items of urban expenditure like paintings, financial obligations and bonds were found in farming households too.[21] Most indicative of this deep urban–rural integration along the more developed coastal areas was the frequent in- and out-migration between urban and rural settlements.[22]

The true rural periphery of the Dutch Republic was located in the Generality Lands, the conquered areas lying mostly to the south. There, towns were not allowed to dominate their hinterland because the entire

---

[18] Bos, *Het Groningsche gild- en stapelrecht*, p. 331.

[19] R. Dekker, *Holland in beroering. Oproeren in de 17de en 18de eeuw* (Baarn, 1982), p. 123; Noordam, *Leven in Maasland*, p. 34.

[20] J. de Vries, *The Dutch rural economy in the Golden Age 1500–1700* (New Haven, 1974), p. 99; J. A. Faber, *Drie eeuwen Friesland. Economische en sociale ontwikkelingen van 1500 tot 1800* (Leeuwarden, 1973), pp. 101, 124–5; Noordam, *Leven in Maasland*, p. 44; C. Lesger, *Hoorn als stedelijk knooppunt. Stedensystemen tijdens de late middeleeuwen en vroegmoderne tijd* (Hilversum, 1990), p. 34.

[21] H. van Koolbergen, 'De materiële cultuur van Weesp en Weesperkarspel in de zeventiende en achttiende eeuw', in A. Schuurman, J. de Vries, and A. van der Woude (eds.), *Aards geluk. De Nederlanders en hun spullen van 1550 tot 1850* (Amsterdam, 1997), pp. 152–3.

[22] R. Rommes, *Oost, west, Utrecht best? Driehonderd jaar migratie en migranten in de stad Utrecht (begin 16e-begin 19e eeuw)* (Amsterdam, 1998), p. 132.

district was placed under the jurisdiction of the Council of State.[23] Dutch Flanders suffered the most far-reaching consequences of these institutional changes, for its towns were only allowed to engage in local trade and the countryside was forced to specialise in agricultural produce, above all wheat; the grain, which was exported to Holland's markets, was not even allowed to be milled within Dutch Flanders. Formerly thriving towns like Hulst and Axel were forcibly ruralised and underwent rapid decline.[24]

The situation in Dutch Brabant was slightly different again. Upon surrender, the major centres of Bois-le-Duc ('s-Hertogenbosch) and Breda were granted some of their former political and tax privileges and were exempted from the high tariffs imposed on goods from the 'foreign' Generality Lands. In the decades following conquest, the Brabant beer, pottery and textile industries clearly benefited from Holland's urban demand.[25] The Brabantine countryside and its manufacture may have benefited even more, as its nearly self-sufficient peasant communities were drawn into the broader Dutch market and took advantage of the area's lower wages compared with the seaboard communities of Holland and Zeeland.

Conflicts between town and country: trade and industry

Higher wages in Holland's countryside were a result of the province's advanced level of specialisation since the later middle ages.[26] During the fifteenth century a large proportion of the rural population had been forced to give up tillage because of the sinking of the peatland (*inklinking*), which rendered it uncultivable. Many had taken to dairy production, fishing, peat digging, shipbuilding, textile production or other artisan activities instead.[27] For some north Holland villages, such as Graft and Zuidschermer, fishing and shipping grew to provide a living for 31–2 per cent of the households. In neighbouring places, like

---

[23] An exception was Westerwolde, to the east of the Oldambt, which was ruled by Groningen and Friesland.

[24] Rottier, *Stedelijke strukturen*, pp. 72–7.

[25] T. Kappelhof, 'Noord-Brabant en de Hollandse stapelmarkt', in K. Davids et al. (eds.), *De Republiek tussen zee en vasteland* (Louvain, 1995), p. 196.

[26] de Vries, *Dutch rural economy*, p. 173. This development had started even earlier than de Vries assumed; see J. L. van Zanden, 'Prijs van de vooruitgang? Economische modernisering en sociale polarisatie op het Nederlandse platteland na 1500', *Economisch- en sociaal-historisch jaarboek* 51 (1988), 82–7.

[27] J. Lucassen, 'Beschouwingen over seizoengebonden trekarbeid', *Tijdschrift voor sociale geschiedenis* 8 (1982), 333; J. L. van Zanden, *The rise and decline of Holland's economy. Merchant capitalism and the labour market* (Manchester, 1993), pp. 32–3; Bieleman, *Geschiedenis*, p. 37.

Wormer, a similar proportion was engaged in textile manufacture.[28] Even long-distance trade in grain constituted a regular part of rural activities.

Farmers in the low peat districts of south Holland and Utrecht combined dairy production with the cultivation of hemp for the production of cordage and subsequently also sailcloth for the maritime industries.[29] The Zaanstreek, just north of Amsterdam, underwent an extraordinary industrial development. Benefiting from the growth of neighbouring consumer markets, in particular of Amsterdam, production was mechanised to an extent impossible in guild-controlled urban settings. By 1731, 584 Zaan windmills were in use for the production of flour, oils, timber, paper, tobacco, paints, mustard, hemp, the fulling of woollens and more. The region's naval industry was especially famous.[30] Virtually none of these rural industries was controlled directly by urban entrepreneurs. This was connected to the fact that the countryside in Holland was not populated by peasants, that is, by largely self-sufficient farmers. Rather, hired labour was extensively used in dairy production and horticulture, in peateries and at dike works. Industrial activities were performed in independent workshops, mills and wharves. Rural wages might be somewhat lower but were on the whole comparable to urban ones.[31] The putting-out system as such was not uncommon, but was concentrated among urban spinners and weavers. During the sixteenth century much of Holland's textile production was concentrated into several larger manufactures, a development which restricted subsequent opportunities for putting-out among the region's draperies.[32]

Many urban guilds observed the rural enterprises with envy. Although the majority of Holland's guilds had been formed recently and were not officially represented in urban governments (by contrast with some of the older towns inland), the town magistrates did not turn a deaf ear to the guilds' complaints. After all, it was often these same officials who had supported the establishment of guilds in order to secure a produc-

[28] A. van der Woude, *Het Noorderkwartier. Een regionaal-historisch onderzoek in de demografische en economische geschiedenis van westelijk Nederland van de late middeleeuwen tot het begin van de negentiende eeuw* (Utrecht, 1983), pp. 312–13.
[29] H. Hoogendoorn, 'En agrarisch-historische schets van het Groene Hart (1500–1950)', *Jaarverslag Stichting Boerderij-Historisch Onderzvek* (Arnhem, 1997), pp. 34–46.
[30] Ibid., pp. 317–20.
[31] de Vries, *Dutch rural economy*, p. 104; J. de Vries, 'The labour market', in K. Davids and L. Noordegraaf (eds.), *The Dutch economy in the Golden Age* (Amsterdam, 1993), pp. 63–5.
[32] L. Noordegraaf, 'The new draperies in the northern Netherlands, 1500–1800', in N. B. Harte (ed.), *The new draperies in the Low Countries and England, 1300–1800* (Oxford, 1997), pp. 180–1.

tive livelihood for the members.[33] Many guilds specified rules about the maximum numbers of artisans, the payment for sick-funds, the raw materials to be used, and the quality of the final product, all of which made guild members less flexible than rural artisans. In addition, urban wages were under pressure from guild duties and urban taxes, which were often higher than rural ones.[34]

In their struggle to suppress rural industries, the towns restricted or prohibited the sale of certain 'foreign' products on their markets and streets.[35] They could also invoke the *banmijl* and the Order op de Buitennering. The first was a franchise that banned all trade and industry within the immediate environs of the town walls; the second was an act dating from 1531 that prohibited the creation of new industries in the countryside.[36] These measures were generally ineffective. Individual merchants like the Directors of the Amsterdam Baltic trade were interested in supporting rural industries.[37] Zaan products were both cheaper and more likely to be in stock (because of lower storage costs) than products in the towns, and the Zaan wharves practised longer working days, which was a major advantage when repairs were needed at short notice.[38] Since fines did not always match the difference in price between urban and rural products, many Amsterdam and Hoorn merchants continued to buy Zaan timber, vessels and ships' provisions.

An additional problem for urban guilds was that low-quality rural products – cloth being the most common example – could damage the urban industries' reputation. The provincial Estates provided a stage to voice urban grievances about these matters. Individual towns, mostly spurred by the guilds, urged the province to restrict rural industries. Certain trades, like drapers, brewers and dealers in groats, had associ-

---

[33] H. Kaptein, *De Hollandse textielnijverheid 1350–1600. Conjunctuur en continuïteit* (Hilversum, 1998), pp. 152–3; K. Goudriaan et al., *De gilden in Gouda* (Zwolle, 1996), pp. 16, 65ff.

[34] Some rural guilds were established as well, but their regulations were limited. See A. J. van Braam, *Bloei en verval van het economisch-sociale leven aan de Zaan in de 17de en de 18de eeuw* (Wormerveer, 1944), p. 61; on inland guilds see also F. D. Zeiler, 'Men segt, dat hier so een gilde is . . . Semi- en buitenstedelijke gilden in noordwest-Overijssel in de zeventiende en de achttiende eeuw', *NEHA-Jaarboek voor economische, bedrijfs- en techniekgeschiedenis* 67 (1994), 105. In some cases, guild regulations pushed up wages considerably higher. Amsterdam ship-carpenters earned 40 to 50 per cent above those in Zaan. J. G. van Dillen, *Bronnen tot de geschiedenis van het bedrijfsleven en het gildewezen van Amsterdam* (The Hague, 1974), p. 291.

[35] Ibid., pp. 154–5, 687; van Braam, *Bloei en verval*, pp. 125–8.

[36] E. C. G. Brünner, *De Order op de Buitennering van 1531. Bijdrage tot de kennis van de economische geschiedenis van het Graafschap Holland in den tijd van Karel V* (Utrecht, 1918), p. 163.

[37] Aten, *Als het gewelt comt*, pp. 256–7.

[38] R. W. Unger, *Dutch shipbuilding before 1800* (Assen, 1978), pp. 8, 84; van Braam, *Bloei en verval*, pp. 62, 129; Aten, *Als het gewelt comt*, p. 243.

ations representing several cities, which sometimes appealed to the provincial government to act on their behalf.[39]

The provincial authorities had their own reasons to combat the spread of rural industries. Since the majority of public funds came from excise, weighing and market dues, the uncontrolled rise of rural traders and producers made it harder to control tax evasion and fraud.[40] In several instances, such as the baking of a certain kind of cake, the provincial government acceded to the cities' complaints. But provincially sponsored restrictions were mostly rather ineffective. In 1602 a scheme was launched to ban international grain trade from the countryside, probably instigated by Amsterdam merchants. Representatives of over twenty villages demanded that the act be repealed. A compromise was struck, in accordance with the previously mentioned Order of 1531 that condoned established rural activities, whereby the international grain trade was allowed where it constituted 'ancient practice'. The villages saw no difficulty in having elderly inhabitants declare that such was indeed the case, and the foreign grain trade continued to be plied in the countryside thereafter.[41]

In the following decades the towns in northern Holland drafted numerous acts banning the beer trade, candle production, weighhouses, pedlars, and so on in the countryside. The affected villages responded with collective petitions supported by the nobility in the provincial estates. Representatives from an increasing number of villages joined the protest. In 1620 three permanent rural deputies were assigned the task of defending north Holland's countryside; their number increased to five in 1631. The original core of the movement was the Zaanstreek, but gradually other districts also became involved. Although the meetings of the village deputies were declared unlawful by the provincial government, no decisive measures were undertaken because the nobility rose in their defence.[42] The villages did not only manage to get the nobility on their side, they also exploited rivalries between towns. In response to an act of 1668 that prohibited the rural beer trade, the rural representatives threatened to boycott Haarlem's markets in favour of neighbouring Alkmaar's if Haarlem's government voted in favour of the restrictions. The outcome was, as usual, a compromise brokered between the nobility and the Haarlem council, in

[39] Ibid., pp. 319–27.
[40] van Braam, *Bloei en verval*, p. 126; M. 't Hart, *The making of a bourgeois state. War, politics and finance during the Dutch revolt* (Manchester, 1993), p. 123.
[41] Aten, *Als het gewelt comt*, pp. 309, 333.
[42] Ibid., pp. 334–5; van Deursen, *Een dorp in de polder*, pp. 274–5.

which all beer traders were enrolled on a new register and they were allowed to continue their activities.[43]

After 1679–80, urban attacks on the countryside subsided as the emphasis of Holland's fiscal policy shifted from excise to direct taxation, and the need to control rural industries and trade for the purposes of provincial revenues declined. The secular economic downturn after 1650 also hit the rural industries, so new businesses in the countryside were rare and less threatening for urban guilds.[44] With support from the nobility and, at times, by skilfully exploiting inter-urban rivalries, Holland's villages were thus able to defend themselves quite effectively against plans by urban elites to suppress their industries. Towns in Holland might be dominant, but they obviously could not subject the countryside at will. What was most remarkable during this period was the high degree of institutionalised bargaining between town and country which resulted overall in a relatively pacific relationship.

Rural industry

Holland's industrial elites followed an entirely different strategy in the two more peripheral areas of Dutch Brabant and Twente where rural industry was particularly developed.[45] Both were sandy-soil economies with a strong rural cottar class. Once the borders of the Dutch Republic were secured, and in particular after the Peace of Westphalia (1648), investments in these areas carried fewer risks.[46] After 1635, Leiden entrepreneurs established a putting-out system around Tilburg in Dutch Brabant, where peasants were already used to spinning and weaving on their own account or for Flemish and Brabantine entrepreneurs. The Leiden intermediaries prepared the wool, had the peasants spin and weave, and brought the cloths back to Leiden for finishing. Urban capitalists therefore dominated the production process.

The distance to Leiden, the costs of mediation and the customs dues (Dutch Brabant was taxed as foreign, conquered territory) all raised the

[43] Ibid., pp. 245, 279; Aten, *Als het gewelt comt,* p. 344.
[44] Unhampered by provincial restrictions the Zaan industry remained vigorous up to the mid-eighteenth century. Then it lost its technological edge and succumbed to international competition. See de Vries and van der Woude, *The first modern economy,* pp. 302–3.
[45] Noordegraaf, 'The new draperies', p. 183. The Dutch 'semi-periphery' also became involved in rural industry, albeit at a lesser scale. Friesian rural weavers received wool from Holland and sold woven cloth for finishing in Holland's industrial towns (Faber, *Drie eeuwen Friesland,* p. 227).
[46] One finds similar investments in other regions that had been subjected to invasion before the 1630s, such as around Maastricht or on the Veluwe (Verstegen, *Gegoede ingezetenen,* p. 45; Jansen, 'De relatie', p. 80).

costs of production. However, these additional expenses were balanced by fiscal privileges – the Tilburg region was granted lower tariffs on woollen textiles – and, especially, by the large difference in wages, which stood 20–45 per cent lower than in Holland. With 42 per cent of the final production cost being determined by wages, the new ventures proved to be highly profitable.[47] Although most of the peasants in the Tilburg region were employed by Leiden, entrepreneurs from Amsterdam, Delft and Haarlem also established business intermediaries. Haarlem merchants were particularly dominant in the areas around Helmond and Eindhoven, where they commissioned linen and *bonten* cloth (a type of fustian combining linen and cotton). Here too, a reduction in tariffs on textiles was eventually granted.

A significant corollary of rural industrial expansion was the development of the smaller Brabant towns. Growth was further stimulated by the merchants' intermediaries, who set up fulling mills and dye-houses and organised transport. The growth of Tilburg from a small village to 9,000 inhabitants within a couple of decades was a particularly striking example of rural industry-led expansion.[48] By the end of the seventeenth century, the merchant intermediaries began to set themselves up independently on the basis of direct trade links with Amsterdam. Several Leiden entrepreneurs moved their quarters to Tilburg itself, thereby reducing the rural industry's distance from the commercial 'core'.

A different type of rural manufacture developed in Twente. Overijssel linen entrepreneurs, who had long been engaged in regional trade in flax, yarn and linen, gradually replaced local flax production with higher quality imports.[49] Woven cloth was often sent on behalf of local traders to Haarlem to be bleached, finished and exported. The introduction of *bombazijn*, another mixed linen and cotton cloth, injected a new dynamism into the area. This industry had first been established in Amersfoort, a town in the province of Utrecht, probably by refugees from the southern Netherlands. Amersfoort had the advantage of low wages because of its landlocked position and was also conveniently located along the trade routes followed by the linen yarn from Twente and the cotton imports from Amsterdam. The local guild issued highly restrictive rules, concerning in particular the maximum number of licensed artisans and the obligation to sell the yarn in small lots to make it easier

[47] H. F. J. M. van den Eerenbeemt, *Bestaan en bedrijvigheid. Aspecten van het sociaal en economisch leven in Stad en Meijerij van 's-Hertogenbosch* (Tilburg, 1975), p. 122; Kappelhof, 'Noord-Brabant', p. 197.
[48] Ibid., pp. 199, 201.
[49] J. A. P. G. Boot, *De Twentsche katoennijverheid 1830–1873* (Amsterdam, 1935), p. 6.

for the craftsmen to buy.[50] After 1727, however, Twente entrepreneurs started to have *bombazijn* made in the countryside, their workers being unhindered by guild restrictions. The rate of industrial growth was explosive and neighbouring towns grew rapidly at the expense of Amersfoort.[51] As a result of these developments, peasant households became increasingly dependent upon urban intermediaries. Whereas previously they had been able to buy the necessary flax or wool themselves, the growing importance of foreign trade (in particular the export of woollens and the import of raw cotton) made reliance on urban networks indispensable. In Brabant, entrepreneurs also often provided the industrial tools.[52]

Rural industry forged strong links between the urbanised west and the agrarian east and south of the Netherlands. As a result, after the downfall of the urban industries in the later seventeenth century, some sectors of the towns' economy managed to survive thanks to rural putting-out. But towards the middle of the eighteenth century the Dutch rural industry was also hit by foreign competition. Unlike other nations, the Dutch republican state avoided the use of tariffs to protect its home industries, for the commercial urban elites of Holland remained intensely preoccupied with upholding Amsterdam's international trading position, and this required low tariffs on all imports including cloth.[53] The maritime west and the inland communities engaged in a long-running conflict over tariff policy, in which the elites, whose main interests lay with industry and agriculture, fought a losing battle to impose protective barriers for their products.

Drainage, taxation and peasant revolts

Whereas external tariff policies were decided by the upper circles of the Republic, taxation and the management of drainage boards with their attendant dike duties were issues resolved at the regional and local level. The mobilisation of the north Holland villages discussed previously

---

[50] P. Brusse and M. Winthorst, 'Tot welvaren van de stadt ende verbeteringh van de neringhe. Arbeidsmarktregulering en economische ontwikkeling in de Amersfoortse textiel 1450–1800', *Textielhistorische Bijdragen* 30 (1990), 15.

[51] C. Trompetter, *Agriculture, proto-industry and Mennonite entrepreneurship. A history of the textile industry in Twente 1600–1815* (Amsterdam, 1997), p. 57; Frijhoff, 'Zutphen's geschiedenis', p. 110.

[52] H. D. Tjalsma, 'Textielnijverheid en modernisering van gezins- en huishoudenstructuur in stad en platteland in de achttiende en de negentiende eeuw', in H. Diederiks, J. T. Lindblad and B. de Vries (eds.), *Het platteland in een veranderende wereld. Boeren en het proces van modernisering* (Hilversum, 1994), p. 157. Cotton printing was also concentrated in Amsterdam.

[53] Israel, *The Dutch Republic*, p. 1002.

illustrates the potential political and economic impact of provincial taxation on town–country relations. Although towns nearly always had a disproportionate influence in devising the arrangements for polders, which involved significant local taxation,[54] the fact that large numbers of burghers also owned the newly drained lands and that dike duties had to be borne both by farmers and landowners meant that town and country interests often coincided. On the other hand, representation on the drainage boards, the handling of sluices, the height of the waterline, the construction of canals and the exploitation of peateries were all issues that could give rise to confrontation.

A conflict over the drainage board on the isle of Walcheren in the province of Zeeland illustrates several of these controversies. In the early 1650s, the Walcheren polder board decided to increase the dike duties by 25 per cent. As these levies were not justified by threats of inundation or by major dike improvements, a substantial group of farmers and landowners refused to pay, on grounds of financial mismanagement by the board and of insufficient representation of farmers and landowners in the polder's administration.[55] The latter seems a legitimate complaint. In Walcheren, the polder's directory traditionally consisted of four voting seats, but the vacancy of the Stadhouder/Prince of Orange's seat after the death of William II in 1650 meant that only three votes were cast. The city of Middelburg, the most powerful in the region, held the chair and one vote; the two other Walcheren towns, Veere and Vlissingen, shared one vote; and two representatives of the landowners held the last vote jointly.

A gathering of the farmers and landowners appointed twenty-four *commissarissen* from their midst, who established a permanent forum for rural discontent in early 1656. They convened in Middelburg at a meeting place provided by the town guilds. Some of their leaders, including their spokesman Gillis de Mailliaerts, were also prominent Middelburg burghers.[56] Among the demands to be considered was that the rural representation should be increased to four votes. Conditions for election to the board were also to be widened from a minimum

[54] A. Hendriksen, *Watergraafsmeer. Binnenzee, polder, lustoord, stadsdeel* (Amsterdam, 1998), p. 28; H. S. Danner, 'Droogmakerijen in de zeventiende eeuw', in E. H. Walhuis and M. H. Boetes (eds.), *Strijd tegen het water. Het beheer van land en water in het Zuiderzeegebied* (Zutphen, 1992), p. 53; C. Postma, *Het hoogheemraadschap van Delfland in de middeleeuwen 1289–1589* (Hilversum, 1989), p. 84.

[55] For a full account of this peasant revolt, see M. 't Hart, 'Een boerenopstand op Walcheren. De strijd om het waterschap 1655–1657', *Tijdschrift voor sociale geschiedenis* 20 (1994), 265–81.

[56] M. van der Bijl, *Idee en interest. Voorgeschiedenis, verloop en achtergronden van de politieke twisten in Zeeland en vooral in Middelburg tussen 1702 en 1715* (Groningen, 1981), p. 351.

ownership of 50 *gemet* (20 hectares) to one of 30 *gemet* (12 hectares). Lastly, the *commissarissen* engaged directly in the drainage board's activities by inspecting the dikes and by paying the labourers on the drainage works, who were often small farmers and farmers' sons, in lieu of the official board itself, which lacked funds.

After initially ignoring the rebels' meetings, the directors of the board soon caved in, probably under pressure from the many landowners who lived within the town walls. The next to acquiesce was the town of Vlissingen, won over by Middelburg's proposed compromise: Middelburg was to have two votes, Veere and Vlissingen one each, and the landowners four, a total of eight. Veere, however, refused to accept the settlement. Instead, the town appealed to tradition, and in addition claimed the former vote of the Stadhouder, thereby increasing its vote to one and a half out of the original four. Veere invoked the ancient institution of the marquisate (*markiezaat*) of Veere, a title granted to the Prince of Orange in the sixteenth century that gave their bailiff the right to preserve the seat with the consent and order of the Royal Princess (mother at this time of the infant William of Orange, later King and Stadhouder William III).

Veere's tactics were not so bizarre if one takes into account the distribution of economic opportunities in the region. Unlike Middelburg, few landowners lived in the town itself. Much of Veere's wealth had come from its seaport. By the seventeenth century, however, Veere had been overtaken by Middelburg and Vlissingen. Vlissingen had become a notorious haven for privateers; Middelburg had developed into an international trade centre that included a staple for French wines, a Bank of Exchange, a Chamber for the West India Company, and the seat of the Zeeland admiralty. Veere had few economic opportunities, so the value of rent-seeking from offices and prerogatives was enhanced.

In the countryside, the previously peaceful protests turned into acts of violence focused mainly upon the magistrates of Veere. Arbitration by the provincial diet resulted in the landowners obtaining half the new total of eight votes and in the concession of a general amnesty. Compared to the contestation by the north Holland villages, a powerful city in the provincial government rather than the nobility had defended the interests of the countryside. The support provided by the Middelburg guilds was also remarkable, and it resurfaced during the Walcheren revolt of 1672, when the farmers sided with Middelburg's craftsmen against the urban oligarchy.[57]

---

[57] P. J. Meertens, 'J. Beronicius en de opstand der Walcherse boeren in juli 1672', *Historia* 9 (1943), 224–32. The craftsmen may have been more willing to provide support

In contrast with Middelburg, the policies of Groningen in the far north were firmly set within a town–country dichotomy. Groningen's position within the region was unchallenged: no other urban centres could compete. The provincial estates were often split between town and country; in the diet, the city and the Ommelanden (the surrounding countryside represented by the Groningen gentry, the jonkers) each had a casting vote and a separate administration.

By the early seventeenth century, Groningen's growth had ground to a halt, largely because its former links with the German territories were restricted by the new national frontiers. The city's budgets displayed regular deficits. The exploitation of former monastic goods proved to be only a temporary solution, and in 1618 the possibility was raised of exploiting peat to the neighbouring south-east as a way out of the city's problems.[58] Up to then Holland and Utrecht had produced the bulk of the country's fuel, dug from low peat bogs in close proximity to the maritime cities, but by the early seventeenth century alternative sources were being urgently sought, as the expanding peat lakes were endangering local agriculture, dike-systems and provincial tax revenues. High-lying peat bogs in the inland provinces of Friesland, Drenthe, Overijssel and Groningen began to be exploited. However, this required large-scale financial investments, particularly for digging the canals, for by contrast with the easier low-peat exploitation in the west, the bogs in higher inland districts took one to two decades to yield a profit.

Seventeenth-century urban expansion and the concomitant demand for fuel gave the morasses of the Oldambt a new significance. Wedged between the Gorecht, south of Groningen, and Westerwolde, both of which were under Groningen lordship, this district had long been marginal. Inundations and recent military invasions, the last in 1624, exacerbated the area's poor reputation. Its seemingly poor resource base had meant that no one had bothered to define its constitutional status when the province and the city joined the Union. For several decades, Groningen acted as an *ad hoc* overseer for its administrative and jurisdictional needs.

During the 1620s the Groningen authorities decided to take the initiative in an area they regarded as the city's hinterland. Canals were projected and peat fields were laid out. All turf was to be shipped solely by Groningen skippers. Sluices were handled for the benefit of the

because rural households in Walcheren only produced coarse textiles for personal consumption.

[58] For a full account of the Oldambt revolt, see M. 't Hart, 'Rules and repertoires. The revolt of a farmers' republic in the early modern Netherlands', in M. Hanagan, L. Page Moch, and W. te Brake (eds.), *Challenging authority. The historical study of contentious politics* (Minneapolis, 1998).

peateries, sometimes against the interests of the neighbouring farmers. Monastic goods were seized and administered as if they were the city's property. Groningen began to enforce staple rights in the Oldambt and raised tolls and other barriers to trade. A reform of the land tax was followed by tax increases, and the building of canals and dikes raised the duties paid by farmers to the drainage board. In the 1630s the urban authorities even ordered village inhabitants to cut the new canals themselves, or face a fine equivalent to double the costs. Five major Oldambt landowners who requested proper compensation for their loss of land were gaoled by the town magistrates. Finally, in 1639 the Groningen government issued the Acte van Souverainiteyt declaring the city's sovereignty over the district, a decree that had to be signed by the village representatives (*volmachten*) and other notables.[59]

The *volmachten* refused to sign and the villagers convened an assembly which drew up a declaration (*procuratie*) stating their immemorial freedom. Three general deputies were elected and were backed by the gentry. This caused a stalemate in the provincial administration where no major decisions could be taken without both the city's and the countryside's vote. Meanwhile, in the Oldambt region the Groningen tax officers were attacked, city labourers at new dike projects were chased away, dug-out canals were refilled overnight, sluices and dikes were destroyed, and the peat of the town's tenants was trampled down. Village representatives drafted their own laws, exercised their own jurisdiction, and collected their own taxes. Soldiers sent by the city in an attempt to restore order were chased off by the village militias.

The deadlock within the provincial administration forced the States General to intervene. Groningen demanded to be recognised as lord of the Oldambt; the Oldambt wished to retain its sovereignty and to send delegates to the provincial diet; the Ommelanden argued that sovereignty over the Oldambt, including the say over all former monastic goods, pertained to the province. Finally, in 1649 the States General resolved that, as the district had failed to show the necessary documents (the files having always been kept by the city),[60] the independent government of the Oldambt should be dissolved. In exchange, all participants were granted a general amnesty, and the revolt subsided. Although the city's former jurisdiction was formally restored, the countryside won several points of substance. The new tolls were withdrawn,

---

[59] C. E. Dijkstra, 'De oldambten tegen de stad . . . een vruchteloze strijd', *Groningsche Volksalmanak. Historisch Jaarboek voor Groningen* 1974–1975, pp. 56–8.

[60] A. S. de Blécourt, *Oldambt en de Ommelanden* (Assen, 1935), p. 144 suggested the city might have destroyed the evidence.

compensation was paid for lost lands, and new boundaries were drawn in the peat fields.[61] While the claim to sovereignty and to representation in the provincial diet was refused to the Oldambt *volmachten*, the city's seigniorial claims were also deemed illegitimate. Sovereignty, it was restated, rested with the diet, thus with the gentry and the city together.

Groningen's power over its hinterland was therefore checked by the highest authority in the land, the States General. Middelburg, by contrast, operated within the typical competitive setting of the maritime west with its frequent inter-urban rivalries; there the conflict was finally solved by the Zeeland provincial government. Most striking in both cases was the emphasis on legal rights and proper representation, on the value of traditions and on the amelioration of rules. The extent of the violence resorted to in these revolts was quite uncommon in Dutch town–country relations, and the resort in both instances to a general pardon shows the willingness by all parties to accede to compromise.

Urban decline, agrarian recovery, and taxation

Even though Middelburg and Groningen could not reign supreme over their hinterland, the events we have just recalled testify to the huge political and economic strength of Dutch cities. The latter's advantage was most apparent in terms of political rights, which in some cases took on an economic significance, as in the case of Groningen and Dordrecht's staple rights. Conversely, the entire fiscal–military machine of the Dutch state rested upon the country's urban economies, for by far the largest proportion of public funds came from taxes levied in the towns, above all from excise dues. The towns might well be overrepresented in the political system, but they generally also paid a disproportionate share of total taxation.[62]

As long as trade expanded, the major towns grew and immigration continued. But the high rates of urbanisation upon which the Dutch state's fiscal–military apparatus rested began to falter from the last quarter of the seventeenth century, even though the overall proportion of people living in cities remained approximately a third. International trade passed Dutch harbours by; improvements and extensions to ports were halted; urban industries suffered, initially from rural competition, but increasingly also from foreign competitors. Rates of innovation

---

[61] Still, in the following decades, the town profited substantially from the peateries because of its advantages in scale. M. A. W. Gerding, *Vier eeuwen turfwinning. De verveningen in Groningen, Friesland, Drenthe en Overijssel tussen 1550 en 1950* (Wageningen, 1995), p. 360.

[62] 't Hart, *The making*, p. 208.

dropped,[63] and high wage levels became a source of comparative disadvantage.

High wages were, in part, a consequence of the socio-political setting. The urban elites invested a growing proportion of their assets in securities issued by the municipalities, the provinces, the Union and the admiralties. Bond revenues became the patriciate's most important source of income.[64] The ongoing pressures of war made it hard to change the prevailing institutional set-up. The soaring state debt had to be serviced by means of excise taxes that raised the level of nominal wages and damaged Holland's industrial competitiveness – all the more since the urban retail price of several industrial products actually decreased between 1645 and 1665.[65] The important textile centres of Leiden and Haarlem could put off the worst by specialising in luxury items and by employing rural spinners and weavers. By the early eighteenth century, however, overall decline could no longer be averted. The contraction of the domestic market and the slowing down of population growth constituted serious constraints, in particular for brewing, the building sector and the potteries.

The immediate causes of decline differed from one town to another. Foreign industrial competition affected the textile industries. Several north Holland towns, in particular Enkhuizen, suffered from the drop in herring catches, which by the later eighteenth century were only a quarter of seventeenth-century levels. Zeeland towns disintegrated as Antwerp's trade declined. Unrelenting competition by Amsterdam reduced several neighbouring international harbours to localities of purely regional importance. Besides Amsterdam, only Rotterdam managed to maintain a significant share of international trade. Between 1650 and 1800 Middelburg, Delft, Alkmaar and Hoorn lost 30 to 40 per cent of their population; Haarlem lost 45, Leiden 54 and Enkhuizen up to 68 per cent.[66]

[63] K. Davids, 'Shifts of technological leadership in early modern Europe', in K. Davids and J. Lucassen (eds.), *A miracle mirrored. The Dutch republic in European perspective* (Cambridge, 1995), pp. 354–5.

[64] See the calculations by de Vries and van der Woude, *The first modern economy*, pp. 120, 124–5. On the pattern of investments of regents in Leiden see M. Prak, *Gezeten burgers. De elite in een Hollandse stad, Leiden 1700–1780* (The Hague, 1985), pp. 274–80.

[65] van Zanden, *The rise*, pp. 138–9; de Vries and van der Woude, *The first modern economy*, p. 295. For most of the seventeenth and eighteenth centuries, labourers and artisans on the sandy soils inland received a wage 60–75 per cent of that paid in the urban west; de Vries, 'The labour market', p. 63. Urban price declines occurred largely as a result of competition from the rural textile industries (de Vries and van der Woude, *The first modern economy*, pp. 286–7).

[66] H. Schmal, 'Patterns of de-urbanisation in the Netherlands between 1650 and 1850', in H. van der Wee (ed.), *The rise and decline of urban industries in Italy and in the Low Countries* (Louvain, 1988), pp. 290–2.

De-urbanisation reduced demand for rural products like hemp that had fed the shipping and fishing industries.[67] Coupled with a general drop in the price of foodstuffs, the rural depression in the Netherlands lasted from the mid-seventeenth to the mid-eighteenth century. Several disasters added to the general misery. In the 1730s, a sea-worm weakened the wooden dike systems, causing huge damage for the drainage boards and all landowners, since stone replacements were required at short notice. In the same period, cattle epizootics reduced the livestock by as much as three-quarters.[68] Farmers in the maritime north and west, who had invested large sums in their farms and had larger numbers of cattle, suffered particularly from these crises. Declining agricultural prices increased the tax burden in real terms. Low revenues hampered repayment of borrowed capital. Large-scale land reclamation came to an end; land was put up for sale by nobles, burghers and urban institutions; the price of farmland fell.

Inland the signs of agrarian regression were less common, because agrarian specialisation and investments had not progressed as far. Eastern rural communities had fixed investments and were therefore able to respond more flexibly to the crisis compared to those in the coastal provinces.[69] Cattle breeding was more easily replaced with rye cultivation and horticulture. An increasing number of peasant families began to grow hops, flax, madder, hemp, fruit and tobacco in response to demand from Amsterdam merchants.[70] While the population in the coastal west contracted, the number of inhabitants inland increased. Twente more than doubled its population between 1682 and 1809, and living standards seem to have risen too.[71]

Inevitably, of course, inland towns were also hurt by the contraction of Holland's urban system.[72] Zwolle, for example, which had handled much of the linen trade between the eastern territories and the Haarlem industries, suffered from the latter's decline.[73] Nevertheless, inland

---

[67] Hoogendoorn, 'Een agrarisch-historische schets', pp. 40–4.

[68] Bieleman, *Geschiedenis*, pp. 106–7.

[69] J. L. van Zanden, 'De landbouw op de zandgronden van Oost-Nederland', *Tijdschrift voor geschiedenis* 101 (1988), 190–205.

[70] H. K. Roessingh, *Inlandse tabak. Expansie en contractie van een handelsgewas in de 17e en 18e eeuw in Nederland* (Wageningen, 1976), pp. 252–53.

[71] Trompetter, *Agriculture*, pp. 45–50; L. Noordegraaf and J. L. van Zanden, 'Early modern economic growth and the standard of living: did labour benefit from Holland's Golden Age?', in Davids and Lucassen, *A miracle mirrored*, p. 434.

[72] Frijhoff, 'Zutphen's geschiedenis', p. 120. See also Kappelhof, 'Noord-Brabant', pp. 192–8, on the dependence of Dutch Brabant's breweries, potteries and textiles upon Holland's markets.

[73] Streng, *Stemme in staat*, p. 78.

towns contracted less than those in the west; although the proportion living in cities may have declined, several non-maritime towns continued to grow in absolute terms thanks in part to the expansion of rural industrial activities.[74]

Meanwhile, the tax distribution between the eastern and western halves of the country became increasingly inequitable. Provincial tax quotas remained fixed from the early seventeenth to the end of the eighteenth century, and took no account of the changing economic and demographic balance between the regions. By the eighteenth century, the maritime communities of Holland, Friesland and Zeeland bore a disproportionate tax burden. On the other hand, virtually all inland sandy-soil provinces and in particular Gelderland appear to have profited from the outdated quota system. Figures provided by Slicher van Bath confirm the light tax burden in the Overijssel countryside, in particular in Twente, which based its wealth on its expanding industry. Wantje Fritschy has calculated that in 1720 a Hollander paid 23 guilders per capita towards provincial taxation, an inhabitant of Overijssel only 10 guilders; in 1790 this burden was respectively 26 and 6 guilders.[75] Tax burdens rose also in Holland's countryside, albeit at a slower rate than in the towns.[76] By contrast, a case study of the small Brabantine town of Woensel has revealed a negligible increase in the tax burden in nominal terms and a significant decline in real terms.[77]

From the mid-eighteenth century, the countryside began to profit from the recovery in agricultural prices. In some regions, the average size of farms increased.[78] Investments in land reclamation and peateries, which had halted during the agrarian depression, were resumed. The sea-worm disaster of the 1730s ultimately brought about a huge improvement in the dike system, as the stone replacements required fewer repairs. Rich benefits were reaped from innovations like the potato, widely adopted during the 1770s. In the neighbourhood of Holland's larger towns, vegetable and fruit production expanded and became

---

[74] J.-C. Boyer, *L'évolution de l'organisation urbaine des Pays-Bas* (Lille, 1978), p. 175; Schmal, 'Patterns of de-urbanisation', pp. 291–2.

[75] W. Fritschy, 'Taxation in Britain, France and the Netherlands in the 18th century', *Social and Economic History in the Netherlands* 2 (1990), 60. See also B. H. Slicher van Bath, *Een samenleving onder spanning. Geschiedenis van het platteland in Overijssel* (Assen, 1957), p. 375, and J. Bieleman, *Boeren op het Drentse zand 1600–1910. Een nieuwe visie op de oude landbouw* (Wageningen, 1987), pp. 176, 707.

[76] de Vries and van der Woude, *The first modern economy*, p. 112; Noordam, *Leven in Maasland*, p. 40.

[77] G. van den Brink, *De grote overgang. Een lokaal onderzoek naar de modernisering van het bestaan* (Nijmegen, 1996), p. 255.

[78] Bieleman, *Geschiedenis*, p. 169; van Zanden, 'De prijs van de vooruitgang?', p. 9; Faber, *Drie eeuwen Friesland*, p. 222.

increasingly directed towards international markets. Grain imports for domestic consumption slowed down as local productivity increased. By the end of the eighteenth century, Dutch agriculture both in the coastal west and in the east had achieved levels of productivity unrivalled elsewhere in the economy.[79]

Most of the population increase of the later eighteenth century was confined to the countryside. In some communities, for example in Krommenie between 1742 and 1797, the number of households engaged in agriculture doubled.[80] Often, long-distance migrants came to work in the countryside and avoided the cities entirely.[81] Several artisans in larger towns reorientated their production to the rural markets. In Delft, the collapse of the traditional brewing, textile and pottery industries was matched by renewed expansion in the building trade, faced with burgeoning demand to improve old farmsteads and build new ones.[82]

Conclusion

Town–country relations in the early modern northern Netherlands were characterised by exceptionally high rates of urbanisation and commercialisation. In political and constitutional terms, the countryside was obviously at a disadvantage compared with the towns. Following the Revolt of the late sixteenth century, the urban elites also wielded enormous economic power through their links to the international trade networks, through industrial activities in the rural periphery and, in some cases, through extensive staple rights or tax privileges. Towns did not shy away from wielding these powers to restrain rural industrial competition, to co-ordinate flood control in the face of a disorderly dike system and of the excessive exploitation of peateries, to divert trade and sales from rival towns, to profit from peateries and land reclamation, or simply to raise tax and toll revenues.

---

[79] J. L. van Zanden, *De economische ontwikkeling van de Nederlandse landbouw in de negentiende eeuw, 1800–1914* (Wageningen, 1985), pp. 48, 219; for Zeeland see P. Priester, *Geschiedenis van de Zeeuwse landbouw circa 1610–1910* (Wageningen, 1998), pp. 49, 55.

[80] van der Woude, *Het Noorderkwartier*, p. 310. In the islands off South Holland, however, English and Flemish demand for flax stimulated a revival of industrial activities. See D. Damsma and L. Noordegraaf, 'Een vergeten plattelandsnijverheid. Vlasarbeid, bevolkingsgroei en proto-industrialisatie in Zuid-West Nederland, 1700–1950', *Economisch- en sociaal-historisch jaarboek* 44 (1981), p. 149.

[81] Rommes, *Oost, west*, p. 130; Faber, *Drie eeuwen Friesland*, p. 234.

[82] T. Wijsenbeek-Olthuis, 'Stedelijk verval en cultuurpatronen', in Schuurman, de Vries, and van der Woude, *Aards geluk*, p. 206.

Despite this, the urban elites could not control the countryside at will. Villages enjoyed a certain degree of political autonomy too, even though their access to the sovereign diets was only indirect. Most rural communities were able to invoke the support of their seigniorial lords, of the provincial nobility, of rival cities, of the urban artisan classes, or even of the States General to protect their rights against urban incursion. The overall result was a highly institutionalised bargaining system in which towns were powerful but not overwhelmingly so. Urban–rural controversies were generally resolved along established lines of conflict resolution. The formally illegal election of *volmachten, commissarissen* or other landowners or village representatives was often the first step towards accommodation. The violent movements around Middelburg and Groningen underscore the relative balance of power between town and countryside, but they were actually quite exceptional for the republican period.

The towns' greater political power was sustained by the fiscal–military regime's reliance on the highly urbanised maritime economy, but towns paid a price for their over-representation in the Republic's sovereign bodies. In the long run, however, the fiscal system ran into limits of its own making. Ongoing warfare forced state debt higher, while payments on state bonds became an ever-growing source of income for the urban elites, who were reluctant to change a highly lucrative redistributive system; the debt had to be paid by raising the excise, which in turn made Dutch industry less competitive and reduced the country's relative wealth. In addition, the Dutch authorities were preoccupied with maintaining Amsterdam's position in international trade, which implied providing virtually no protection for domestic industries.

When the economic momentum of the Republic shifted from the maritime west to the agrarian east, the Dutch state proved incapable of changing existing fiscal arrangements, at least in part because the prevailing tax regime relied upon the extensive political privileges granted to urban elites. From about 1740, the number of urban poor increased, in particular in the maritime west, whereas the farming population experienced a phase of specialisation and growth in productivity. The smaller towns inland profited from the outdated system of quotas, which gave them lower tax burdens and lower wages. On the other hand, although the small town notables resented the fact that they were not represented on the Republic's sovereign bodies, the country's political institutions also suffered from inertia and resistance to change. The number of constituent cities was frozen, their elites being unwilling to give up ancient prerogatives. In the 1780s, the ossified oligarchy was challenged by a widespread revolt, the so-called Patriot Movement. Small towns inland sided with rural militias in demanding proper political and economic reforms.[83] The regents, however, managed to restore their power up to 1795. The wealthy small towns and rural communities had to wait for the centralised state of the nineteenth century to gain their rightful place in the national political system.

[83] W. Fritschy, 'Financiële unificatie en natievorming. Een onderzoek in Overijssel', *Bijdragen en Mededelingen betreffende de Geschiedenis der Nederlanden* 104 (1988), 672–3; W. P. te Brake, 'Burgers and boeren in the Dutch patriot revolution', in Th.S. M. van der Zee et al. (eds.), *1787: De Nederlandse Revolutie?* (Amsterdam, 1988), pp. 84–99.

5   Town and country in England, 1300–1570[1]

James A. Galloway

Urbanisation

By the close of the thirteenth century, the population of England had reached or was close to its medieval peak. Although there is no unanimity as to the precise magnitude, it is widely believed that there were more people in the country *c.*1300 than there were to be for some 300 years thereafter and perhaps considerably longer.[2] Until comparatively recently it has been a commonplace to stress the overwhelmingly rural nature of that population and of the economy which sustained it, and the most influential writer on the medieval English economy, M. M. Postan, has stressed the fragile nature of the ecological balance within which it operated, portraying the relation between people and resources in neo-Malthusian terms.[3] New research directions since the 1970s have substantially modified that picture, placing increased emphasis upon the adaptive and innovative character of pre-Black Death England, and upon the degree to which its economy had developed a commercialised character. Parallels are sought with the England of the later sixteenth century, and continuities in the fundamentals of economic and social life receive increasing stress. England's towns *c.*1300 were bigger than previously thought, and its agrarian base more varied and responsive to

---

[1] I would like to thank Derek Keene and Margaret Murphy for their comments on an earlier version of this chapter.

[2] Recent estimates of the population *c.*1300 have ranged from *c.*4 million to 6 million and above. If the former were correct, then population levels would have been regained by the last decade of the sixteenth century, if the latter, not until after 1750. See B. M. S. Campbell, J. A. Galloway, D. Keene and M. Murphy, *A medieval capital and its grain supply: agrarian production and distribution in the London region c.1300* (Historical Geography Research Group, Research Series no. 30, 1993), p. 44; R. M. Smith, 'Demographic developments in rural England, 1300–1348: a survey', in B. M. S. Campbell (ed.), *Before the Black Death: studies in the 'crisis' of the early fourteenth century* (Manchester, 1991), p. 49; E. A. Wrigley and R. S. Schofield, *The population history of England 1541–1871: a reconstruction* (Cambridge, 1981), pp. 208–9.

[3] This aspect of Postan's work is most fully developed in his 'Medieval agrarian society in its prime: England', in M. M. Postan (ed.), *The Cambridge economic history of Europe*, vol. I: *The agrarian life of the middle ages*, 2nd edn (Cambridge, 1966), pp. 549–632.

Figure 5.1   Late medieval England (places mentioned in the text)

the stimulus provided by concentrated market demand. Consequently, the interrelations of town and country have assumed greater significance and are viewed in a more dynamic light, with greater emphasis placed upon interconnection and mutual stimuli.

This tendency has been associated with a shift in perspective, from the study of the particular to the general, and from the individual place to the regional and national setting. Detailed studies of individual manors, estates, villages and towns have been supplemented by approaches which seek to identify the wider structures and processes within which these particular places existed and interacted.[4] Studies of

---

[4] In some ways a revival of the historical geography tradition associated with H. C. Darby, R. A. Pelham and others, wherein mapping of national or supraregional datasets provided a central tool. Ironically, such approaches lost their centrality within historical geography just as historians were discovering their worth.

agricultural specialisation, of the diffusion of innovations, and of animate and non-animate sources of power and traction have all adopted these supralocal approaches, and these have recently been supplemented by new studies of regional settlement patterns, of urban hierarchy and of commercial networks.[5]

One of the most powerful stimuli to reappraising the relations between town and country, and to reconceptualising the economy as a whole, has been the revision of the estimated populations of individual towns and of the total urban system. Substantial upward revisions of pre-Black Death population levels have been suggested for a number of important provincial towns, including Norwich and Winchester, as well as for the capital, London, which may have had 80,000 inhabitants in 1300.[6] At the same time, a recent estimate suggests that at any one time between *c*.1270 and *c*.1540 around 600 small towns were in existence; this number represents places whose estimated populations ranged from 2,000 down to as few as 300, but which performed genuinely urban functions.[7] If such places are counted as towns, then the urban share of England's total population may have fluctuated around 20 per cent throughout the later medieval period. Although a considerable degree of uncertainty remains, the exercise suggests a rate of urbanisation mark-

[5] B. M. S. Campbell, 'People and land in the middle ages, 1066–1500', in R. A. Dodgshon and R. A. Butlin (eds.), *An historical geography of England and Wales*, 2nd edn (London, 1990), pp. 69–122; J. Langdon, *Horses, oxen and technological innovation: the use of draught animals in English farming from 1066–1500* (Cambridge, 1986); J. Langdon, 'Lordship and peasant consumerism in the milling industry of early fourteenth century England', *Past and Present* 145 (1994), 3–46; Campbell et al., *Medieval capital, passim,* and references therein; M. Kowaleski, *Local markets and regional trade in medieval Exeter* (Cambridge, 1995); C. Lewis, P. Mitchell-Fox and C. Dyer, *Village, hamlet and field: changing medieval settlements in central England* (Manchester, 1997); P. Clark and J. Hosking, *Population estimates of English towns 1550–1851* (Centre for Urban History, University of Leicester, Working Paper no. 3, revised edn, 1996). Commercial networks in the London region and England as a whole are the subject of continuing research at the Centre for Metropolitan History, Institute of Historical Research, in the projects 'Market networks in the London region: the trade in agrarian produce *c*.1400', funded by the Leverhulme Trust from 1994 to 1997, and its successor, 'Metropolitan market networks *c*.1300–1600', funded by the Economic and Social Research Council (award no. R000237253).

[6] Campbell et al., *Medieval capital*, pp. 9–10. P. Nightingale advocates a more conservative figure of 60,000 in 'The growth of London in the medieval English economy', in R. H. Britnell and J. Hatcher (eds.), *Progress and problems in medieval England: essays in honour of Edward Miller* (Cambridge, 1996), pp. 96–7. For the location of places mentioned in the text, see Figure 5.1. The divisions shown for England are historic (pre-1974) county boundaries. These boundaries are approximate only, and should not be taken as definitive. They constitute a modified version of a map first produced by Professor Marjorie K. McIntosh of the University of Colorado. I am grateful to Professor McIntosh for permission to use and modify her map.

[7] See C. Dyer, 'Small towns 1270–1540', in D. Palliser (ed.), *The Cambridge urban history of Britain*, vol. I: *c*.600–*c*.1540 (Cambridge, 2001).

edly higher than virtually all previous estimates based upon minimum population criteria for urban status.[8] It may be usefully compared with Wrigley's estimate of 24 per cent for the non-agricultural element of England's population in 1520; this comprises 5.5 per cent in towns of 5,000 and more people, and 18.5 per cent as the 'rural non-agricultural' element, which plainly would include the residents of the many small and middling towns.[9]

Commercialisation and markets

The possibility that up to one-quarter of the population may have supported themselves by non-agricultural means throughout the later medieval period has important implications for our view of both urban and rural economies, and for the ways in which they interacted. The domestic trade in agrarian produce, in the absence of substantial net inflows of foodstuffs from overseas, must have been quite well developed from an early date, and a significant degree of regional differentiation and specialised production for extra-local markets is implied. Conversely, the concentration of population in towns implies the existence of significant demand for the products of urban crafts and industries from far more than an elite market of upper-class consumers, whose needs could probably have been met by a significantly less urbanised economy, and suggests that the manufacture of lower-valued consumer goods had begun to form a significant element of production before 1300.

Levels of market involvement in later medieval England were high, and much of the growth in trade and in the institutions which channelled and underpinned it had taken place before the end of the thirteenth century. The urban share of England's population almost certainly rose significantly between the Domesday survey of 1086 and the year 1300, while the volume of coin in circulation appears to have risen several times faster than the population over the same period.[10] New towns, markets and fairs were established throughout England; several thousand places, urban and rural, had obtained the right to hold

[8] C. Dyer, 'How urbanised was medieval England?', in J.-M. Duvosquel and E. Thoen (eds.), *Peasants and townsmen in medieval Europe. Studia in honorem Adriaan Verhulst* (Ghent, 1995), pp. 169–83. J. de Vries, *European urbanisation 1500–1800* (London, 1985), p. 39, put England's urban share at 3.1 per cent in 1500 using minimum urban populations of 10,000.

[9] E. A. Wrigley, 'Urban growth and agricultural change: England and the Continent in the early modern period', *Journal of Interdisciplinary History* 15 (1985), 683–728.

[10] R. H. Britnell, 'Commercialisation and economic development in England, 1000–1300', in Britnell and B. M. S. Campbell (eds.), *A commercialising economy: England 1086–c.1300* (Manchester, 1995), pp. 7–26.

a market by 1349 as lords sought to cash in on the growth in commercial activity.[11]

The seigniorial class also participated in the growth of trade through the marketing of agrarian produce from their directly managed demesnes. While some manors and estates were run principally to provide produce for direct consumption in lordly households, others sold a high proportion of their output. In ten counties around London, an average 38 per cent by value of all available grain[12] was sold from a sample of demesnes in the period 1288–1315, and an almost identical proportion from a similar sample covering the period 1375–1400.[13] Individual demesnes and estates might market much higher proportions, while major estates often chose to use the market to purchase as well as to sell produce.[14] There is reason to believe that commercialisation of the pastoral sector of the agrarian economy, although more difficult to measure, may have been even more developed than in the case of grain.[15]

Furthermore, this involvement in commerce was not restricted to the demesne sector. The peasantry, whose needs for cash grew with the burden of taxation under Edward I and his successors, were, together with small-scale traders and artisans, the principal patrons of England's dense network of small town and village markets, using them to sell their surplus crops and animals and to purchase a limited range of processed foods and manufactures.[16] Although difficult to quantify, by the fourteenth century peasant agriculture may have been at least as market-oriented as was the demesne sector, and for certain types of product it was the principal source of commercial supply.[17]

The market network which handled this extensive trade had some of

---

[11] R. H. Britnell, 'The proliferation of markets in England, 1200–1349', *Economic History Review*, 2nd ser., 34 (1981), 209–21.

[12] That is, after the deduction of tithe and seed-corn. Most tithe grain would subsequently have been sold, so these figures are almost certainly underestimates.

[13] Campbell et al., *Medieval capital*, p. 38; J. A. Galloway, D. Keene, M. Murphy and B. M. S. Campbell, 'The impact of London's changing demand for grain upon its rural hinterland *c*.1300–1400', unpublished MS.

[14] R. H. Britnell, *The commercialisation of English society, 1000–1500* (Cambridge, 1993), p. 121; Campbell et al., *Medieval capital*, pp. 155, 204–5.

[15] B. M. S. Campbell, 'Measuring the commercialisation of seigneurial agriculture *c*.1300', in Britnell and Campbell, *Commercialising economy*, pp. 163–74.

[16] J. R. Maddicott, 'The English peasantry and the demands of the crown 1294–1341', in T. H. Aston (ed.), *Landlords, peasants and politics in medieval England* (Cambridge, 1987), pp. 285–360; C. Dyer, 'The consumer and the market in the later middle ages', *Economic History Review*, 2nd ser., 42 (1989), 305–26.

[17] B. M. S. Campbell, 'Ecology versus economics in late thirteenth- and early fourteenth-century English agriculture', in D. Sweeney (ed.), *Agriculture in the middle ages: technology, practice and representation* (Philadelphia, 1995), pp. 90–1.

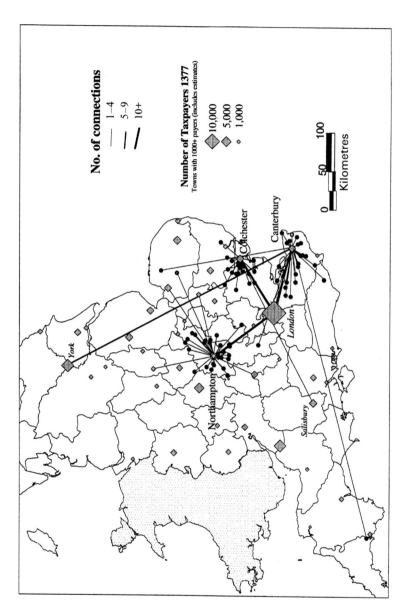

No. of connections

— 1–4
— 5–9
— 10+

Number of Taxpayers 1377
Towns with 1000+ payers (includes estimates)

◆ 10,000
◆ 5,000
◇ 1,000

York

Colchester

Canterbury

Northampton

London

Salisbury

0   50   100

Kilometres

Figure 5.2   Debt connections of Canterbury, Colchester and Northampton, c.1400. Source: see note 20.

the characteristics of a 'central place' system.[18] The larger centres were quite evenly distributed across lowland England and acted as regional foci for the trade of smaller towns, villages and hamlets. Size was to a significant degree associated with functional differentiation, so towns of similar size or rank had relatively little cause to interact. 'One smaller town', comments Shaw, 'had little to offer another',[19] and the point is also applicable to larger centres. Thus, the contacts revealed by a sample of debt litigation involving inhabitants of three important boroughs of south-eastern and midland England c.1400 show a predominance of interaction with villages and smaller towns in the hinterland of each, some links with larger centres (including in each case a strong connection with London), but hardly any contact with other towns of rank equivalent to their own (Figure 5.2).[20]

Towns of widely varying population tended to have quite similarly sized hinterlands of intensive interaction, within which three-quarters or more of all their recorded contacts fell, corresponding to the local trade areas predicted by central place models.[21] In the West Midlands and in the South-East these local trade areas characteristically had radii of 10–20 km, and were dominated by the trade in raw and processed foodstuffs and in low-value manufactures.[22] In addition, larger towns had more extensive economic regions which looked to them for the provision of goods and services of higher value. The concentrated contacts mapped for Canterbury, Colchester and Northampton in part reflect these higher-order linkages, extending up to 40–50 km from the town.[23]

Patterns of trade and interaction thus to some degree reflect central place structures, although these were overlain by cross-currents of longer-distance trade and by the overarching influence of London,

[18] For a recent reworking of central place theory, see J. U. Marshall, *The structure of urban systems* (Toronto, 1989).

[19] D. G. Shaw, *The creation of a community: the city of Wells in the middle ages* (Oxford, 1993), p. 94.

[20] Based upon analysis of a database compiled during the 'Market networks in the London region c.1400' project, drawn from a sample of debt litigation in the central Court of Common Pleas from the Michaelmas law terms of 1384, 1403 and 1424. The original records are in the Public Record Office, London (Class CP40).

[21] Marshall, *Structure*, pp. 139–77.

[22] C. Dyer, 'Market towns and the countryside in late medieval England', *Canadian Journal of History* 31 (1996), 2–20; 'Market networks c.1400' project database.

[23] Common Pleas debt cases have a minimum value of £2, and consequently exclude the petty and peasant debts which dominate local court records. Although probably the largest of the three towns, Colchester's hinterland appears more restricted than those of Northampton and Canterbury, perhaps reflecting the fact that its primary role was that of manufacturing town rather than regionally important central place. For an earlier period, see J. Masschaele, *Peasants, merchants and markets: inland trade in medieval England, 1150–1350* (Basingstoke–London, 1997), pp. 81–2.

which had links with settlements of all sizes, often unmediated by second- or third-rank centres. An important role in inter-regional trade was played by the fairs which, like markets, were numerous and differentiated by wealth and importance. Although the 'great fairs', specialising particularly in cloth and attended by wealthy foreign merchants, were in decline before 1300, many regional fairs retained or increased their importance in the later middle ages, attracting buyers and sellers from considerably further afield than most markets. Fairs such as Stourbridge near Cambridge formed particularly active foci of trade in the fifteenth century, both promoting and reflecting an increased degree of spatial integration within the economy. A ring of fairs around London, among them Kingston (Surrey), Uxbridge (Middlesex) and Stortford (Essex), saw active trade in livestock and other produce in the later fourteenth century and played an important role in the capital's food supply system.[24]

London and its region

The demands of significant urban and other non-agricultural populations, acting within an economy where the means and rules of market-based exchange were well established, were sufficient to begin to produce identifiable patterns of local and regional specialisation by c.1300. This was most pronounced in the vicinity of London, the only one of England's towns and cities which stood comparison with those of Italy or north-western continental Europe in terms of size and wealth. There are distinct signs that in the hinterland of medieval London the factor of distance was influencing the uses to which land was put, in ways broadly consonant with the well-known model of J. H. von Thünen.[25]

A tendency towards zoning of land-uses is manifest in distinct biases towards particular uses at particular locations, explicable in terms of distance from the London market. Thus, the commercial production of firewood, bulky but essential to the pre-industrial city, displayed a strong concentration in areas within some 20 km of London or of navigable stretches of the river Thames.[26] Within the grain sector the

[24] E. Miller and J. Hatcher, *Medieval England: towns, commerce and crafts 1086–1348* (London, 1995), pp. 166–7; S. R. Epstein, 'Regional fairs, institutional innovation and economic growth in late medieval Europe', *Economic History Review*, 2nd ser., 47 (1994), 459–82. Data on the use of fairs in the London region has been compiled from various sources during the 'Market networks' projects.
[25] P. Hall (ed.), *Von Thünen's isolated state: an English edition of 'Der Isolierte Staat' by Johann Heinrich von Thünen* (London, 1966).
[26] J. A. Galloway, D. Keene and M. Murphy, 'Fuelling the city: production and

influence of distance from the London market can be seen in the tendency for manorial demesnes to concentrate upon the bulky, lower-valued crops such as oats in areas close to the city, while higher-valued wheat predominated at a greater distance. Environmental factors played their part, but only the factors of urban demand and transport cost can explain the strength of these specialisms.[27]

These specialised land-use regimes were dynamic, and reconfiguration occurred after the Black Death as relative prices shifted in response to changes in the scale and structure of demand. The clearest evidence from the period under consideration concerns changes observable in the later fourteenth century, after famine and repeated outbreaks of plague had seen the population of England halve from the levels of *c.*1300. Real living standards rose, despite attempts to curtail labour mobility and wage increases, and a substantial section of the surviving population was in a position to consume larger quantities and more diverse types of food, drink and manufactured goods.[28]

Per caput consumption of ale undoubtedly increased after 1350 in both town and country, stimulating an expansion in barley production across England, which was particularly marked in counties to the north and north-west of London that supplied the metropolitan market.[29] This specialised system of production and distribution, once established, appears to have persisted, undoubtedly expanding in scale and complexity during the sixteenth and seventeenth centuries, but in essence continuing upon its medieval foundations. Other specialisms were more volatile; the emphasis upon rye cultivation in the Thames valley declined markedly after the Black Death, as the market for non-wheaten bread contracted in both London and the countryside, but it appears likely that cultivation of this cheaper grain staged a recovery in many parts of England with the renewed population growth and falling

---

distribution of firewood and fuel in London's region, 1290–1400', *Economic History Review*, 2nd ser., 49 (1996), 447–72.

[27] Campbell et al., *Medieval capital*, pp. 116–23.

[28] C. Dyer, *Standards of living in the later middle ages: social change in England 1200–1520* (Cambridge, 1989), pp. 158–78, 207.

[29] J. A. Galloway, 'Driven by drink? Ale consumption and the agrarian economy of the London region *c.*1300–1400', in M. Carlin and J. Rosenthal (eds.), *Food and eating in medieval society* (London, 1998). The scale of urban ale consumption meant that a late medieval town might consume more barley than wheat; in 1520 the mayor of Coventry found that each week the city's brewers consumed 146 quarters of malt, compared to the 132 quarters of various grains used by the bakers. These figures imply a daily consumption of over 2 pints of ale averaged across the 6,601 adults and children counted by the mayor. Although compiled during a subsistence crisis, these figures seem intended to represent 'normal' weekly grain usage; see M. D. Harris (ed.), *The Coventry Leet Book* (London, 1907–9), pp. 674–5.

living-standards of the sixteenth century, before fading away again thereafter.[30]

The significant post-Black Death restructuring of the grain sector was matched by a decisive shift in the balance between arable and pastoral. The overall size of the market for grain contracted, while per caput and possibly aggregate demand for meat grew with the rise in living standards.[31] At the same time, the decline in exports of raw English wool after 1350 was more than offset by the growing requirements of the domestic woollen textile industry, which expanded markedly in the second half of the fourteenth century. A parallel decline in exports of hides from England almost certainly reflects increased domestic manufacture and consumption of leather goods after the Black Death, rather than any contraction of total output.[32]

Within the demesne sector, the area sown with crops declined by 20–25 per cent during the fourteenth century, while animal numbers increased by a similar factor, and stocking densities (measured against the sown acreage) rose by over 60 per cent. The most striking growth was in sheep–corn husbandry, an extensive type of mixed farming which underwent particular expansion in midland and southern England.[33] These areas were ecologically well suited to this type of farming and geographically well placed to respond to the changing demands of London and the towns of the Midlands and the South. In Warwickshire a significant expansion of grassland is evident between the mid-fourteenth and the later fifteenth centuries, both in areas which had been almost exclusively arable at the earlier date and in the more wooded Arden region. At the same time, the cattle-marketing role of towns like Birmingham and Coventry was expanding to serve both local

---

[30] J. A. Galloway, 'London's grain supply: changes in production, distribution, and consumption during the 14th century', *Franco-British Studies* 20 (1995), 23–34. In Norfolk, rye is calculated to have occupied 13.1 per cent of sown acreage in the period 1250–1349, 6.9 per cent in 1350–1449 and 16.4 per cent in 1584–1640. See B. M. S. Campbell and M. Overton, 'A new perspective on medieval and early modern agriculture: six centuries of Norfolk farming, c.1250–c.1850', *Past and Present* 141 (1993), 54. A similar trend is indicated elsewhere, for example in Hertfordshire, when medieval rye acreages (mapped in Campbell et al., *Medieval capital*, p. 123) are compared with those calculated for the early modern period by P. Glennie, 'Continuity and change in Hertfordshire agriculture 1550–1700: I – patterns of agricultural production', *Agricultural History Review* 36 (1988), 61.

[31] Dyer, *Standards of living*, pp. 158–9.

[32] J. Bolton, *The medieval English economy 1150–1500* (London, 1985), pp. 267ff.; M. Kowaleski, 'Town and country in late medieval England: the hide and leather trade', in D. Keene and P. Corfield (eds.), *Work in towns 850–1850* (Leicester, 1990), pp. 63–4.

[33] B. M. S. Campbell, K. C. Bartley and J. Power, 'The demesne-farming systems of post-Black Death England: a classification', *Agricultural History Review* 44 (1996), 134–5, 177.

needs and those of the drovers who brought Welsh cattle into the region to fatten before selling them on.[34]

Drove routes linked these midland towns with north Wales and Cheshire and with the metropolitan market. Animals for consumption in royal and aristocratic households had been brought to London from Cheshire in the thirteenth century, and from north Wales in the mid-fourteenth.[35] Commercial droving links between Warwickshire, North-amptonshire and London had been established by *c*.1400, and perhaps much earlier, and the trade in livestock became one of the most tenacious links between the capital and more distant parts of England and Wales.[36] By the mid-sixteenth century the system was undergoing considerable expansion, as London embarked upon a period of precipi-tate growth which would take it back to the population levels of 1300, and soon surging beyond them to unprecedented heights.[37] The con-tinuing influence of existing roads and routes meant, however, that metropolitan influence remained markedly linear in its manifestation. Towns such as Retford in Nottinghamshire derived much of their wealth from their locations on or near these major overland routes.[38]

Urban staples and privileges

Unlike many of its continental counterparts, London had to provide for itself without significant political control over its rural hinterland.[39] It is true that hunting rights in Middlesex, Surrey and the Chilterns were enjoyed by twelfth-century Londoners, and that for many centuries the city possessed jurisdiction over the river Thames between Staines in Middlesex and the Yantlet Creek by the Isle of Grain in Kent.[40] London's regulatory power over local and regional trade was quite limited, however. Twelfth-century sources point to restrictions on

---

[34] C. Dyer, *Warwickshire farming 1349–c.1520: preparations for agricultural revolution*, Dugdale Society Occasional Papers no. 27 (1981), pp. 10, 20; R. H. Holt, *The early history of the town of Birmingham, 1166–1600*, Dugdale Society Occasional Papers no. 30 (1985).

[35] H. J. Hewitt, *A history of Cheshire*, vol. V: *Cheshire under the three Edwards* (Chester, 1967), pp. 30–4.

[36] 'Market networks *c*.1400' project databases; N. W. Alcock (ed.), *Warwickshire grazier and London skinner, 1532–1555* (Oxford, 1981), pp. 40–78.

[37] V. Harding, 'The population of London, 1550–1700: a review of the published evidence', *London Journal* 15 (1990), 111–28.

[38] D. Marcombe, *English small town life: Retford 1520–1642* (Nottingham, 1993), p. 102.

[39] D. Nicholas, *The later medieval city* (London, 1997), pp. 87–101.

[40] F. Stenton, 'Norman London: an essay', in William Fitz Stephen, *Norman London, with an essay by Sir Frank Stenton, introduction by F. Donald Logan* (New York, 1990), p. 3; R. R. Sharpe (ed.), *Calendar of Letter-Books of the City of London: Letter-Book A* (London, 1899), p. 186.

trading within a three-mile (5 km) radius of the city,[41] while after 1327 royal charters forbade the establishment of new markets within seven miles (11 km) of London.[42] Rather than exerting any direct control over an extensive rural hinterland, later medieval London, like other English towns, was obliged in its attempts to regulate the trade in agrarian and other hinterland produce to restrict itself to the area within or immediately adjacent to its boundaries.[43] These attempts included the institution of the urban franchise, which in chartered boroughs conferred privileged trading and other rights on the free burgess stratum of the town's population, the related system of tolls or tariffs levied upon outsiders and resident 'foreigners' and from which citizens were normally exempt, the regulation of measures and the price of victuals and other goods, and attempts to prevent the interception of produce on its way to market by 'forestallers'.[44]

The privileges claimed by the larger urban communities could nevertheless appear oppressive to inhabitants of the countryside and of smaller towns, and feature in a number of contexts during the Peasants' Revolt of 1381. Freedom to buy and sell in all urban and rural markets and other places within the kingdom was reported to be one of the rebels' demands at Mile End, and a specific grievance against trade monopolies which had recently been granted to Yarmouth inspired men from smaller Suffolk towns to join in an attack upon the property of that borough's dominant merchants.[45] Townsmen and inhabitants of rural liberties from a broad swathe of southern and midland England periodically challenged payment of tolls in London, but the capital's privileged status within the system was hard to dislodge, and was sometimes given formal recognition in the charters of other boroughs, which granted freedoms 'saving the liberties of London'.[46] This primacy within the

---

[41] F. Liebermann (ed.), *Die Gesetze der Angelsachsen* (Halle, 1903), vol. I, p. 673; M. Bateson (ed.), 'A London municipal collection of the reign of John', *English Historical Review* 17 (1902), 497.

[42] D. Keene, 'Medieval London and its region', *London Journal* 14 (1989), 103.

[43] For an unsuccessful attempt by townsmen to claim a monopoly on trade within their immediate hinterland see D. Keene, *Survey of medieval Winchester* (Oxford, 1985), p. 68.

[44] For the regulation of trade see Britnell, *Commercialisation*, esp. pp. 90–7.

[45] R. H. Hilton, *Bond men made free* (London, 1973), pp. 229–30; E. B. Fryde, *Peasants and landlords in later medieval England, c.1380–1525* (Gloucester, 1996), p. 48.

[46] A. Ballard, *British borough charters, 1042–1216* (Cambridge, 1913), pp. 182, 188–90. London records document numerous attempts by provincial towns to secure freedom from toll in London, but the capital's rulers often ignored apparently valid claims for exemption, even when backed by royal writ; see e.g. R. R. Sharpe (ed.), *Calendar of Letter Books of the City of London: Letter Book H* (London, 1907), pp. 53–4. Much remains to be discovered about the practical operation of the urban tolls system and its economic impact; for tolls and toll disputes in the pre-1350 period, see Masschaele, *Peasants*.

tolls system gave London certain advantages in procuring its necessary supplies, as did its relations with the crown, which facilitated the acquisition of licences to ship grain and other supplies from outlying ports in years of dearth. By the sixteenth century provisioning the rapidly growing capital began to attract more regular government attention, and its needs were sometimes given priority over those of producers and exporters.[47]

The degree to which government policy in this area was shaped by metropolitan needs is open to question, however, as they formed just one strand in a wider approach to food supply and the amelioration of dearth.[48] State intervention in grain distribution and marketing increased after the harvest failure of 1527, through the surveying of grain stocks, attempts to compel the marketing of surpluses and regulation of the activities of middlemen, and was to be codified towards the end of the century in the 1587 Book of Orders for the Relief of Dearth.[49] Above all, however, London depended upon the active endeavours of its own citizens and of middlemen based in the smaller towns of its hinterland to ensure a smooth, regular supply of foodstuffs, fuel and other necessary supplies. These traders benefited from those features of England's centralised political structure which tended to reduce transaction costs[50] – the existence of a dense network of recognised markets and fairs, a stable currency, the standardisation of weights and measures, the existence of effective procedures for the enforcement of contracts and the settlement of disputes – and which in turn reduced the need for urban political control of the countryside.

Beyond London: agrarian specialisation

Most English towns had not reached the critical mass, in terms of population level and aggregation of craft-industrial production, to enable them on their own to mould the agricultural productive system in the way that London was doing from the late thirteenth century

[47] The classic study is N. S. B. Gras, *The evolution of the English corn market* (Cambridge, MA, 1915), esp. pp. 224–8.

[48] The arguments put forward by Gras regarding the growth of extra-local markets and the direction of government policy are substantially modified by V. Ponko, 'N. S. B. Gras and Elizabethan corn policy: a re-examination of the problem', *Economic History Review*, 2nd ser., 18 (1965), 24–42 and E. Kneissel, 'The evolution of the English corn market', *Journal of Economic History* 14 (1954), 46–52. For the earlier period see also Campbell et al., *Medieval capital*.

[49] R. B. Outhwaite, *Dearth, public policy and social disturbance in England, 1550–1800* (Basingstoke–London, 1991), pp. 39–40.

[50] For a consideration of transaction costs within medieval urban trade networks see Kowaleski, *Exeter*, pp. 179–221.

onwards. Later fourteenth-century Exeter, which remained relatively small despite its key role in the commercial networks of south-west England, is a case in point.[51] The somewhat larger town of Colchester also seems to have been unable significantly to modify the economic environment within which the farmers of its hinterland operated, or to exempt them from general recessionary trends in agriculture c.1400.[52] In Norfolk, Norwich was perhaps large enough to make a noticeable impact, although its demands formed just one among a complex of factors which influenced the development of an unusually intensive and highly productive agrarian economy.[53]

Perhaps most towns of medium size or above promoted the development of intensively managed gardens, orchards and meadows in their immediate vicinity.[54] The northern capital, York, was said to draw large quantities of barley from its hinterland and adjoining counties c.1540, and to have 'used up' the woods within a 30 km radius to fuel its malt kilns.[55] The latter claim was doubtless exaggerated, but if the perceived impact of the city's requirements was so dramatic at a time when its population was only beginning to recover from its late medieval nadir, it may be surmised that a century and a half earlier when, with 15,000 or so inhabitants, it ranked second to London in England's urban hierarchy, York must have had a noticeable impact upon its agrarian hinterland. A similar case might be made for Bristol, third in rank and with at least 12,000–13,000 inhabitants in the later fourteenth century.

The combined pull of urban markets might constitute a potent spur to commercialisation and specialisation in rural areas. The strength of that pull varied greatly, however, reflecting the uneven distribution of the larger towns and the fact that in many respects England's urban system had a single focus because of the marked primacy of the capital, which in 1377, and probably also in 1300, was between three and four times larger than its nearest rival. The 'potential' or intensity of inter-action between urban centres, which by extension may be taken to indicate combined urban influence over the countryside, was greater in the immediate vicinity of London than anywhere else in England in the later fourteenth century, but a zone of relatively high potential extended

[51] Ibid., p. 4.
[52] R. H. Britnell, *Growth and decline in Colchester 1300–1525* (Cambridge, 1986), p. 157.
[53] Norwich may have had over 20,000 people in the early fourteenth century, but had contracted considerably by 1377. See E. Rutledge, 'Immigration and population growth in early fourteenth-century Norwich: evidence from the tithing roll', *Urban History Yearbook 1988*, pp. 15–30; Campbell, 'People and land', p. 83.
[54] Keene, *Winchester*, pp. 149–52.
[55] D. M. Palliser, 'York under the Tudors: the trading life of the northern capital', in A. Everitt (ed.), *Perspectives in English urban history* (London, 1973), p. 48.

to the North and North-West, into the Midlands and towards the ports of the Wash. By contrast, most of northern and western England was much more weakly exposed to urban influence. No individual town or group of towns appears to have constituted a distinct, secondary focus within the urban system at this period.[56] The marked primacy of London has been linked to the creation of an integrated national market for wheat by the later seventeenth century,[57] and it may be that a significant degree of market integration had already been achieved by the close of the middle ages. As early as 1300 London influenced grain price levels across at least a part of southern and midland England.[58]

In certain strategically located and environmentally favoured areas the demands of London combined with those of the urban populations of the Low Countries to bolster, if they did not create, unusually intensive and productive agrarian regimes. This was true of eastern Kent, linked to the London market through the ports of Faversham and Sandwich, but also frequented by merchants from Picardy and Flanders.[59] Another such area of intensive agriculture was Norfolk, linked into the coastal and international trade in grain via the ports of Lynn and Yarmouth. Lynn in particular acted as a major grain entrepôt, gathering together produce from an extensive area of East Anglia and the East Midlands.[60] For much of the period between the late thirteenth and later sixteenth century this supply system seems to have acted as a 'safety-valve' for London, drawn upon in years of high prices rather than routinely, diverting supplies which might otherwise have been exported. The crown similarly tapped into this system, drawing supplies northwards to feed its garrisons and armies engaged against Scotland. A further area subject to dual or multiple influences was Sussex; a productive arable system in the coastal area sent intermittent supplies to continental markets, while parts of Wealden Sussex and Kent were linked to the fuel-hungry towns of the Low Countries, to which they regularly sent large quantities of billets and other types of wood fuel.[61]

[56] These observations derive from an attempt to measure the urban potential of English towns at the time of the 1377 poll tax. The calculation is based upon the 'mass' (taxed population) of each town and its distance from every other town in the national urban system. The method derives from that used by de Vries, *European urbanisation*, pp. 154ff. A full presentation of the results will be included in a book arising from the 'Market networks' projects, currently in preparation.

[57] J. Chartres, 'Market integration and agricultural output in seventeenth-, eighteenth-, and early nineteenth-century England', *Agricultural History Review* 43 (1995), 117–38.

[58] Campbell et al., *Medieval capital*, pp. 63–9; analysis of price material from *c.*1300 to 1600 forms part of current research on metropolitan market networks.

[59] Ibid., pp. 126–7, 179–80.

[60] Campbell, 'Ecology versus economics', p. 81 and nn. 35–7.

[61] Campbell et al., *Medieval capital*, p. 181; Galloway, Keene and Murphy, 'Fuelling the city', p. 467.

Migration

Mobility levels were high in both town and country from an early date, but in-migration was probably highest in the larger towns and ports such as Ipswich, where few of the later medieval inhabitants appear to have been natives.[62] Rural–urban migration almost certainly increased in the aftermath of the Black Death, allowing some towns to grow rapidly in the face of national population collapse, with a subsequent decline contributing to the fifteenth-century malaise affecting many of the larger centres.[63] Much mobility was local and fell within urban hinterlands only slightly more extensive than local trade areas. Even the large towns drew the bulk of their recruits from within c.35 km before 1350, with the known exceptions of London and to a lesser extent Winchester. Beyond these intensive migration hinterlands, however, longer-distance movement occurred.[64] The long-distance element was naturally most significant in the case of ports, around one-quarter of new recruits to the freedom at late medieval Romney coming from more than 80 km away.[65] Alien immigration also often followed coastal and overland trade routes. Scots settled in urban and rural locations in East Anglia and south-eastern England close to the eastern seaboard in the fifteenth and earlier sixteenth centuries, reflecting the principal direction of Anglo-Scottish trade at that period,[66] while the presence of numerous Welsh people in sixteenth-century Winchester probably reflects linkages within the cattle-droving and wool trades.[67] Although many of the newcomers to urban society came straight from the countryside, there was a disproportionate tendency for the larger towns to draw migrants from smaller urban centres.[68] There is some evidence to suggest that the movement of the poorest class of migrants was also in part channelled

[62] J. A. Raftis, 'Geographical mobility in Lay Subsidy Rolls', *Medieval Studies* 38 (1976), 385–403. Of fifteen Ipswich residents testifying in surviving Norwich Consistory Court records c.1500, none had been born there; although probably not wholly representative, this sample clearly indicates high mobility levels. See E. D. Stone (ed.), *Norwich Consistory Court depositions 1499–1512 and 1518–30* (Norwich, 1938).

[63] Britnell, *Growth and decline*, pp. 96, 204; A. Dyer, *Decline and growth in English towns 1400–1640* (Basingstoke, 1991), p. 17.

[64] P. McLure, 'Patterns of migration in the late middle ages: the evidence of English place-name surnames', *Economic History Review*, 2nd ser., 32 (1979), 167–82; Keene, *Winchester*, p. 375.

[65] A. F. Butcher, 'The origins of Romney freemen, 1433–1523', *Economic History Review*, 2nd ser., 27 (1974), 16–27.

[66] J. A. Galloway and I. Murray, 'Scottish migration to England, 1400–1560', *Scottish Geographical Magazine* 112 (1996), 29–38. Large numbers of Scots also settled in the English border counties.

[67] Keene, *Winchester*, p. 379.

[68] S. L. Thrupp and H. B. Johnson, 'The earliest Canterbury freemen's rolls, 1298–1363', in F. R. H. Du Boulay (ed.), *Documents illustrative of medieval Kentish*

upwards through the settlement hierarchy, vagrants in sixteenth-century London being more likely to have an urban background than their counterparts in smaller towns.[69]

Urban and rural industry

Intertwined as urban and rural economies and societies were at many levels, their interaction was not always harmonious. One area where conflict between the interests of town and country has often been posited is in the location and organisation of industry, and the supposed drift of industry to the countryside during the later middle ages when important rural textile industries came to prominence in several English regions, most notably in parts of East Anglia, in Somerset, in Wiltshire and in the West Riding of Yorkshire. Lesser centres of production included the Kentish Weald, Westmorland, and Shropshire, plus scattered areas of the Midlands and the South. The idea that this rural development could be explained simply as a successful attempt to escape from the restrictions of 'conservative' or 'guild-dominated' towns has long been regarded as simplistic, while the picture of an industry shifting from urban to rural locations primarily in response to technological innovation is also clearly inadequate.[70]

More recent analyses have sought to relate developing rural industry to social structure and inheritance customs, to the relative strength or weakness of lordship, and to the seasonality of agricultural labour demands, demonstrating a strong association with pastoral farming regimes albeit questioning the ability of fully-fledged proto-industrialisation theory to explain the English case.[71] The difficulty against which any generalised explanation immediately comes up is the sheer diversity

society (Ashford, 1964), p. 176; S. L. Thrupp, *The merchant class of medieval London* (Michigan, 1948), pp. 211–14.

[69] A. L. Beier, *Masterless men: the vagrancy problem in England 1560–1640* (London, 1984), pp. 39, 215.

[70] R. A. Pelham, 'England in the fourteenth century', in H. C. Darby (ed.), *An historical geography of England before AD 1800* (Cambridge, 1936), and E. Carus-Wilson, 'An Industrial Revolution of the thirteenth century', in Carus-Wilson, *Medieval merchant venturers*, 2nd edn (London, 1967), pp. 183–211, argued that cloth-making migrated from eastern to western England, and from lowland to upland locations in response to the development of mechanical fulling. The inadequacy of this picture is shown by the success of urban cloth industries at Colchester (and, less dramatically, Winchester), where fulling mills operated in suburban locations, and Salisbury, where non-mechanical fulling within the town continued, supplemented by the use of rural mills. See Britnell, *Growth and decline*, p. 76; A. R. Bridbury, *Medieval English clothmaking* (London, 1982), pp. 80–1, 114.

[71] J. Thirsk, 'Industries in the countryside', in F. J. Fisher (ed.), *Essays in the economic and social history of Tudor and Stuart England in honour of R. H. Tawney* (Cambridge, 1961), pp. 70–88; M. Zell, *Industry in the countryside: Wealden society in the sixteenth century*

of developments in different regions, and the apparent lack of a clear chronology. Rural cloth manufacture was present in the thirteenth century, and had already begun to prompt urban complaints about competition, although suburban development may have been the principal target. Urban merchants, however, may often have played a role in initiating production in the countryside and in smaller towns at this time.[72] The difficulties of explaining the rapid growth in rural cloth production in several regions during the second half of the fourteenth century as a form of proto-industrialisation are obvious; why should these rural industries have expanded, in some cases spectacularly, during a period of population decline, labour shortage and rising real living standards in the countryside, precisely the opposite conditions to those which, at least in its classic form, proto-industrialisation theory postulates?[73] In the absence of sustained pressure upon rural resources, 'superexploitation' of a part-agricultural, part-industrial workforce appears problematic.

After c.1400 regional divergences became more pronounced. In the industrial region of northern Essex and southern Suffolk, centred upon the valley of the river Stour, the cloth-making industry in the established urban centre of Colchester fared better than that in most of the surrounding industrial villages and small towns between the 1390s and the 1460s.[74] Colchester's output and its share of the total taxed cloth production of Essex increased. Moreover, a tendency to concentrate marketing in fewer hands is apparent in the borough, while in the smaller towns and villages of north-eastern and north-central Essex things may have been moving in the opposite direction.[75] By contrast, in the West Riding a marked advance in the rural industry occurred over the same period, most notably in the valleys of the Aire and the Calder,

(Cambridge, 1994); D. C. Coleman, 'Proto-industrialisation: a concept too many', *Economic History Review*, 2nd ser., 36 (1983), 435–48.

[72] Oxford men were said in 1275 to have supplied looms to weavers at Banbury, Cowley and Islip; see Bolton, *English economy*, p. 158.

[73] Zell, *Industry*, p. 241.

[74] J. A. Galloway, 'Colchester and its region 1310–1560: wealth, industry and rural–urban mobility in a medieval society', unpublished Ph.D. thesis, University of Edinburgh, 1987, pp. 213–17.

[75] Ibid. Older narratives assume that the rural industry in Essex and Suffolk grew continuously between the fourteenth and sixteenth centuries, and was marked from an early stage by 'capitalist' organisation; see e.g. E. Power, *The Paycockes of Coggeshall* (London, 1920). However, the 'slippage' in the rural industry of Essex during the first two-thirds of the fifteenth century indicated by the aulnage accounts may, if real, reflect the absence of genuine proto-industrial characteristics, the concentrated urban labour force of Colchester continuing to have significant advantages over a rural workforce which had no pressing need to expand or even maintain its involvement in industrial production.

while centres of urban manufacture, principally York and Beverley, lost ground.[76] Similarly, it was in the countryside that the greatest expansion of cloth-making occurred in the west of England during the fifteenth century, although its organisation seems to have been quite different. In the West Riding the successful rural industry of the later fifteenth century remained largely in the hands of petty producers, and the penetration of capital would remain relatively slight in later centuries compared to such areas as Wiltshire, where merchant-clothiers were playing a major role well before 1500.[77]

It is clear that there was no simple tendency for rural cloth manufacture to 'undermine' that of the towns, at any rate not before the resumption of sustained demographic growth had begun to reverse the labour scarcity of the later middle ages. In 1561 York could explain its industrial decline in terms of the success of Halifax, Leeds and Wakefield, which, in addition to abundant water power, had the advantage of 'poor folk' to work in the textile crafts who could obtain food and fuel 'good and cheap which is in this citie very deare and wantyng'.[78] A hundred years earlier 'poor folk' would have been considerably thinner on the ground. Moreover, the West Riding industry made products quite different from those of York and Beverley, cheap, coarse woollens principally for domestic consumption, rather than finer dyed cloths for export, hence the decline of old-established urban cloth-making centres must be explained by changes in patterns of demand and market organisation rather than a migration of industry.[79] The two industries were relatively unconnected in the sphere of production, and the economic difficulties of York, Beverley and the port of Hull were exacerbated by the apparent failure of their merchants to develop effective and durable marketing linkages with the West Riding.

That failure has been ascribed to a lack of cash or credit for investment, placing merchants from those boroughs at a disadvantage *vis-à-vis* the Londoners whose superior access to credit and to continental markets enabled them increasingly to penetrate the Yorkshire industry.[80] The case of the Kent broadcloth industry of the sixteenth

[76] H. Heaton, *The Yorkshire woollen and worsted industries*, 2nd edn (Oxford, 1965), pp. 60, 68–76; J. Kermode, 'Merchants, overseas trade and urban decline: York, Beverley and Hull c.1380–1500', *Northern History* 23 (1987), 51–73.
[77] P. Hudson, 'Proto-industrialization in England', in S. C. Ogilvie and M. Cerman (eds.), *European proto-industrialization* (Cambridge, 1996), pp. 49–66; E. Carus-Wilson, 'The woollen industry before 1550', in *Victoria history of the county of Wiltshire* (London, 1959), vol. IV, pp. 134–6; G. D. Ramsay, *The Wiltshire woollen industry in the sixteenth and seventeenth centuries*, 2nd edn (London, 1965), pp. 31ff.
[78] Cited in Heaton, *Yorkshire woollen industries*, pp. 54–5.
[79] Kermode, 'Merchants', p. 63.
[80] Ibid., pp. 59–62.

century shows that where clothiers could successfully raise money for investment locally an industry could flourish without London capital, although ready access to the metropolitan market and the London-centred export trade was crucial.[81] In areas where the products of urban and rural manufacture were less dissimilar than was the case in York-shire, such as the Essex–Suffolk textile zone, the prospects for integra-tion in both production and marketing may have been better. Colchester merchants, and the Germans who dominated cloth exports through that town in the mid-fifteenth century, handled the products of both rural and urban industry.[82] Nevertheless, in the fourteenth and for most of the fifteenth centuries there is only limited evidence of urban–rural integration in the production of cloth rather than in its marketing. Colchester clothiers used country labour to spin thread on occasion, and supplemented the capacity of the town's own fulling mills with those of villages in the hinterland, but all the stages of the manufacturing process are documented within the borough, and there is evidence of considerable flexibility in industrial organisation there. Similarly, some country cloth was brought to the borough for finishing prior to sale,[83] but of a regular and systematic interweaving of urban and rural produc-tion, co-ordinated by large-scale putting-out merchants, there is little sign.

Although both systems probably coexisted throughout the medieval and early modern periods, it seems probable that by 1500 the balance within the Essex/Suffolk textile industry was shifting away from a *Kaufsystem* characterised by independent or semi-independent petty producers towards a *Verlagssystem* dominated by small-town clothiers.[84] This coincided with the late medieval prosperity of certain small towns within the region, and with a rapid growth in English cloth exports after 1470, a trend which continued with relatively little interruption through the first half of the sixteenth century.[85] This period, which in Wiltshire has been characterised as 'a boom period for clothiers', probably also

---

[81] Zell, *Industry*, pp. 237–8, 244.

[82] Britnell, *Growth and decline*, pp. 172–5.

[83] The opposite also occurred, with Colchester cloths being sold in small towns such as Kersey; see Galloway, 'Colchester', p. 151. There is little to suggest that Colchester's relatively modest cloth totals in the aulnage accounts included a significant element of rural manufacture – unlike Salisbury, where the much larger number of aulnaged cloths must, it has been persuasively argued, have included a significant quantity made elsewhere (Bridbury, *Clothmaking*, pp. 68–70).

[84] At Lavenham independent craftsmen were 'fast disappearing' by the early sixteenth century; see D. Dymond and A. Betterton, *Lavenham: 700 years of textile making* (Woodbridge, 1982), p. 13.

[85] Bridbury, *Clothmaking*, Appendix F, pp. 118–22, which supplements E. M. Carus-Wilson and O. Coleman, *England's export trade 1275–1547* (Oxford, 1963).

saw the Essex and Suffolk industries at their height, with buoyant demand allied to renewed population growth prompting the emergence of something more recognisable as a proto-industrial regional economy.[86] At the same time, however, the overall volume of interaction between Colchester and its immediate hinterland was in decline, and longer-distance linkages become increasingly prominent.[87] In several parts of England the early sixteenth century saw complaints from towns about rural competition in the cloth industry, and this often seems to have been a new concern.[88] The 'crisis' experienced by a number of English towns at the close of the middle ages had many causes, but the restructuring of rural–urban relations within the woollen cloth industry as more truly regional economic assemblages emerged was often a contributory factor.

In some other industries, particularly those linked to the victualling trades and those which were less regional in their locational structure, a closer symbiosis of town and country after the Black Death is visible. Towns acted both as centres of concentrated consumption of meat and other animal products and as conduits for the trade in livestock. This trade also linked town and country, and different levels of the urban system, in more complex patterns of interdependence. The by-products which arose from butchering the large number of animals consumed in towns provided raw materials for leather processing, wax- and candle-making, and a range of related crafts and industries. Some of this work was performed in the towns where the animals were slaughtered and eaten, but other materials were sent back into the hinterlands for processing. Tanning in particular was a noxious occupation, which townsmen commonly pushed into suburban or rural locations.[89] Londoners sent large numbers of hides by boat to be tanned at smaller towns within its region, including Maidstone in Kent and Barking in Essex, the tanned hides then probably returning to the capital's leather-workers.[90]

Another aspect of this interrelated spatial economy is illustrated by

---

[86] Carus-Wilson, 'Woollen industry', p. 141; Galloway, 'Colchester', pp. 217–26.

[87] Britnell, *Growth and decline*, pp. 246–50. Amongst these linkages were regular shipments of grain from Norfolk, and there may possibly be a connection between an increasing dependence on food supplies from a distance and a growing industrialisation of the borough's hinterland, with a consequent decline in local agricultural surpluses.

[88] C. Phythian-Adams, *Desolation of a city: Coventry and the urban crisis of the late middle ages* (Cambridge, 1979), p. 40; M. Stanford (ed.), *The Ordinances of Bristol, 1506–98*, Bristol Record Society Publications vol. XLI (1990), p. 4.

[89] Kowaleski, *Exeter*, pp. 301–5; Kowaleski, 'Town and country', pp. 59–62.

[90] R. Holt, 'The medieval market town', in P. Clark and L. Murfin (eds.), *The history of Maidstone* (Stroud, 1995), pp. 20–40.

the small north Essex town of Thaxted. Located near a major corridor of the metropolitan livestock trade, it had emerged by the thirteenth century as a major manufacturer of knives, and by 1381 the industry appears to have sustained at least one-third of the adult male population.[91] Many of the knives produced may have been consumed by an important local tanning industry, which in turn would have provided leather and bone required by the cutlers. At the same time London investment and London markets stimulated the production of high-quality knives for wealthy consumers.[92] Economic specialisation in many other small and medium-sized urban centres similarly reflected not merely local resource endowment, but, crucially, their position within regional and inter-regional networks of urban–rural and urban–urban trade.

Urban involvement in the extractive industries could be equally significant and multi-faceted. In the Cornish tin industry, the ranks of the locally based merchant tinners were dominated by the burgesses of Bodmin, Lostwithiel and other towns, which also acted as centres for the regulation and taxation of the industry. These merchant tinners formed the middle links in a chain of credit, receiving advances from the wealthy tin dealers, mostly Londoners and aliens, who dominated the export trade, and in turn lending money to the labouring tinners.[93] The burgesses of Newcastle upon Tyne's involvement with the development of the Tyne coal trade was complex and riven with conflicts. Whereas in the fourteenth century the prime aim of the Newcastle burgesses seems to have been to route the coal trade through their city in order to benefit from the tolls revenue which accrued, by the later sixteenth century they were both claiming and exercising an effective monopoly over the regional coal trade, and were playing an increasingly dominant role in production. Elsewhere, direct urban involvement in coal-mining was uncommon, however, although boroughs in or adjacent to other coal-fields sometimes sought to develop collieries for their own fuel supply, and Londoners were leasing mines in north Wales and Leicestershire as well as the North-East by the later sixteenth century. More characteristic of urban involvement was the advancing of credit to coal-masters and trade in colliery leases.[94] Most significant of all for the long-term growth of England's extractive industries may have been the size and relative

[91] K. C. Newton, *Thaxted in the fourteenth century* (Chelmsford, 1960), pp. 20–1.

[92] D. Keene, 'Small towns and the metropolis: the experience of England', in Duvosquel and Thoen, *Peasants and townsmen*, p. 235.

[93] J. Hatcher, *English tin production and trade before 1550* (Oxford, 1973), *passim*, esp. pp. 53, 57, 137.

[94] J. Hatcher, *The history of the British coal industry*, vol. I: *Before 1700: towards the age of coal* (Oxford, 1993), pp. 250, 510–13.

reliability of the metropolitan market. Even quite low-value products made at a considerable distance might find a niche in the London market from an early date.[95] Advance payments by London merchants formed a major source of capital for Derbyshire's lead-brenners in the sixteenth century,[96] and the London market seems to have exerted a significant influence on the spread of blast-furnace technology within England and Wales after 1496.[97]

Conclusion

The period under consideration saw many profound changes in the social and economic life of England and in the interrelations of town and country. In some respects it represents one complete cycle of change, beginning and ending in periods of relatively high population and correspondingly low real living standards with, in between, an era of demographic decline and stagnation associated with high real wages. Many towns had achieved their peak medieval size *c.*1300, others did so around a century later, but most struggled to attract sufficient recruits from the countryside during much of the fifteenth century. By 1570, most were once more coping with large-scale immigration and the social problems it brought in its train.[98]

In agriculture, grain yield levels in some of the most favoured and productive areas *c.*1300 were not surpassed until the eighteenth century, and were notably lower in the intervening centuries.[99] In other respects, however, the concept of a cycle may be misleading, as elements of continuity through the fifteenth century are not hard to find, and increasingly historians stress the artificiality of the traditional medieval/ early modern divide. The significance of the apparent contrast between the market networks of the high middle ages and those of the sixteenth and seventeenth centuries, once seen as pointing to a fundamental economic disjuncture, is being reappraised. The large number of markets founded in the twelfth and thirteenth centuries, it is argued, included many which were speculative and never met a real economic need, and often may never have functioned at all. Consequently, their

---

[95] Galloway, Keene and Murphy, 'Fuelling the city', p. 448; H. Cleere and D. Crossley, *The iron industry of the Weald* (Leicester, 1985), pp. 103–4.

[96] D. Kiernan, *The Derbyshire lead industry in the sixteenth century*, Derbyshire Record Society, xiv (1989), 53.

[97] Individual London craftsmen and merchants were also intimately involved in the early establishment of blast-furnaces and steel forges in the Weald; see Cleere and Crossley, *Iron industry*, pp. 110–20.

[98] Beier, *Masterless men*, pp. 14ff., 30–1, 39–48.

[99] Campbell and Overton, 'New perspective', p. 70.

'disappearance' in the later middle ages has less significance than the fundamental continuity of a core of markets which were central to the trade of both the thirteenth and the sixteenth centuries.[100] Again, agricultural productivity in areas characterised by less intensive regimes *c.*1300 may not have experienced the same subsequent decline as did Norfolk and perhaps Kent, but may rather have seen a broad (although doubtless not continuous) rise in yields, particularly in areas most exposed to metropolitan demand. This may be true of Hertfordshire, where, although strict comparison is difficult, sixteenth- and seventeenth-century grain yields appear to have been higher than those obtained before the Black Death.[101]

Clearly, neither cyclical change nor structural continuity adequately describes the period. In some respects, the Black Death emerges as a major watershed in rural–urban relations as in other aspects of social and economic life. The brewing industry became more strongly differentiated in scale and organisation, with an increasingly capitalist (and male-dominated) industry characterising the urban sector after 1349, while country brewers remained mostly small-scale.[102] In the countryside, the reduction in the pressure to grow bread grains may have permitted an increased level of agricultural and industrial specialisation, the redistribution of incomes adding a further stimulus to the processes of regional differentiation visible before the Black Death. Although it has been argued that by the mid-fifteenth century the effects of population stagnation had become almost entirely negative,[103] the very weakness of the economy may have released yet more forces for longer-term change, accelerating the conversion of arable to pasture and in some cases prompting the desertion of settlements.[104] Although difficult to prove, it may also have diverted some investment away from land towards the textile industry.

Perhaps the most profound process of change at work throughout the period of recession, laying the foundations for future transformations, was the continued growth of London's economic centrality, as networks of credit and trade came more and more to operate out of and through

[100] J. Masschaele, 'The multiplicity of medieval markets reconsidered', *Journal of Historical Geography* 20 (1994), 255–71.
[101] P. Glennie, 'Continuity and change in Hertfordshire agriculture: II – trends in crop yields and their determinants', *Agricultural History Review* 36 (1988), 147; Campbell et al., *Medieval capital*, pp. 126–7. The conclusion can only be tentative due to the different basis on which yields or yield trends must be calculated in the two periods.
[102] J. Bennett, *Ale, beer and brewsters in England* (Oxford, 1996), esp. pp. 46–51.
[103] J. Hatcher, 'The great slump of the mid-fifteenth century', in Britnell and Hatcher, *Progress and problems*, p. 241.
[104] C. Dyer, 'Deserted medieval villages in the West Midlands', *Economic History Review*, 2nd ser., 35 (1982), 19–34.

the capital. Recession acted to the capital's relative advantage, as its merchants had greater resources to withstand the slump and could draw manpower and trade away from provincial centres, especially the ports, exerting a stranglehold over the export and distributive trades.[105] London's share of England's overseas trade, which had stood at around 35 per cent in 1300 and in 1400, had risen to 68 per cent by 1500, and would peak at 85 per cent in 1540, reflecting the growing centrality of the London–Bruges and subsequently the London–Antwerp axis.[106] This trend was associated with a diminished control by many regional centres over their own hinterlands, as Londoners became increasingly involved in the direct supply of imports to consumers and middlemen, and in the marketing of rural manufactures.[107] Many provincial merchants were drawn to the capital, a process which had been evident during the fourteenth century at Winchester.[108] By the early sixteenth century merchants from major ports like Bristol were relocating their businesses in the capital, drawn by the superior access to markets and the greater capacity for integration within the cloth industry. Londoners, new or established, were capturing business in Bristol's industrial hinterland, extending better credit terms to producers than local merchants could offer.[109]

This concentration of trade further increased London's primacy within the English urban system. By the 1520s the capital's taxable wealth was greater than that of the largest of its rivals by a factor of ten, compared to a factor of five in 1334, despite the fact that its population probably still lay below the level achieved *c.*1300.[110] What had changed was the degree to which infrastructure and trade networks, and the associated flows of credit and goods, were focused upon London, reflected in the outstanding wealth of London's merchant community. Where money flowed, so too did population, and when the demographic upswing came it was London that gained more than any other urban community. Indeed, some regional centres and other large towns appear to have experienced a period of particular economic difficulty during the period *c.*1520–60, while London grew rapidly.[111] That expansion con-

---

[105] P. Nightingale, 'The growth of London in the medieval English economy', in Britnell and Hatcher, *Progress and problems*, pp. 104–6.

[106] Keene, 'Medieval London', p. 99; Bolton, *English economy*, pp. 315–19.

[107] Kermode, 'Merchants', pp. 70–1; D. M. Owen, *The making of King's Lynn: a documentary survey* (Oxford, 1984), pp. 44, 51.

[108] Keene, *Winchester*, p. 99.

[109] D. H. Sacks, *The widening gate: Bristol and the Atlantic economy 1450–1700* (Berkeley–Oxford, 1991), pp. 30–2.

[110] Keene, 'Medieval London', p. 99.

[111] Dyer, *Decline and growth*, pp. 35–6.

tinued apace thereafter despite renewed population growth and economic diversification elsewhere in the urban system.

Channels of trade, provisioning and population movement did not have to be invented anew in the sixteenth century. They were already in place, as were many of those aspects of spatial specialisation within the economy which both resulted from and further fuelled urban, and most particularly metropolitan, growth. Town and country were inextricably linked by market relations before 1300. The period 1300–1570 saw some significant restructuring of those relations in response to demographic and political stimuli. Central place factors perhaps weakened as an organising principle, while London's links with dynamic urban economies outside England assumed greater importance and the capital's merchants increasingly intervened in the hinterlands of provincial centres. The relative eclipse, albeit temporary, of many of the most important towns in the English regions, and the apparent weakening of their influence over their 'natural' hinterlands, may represent a crucial stage in the development of integrated metropolitan and eventually national markets.

Paul Glennie

Introduction

By European standards, late sixteenth-century England was lightly urbanised; London aside, a land of small towns. Two centuries later England had become entrained in urban growth that was without European parallel. This transformation raises many questions about the town–country relations and the economic and cultural context within which it occurred.

Discussion of town–country relations involves tensions, sometimes contradictions, among themes of *contrast* (the divergent experiences of 'town' and 'country'), *diversity* (a variety of experiences in particular places that undermines the categories 'urban' and 'rural') and *integration* (connections among places). There is no inevitability about how these themes are interrelated. For example, places frequently became increasingly differentiated as spatial divisions of labour increased within a more integrated economy, while other facets of spatial integration were associated with reduced diversity, such as the diffusion of more uniform attitudes to work or consumption. Moreover, a dualism of town and country may not provide the most important categories within which to analyse integration and differentiation. For example, analyses of industrial change may reject perspectives based on competition between urban and rural industries, in favour of an emphasis on changing regional town–country networks, and the intertwining of urban and rural life.

The chapter is divided into four main sections. The first section examines institutional factors bearing on town–country relations and regional economic change in early modern England, which have a lower historiographical profile than in continental Europe. The second section examines various economic connections between urban and rural populations, and the third focuses on administrative and cultural connections. The fourth section shifts the scale of attention from the specifics of towns to characteristics of the whole urban system, both quantitative

Figure 6.1   Early modern England (places mentioned in text)

and qualitative. The conclusion briefly considers the long-run context of this complex period.

Institutions and economic change

Several fields of European history, notably urban history and 'proto-industrialisation' debates, have recently witnessed an 'institutional turn', in which political and social institutions have been analysed as major determinants of long-run socio-economic change. In these accounts, the cost advantages of particular locations for, say, textile production were less important than the 'regional political institutions [that] played a major role in establishing the division of labour between town and country'.[1] Attention is here being directed to the potential abilities of towns to control their rural hinterlands: through a combination of direct territorial control, oppressive fiscal policies, tenurial arrangements, and influence over crown or state policies, urban corporations attempted to discourage or subordinate industrial competition from rural producers in their territories.

However, relatively few historians working on England have been prominent in the institutional turn. Two major reasons may be adduced for this. One is thematic, in that institutions have been inconspicuous in writing on early modern English economic history, in contrast to their prominence in 'transition debates' on feudalism and emergent agrarian capitalism. Although the English state consistently sought to avoid potentially damaging reliance on strategic imports, it did little directly to organise agricultural or industrial production, and was neither strongly supportive nor hostile towards institutions such as urban guilds. Crown attempts to promote certain activities by granting monopolies, such as to Elizabethan metallurgical 'companies', were not sustained.[2] Economic regions in England were not defined by institutional constraints on trade as they were in much of southern and eastern Europe. England provides several dramatic examples of 'free market' (that is, 'not institutionally directed') proto-industrial growth, whereas active feudal or crown intervention underlay proto-industrial-isation in areas such as Wurttemburg, Bohemia, central Sweden and northern Italy.[3]

The jurisdictional privileges enjoyed by early modern English towns rarely amounted to effective political authority over a defined territory, and they struggled to maintain powers confining trade to their marketplaces. With government highly centralised in London, English towns lacked formal political and financial powers. Oligarch-ical urban self-government was unusual, especially before c.1750, partly because of long run shifts in towns' economic bases. Most small towns were unincorporated, adapting their frameworks of part-time manorial and parish officers with changing circumstances, as various town and market officials were attached to Manchester's

[1] S. R. Epstein, 'Town and country: economy and institutions in late-medieval Italy', *Economic Review*, 2nd ser., 46 (1993), 466.
[2] D. Palliser, *The age of Elizabeth* (London, 1983), pp. 318–25; J. Thirsk, *Economic policy and projects* (Oxford, 1978).
[3] S. Ogilvie and M. Cerman (eds.), *European proto-industrialization* (Cambridge, 1996); P. Glennie, 'Industrial change 1540–1700 and the problem of proto-industrialisation', in R. Butlin and R. Dodgshon (eds.), *An historical geography of Europe* (Oxford, 1998); C. Tilly and W. Blockmans (eds.), *Cities and the rise of states in Europe, AD 1000 to 1800* (Oxford, 1994).

manorial court leet.[4] Co-operation among larger English towns remained informal and opportunistic, rather than an effective political lobby comparable to the Convention of Royal Burghs in Scotland. Overall, institutions play a minor role in narratives of English economic development.

Secondly, English historians have defined 'institutions' relatively narrowly, as obstacles obstructing the 'natural', efficient operation of free markets, thereby constraining economic development. Thus, manufacturing and trading privileges of urban guilds and merchant companies; feudal or customary land tenures; and common-field agricultural systems, were all eroded by the market allocation of resources in creating a modern economy. Informal institutions and loose regulatory frameworks were equated with economic flexibility. However, many of these practices would fall under current definitions of 'social institutions' such as the 'rules and practices through which people organised their economic, social, demographic, political and cultural activities'[5] which seek to span both cultural and moral, and political and socio-economic factors and which could promote or inhibit agricultural or industrial activities, or channel them into particular forms. Local cultures; long-run shifts in property holding; settlement customs; devolution of local administration; conventions of family, household and community organisation; and attitudes to household roles and resources, land, work, wages, saving and domestic tasks, were all factors shaping households' and employers' perceptions and everyday decision-making, and therefore affecting the costs and availability of labour, raw materials, transport, exchange, information and household security.

Economic connections

Urban provisioning

Notwithstanding food production from gardens, livestock keeping and town fields and commons, all towns depended on supplies from their hinterlands. A small town's annual food consumption amounted to the produce of several square kilometres, and London's annual grain consumption in c.1700 (estimated at 3.8 million hectolitres) represented the total output of up to 6,700 km^2 of arable land, depending

---

[4] T. S. Willan, *Elizabethan Manchester* (Manchester, 1980); R. Tittler, *Architecture and power: the town hall and the English urban community c.1500–1640* (Oxford, 1991).
[5] Ogilvie and Cerman, *European proto-industrialization*, pp. 23–4, 37.

on harvest conditions.[6] In addition, much larger areas of grazing lands, pastures, wood and coppice were required to produce livestock, dairy products and eggs; leather and tallow; the fodder consumed by London's horses; timber and firewood. In practice, London's environs contained substantial populations, and much output was consumed locally, so London's requirements impinged on areas throughout Britain, especially along major arteries of coastal, river or road communications.

Likewise, Bristol drew on much of the Severn basin, and Newcastle on many eastern coastal districts in England and Scotland. Significant increases in demand for food came also from rural industrial districts, West Riding textile districts relying on grain from the East Riding and East Midlands, while West Midlands metalworking districts stimulated adjacent areas of commercialised arable farming.[7] Supply areas could change dramatically from year to year, with quantitative and qualitative variations in harvests, changes in the product mix and productivity of agriculture in different areas, and in farmers' market orientation, and with transport innovations. Several otherwise unprepossessing ports and towns, like Ware or Lichfield, became important nodes in regional or export trading networks, and centres of grain-processing industries, though this could be short-lived in the face of inter-town competition, as market networks were rationalised. Numerous markets, disproportionately among those not situated on major highways, disappeared,[8] and others fought to avoid the same fate.

The most extensive supply networks were important both because of their scale and as sites of more sophisticated structures of wholesale trade as supply chains were articulated through tiers of intermediate markets, whose civic authorities sometimes provided trading infrastructure.[9]

---

[6] J. Chartres, 'Food consumption and internal trade', in A. Beier and R. Finlay (eds.), *London 1500–1700: the making of the metropolis* (London, 1986), pp. 168–96, estimates at p. 178; P. Glennie and I. Whyte, 'Towns in an agrarian economy 1540–1700', in P. Clark (ed.), *Urban history of Britain*, vol. II: *1540–1840* (Cambridge, 2000), pp. 167–94 (volume hereafter abbreviated to *UHB2*).

[7] J. Thirsk, *English agricultural regions and agrarian history* (London, 1985), pp. 17–19; P. Large, 'Urban growth and agricultural change in the West Midlands', in P. Clark (ed.), *The transformation of English provincial towns* (Leicester, 1984), pp. 169–89; M. Rowlands, 'Continuity and change in an industrialising society: the case of the West Midlands industries', in P. Hudson (ed.), *Regions and industries: a perspective on the Industrial Revolution in Britain* (Cambridge, 1991), p. 121.

[8] A. Rosen, 'Winchester in transition', in P. Clark (ed.), *English country towns 1500–1800* (Leicester 1982), p. 152.

[9] F. J. Fisher, 'The development of the London food market', *Economic History Review* 5 (1934); J. Chartres, 'Marketing', in J. Thirsk (ed.), *Agrarian history of England and Wales*, vol. V. *1640–1750* (Cambridge, 1985), pp. 412–13; Chartres, 'Food consumption', pp. 168–96.

Around London, major out-markets at Reading, Henley, Windsor, High Wycombe, Hitchin, Ware, Maldon, Milton, Reigate, Dorking and Guildford each dominated a further group of local markets. Each tier of marketing comprised small groups of purchasers buying from larger numbers of sellers. The resultant downward pressure on prices to farmers was commonly identified as unequal and exploitative, damaging rhetorics of trade as a reciprocal relationship, and creating anti-urban and anti-middlemen feeling among local consumers facing higher prices during food shortages.[10]

As food supply networks became more elaborate, poor harvests periodically revived an enduring political issue: the relative priority attached to food producers, traders and consumers.[11] Especially before the late seventeenth century, the regulation of food markets was dominated by concerns to ensure the availability and prices of grains. Growing exports of grain and malt, especially from East Anglia, touched similar political sensibilities.[12] Over time, the primary concern of the authorities shifted from consumer protection to ensuring free market trading conditions.[13] Albeit at the expense of rural consumers and dwellers in out-markets, English urban grain supplies were robust by European standards.[14] Harvest failures, food shortages and increases in food prices were associated with high mortality, especially pre-1600, but not specifically with urban mortality. The higher mortality was not necessarily due directly to famine, but rather to the increased susceptibility of

[10] Chartres, 'Food consumption', pp. 184–8; R. B. Outhwaite, *Dearth, public policy and social disturbance in England, 1550–1800* (London, 1991), pp. 35–44.

[11] E. P. Thompson 'The moral economy of the English crowd in the eighteenth century', *Past and Present* 50 (1971), 71–136; E. P. Thompson, 'The moral economy revisited', in E. P. Thompson, *Customs in common* (London, 1992), ch. 3. For changes in regulatory priorities, see R. B. Outhwaite, 'Dearth and government intervention in English grain markets, 1590–1700', *Economic History Review*, 2nd ser., 34 (1981), 389–406.

[12] D. Ormrod, *English grain exports and agrarian capitalism, 1700–1760* (Hull, 1985).

[13] Outhwaite, 'Government intervention'; Outhwaite, *Dearth, public policy*; J. Walter and K. Wrightson, 'Dearth and the social order in early modern England', *Past and Present* 71 (1976), 22–42; A. Appleby, *Famine in Tudor and Stuart England* (London, 1978).

[14] A. Appleby, 'Grain prices and subsistence crises in England and France, 1590–1740', *Journal of Economic History* 39 (1978), 865–87; Appleby, *Famine*; E. A. Wrigley and R. S. Schofield, *The population history of England 1541–1871: a reconstruction* (London, 1981), pp. 645–93; P. R. Galloway, 'Basic patterns in annual variations in fertility, nuptiality and mortality, and prices in pre-industrial Europe', *Population Studies* 42 (1988), 275–304; J. Walter and R. Schofield (eds.), *Famine, disease and the social order in early modern society* (Cambridge, 1989); E. A. Wrigley et al., *English population history from family reconstitution studies, 1580–1837* (Cambridge, 1997), ch. 6; S. Scott et al., 'Infant mortality and famine: a study in historical epidemiology in northern England', *Journal of Epidemiological and Community Health* 49 (1995), 244–52; S. Scott et al., 'The origins, interactions and causes of the cycles in grain prices in England, 1450–1812', *Agricultural History Review* 46 (1998), 1–14.

malnourished persons to certain diseases, and to changes in the movements of both people and goods, which affected the numbers of people,
and the localities, exposed to particular infections.

Urban impacts on agriculture extended far beyond commodity movements, although it must be stressed that urban demand for food was just
one of many factors stimulating agrarian change. In the long run,
increasing urbanisation was broadly associated with more market-oriented and more specialised agricultural production; with more intensive
cultivation and higher land productivity; with increasing concentrations
of landholding and larger farm sizes; with capitalist land tenures and
higher rents; with higher investment, some involving urban capital; and
with greater use of wage labour.[15] Significant urban capital was invested
in farmland, often for mixed commercial and status motives, although
the precise connections between agrarian change and the penetration of
urban capital remain unclear for many areas.

Some particularly specialised production, either commercial or institutional, occurred immediately around towns, especially of fruit, vegetables and fresh milk. Slightly further afield was specialised production
of hay, wood and fresh fat livestock, often like market gardeners using
by-products from urban agricultural processing, especially brewing and
milling. The greater meat consumption among urban populations consistently attracted contemporary comment, and encouraged livestock
production around towns. Some specialities could be pursued on
smallholdings, and the greatest concentration of holdings occurred in
the commercial arable areas of southern England and the Midlands,
although even here significant areas remained in smaller holdings.

Indirectly, agrarian changes could affect urbanisation rates, though
here again there were many other factors involved. Enclosures provide a
classic example. The conversion of farmland from common-field systems
to 'several' systems with more independent decision-making by individual
farmers was often accompanied by conversion from arable to pasture, an
increasing scale of arable production, and a reduction in smallholdings.
Besides reducing the agricultural population, these changes transformed
agricultural labour markets, which had hitherto sought to retain popula-

---

[15] M. Overton, *Agricultural revolution in England: the transformation of the agrarian economy,
1500–1850* (Cambridge, 1996), pp. 168–82; J. Yelling, 'Agriculture 1500–1730', in R. A.
dodgshon and R. A. Butlin (eds.) *An historical geography of England and Wales*, 2nd edn
(London, 1990), pp. 181–98; J. V. Beckett, *The agricultural revolution* (London, 1990),
pp. 45–53; R. Allen, *Enclosure and the yeoman* (Oxford, 1992), pp. 78–104; R. B.
Outhwaite 'Progress and backwardness in English agriculture, 1500–1640', *Economic
History Review*, 2nd ser., 39 (1986), 1–18; M. Overton, 'The determinants of crop yields in
early modern England', in B. Campbell and M. Overton (eds.), *Land, labour and livestock:
historical studies in European agricultural productivity* (Manchester, 1991), pp. 284–322.

tion to meet peaks in demand for labour. Their dismantling, especially at enclosures, intensified inter-regional or rural–urban subsistence migration.[16] In turn, this could create urban social problems, where insufficient urban employment was available for in-migrants.[17]

Providing for hinterlands

All towns, however small, produced and distributed everyday items to their own population and that of surrounding areas. High transport and transactions costs accounted for much of goods' prices to consumers, so protecting local producers whilst simultaneously limiting their scale. Towns were the major locations for the provision of food, drink, textiles, clothing, leather, wood and metal items. Their supply was what made micro-towns 'urban', and what made the health of almost all urban economies dependent on general trading conditions, and towns' control over trade. Most sixteenth-century artisans, especially in small towns, sold their output directly to consumers from their workshops, with some ancillary retailing of goods made elsewhere.

The subsequent proliferation of specialist retail shops, and people's greater reliance on retail access to goods, are key themes in early modern consumption history.[18] Regional and household specialisation meant that many items hitherto produced locally or domestically were bought from retailers increasingly operating from private premises rather than public markets. Shops were sustained by sales of new consumer durables and semi-perishables, and of familiar goods formerly obtained

[16] Subsistence migration, the result of 'push' factors, is conventionally distinguished from 'betterment' migration, in response to 'pull' factors. P. Clark, 'Migration in England during the late-seventeenth and early eighteenth centuries', in P. Clark and D. Souden (eds.), *Migration and society in early modern England* (Brighton, 1987), p. 279; Allen, *Enclosure and the yeoman*, especially pp. 235–80, relates migration surges from the south Midlands to London to enclosures.

[17] The gender composition of migrants, depending on sex-specific structures of urban livelihood opportunities, had important implications for urban demography: C. Galley, 'A model of early modern urban demography', *Economic History Review*, 2nd ser., 38 (1995), 448–69.

[18] J. Patten, 'Urban occupations in pre-industrial England', *Transactions of the Institute of British Geographers* n.s. 2 (1977), 296–313; H.-C. Mui and L. Mui, *Shops and shopkeeping in eighteenth century England* (London 1985); C. Shammas, *The pre-industrial consumer in England and America* (Oxford, 1990); P. Glennie and N. Thrift, 'Consumers, identities and consumption spaces in early-modern England', *Environment and Planning A* 28 (1996), 28–45; P. Ripley, 'Village and town: occupations and wealth in the hinterland of Gloucester, 1660–1700', *Agricultural History Review* 32 (1984), 170–8; Large, 'Urban growth'; J. Pennington and J. Sleights, 'Steyning trades 1559–1787', *Sussex Archaeological Collections* 130 (1992), 164–88; J. Stobart, 'The spatial organisation of a regional economy: central places in north-west England in the early eighteenth century', *Journal of Historical Geography* 22 (1996), 147–59; P. Glennie, 'Shops and shopkeepers in early modern Hertfordshire' (forthcoming).

elsewhere, whose prodigious variety is evident from stock lists, probate inventories and advertisements. For example, handbills issued by John Jones, a shopkeeper from Bishops Stortford (Hertfordshire), in *c.*1750 included well over two hundred items, from many parts of the world. Some starches and soaps were described as 'Spanish', 'Nankeen', or 'Poland'; powders and perfumes were called 'Cyprus', 'French', 'Venice' or 'Hungary'; various items were described as 'Dutch', 'Indian', 'Bengal', or 'Morocco'; and flutes and fifes had been imported from Germany. In addition, some English-made goods were of exotic types, from 'Japanned' wooden furniture to objects of ivory and tortoiseshell, 'Sanative English tea' and 'Rose's English coffee'. Produced closer to home were the likes of 'Hampshire millers' rat powder', 'Dalmahoys' tasteless salts', and cricket bats and balls. For almost all goods, except patent medicines, geographical provenance served as useful description.[19]

Early retail shops mainly obtained goods of distant origin directly from London or provincial port-based dealers and importers. Over time, more hierarchical supply networks formed, especially where principal shopkeepers in provincial and county towns became wholesalers to small town and village shopkeepers. Multiple shop ownership appeared, a late seventeenth-century Leicester haberdasher having branches in Lutterworth and Melton Mowbray, and a Leicester ironmonger owning other shops in Loughborough and Hinckley.[20]

The widespread distribution of shops by *c.*1750 is clear from militia ballot lists, a somewhat neglected source. From 1757, parish lists of men aged 18 to 45 or 50 years, and their occupations, were compiled almost annually in most English counties, for balloting county militias.[21] Their survival is very uneven, the fullest extant returns being for Hertfordshire's 132 parishes, including 20 small towns with populations of between 800 and 3,000 people. Leaving aside the most specialised urban retailers, between 1758 and 1786 more than 530 men, most appearing in several consecutive lists, were described as shopkeeper, grocer, draper, mercer, or haberdasher. Nearly 70 per cent lived in the small towns, with more than 20 shopkeepers recorded at St Albans, Hertford, Hitchin, Ware, Watford, Royston, Hemel Hempstead, Barnet, Bishops Stortford and Cheshunt. Half of the rural parishes had no retailer listed.[22] But rural shops were not unusual in the 1750s – some

19 Shammas, *Pre-industrial consumer*, pp. 197–265; Hertfordshire Record Office, Hertford, D/Ex/279/B1.
20 A. Dyer, 'Urban networks in the English Midlands', in *UHB2*, citing *Victoria county history of Leicestershire*, vol. IV (London 1958), pp. 81, 97.
21 For an introduction, see P. D. Glennie *'Distinguishing men's trades': occupational sources and debates for pre-census England* (Cheltenham, 1990), esp. pp. 46–65.
22 Which is not to say there were none, conducted either as by-occupations or by men not

had existed a century earlier – and they became more widespread: shopkeepers are first recorded between 1771 and 1786 in at least seven small parishes, whose median population was under 300 people. The effects of shops on urban–rural distinctions were complex. As village shops spread, small towns became less distinctive as access points to consumer goods and exotic items.

Partly because of marketing, retailing and informal trading, towns were important nodes in networks of credit and debt that routinely involved much of the population. Credit originated both through cash loans and through forms of deferred payment, especially of wages and payments to retailers. Rural households received credit through urban merchants, craftsmen and shopkeepers, and farmers extended credit to urban-based dealers, drovers and processors.[23] Like commodity networks, networks of capital flows became more structured and integrated, rather than opportunistic and isolated.

Specialised industrial districts

Beyond basic craft provision for their immediate localities, some towns possessed more significant concentrations of 'manufactures', especially in textiles and metalworking. However, urban locations were not a prerequisite for these activities, whose occurrence in rural districts underlies theories of proto-industrialisation.[24] Regional concentrations of craft activities in diverse settings have been attributed to equally varied causes, including the distribution of particular resources (iron, water, coal); local agro-environmental conditions, especially pastoral products (wool, leather, wood);[25] inheritance and landholding customs, where subdivision of farm holdings encouraged craft by-employments to supplement household incomes;[26] accessible locations close to major

liable for the ballot. That shops were more common than men described as shopkeepers is evident from retail shop stocks and fittings which were listed in the inventories of men ascribed other occupations, and from the prosecution of men in other occupations for trading as grocers without having served an apprenticeship.

[23] A. Dyer, *The city of Worcester in the sixteenth century* (London, 1973), pp. 68–9; C. Muldrew, 'Credit and the courts: debt litigation in a seventeenth-century urban community', *Economic History Review*, 2nd ser., 46 (1993), 23–38.

[24] For recent reviews, see Ogilvie and Cerman, *European proto-industrialization*; Glennie 'Problem of proto-industrialization'.

[25] A. Kussmaul, *A general view of the rural economy of England, 1538–1840* (Cambridge, 1990).

[26] J. Thirsk, 'Industries in the countryside', in F. J. Fisher (ed.), *Essays in the economic and social history of Tudor and Stuart England, in honour of R. H. Tawney* (London, 1961), pp. 70–88.

markets and transport routes;[27] and non-location-specific cumulative 'human capital', or the skills and experience of workers, entrepreneurs and traders.[28] Only the latter two factors are town-specific.

In 1570 few towns apart from London[29] contained industrial activities supplying regional or national markets. The likes of the Worcester cloth industry were unusual. Some urban manufacturing appeared from *c.*1600, especially around (and for) London, for example the production of cutlery at Tonbridge. Other industries migrated from London in the face of high costs there, notably the hosiery, hat and silk production that resettled in some east midlands towns. Glass-making, salt extraction and other fuel-intensive industries expanded in and around Newcastle, where coal was abundant and cheap. All these were small-scale employers compared with the rural textile industries thriving in the West Country, East Anglia and the West Riding, or metalware industries in parts of the West Midlands and South Yorkshire.[30]

Several historians have linked sluggish European urban growth, 1600–1750, to rural proto-industries.[31] Broad concepts of proto-industrialisation (the development of rural regions, in which much of the population lives largely from household industrial production for eventual sale outside the region, experiencing internal pressures towards capitalist industrial production) first emerged in the 1970s, but have subsequently been significantly refined. It has become increasingly clear that English proto-industrialisation, with weak institutional controls over production and marketing, differed from that elsewhere in Europe, where control was commonly exercised by guilds, merchant companies or product-finishers, backed by state-protected production or trading monopolies, and sometimes by legal wage controls. Simultaneously, the relationships among proto-industries, demographic change, and agrarian household structures have come to appear contingent rather than necessary, and very much more complex than was originally envisaged. Still, proto-industrialisation concepts usefully highlight the spatial dynamics of industrial processes, and the relations between local institutional contexts and households' flexibility in entering or leaving

27 A. Everitt, 'Country, county and town: patterns of regional evolution in England', *Transactions of the Royal Historical Society*, 5th ser., 29 (1979), 79–108.
28 M. Berg (ed.), *Markets and manufactures in early modern Europe* (London, 1991).
29 On London, see also A. Beier, 'Engines of manufacture: the trades of London', in Beier and Finlay, *London 1500–1700*, pp. 141–67; N. Zahedieh, 'London and the colonial consumer in the late seventeenth century', *Economic History Review*, 2nd ser., 47 (1994), 239–61.
30 P. J. Bowden, *The wool trade in Tudor and Stuart England* (London, 1962).
31 J. de Vries, *European urbanisation, 1500–1800* (London, 1984).

production, especially where production was very sensitive to market conditions. Local social variations gave rise to considerable short-distance variations in proto-industrial forms. Thus Hudson discusses a patchwork of localities in the West Riding, with diverse product special-isations, scales of production and forms of organisation.[32]

At all events, it is hard to argue that proto-industrial growth was antithetical to urbanisation in England, the most rapidly urbanising country in Europe, and among the most heavily proto-industrialised.[33] Almost all regions of rural industry were organised around urban commercial and financial centres, in which finance, trading, provision of materials, and the most highly skilled stages of production and finishing were concentrated, although few of these centres in England had been specifically privileged or planned. The small workshop-based hardware industry of the Black Country area, for example, focused on the inns and warehouses of Wolverhampton, which had outcompeted the rival centres of Walsall, Dudley and Stourbridge.[34] Here, and elsewhere, the boundaries between 'urban' and 'rural' became increas-ingly blurred as industrial production took place in towns, and booming proto-industrial villages became recognisably urban in land-scape, population and functions.

Through the seventeenth century, many older cloth production centres revived, sometimes by switching to lighter New Draperies, and several towns rapidly expanded their craft production of everyday items for regional or national markets: shoes in Northampton; buttons in Macclesfield; glass in Stourbridge and Nottingham; nets in Bridport.[35] The origins of these industrial specialisms may be obscure, but once established they accumulated important advantages in human capital. Older labelling of their persistence as 'inertia' has been discarded as too passive, to be replaced by concepts of 'skill regions'.[36]

During depressions, corporate measures to encourage trade centred on unregulated activities, rather than reinforcing protective restrictions, as where Leicester's stocking-makers successfully argued that the trade should not be restricted to freemen: 'it is not the curious making of a

---

[32] P. Hudson, 'Proto-industrialisation: the West Riding wool textile industry', *History Workshop Journal* 12 (1981), 34–61; P. Hudson (ed.), *Regions and industries*; R. Burt, 'The transformation of the non-ferrous metal industries in the seventeenth and eighteenth centuries', *Economic History Review*, 2nd ser., 38 (1995), 23–45.

[33] E. A. Wrigley, *People, cities and wealth* (Cambridge, 1987), esp. pp. 157–93.

[34] B. Trinder, 'Industrialising towns, 1700–1840', in *UHB2*, pp. 805–30.

[35] Everitt, 'Country, county and town'; Thirsk, *Economic policy*; A. Dyer, *Decline and growth in English towns 1400–1640* (London, 1990), pp. 56–7; J. Houghton, *Collection for the improvement of husbandry and trade* (London, 1692–1703).

[36] Berg, *Markets*.

few stockings, but the general making of many that is most for the public good, for that sets more people on work'.[37]

Administrative and socio-cultural connections

Paradoxically, while English state power was highly centralised, it involved a comparatively small full-time bureaucracy. Much county and sub-county administration was performed by county or parish office-holders, of both elite and humble status. Towns were important centres for judicial and religious administration, charitable provision, and for taxation.[38] Some administration was necessarily urban, but the convenience of urban meeting points was frequently remarked. Much administration (including sessions, visitations and musters) was implemented from small towns, through churchwardens, constables or other parish officers, who mediated between local communities and vestries, and civil and ecclesiastical authorities. Their responsibilities entailed considerable geographical mobility, in attending diocesan and archdeaconry visitations that monitored the physical and moral condition of parish life, and assizes or quarter sessions. Some meetings were held in one place year after year but others, especially visitations, successively visited different centres.

During the 1560s, the churchwardens of Kingston-upon-Thames represented the parish at London, Winchester, Reading, Maidenhead, Staines, Leatherhead, Dorking, Ewell, Sutton and Ditton. Their successors also visited Southwark, Chertsey, Guildford, Carshalton and Chichester in the 1590s, while the wardens of Steeple Ashton (Wiltshire) attended visitations or sessions at Trowbridge, Devizes, Lavington and elsewhere. Twenty years later, wardens from Highworth and Christian Malford were among those assembled at Marlborough, Salisbury, Devizes, Malmesbury, Wootton Bassett, Chippenham and Farringdon. In mid-seventeenth-century Lancashire, the churchwardens of Padiham attended at Wigan, Blackburn, Whalley, Clitheroe, Bolton, Chester, Colne and Burnley, while their counterparts at

---

[37] P. Slack, 'Great and good towns 1540–1700', in *UHB2*, pp. 347–76.

[38] Changes in taxation, which was becoming the chief source of English state finance, themselves affected town–country relations. Towns contributed an increasing proportion of the fiscal burden, as their share of national wealth grew, and as urban activities and populations were specifically targeted through the introduction of the excise and other indirect taxes on spending. New taxes, especially the excise, whose administration involved some 1500 men in *c*.1700, were mainly administered from provincial centres and small towns; J. Brewer, *The sinews of power: war, money and the English state* (London, 1989).

Whalley attended at Blackburn, Chester, Burnley, Padiham, Preston and Lancaster.[39]

Similar instances from all parts of England illustrate how visitations and sessions assembled parish officeholders in small towns. Such meetings provided direct channels between national or diocesan administrators and local communities. They were also important for the spread of information outside the official purposes of the gathering. For example, churchwardens at visitations informally discussed parish building activities and the skill and reliability of craftsmen. Meetings were also economically important for their venues, through the provision of accommodation, stabling and victuals. This was one factor in their being held in different places, whose significance is suggested by the numerous attempts by parish vestries to limit wardens' spending at visitations.

Towns, large and small, were also focal points for nonconformist sects. Most Quakers and Presbyterians were townspeople, and the country-dwelling majority of other dissenters usually held assemblies at urban inns or meeting-houses. Margaret Spufford's verdict that 'the typical territory of non-conformist meetings was the market area'[40] conveys how ostensibly separate urban functions were typically experienced in conjunction: a countryman attending a market, a prayer meeting and a hardware shop was not separately being 'a producer', 'religious' and 'a consumer'; though historians may distinguish those roles, he could live all three roles in a single journey.

Urban gatherings, whether for administration or business, conscience or pleasure, had significant economic dimensions, through the provision of facilities, sustenance, equipment and entertainment, often promoted by innkeepers.[41] Urban social facilities and professional expertise typically reinforced one another, encouraging further expansion of activities and facilities. Several new types of consumer-oriented urban space were widespread by c.1700, including coffee houses, which, like inns, were both nodes in information and carrying networks, and centres for recreation.[42]

[39] Kingston Borough Archives, KG/2/2–3; Wiltshire Record Office, Trowbridge, 1184/19, 1710/32; Lancashire Record Office, Preston, PR. 2863/2/1, PR. 8.

[40] M. Spufford et al., *The world of rural dissenters* (Cambridge, 1995), pp. 30, 390.

[41] P. Borsay, *The English urban renaissance: culture and society in the provincial town, 1660–1760* (Oxford, 1989); P. Clark, *Sociability and urbanity: clubs and societies in the eighteenth century* (Leicester, 1986), pp. 1–22; P. Earle, *The making of the English middle class: business, society and family life in London, 1660–1730* (London, 1989); J. Barry, 'Provincial urban culture, 1640–1750: urbane or civic?', in J. Pittock and A. Webb (eds.), *Interpretation and cultural history* (Basingstoke, 1991), pp. 198–234.

[42] A. Everitt (ed.), *Perspectives in English urban history* (London, 1973), pp. 91–137; P. Clark, *The English alehouse: a social history* (London, 1983).

The role of the larger towns as social centres of fundamental importance from at least the 1560s decisively accelerated after the Restoration in 1660. Participants spanned a considerable range of the social spectrum, with the urban 'middling sort' both providing and consuming a range of professional and cultural services. New social events, recreations and spectacle were widespread, although they attracted particular comment from contemporaries where they dominated 'leisure town' economies. More hyperbolic accounts of new urban cultures and meetings, with their emphasis on assemblies, science, and swimming crocodiles, may require some qualification in the cases of very small towns, where the tedium of small scale sociability among a small pool of people has perhaps been glossed over.

The relationship of services to town size was made complex by local factors such as active gentry, entrepreneurial or innkeeper promoters, and highway locations with substantial through traffic.[43] Small towns accumulated service and social functions in an eclectic fashion, but they could as easily be lost, for there was at least as much competition among towns regarding the service sector as any other, with a ratcheting up of notions of 'good' shops, or 'fine' entertainments or facilities. Thus a visitor in 1760 complained that Exeter's shops were 'of a very ancient model', demolishing the city's claim as the 'London of the West'. Such labels were also threatened by improving communications, giving wealthy consumers more scope to travel to the real London rather than a regional substitute.

Growing per caput consumption of commodities in Restoration England is often seen as central to 'urban renaissance' and, especially since the late 1980s, has been systematically explored.[44] Numerous new goods were bought and owned by households comprising the wealthier two-thirds of the English population after *c*.1660, many made more widely available by the proliferation of retail shops. Extensive consumption, varying with wealth, gender and location, of items ranging from new styles of furnishing to glass and ceramics, and from clocks and globes to teapots and toys, took place within changing layouts and

---

[43] Clark, *Sociability*; Barry, 'Provincial urban culture', also stresses the importance of thoroughfare locations for the smallest towns.

[44] N. McKendrick, J. Brewer and J. Plumb, *The birth of a consumer society: the commercialization of eighteenth century England* (London, 1982); L. Weatherill, *Consumer behaviour and material culture in Britain 1660–1760* (London, 1988); Earle, *Making of the English middle class*; Shammas, *Pre-industrial consumer*; J. de Vries, 'Between consumption and the world of goods', in J. Brewer and R. Porter (eds.), *Consumption and the world of goods* (London, 1993), pp. 85–132; P. Glennie, 'Consumption in historical studies', in D. Miller (ed.), *Acknowledging consumption: interdisciplinary studies* (London, 1995), pp. 164–203.

decoration within private houses, and in new public spaces such as assemblies and promenades.

Although many facets of consumption behaviour await detailed study,[45] urban consumption changes were clearly precocious, reflecting the wealth and status of urban consumers and their greater access to new commodities, besides changing preferences. Townspeople and artisans, as well as professionals and traders, seem to have spent more heavily on so-called 'positional goods' than comparably wealthy country dwellers, prompting suggestions of a distinctive urban 'consumption ethic'.[46] The capacities of certain sorts of consumption to signal new sensibilities provided – at a price – new bases for social identifications, supplementing those determined by social origins. In Jonathan Barry's words, by the early eighteenth century 'the forms of culture now seen as dominating town life were essentially there to be purchased by consumers'.[47]

Much sociability bore on establishing the relations of trust central to urban economic relationships and administrative co-operation, both within towns and between mercantile, professional and rural elites.[48] Hence the social as well as the cultural importance of education, manners, reliability and shared participation in cultural activities. One outcome of the Civil War, Commonwealth and Restoration was improved relations between towns and the provincial elites, and urban appreciation of the value of socio-political links to the gentry as a whole, rather than to individual magnates or patrons, though the latter could still be important in sponsoring commercial and charitable schemes. This was a key factor in the post-Restoration 'urban renaissance' of leisure and cultural activities, because of both elite spending and the role of lawyers and other professionals as financial and cultural brokers between rural elites and urban merchants and entrepreneurs.

---

[45] J. Styles, 'Manufacture, consumption and design in the eighteenth century', in Brewer and Porter, *Consumption and world of goods*, p. 540; N. Harte, 'The economics of clothing in the seventeenth century', *Textile History* 22 (1991), 277–96.

[46] Weatherill, *Consumer behaviour*, pp. 78–9; Earle, *Making of the English middle class*; H. R. French, 'Chief inhabitants and their areas of influence: local ruling groups in Essex and Suffolk 1630–1720', Ph.D. thesis, University of Cambridge, 1993. The social depth of markets for consumer goods remains controversial. See Glennie, 'Consumption', esp. pp. 173–4, 177–8; P. King, 'Pauper inventories and the material lives of the poor', in T. Hitchcock, P. King and P. Sharpe (eds.), *Chronicling poverty: the voices and strategies of the English poor, 1640–1840* (Basingstoke, 1996) pp. 155–91.

[47] Barry, 'Provincial urban culture', p. 208.

[48] Clark, *Sociability*; C. Brooks, 'Apprenticeship, social mobility and the middling sort', in J. Barry and C. Brooks (eds.), *The middling sort of people: culture, society and politics, 1550–1800* (Basingstoke, 1994), p. 77; J. Barry, 'Bourgeois collectivism? Urban association and the middling sort', in Barry and Brooks, *Middling sort*, p. 101.

Links between town and country were ceremonially presented, in ceremonial processions and similar public events, as close and co-operative. The relative cultural consensus underlying many of these events relied, though, on the willingness of gentry and urban elites to derive mutually acceptable conceptions of their relative status, and especially on urban elites deferring to their rural social superiors. The corollary was change in the cultural status of urban residence, especially in rural elites' greater use of urban houses and patronage of recreational activities. A by-product of rural and urban elites becoming increasingly interconnected by family ties, mercantile investments, professional services and shared administrative and cultural activities was a regenerated sense of urban social cohesion, among those elites – if not among the population at large.

Urban systems and market integration

By European standards, before *c.*1700 England was a land of many small towns, a massively primate capital city, and few large provincial cities.[49] A population threshold of 5,000, widely used in international comparisons, excludes all but 10 English towns in *c.*1520, and 31 in *c.*1700.[50] Even in 1801, under 100 of the 700 or so urban places in England exceeded this threshold, though England now contained several of Europe's largest provincial centres. The intervening transformation was undeniably dramatic, although Tudor and Stuart England does appear significantly more urbanised when account is taken of its many small towns. In *c.*1700, for example, counting some 750,000 persons in small towns as townspeople raises the urban proportion from one-sixth (using the 5,000 threshold) to more than one-third of English population.[51] Lowering the urban population threshold also affects regional patterns of urbanisation. Until *c.*1700, even counties like Hertfordshire were relatively highly urbanised because they contained so many small towns.

Before *c.*1650, London aside, the urban proportion of the English population grew only slightly. Given the weakly integrated national space economy, established regional and county centres, small as many of them appear, were central to town–country relations. Newcastle,

---

[49] Shortage, that is, compared both with other countries (de Vries, *European urbanisation*), and with geographical models of settlement rank-size change.

[50] P. Clark and J. Hosking, *Population estimates for English small towns, 1563–1801* (Leicester, 1993); R. Lawton and C. Pooley, *Britain 1740–1950: an historical geography* (London, 1992), p. 94.

[51] These figures are based on data assembled by Langton, 'Urban growth', in *UHB2*, pp. 453–90, which substantially improve on all earlier estimates for the period 1660–1841.

Bristol, York, Norwich and Exeter were each influential over considerable areas of England, and of Wales in the cases of Bristol, Chester and
Shrewsbury (where Defoe remarked on hearing Welsh spoken on
market days). The county towns, especially, exemplify a combination of
modest size and slow growth, with diverse functions. They made up a
varied group: substantial towns like Worcester or Ipswich being several
times the size of Buckingham and Dorchester, but all facing a combination of rural competition, low investment and weak consumer demand.

The relative fortunes of small and large towns has been much
debated, and there were clearly major geographical variations in the
growth of small towns.[52] Even if, nationally, small towns grew more
slowly than larger towns, or the national population, there are considerable local variations. In the Gloucestershire Cotswolds, the small-town
hubs of rural cloth production grew fastest of all, while the larger towns
of Gloucester, Cirencester and Tewkesbury grew more slowly than
either small towns or rural parishes. Elsewhere in the Midlands, Dyer
suggests that small and large towns grew at similar rates. In Hertfordshire, small-town populations grew rapidly – but no more rapidly than
the population at large – until about 1640, after which small-town
population growth accelerated while rural population declined. And
Cumbrian small-town populations increased faster than rural parishes,
though their markets were 'rudimentary in scope and function', as new
markets were established around larger centres of wholesaling and
professional services at Carlisle, Kendal and Penrith.[53]

The period between c.1650 and c.1750 saw significant expansion and
reshaping of more economically and socially integrated urban networks.
Urban populations grew significantly, while national population remained stable. London's dominance increased, its influence now increasingly mediated through provincial capitals like Bristol, Newcastle
and Norwich. Several small towns began their transformation into
major industrial centres. A few new towns appeared in hitherto remote
areas, reflecting growing marketing opportunities and slightly reducing
regional contrast in urban density.[54] Scores of places fell away at the
bottom of the hierarchy, too small, inappropriately sited, or outcompeted by local rivals.[55] Improved transport and communications were

[52] Ibid.; P. Clark, 'Small towns in England 1550–1850: national and regional population
trends', in P. Clark (ed.), *Small towns in early modern Europe* (Cambridge, 1995).
[53] D. J. Rollison, *The local origins of modern society: Gloucestershire 1500–1800* (Cambridge,
1992), pp. 27–31; A. Dyer, 'Midlands', in *UHB2*, pp. 93–110; P. D. Glennie, 'A
commercialising agrarian region: late medieval and early modern Hertfordshire', Ph.D.
thesis, Cambridge University, 1983, pp. 91–119; J. D. Marshall, 'The rise of the
Cumbrian market town', *Northern History* 25 (1989), 134.
[54] Marshall, 'Rise of the Cumbrian market town', 145.

double-edged developments as towns competed for trade. The protection hitherto offered to isolated towns, including some county towns, by high transport and transactions costs was lost, and many such places lost out to larger towns with expanding spheres of influence. Improved communications networks were associated with fewer towns, possessing better facilities. Over time, places benefiting from these changes at one time could be threatened by them later, as trade became further concentrated in better placed towns.

After *c.*1750, the pace of change quickened further. The continuing growth of towns like Manchester, Leeds, Birmingham and Halifax was so rapid that existing hierarchies were severely disrupted. New regional commercial economies around such centres rapidly became the most striking features of urbanisation, while southern England and East Anglia, which retained their many small towns but generated few new large centres, became much more peripheral to urban systems. The massive growth of urban industrial labour undermined any remaining idea that a town's size provided a guide to its range of functions. Many regional capitals and county towns, among them Reading, Northampton, St Albans, Maidstone, Rochester, Huntingdon, Lichfield, Ely, Hereford, Chelmsford and Beverley, rapidly slipped down the size-ranking of English towns. Though they retained or expanded most of their traditional roles, their populations grew slowly, if at all. If taken only as a rule-of-thumb, Wrigley's comment that these towns were modern, but not industrial, whereas the most rapid growth came in towns that were industrial, but not modern, succinctly conveys the contrast.[56]

As the total urban population grew, and towns developed more specialised roles, urban networks became much more coherently integrated as systems of central places. Geographers have been particularly concerned to identify coherent hierarchies of places, defined in 'orders' according to their distinct arrays of functions, and by interdependence among towns linked by flows of objects, people and information. For example, Patten analysed occupational scalograms of East Anglian towns and villages, to show functional changes within a rather stable regional urban system.[57] More recently, Stobart has shown the dynamism of urban networks in north-west England. He identifies an

[55] Chartres, 'Marketing', pp. 412–13.
[56] E. A. Wrigley, 'The process of modernisation and the Industrial Revolution in England', *Journal of Interdisciplinary History* 3 (1972), 225–59.
[57] J. Patten, *English towns, 1500–1700* (Folkestone, 1975); J. Patten, 'Changing occupational structures in the East Anglian countryside, 1550–1700' in H. S. A. Fox and R. A. Butlin (eds.), *Change in the countryside: essays on rural England 1500–1900* (London, 1979), pp. 103–21. Patten's view in the late 1970s, that East Anglia was a 'leading region' in English economic change, requires revision in the light of work on other areas.

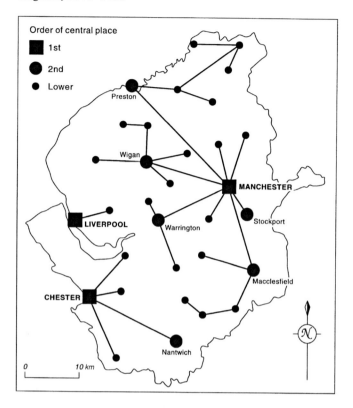

Figure 6.2   Urban networks in eighteenth-century north-west England

established regional urban hierarchy, comprising several 'orders' of central places (Figure 6.2), which was, however, cut across by various rapidly growing service occupations, 'making a nonsense of the idea that high order functions should be located only in high order centres'.[58]

The economic integration implied by functional differentiation among towns (and rural areas) is directly attested by evidence for commercial movements of goods, for the existence or payment of debts, and for changes in the scale and organisation of commodity trades.[59] Indirect evidence comes from coherent space-time patterns in prices and price

[58] J. Stobart, 'The spatial organization of a regional economy: central places in north-west England in the early eighteenth century', *Journal of Historical Geography* 22 (1996), 147–59, quote at p. 155.

[59] J. Langton, 'The Industrial Revolution and the regional geography of England', *Transactions of the Institute of British Geographers*, n.s. 9 (1984), 145–67; D. J. Gregory, 'The production of regions in England's Industrial Revolution', *Journal of Historical Geography* 14 (1988), 50–8; Kussmaul, *General view*. Changes in grain trading have

movements, that imply well-integrated market areas. English grain
prices were systematically collected and published from the late 1680s
by John Houghton, in his commercial newspaper *Collections Relating to
Husbandry and Trade.*[60] Analyses of Houghton's data reveal a coherent
geographical pattern in wheat prices (Figure 6.3), and that wheat prices
in different markets changed in a co-ordinated way in response to
harvest and market conditions, implying considerable spatial integration.[61] The same features are evident, though less strongly, for barley,
but are rather weak for rye and oats, implying that these crops remained
more locally marketed, with much less inter-regional trade.

Geographies of the price of labour, i.e. wages, are more problematic.
Data, especially outside large towns, are less abundant, and the product
is less standardised. With wages increasingly important within household incomes, geographies of wages have implications for plebeian
standards of living as well as production costs. That a north-south
differential existed in wage rates by *c.*1800 is clear.[62] Earlier patterns
remain uncertain. Woodward identifies two major wage regions among
larger towns in northern England, with higher wages in north-east
England (Newcastle, York, Hull, Beverley) than elsewhere (including
Kendal, Carlisle, Lincoln). In both areas, wage rates were significantly
lower than in and around London, or in Bristol, although not dissimilar
from those of other southern English towns (Table 6.1).

Given current knowledge, it is hazardous to generalise about geographies of wages beyond the premium rates paid in the metropolitan
counties and in provincial centres. Current data on small town and rural
wage rates before the late eighteenth century are too sparse to permit
detailed conclusions. Similarly, assertions that attempts at wage regulation had negligible effects currently rest on limited material, especially
for the wages of rural craftsmen.

Conclusions

The recent tendency among economic historians to downplay the
rapidity of economic change in the eighteenth century ought not to be

already been mentioned; similar changes affected trading in commodities such as wool,
timber and coal.
[60] J. E. T. Rogers, *A history of agriculture and prices in England*, 7 vols. (Oxford, 1866–92),
vol. IV; Chartres, 'Marketing', pp. 460–5. The relative abundance of grain price data,
and product variability among livestock and consumer goods, mean that similar
mapping is more difficult for other commodities.
[61] Chartres, 'Marketing', p. 460.
[62] E. Hunt, 'Industrialization and regional inequality: wages in Britain 1760–1914',
Journal of Economic History 46 (1986), 965.

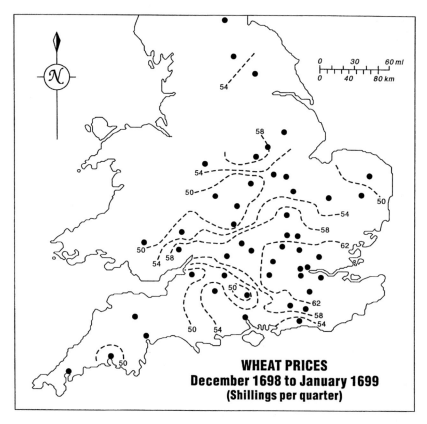

Figure 6.3   Integration of the English wheat market, 1698–9

extended to the magnitude, the character and the spatial-temporal patterning of late seventeenth- and eighteenth-century urbanisation. While town–country relations, in their various forms, need not change in synchrony with shifts in the urban–rural split of population, the discontinuity between urbanisation in the sixteenth and eighteenth centuries is dramatic. This discontinuity was not a departure from an unchanged medieval urban system, but from a complex of slower commercial, administrative and cultural changes under way in the late sixteenth and seventeenth centuries. Changes in urban roles based on a very heterogeneous set of economic, socio-political and cultural changes, singly or in combination, had, unsurprisingly, already created a kaleidoscopic variety of experiences among towns. As the preceding discussion has attempted to convey, although marketing and distribu-

Table 6.1. *Carpenters' daily wage rates in selected English towns,*
c.1540–c.1660

Pence per day (d.) in	c.1540	c.1560	c.1580	c.1600	c.1620	c.1640	c.1660
Northern England							
York	6	8	8–10	12	12–14	14	18
Newcastle		8	8–10	10–12		16–18	20–22
Durham	5–7	8–10	8–10	9			16–18
Chester	6	8–10	8–10	10–12	12–15	13–18	14–18
Hull	6	8–10	9–10	10	12	12–14	18–21
Southern England							
London			16	18	24–30	30	36
Kingston	8	12	12	14–18	20	24	24
Reading	6–8	10	12	14–16	15	16–20	
Winchester	6	8–9	10	12	13–16	14–16	18–20
Salisbury	6	8–11	12	12	12–16	16	18–24
Bristol	8	12	12	12	12–14	16–24	20–30

Sources: For northern England from D. Woodward, *Men at work: building craftsmen and labourers in northern English towns 1450–1750* (Cambridge, 1995); London rates from J. Boulton, 'Wage rates in London', *Economic History Review*, 2nd ser., 49 (1996), 288–9; other southern towns from author's work in progress, based on churchwardens' and borough accounts at Kingston Borough Archives (Kingston), Berkshire Record Office (Reading), Hampshire Record Office (Winchester), Wiltshire Records Office (Trowbridge), City of Bristol Record Office (Bristol).

tion, finance and industrial production, were central to urbanisation, several other factors were involved, not least institutional and cultural influences of various kinds. Consequently, trajectories of change in early modern urban economies were neither uniform nor unidirectional.

A, if not the, central question remains exactly why English urban growth departed so dramatically from its own earlier history, and from the experience of other areas of seventeenth- and eighteenth-century Europe. The current state of the literature leaves this question without decisive answer, and no consensus as to whether the key lay within the urban sector itself, in its wider setting, or in the relationship between the two. Once under way, rising agricultural labour productivity and urban growth were mutually reinforcing, but in which sector did the reshaping begin? And how much was due to changes in the integration among regions and economic sectors, rather than to initial changes in techniques or technologies?[63]

[63] E. A. Wrigley, 'Urban growth and agricultural change: England and the Continent in the early modern period', *Journal of Interdisciplinary History* 15 (1985), 683–728; M. Darnton, 'Integration and specialisation', in M. Darnton, *Progress and poverty: an economic and social history of Britain 1700–1850* (Oxford, 1995).

At the same time, as the use of 1570 to divide the two chapters on England implies, there appear considerable continuities across the conventional medieval–modern divides of 1500 or 1540. This is not to ignore either the immediate impact, or the long-run ramifications, of major social changes such as the massive post-Reformation redistribution of ecclesiastical urban property to individuals or corporations. Some major changes in late medieval urban relations raise interesting comparative questions with changes mentioned in this chapter. For example, how does the way in which late medieval London drew to itself many major provincial merchants, and much hitherto provincial business, compare with the similar developments that characterised much of the sixteenth century, and changes in the opposite direction from the mid-seventeenth? It would be premature to interpret the similarities as a continuation of the same process, not least because so much had changed in town–country relations, and in the demographic situation, but the question is worth asking. Likewise, in what other ways were changes in town–country relations during the early modern demographic expansion paralleling or departing from those during population growth three centuries earlier?

Alongside those very large questions, a possible research agenda would include a multitude of smaller though still substantial topics, several of which have already been mentioned. The following brief list is very much a personal one, though it is intended to convey the diversity of work for which there is scope. With no pretensions to comprehensiveness, work would be welcome on the demography of small towns; on the demographic impacts, urban and rural, of much greater movements of people and goods; on the transmission of, and audience for, commercial information; on the history of urban service and recreational facilities prior to the date of 1660 which conventionally defines the 'urban renaissance'; on geographical variations in wage rates; on the significance of wages as against other components of plebeian household incomes; on the impact of attempts at wage regulation; on physical geographical influences on proto-industries (which have now almost disappeared from discussion); and on relations between English and Scottish economic change after the Union of 1707.

7   Town and country in the Polish Commonwealth, 1350–1650

Andrzej Janeczek

Translated by P. Rutkowski and S. R. Epstein

Introduction

During the fourteenth century new prospects opened up for east-central Europe. Poland, Bohemia, Hungary and Lithuania underwent intensive economic development, consolidated and strengthened their polities, and initiated a period of external expansion.[1] In 1340 the newly united Polish state began a struggle to succeed the disintegrating duchies of the western Rus'. Lithuania gained vast tracts of the northern Rus' and Kievan Duchy. A union between Poland and Lithuania, formed in 1385 and made permanent in 1569, created one of the biggest states in Europe at the time, known as the Commonwealth of the Two Nations, which by 1500 covered 1,140,000 km^2, of which the territory of the Polish crown accounted for only 255,000 km^2. The Commonwealth extended from the Baltic to the Black Sea and from the Carpathian mountains to the outskirts of Moscow. It formed a vast cultural frontier between the Latin West and the Byzantine and Orthodox East, and after the Turks expanded into Europe it also became a gate to the Muslim world. The Commonwealth also displayed considerable internal diversity. Poland, especially its eastern lands, included a particularly heterogeneous mixture of ethnic groups, religions and cultures, with corresponding differences in development ranging from simple barter economies to sophisticated forms of market exchange.

Although Poland was rich in land, this was not the main source of the country's wealth. The most important natural resource for a feudal economy was men, and Poland was one of the most sparsely populated countries in Europe. To the west, where it was surrounded by Bohemia, Saxony, Brandenburg and Denmark, population density in the fifteenth century approximated 10–15 persons/km^2. This compared poorly with

[1] A. Mączak, H. Samsonowicz, and P. Burke (eds.), *East-central Europe in transition. From the fourteenth to the seventeenth century* (Cambridge, 1985); J. Kłoczowski, *Europa słowiańska w XIV–XV wieku* (Warsaw, 1984).

156

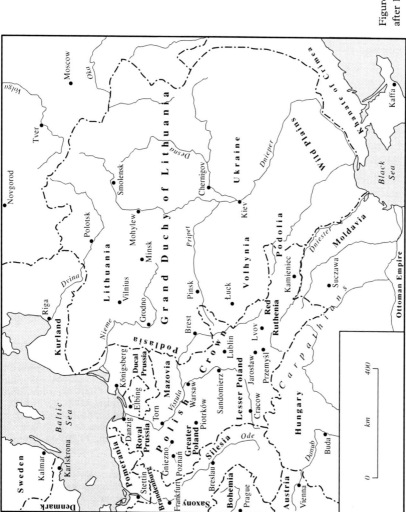

Figure 7.1 Poland and Lithuania after 1466

most other developed European regions which had densities exceeding 20–30 inhabitants/km². The contrast became sharper as one moved further to the east. Population in Red Ruthenia and in the Grand Duchy of Lithuania was even sparser (3–5 persons/km²), while the Ukrainian steppes, the so-called Wild Plains, were practically uninhabited.[2]

Nevertheless, we have deliberately drawn the comparison in the most flattering period for Poland, for during the late middle ages the erstwhile disparities between the Polish and western European economies narrowed.[3] Whereas after the mid-fourteenth century the West experienced economic disarray, Poland underwent a boom based upon demographic growth, internal colonisation, agricultural expansion and the growth of towns, crafts, trade and credit as witnessed by the diffusion of petty coinage for small-scale transactions.[4] Fourteenth-century Poland's external trading relations were also fundamentally transformed. The country was gradually drawn from a peripheral position into Europe's commercial mainstream, resulting in patterns of economic co-operation and specialisation.[5] Western Europe became Poland's main commercial partner. Foreign trade, which had had a transient character and had been restricted to luxury items, now began to influence home markets by stimulating local production and finding commercial outlets abroad. Both Poland and Lithuania supplied the west European commercial system with timber. From the second half of the fifteenth century they also exported cereals and oxen, in addition to other forestry products like ash, wax and honey. The newly developed mining industries in the Carpathians provided lead, silver and salt.

Connections between domestic and international markets were facilitated by Poland's favourable location in relation to the main centres of production and trade routes. After the annexation of Red Ruthenia (1340–87), Poland came to include much of Europe's Baltic–Pontic axis between Danzig and Kaffa and became part of the great east-central

---

[2] *Economic history of Poland in numbers* (Warsaw, 1994); H. Łowmiański, *Zaludnienie państwa litewskiego w wieku XVI* (Poznań, 1998).

[3] M. Małowist, 'The problem of the inequality of economic development in Europe in the later middle ages', *Economic History Review*, 2nd ser., 19 (1966), 15–28; H. Samsonowicz, 'Polska w gospodarce europejskiej XIV i XV wieku', in A. Gieysztor (ed.), *Polska dzielnicowa i zjednoczona. Państwo – społeczeństwo – kultura* (Warsaw, 1972), pp. 368–98.

[4] S. Trawkowski, 'Die Rolle der deutschen Dorfkolonisation und des deutsches Rechtes in Polen im 13. Jahrhundert', in W. Schlesinger (ed.), *Die deutsche Ostsiedlung des Mittelalters als Problem der europäischen Geschichte* (Sigmaringen, 1975), pp. 349–68; R. C. Hoffmann, *Land, liberties and lordship in a late medieval countryside. Agrarian structures and change in the duchy of Wrocław* (Philadelphia, 1989).

[5] M. Małowist, *Wschód a Zachód Europy w XIII–XVI wieku. Konfrontacja struktur społeczno-gospodarczych* (Warsaw, 1973); M. Małowist, 'Podziały gospodarcze i polityczne w Europie w średniowieczu i w dobie wczesnej nowożytności', *Przegląd Historyczny* 82 (1991), 233–44.

European and Levantine system of trade. In addition, the recapture of
Pomerania (1466) and of its main town, Danzig, gave Poland direct
access to the sea, which facilitated contacts between the vast basin of the
Vistula river and other economic zones. The Vistula, which was used to
float goods to Danzig and from there across the Baltic to foreign
destinations, became Poland's most important water-borne trade route,
in addition to older land routes leading from the east through Silesia and
Bohemia, or Saxony. These roads were used to transport cheap commodities for popular consumption.[6] In exchange for raw materials,
Poland imported high-value industrial goods, a pattern of trade that
over time would strongly affect its economic and social organisation.

Rather than following the traditional chronological divide between
medieval and early modern times, the period between the fourteenth
and sixteenth centuries when these changes first occurred and came to
fruition is best examined as a unit. It was a period that established
Poland's position in European politics and in its economy saw a
reorganisation of land ownership and the development of the manorial
economy, witnessed the crystallisation of the late feudal social order and
the nobility's political offensive, and established patterns of urban
development that remained in place until the nineteenth century.

Towns and the nobility

The Polish political system, often described as a democracy of nobles, in
fact gave the nobility a virtual monopoly on power.[7] Town burghers
played no part in public life; they had no access to public offices except
in local government. Only a few of the largest towns were represented in
the national parliament, the Seym, where, however, they had no right to
make laws. All decisions concerning towns were made by the nobility in
the Seym and in regional assemblies.

The monarchy, whose authority was undermined by its dependence
on competing groups of magnates and noblemen, was gradually deprived of real powers. During the sixteenth century the king pursued no
specific municipal policy, but he still maintained the right to grant

---

[6] H. Samsonowicz, 'Przemiany osi drożnych w Polsce późnego średniowiecza', *Przegląd
Historyczny* 64 (1973), 697–715.

[7] A. Wyczański, 'The problem of authority in sixteenth-century Poland: an essay in
reinterpretation', in J. K. Fedorowicz (ed.), *A republic of nobles. Studies in Polish history to
1864* (Cambridge, 1982), pp. 96–108; A. Mączak, 'The structure of power in the
Commonwealth of the sixteenth and seventeenth centuries', in ibidem, pp. 113–34;
A. Mączak, 'The space of power: Poland-Lithuania in the sixteenth and seventeenth
centuries', in W. Feldenkirchen et al. (eds.), *Wirtschaft – Gesellschaft – Unternehmen.
Festschrift für Hans Pohl zum 60. Geburtstag* (Stuttgart, 1995), pp. 633–40.

special privileges, new town foundations and new markets and fairs. By then, however, even these rights were devoid of much significance. In the duchy of Lithuania after 1588 a lord no longer needed to gain royal assent to found a new town, whose entire administration fell under his control. Although about one-third of the towns were formally part of the royal demesne, in practice they differed little from seigniorial towns, for either a nobleman or magnate took out a long-term, frequently hereditary, lease on them, or they were managed by royal officials who administered the towns like private property. The monarchy and towns were therefore never able to forge a strategic alliance within the Commonwealth against the nobility. The reason seems to have been the latter's peculiarly powerful position, which both controlled the state apparatus and the commanding heights of legislation and owned huge tracts of urban and rural property.

The nobility exploited their control over state offices and legislation ruthlessly to eliminate urban competition. The Seym began passing anti-municipal legislation as early as the fifteenth century by curbing the towns' fiscal autonomy, banning land ownership by townspeople, and fixing prices for craftsmen's products and labour. During the sixteenth century the law established further restrictions on the towns' domestic affairs, including a prohibition of active participation by Polish merchants in foreign trade (1565).[8] Although the law was seldom enforced, its very existence testifies to the legal and political hostility surrounding the Commonwealth towns.[9] But the nobility's most significant achievement was the complex bundle of rights over the valuable grain trade, which included exemption from customs, free navigation on rivers used for shipping goods, free trade on town markets, and price controls that set favourable terms of trade between farm produce and goods distributed by towns. The nobility also managed to obtain the right to brew beer on the manorial farm, thus depriving towns of this important consumer market in the countryside.

Under such circumstances the burghers could only take a subsidiary role. During the sixteenth century they became even more marginalised as landlords took a growing interest in manufacture and trade, as was indeed characteristic of much of east-central Europe at the

[8] J. Bieniarzówna, 'Proces organiczania autonomii miast małopolskich w pierwszej połowie XVI w.', *Małopolskie Studia Historyczne* 6 (1963), 53–73; A. Popioł-Szymańska, 'Problematyka handlowa w polityce "miejskiej" szlachty w Polsce centralnej w XV i XVI wieku', *Roczniki Dziejów Społecznych i Gospodarczych* 31 (1970), 45–83; A. Popioł-Szymańska, 'Poglądy szlachty i mieszczan na handel wewnętrzny w Polsce od końca XV wieku do połowy XVII wieku', *Roczniki Historyczne* 37 (1971), 39–83.
[9] M. Bogucka, 'Polish towns between the sixteenth and eighteenth centuries', in Fedorowicz, *A republic of nobles*, pp. 138–52.

time.[10] Statutes concerned specifically with seigniorial towns began to appear in the second half of the sixteenth century. They delegated a broad swathe of powers concerning judicial and religious matters – previously under the state's remit – to the noble and religious lords of the towns, which further weakened the ties between towns and the state.[11]

Under these conditions, the nobility's political, social and economic strategy regarding urban affairs might seem to be essential. Study of its attitudes towards towns fails, however, to reveal any coherent body of thought; rather, the nobility sought pragmatic solutions to everyday concerns. They tried to strike a balance between the tendency to levy heavy taxes on towns; fix low prices on domestic and imported industrial products; raise prices on farm products; eliminate all forms of urban monopoly such as craft guilds and staple rights, and their concern not to kill the goose that laid the golden eggs. The nobility's attitude towards urban affairs was not unconditionally negative, so long as their interests and profits were not under threat. They were perfectly aware of the link between urban prosperity and the success of their own farming activities. Quite simply, towns were to provide sources of income that could not be provided by the country. They were viewed as complementary rather than alternative to the farming economy.[12]

Urban foundations

The agrarian character of Poland and its social, economic and political domination by the nobility make it all the more surprising that the country should undergo an urban boom during the late middle ages and sixteenth century. The first forms of urbanisation in this part of Europe had begun as late as the ninth and tenth centuries, and they took on a new impetus and new legal and social forms during the thirteenth century under the influence of so-called German law (*ius theutonicum*). This was a set of liberties and customs imported from German-speaking lands to east-central Europe that ensured personal liberty, inheritance rights and judicial autonomy to town-dwellers along west European

[10] M. Małowist, 'Über die Frage der Handelspolitik des Adels in den Ostseeländern im 15. und 16. Jahrhundert', *Hansische Geschichtsblätter* 75 (1957), 29–47; H. Samsonowicz, 'War Jagiellonisches Ostmitteleuropa eine Wirtschaftseinheit?', *Acta Poloniae Historica* 41 (1980), 85–97.

[11] T. Opas, 'Miasta prywatne a Rzeczpospolita', *Kwartalnik Historyczny* 87 (1971), 28–47.

[12] A. Wyrobisz, 'Attitude of the Polish nobility towards towns in the first half of the 17th century', *Acta Poloniae Historica* 48 (1983), 77–94; A. Wyrobisz, 'Power and towns in the Polish gentry Commonwealth. The Polish Lithuanian state in the sixteenth and seventeenth centuries', *Theory and Society* 18 (1989), 611–30.

lines. The introduction of German law also witnessed the gradual introduction of forms of municipal government and institutions, craft and merchant guilds, and, more generally, a distinctly urban way of life.

German law was the only canon of urban organisation employed in late medieval and early modern times. Although during the first half of the thirteenth century there were attempts to find other ways of organising a town as a separate community, none of those alternatives was adopted, and the German law model continued to be used on the eastern peripheries of the Commonwealth as late as the eighteenth century. Until the political catastrophe of the late eighteenth century it served as the country's only form of urban government, regardless of status, size and function.

The political, social and economic reorganisation of an existing town or the foundation of a new one occurred on the basis of a royal charter or lease (*locatio*). From the thirteenth century towns were therefore defined as such by law, and we will follow this usage here. They had the rights to a variety of privileges and immunities and were termed *oppida* (boroughs) or *civitates* (cities) in the sources; they were thus legally, politically and socially distinct from the countryside. The foundation of a town consisted in measuring and marking out an area separate from the fields, after which the streets, building blocks, churches, public buildings, marketplaces and garden plots were drawn out. Most surviving town plans are geometrical and regular, suggesting that they were prepared before building began.[13] Town fortifications, which rarely consisted of stone walls and were most often simple earth ramparts, set the urban space clearly apart from the surrounding countryside.

After its beginnings in the thirteenth century, the phenomenon of new foundations intensified markedly during the fourteenth, fifteenth and sixteenth centuries,[14] abated during the seventeenth, only to revive for a

[13] B. Zientara, 'Socio-economic and spatial transformation of Polish towns during the period of location', *Acta Poloniae Historica* 34 (1976), 57–83.

[14] R. Roepell, 'Über die Verbreitung des Magdeburgischen Stadtrechtes im Gebiete des alten polnischen Reichs ostwärst der Weichsel', *Verhandlungen der Historisch-Philoso-phischen Gesellschaft in Breslau*, vol. I (Breslau, 1857); O. Lange, *Lokacja miast w Wielkopolsce właściwej na prawie niemieckim w wiekach średnich* (Lvov, 1925); S. Pazyra, *Geneza i rozwój miast mazowieckich* (Warsaw, 1959); Z. Kulejewska-Topolska, *Nowe lokacje miejskie w Wielkopolsce od XVI do końca XVIII wieku* (Poznań, 1964); S. Alexandrowicz, 'Powstanie i rozwój miast województwa podlaskiego (XV–XVII wieku)', *Acta Baltico-Slavica* 1 (1964), 137–56; W. Kuhn, 'Die deutschrechtlichen Stadtgründungen in Kleinpolen', in H. Stoob (ed.), *Die mittelalterliche Städtebildung im südöstlichen Europa* (Cologne, 1977), pp. 39–89; M. Horn, 'Miejski ruch osadniczy na Rusi Czerwonej do końca XV wieku', *Roczniki Dziejów Społecznych i Gospodarczych* 35 (1974), 49–74; M. Horn, 'Miejski ruch osadniczy na Rusi Czerwonej w latach 1501–1648', *Zeszyty Naukowe Wyższej Szkoły Pedagogicznej w Opolu, ser. A, Historia* 13 (1975), 29–36; H. Samsonowicz, 'Liczba i wielkość miast późnego średniowiecza Polski',

time during the second half of the eighteenth century. Polish pre-industrial towns were therefore almost exclusively products of the late medieval and early modern period. Within this period, over the duration of the three centuries and in each of the three main provinces of the Polish crown (Greater Poland, Lesser Poland and Red Ruthenia), a similar number of towns was founded. However, a more detailed analysis reveals interesting local differences, especially as far as the timing and intensity of new plantations in the different provinces are concerned.

The plantation movement can be described as a wave of innovations that moved from west to east and followed a common pattern of rise, climax and fall. It began in Silesia outside the crown, then moved to Prussia and to Lesser and Greater Poland, and then, after a delay of a century, to Mazovia. At an even later date it reached the eastern part of Lesser Poland and, finally, came to Western Rus'. The duchy of Lithuania also underwent an intense period of urbanisation, but there the climax was reached during the second half of the sixteenth and at the beginning of the seventeenth century.[15] Although the precise number of new towns in the duchy is hard to establish, according to some estimates the country achieved a total of about 920 towns.[16] Consequently, between the fourteenth and the first half of the seventeenth century there were altogether about 2,350–2,400 town plantations in the Commonwealth of the Two Nations including Ukraine, Podolia, Volhynia and Podlasia.

Kwartalnik Historyczny 86 (1979), 917–31; M. Biskup, 'Rozwój sieci miast pruskich do drugiej połowy XVII w.', *Kwartalnik Historii Kultury Materialnej* 28 (1980), 401–12; A. Berdecka, *Lokacje i zagospodarowanie miast królewskich w Małopolsce za Kazimierza Wielkiego (1333–1370)* (Wrocław, 1982); A. Berdecka, 'Lokacje miast małopolskich za Władysława Łokietka (1306–1333)', *Kwartalnik Historii Kultury Materialnej* 31 (1983), 335–44; W. Jarmolik, 'Rozwój niemieckiego prawa miejskiego na Podlasiu do unii lubelskiej 1569 roku', *Przegląd Historyczny* 73 (1982), 23–46; F. Kiryk, 'Z badań nad urbanizacją Lubelszczyzny w dobie jagiellońskiej', *Rocznik Naukowo-Dydaktyczny WSP w Krakowie* 43 (1972), 93–164; F. Kiryk, *Rozwój urbanizacji Małopolski XIII–XVI w. Województwo krakowskie* (Cracow, 1985); F. Kiryk, *Urbanizacja Małopolski. Województwo sandomierskie, XIII–XVI wiek* (Kielce, 1994); M. Bogucka, 'Le réseau urbain et les campagnes en Pologne (1500–1800)', *Storia della città* 36 (1986), 77–84; M. Bogucka and H. Samsonowicz, *Dzieje miast i mieszczaństwa w Polsce przedrozbiorowej* (Wrocław, 1986); R. Szczygieł, *Lokacje miast w Polsce XVI wieku* (Lublin, 1989); K. Kamińska, *Lokacje miast na prawie magdeburskim na ziemiach polskich do 1370 r.* (Toruń, 1990).

[15] J. Bardach, 'Miasta na prawie magdeburskim w Wielkim Księstwie Litewskim od schyłku XIV do połowy XVII stulecia', *Kwartalnik Historyczny* 87 (1980), 21–51.

[16] S. Alexandrowicz, 'Powstanie sieci miejskiej Podlasia na tle wczesnych procesów urbanizacyjnych w Wielkim Księstwie Litewskim', *Kwartalnik Historii Kultury Materialnej* 28 (1980), 413–28; A. Wyrobisz, 'Townships in the grand duchy of Lithuania during the agrarian and urban reform called "pomera na voloki" (2nd half of 16th–first half of 17th centuries)', in A. Mączak and C. Smout (eds.), *Gründung und Bedeutung kleinerer Städte im nördlichen Europa der frühen Neuzeit* (Wiesbaden, 1991), pp. 193–204.

Table 7.1. *Town foundations in the Polish Commonwealth, 1200–1650*

	1200–99	1300–99	1400–99	1500–99	1600–50	Total[a]
Greater Poland	64	94	95	13	8	274
Lesser Poland	35	81	58	59	18	251
Mazovia	3	36	43	31	1	114
Royal Prussia[b]	13	22	2	0	1	38
Red Ruthenia	0	38	96	153	38	325
Total[a]	115	271	294	256	66	1,002

Notes:
[a] Territory before 1569.
[b] Territory after 1466.

Urban networks

Despite its failures (towns that never took off, others that disappeared), the plantation movement established from scratch an urban network, or rather, urban networks – for the distribution of towns was regionally uneven between the crown provinces (Table 7.1). The fourteenth-century data show this very clearly. In Red Ruthenia, whose undeveloped system was built up over only a few decades, urban functions were probably still fulfilled by old towns that had yet to be reformed according to German law. Although Mazovia had a slightly more developed urban system, each town had to satisfy the needs of a huge territory. Regional differences were still apparent by about 1500 but there had also been a noticeable levelling off. The two regional extremes were then Greater Poland, which already had a fully developed town system, and the eastern regions of Mazovia, Red Ruthenia and part of Lesser Poland, where the plantation movement was still in progress. A century later the process of convergence had been completed. The average radius of the territory serviced by each town had dropped from 14 to 9 km, its area from 600 to 270 km^2, a decline of nearly 55 per cent. Perhaps more significantly, regional extremes had narrowed from a minimum of 11 and a maximum of 26 km in the fourteenth century to 8 and 10 km respectively in the sixteenth. The only significant exception was Royal Prussia, where there were virtually no new foundations after 1400, and which perhaps as a consequence also contained the largest towns in the country.[17]

[17] Calculations from data listed by Szczygieł, *Lokacje miast*; Horn, 'Miejski ruch osadniczy'; F. Kiryk, 'Lokacje miejskie nieudane, translacje miast i miasta zanikłe w Małopolsce do połowy XVII stulecia', *Kwartalnik Historii Kultury Materialnej* 28

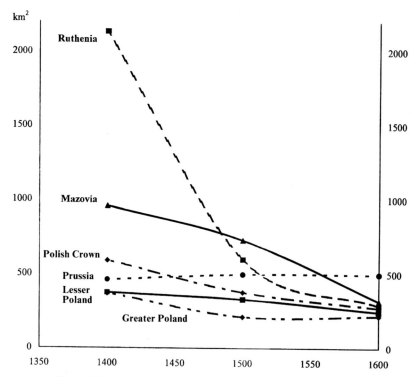

Figure 7.2 Average size of urban territory in the Polish Commonwealth, 1400–1600

The average radius of just over 9 km of the zone under town influence in the Polish crown at the end of the sixteenth century was only a little larger than a town mile, or a two-hour walk at the most.[18] While the high degree of urban concentration and ease of access implied by these figures fails to reflect more subtle regional differences, it also underestimates the degree of urban density by including uninhabited forests, swamps and mountains. For this reason also one should not consider such notional urban hinterlands as mutually exclusive; many rural settlements could be within the sphere of influence of several towns at the same time. As research on the territorial functions of medieval towns

(1980), 373–84; H. Samsonowicz, 'Gospodarka i społeczeństwo (XIII–początek XVI w.)', in A. Gieysztor and H. Samsonowicz (eds.), *Dzieje Mazowsza do 1526 roku* (Warsaw, 1994), pp. 271–6; J. Wiesiołowski, 'Le réseau urbain en Grand Pologne aux 13e–16e ss.', *Acta Poloniae Historica* 43 (1981), 5–29.

[18] W. Küchler, *Das Bannmeilenrecht. Ein Beitrag der mittelalterlichen Ostsiedlung zur wirtschaftlichen und rechtlichen Verschränkung von Stadt und Land* (Würzburg, 1964).

in Greater Poland has shown, the spheres of domination (*inland*), of direct influence (*hinterland*), and of indirect influence, made up an extremely complex structure of overlapping elements that was the basis for a changeable hierarchy of multi-functional towns.[19]

The system was by no means homogeneous. It is sufficient to compare Royal Prussia, the most urbanised province of the crown, in which between 27 and 37 per cent of the population lived in towns,[20] with the duchy of Lithuania, where, although towns were thicker on the ground, only about 14 per cent of the population was urbanised.[21] While differing significantly from other Polish provinces, conditions in Prussia were quite comparable with the more urbanised regions of western Europe like Flanders and the Rhineland. Three of the seven Polish towns with over 10,000 inhabitants at the end of the sixteenth century were situated in Prussia. They included Danzig, the main Polish emporium and largest Baltic port, which was easily the most populous town of the Commonwealth, with 40,000 inhabitants. The remaining four cities were Cracow, Lvov, Poznań and Warsaw, all of them provincial capitals.[22]

By the end of the sixteenth century only 12 per cent of Polish towns were medium-sized, defined as centres with a population between 2,000 and 10,000.[23] Small towns with fewer than 2,000 inhabitants made up the rest.[24] The vast majority of towns thus fell below the urban threshold of 2,000–5,000 established by west European scholars; several were comparable in size to large villages. The fact that burghers often engaged in farming also meant that they sometimes failed to meet the criterion of predominance of craft production and services over other functions. Yet, even though the Polish language has retained no special term for these semi- or quasi-urban settlements, with the exception of the diminutive 'small town' (*miasteczko*) – contemporaries used only two basic words: town (*miasto*) and country (*wieś*) – in Poland and east-

[19] J. Wiesiołowski, 'Miasto w przestrzeni społecznej późnego średniowiecza', in *Społeczeństwo Polski średniowiecznej* (Warsaw, 1985), vol. III, pp. 305–86.

[20] *Atlas historyczny Polski. Prusy Królewskie w drugiej połowie XVI w.* (Warsaw, 1961).

[21] Wyrobisz, 'Townships'; S. Alexandrowicz, 'Zaludnienie miasteczek Litwy i Białorusi w XVI i pierwszej połowie XVII wieku', *Roczniki Dziejów Społecznych i Gospodarczych* 27 (1965), 35–65; Alexandrowicz, 'Powstanie sieci'.

[22] M. Bogucka, 'Miasta Europy Środkowej w XIV–XVII w. Problemy rozwoju', *Roczniki Dziejów Społecznych i Gospodarczych* 42 (1981), 5–24; Bogucka and Samsonowicz, *Dzieje miast*.

[23] Bogucka and Samsonowicz, *Dzieje miast*.

[24] Alexandrowicz, 'Zaludnienie miasteczek'; M. Horn, 'Zaludnienie miast ziemi przemyskiej i sanockiej w drugiej połowie XVI i pierwszej połowie XVII wieku', *Roczniki Dziejów Społecznych i Gospodarczych* 31 (1970), 85–101.

central Europe as elsewhere these centres were clearly a distinctive form of non-rural settlement.[25]

One must nevertheless wonder what was the purpose of a phenomenon that produced settlements that were urban only in name, whose size and economic functions frequently failed to differentiate them from country villages. The movement was certainly not promoted by the old-established towns, which were customarily wary of any competitors that might challenge their functional monopolies, nor was it generally the result of any nationwide programme initiated by the monarchy. The main exception to this picture was Red Ruthenia, which had been practically untouched by German law until the region was incorporated into the crown in 1340–87. The dissemination thereafter of the new model of urbanisation was one aspect of the importation of west European institutions to the Byzantine and Russian worlds which triggered simultaneous political, social and economic reforms and was accompanied by strong internal colonisation and demographic growth.[26] In late medieval Ruthenia, by contrast with other parts of Poland, town plantations were promoted by the state, just as were western colonisation and the settlement of Polish nobility. Urban foundations during the second half of the fourteenth and the first half of the fifteenth century were part of a strategy to integrate the newly incorporated country into the Polish crown. They were also helped by favourable economic circumstances. By the sixteenth century, however, the former political and economic impetus no longer existed, but urban settlements continued, if anything with even greater impetus.[27] New foundations occurred at a time of devastating invasions by Wallachians, Tatars and Turks, in economically peripheral areas where no lasting relations with the countryside could be established.

Who, then, was so anxious to found towns in law though not necessarily in fact? And what were their motives? Founding a new town and ensuring its development was not an effortless or costless undertaking. It was an investment that needed both entrepreneurial flair and successful lobbying to gain a royal charter. It required drawing up a building and settlement plan and bringing it to fruition by attracting

---

[25] Z. Kulejewska-Topolska, 'Oznaczenia i klasyfikacje miast w dawnej Polsce (XVI–XVIII w.)', *Czasopismo Prawno-Historyczne* 8 (1956), 253–68.

[26] A. Janeczek, 'Miasta Rusi Czerwonej w nurcie modernizacji. Kontekst reform XIV–XVI w.', *Kwartalnik Historii Kultury Materialnej* 43 (1995), 55–66.

[27] A. Janeczek, *Osadnictwo pogranicza polsko-ruskiego. Województwo bełskie od schyłku XIV do początku XVII w.* (Warsaw, 1991); A. Janeczek, 'Settlement of Polish–Ruthenian borderland. County of Bełz from the late fourteenth century to the beginnings of the seventeenth century', in *Recent doctoral research in economic history. Proceedings, Eleventh International Economic History Congress* (Milan, 1994), pp. 19–27.

settlers with allowances and privileges, a process which could take a dozen or more years to complete. That it was a risky enterprise is confirmed by the fact that some towns, although granted the necessary charters, remained on paper, others were never finished, and others still, after initial success, proved in the longer run to be failures. Nevertheless, urban plantations proved attractive to a considerable number of land-owners, which included besides the nobility also the crown and the Catholic Church. As a rule, the state and religious landlords, especially monasteries, took the initiative in the earlier stages. The magnates and nobility followed, but with increasing enthusiasm, so that during the sixteenth century only 15 per cent of all new towns were founded on royal lands. The aristocracy's change of heart is closely connected with the early modern 'aristocratic offensive', which included the reorganisa-tion of landed estates, the colonisation of new land, and the introduction of serfdom in the manorial economy.[28]

Small towns

Although the small town was a feature of most pre-modern European societies, it was especially characteristic of urbanisation in Poland and on the periphery of western Europe.[29] The peculiarities of these regions consisted of a lack of ancient municipal traditions, delayed urbanisation, an imbalance between the small number of big towns and the large number of small ones, a relatively high density of centres with an urban charter and a low development of urban modes of life, strong links with the landlord or manorial economy, and low rates of urbanisation (between 20 and 25 per cent in late sixteenth-century Poland including the centres with fewer than 2,000 inhabitants). In sum, the legal status

[28] Szczygieł, *Lokacje miast*; A. Wyrobisz, 'Rola miast prywatnych w Polsce w XVI i XVII wieku', *Przegląd Historyczny* 65 (1974), 19–45; T. Lalik, 'La genèse du réseau urbain en Pologne médiévale', *Acta Poloniae Historica* 34 (1976), 97–120.

[29] See P. Clark (ed.), *Small towns in early modern Europe* (Cambridge, 1995); F.-E. Eliassen, 'The urbanisation of the periphery. Landowners and small towns in early modern Norway and northern Europe', *Acta Poloniae Historica* 70 (1994), 49–74. For Polish small towns see M. Bogucka, 'Miasta Europy'; M. Bogucka, 'The network and functions of small towns in Poland in early modern times (from the 16th to the first half of the 17th century)', in Mączak and Smout, *Gründung*, pp. 219–33; H. Samsonowicz, 'Die kleinen Städte im Zentraleuropa des Spätmittelalters. Versuch eines Modells', in ibidem, pp. 205–17; H. Samsonowicz, 'Soziale und wirtschaftliche Funktionen der Kleinstädte in Polen des 15. Jahrhunderts', *Jahrbuch für Geschichte des Feudalismus* 2 (1978), 191–205; A. Wyrobisz, 'Small towns in 16th and 17th-century Poland', *Acta Poloniae Historica* 34 (1976), 153–63; T. Lalik, 'Les fonctions des petites villes en Pologne au bas moyen âge', *Acta Poloniae Historica* 37 (1978), 5–28. For Lithuania see S. Alexandrowicz, 'Miasteczka Białorusi i Litwy jako ośrodki handlu w XVI i w 1 połowie XVII w.', *Rocznik Białostocki* 1 (1961), 63–127; Alexandrowicz, 'Zaludnienie miasteczek'; Wyrobisz, 'Townships'.

of small towns was not fully matched by their economic and social functions.

This imbalance between form and content was a characteristic feature of pre-modern Poland, especially in the sixteenth century.[30] We should not, however, treat it purely as a symptom of backwardness. On the contrary, the growth of small towns was a consequence of the general late medieval economic revival in the countryside, in colonisation, in population, and in the monetisation of the economy, which had stimulated this process of urbanisation. Independently of the landowners' initiatives, urbanisation was a response to rural demand for better and more efficient systems of urban production and distribution. The processing and distribution of farm products was perhaps the most important activity linking town and country conducted by the inhabitants of small towns.[31] Although town charters often provided the means to set the terms of trade with the countryside, increasing competition gradually undermined these powers, to the benefit of the peasantry.

Late medieval colonisation of new land and improvements in agricultural implements and techniques raised agricultural output. Living standards and diets improved and price volatility in the period preceding the new harvest declined.[32] As early as the fifteenth century, thus well before the heyday of the grain export market, cereals were traded nationwide to supply the developing towns with food and with the wherewithal to make alcoholic beverages, especially beer, which they sold on, together with other processed goods, to the countryside. The new local markets that arose formed the basis for economic co-operation with the country.

In the longer run, these positive developments would be partly counteracted by contemporary changes in agrarian structure. A typical feature of the Polish economy was the large manorial farm, which produced cereals and other crops and sometimes livestock, using servile labour or hired hands. From the fourteenth century onwards, such farms became more commonly established in response to growing local demand. During the sixteenth century a variant of the manorial demesne became popular among the nobility, either for growing cereals for foreign markets or for satisfying the landlord's own needs for food, livestock and processed goods.[33] The manorial system was consolidated by legal changes to the peasants' status, including the enforcement of

[30] Wyrobisz, 'Small towns'; Bogucka, 'The network'; Bogucka and Samsonowicz, *Dzieje miast.*

[31] Lalik, 'Les fonctions'.

[32] T. Lalik, 'Ze studiów nad rynkiem spożywczym w Polsce XVI wieku', *Kwartalnik Historii Kultury Materialnej* 24 (1976), 3–33.

[33] J. Topolski, 'The origins of the early modern manorial economy in Europe', in

seigniorial jurisdiction over subjects in 1518, and statutes imposing compulsory and unremunerated labour services on the lords' demesnes, passed in 1520.

The diffusion of the manorial system tended to reinforce the subsistence economy and to restrict trade between town and country. As it was, town burghers acted largely as intermediaries in the grain trade and as consumers of luxury or technologically advanced goods that demesne farms were unable to provide, but during the sixteenth century even the towns' role in the grain trade was curtailed. Manorial landlords attempted to bypass the town merchants by shipping their grain independently to the Baltic ports, where they dealt directly with the great Danzig wholesalers, who monopolised exports by advancing cash to their suppliers and acting as brokers for foreign commodities.[34] None of these developments helped to foster a sturdy commercial and manufacturing base in the towns.

Trade nevertheless did increase. Most of it was conducted during the weekly markets and fairs organised by virtually every town, no matter how small. Weekly markets served local trade, while fairs served regional exchanges.[35] Trade at markets could be activated through small-scale credit.[36] Fairs, which were frequented also by foreign merchants, were occasions not only for trading but also for negotiating future deliveries and settling old debts. Thus small towns served as intermediaries between large town merchants and rural producers and consumers, collecting rural surpluses to be redistributed further up in the urban hierarchy and gathering information for national and international traders.

Some strategically situated towns helped establish commercial relations between Lesser Poland and Hungary, Greater Poland and Germany, Red Ruthenia and the Levant and Pontic colonies, and Mazovia and Lithuania. Towns located along navigable rivers like the Vistula, or the Niemen and Dvina rivers in Lithuania, acted as staging and customs posts for the sixteenth-century trade through Danzig, Königsberg and Riga to western markets of timber, forestry products (ash, wax), grain and grain products (vodka), and hemp, linen, hops and

J. Pelenski (ed.), *State and society in Europe from the fifteenth to the eighteenth century* (Warsaw, 1985), pp. 219–29.

[34] M. Małowist, 'A certain trade technique in the Baltic countries in the 15th–17th centuries', in *Poland at the XIth International Congress of Historical Sciences in Stockholm* (Warsaw, 1960), pp. 103–16.

[35] S. Gierszewski, *Struktura gospodarcza i funkcje rynkowe mniejszych miast województwa pomorskiego w XVI i XVII w.* (Danzig, 1966).

[36] H. Samsonowicz, 'Local credit in mediaeval Poland', *Studia Historiae Oeconomicae* 21 (1994), 51–7.

soap. River transport was also used to ship salt, fish, wine, beer, fruit, spices, sugar, paper, cloth and other products inland.[37] Danzig's wealth and its dominant position in the Commonwealth was based on its unique function as the gateway between the national market and the external world.[38]

A characteristic feature of all small towns was their agrarianism. New towns were granted large allotments, half or more of the urban population consisted of burgher-farmers, and there were distinct ploughmen's confraternities (*contubernia agricolarum, fraternitas rusticorum*). Farming and animal breeding were a fundamental and sometimes dominant aspect of the Polish town economy. Nevertheless, the burghers' farms were too small to maintain their owners without their engaging in other occupations including crafts, retailing and other services. Towns were thus unlikely to produce agricultural surpluses for sale. As a rule the burghers' farms were run to feed the town and did not compete significantly with rural output in supplying the regional and foreign markets. On the other hand, urban farming did restrict demand for rural produce by the small towns and hence undercut exchange relations between town and country.[39]

Most artisan workshops were situated in the larger towns; luxury production could be found only there. These towns could have from a few hundred to a few thousand artisans, representing 70 to 200 or so crafts. The biggest production centre was Danzig with about 3,000 workshops, the others in Prussia being Thorn and Elbing. Among the larger manufacturing centres were Poznań and Gniezno in Greater Poland, Cracow (with about 700 workshops) in Lesser Poland, Warsaw (*c.*500) in Mazovia, Lvov, Przeworsk, Przemyśl and Jarosław in Russia, and Vilnius and Mohylew in Lithuania. Urban craftsmen worked outside the guilds within noble and church enclaves as well as in the suburbs. The organisation of production did not change much in the period we are concerned with, and followed the customary structure of a small workshop headed by a master employing a few journeymen and apprentices.

[37] Alexandrowicz, 'Miasteczka'.

[38] S. Mielczarski, *Rynek zbożowy na ziemiach polskich w drugiej połowie XVI i pierwszej połowie XVII wieku. Próba rejonizacji* (Danzig, 1962); J. M. Małecki, *Związki handlowe miast polskich z Gdańskiem w XVI i pierwszej połowie XVII wieku* (Wrocław, 1968); M. Bogucka, 'Danzig's Bedeutung für die Wirtschaft des Ostseeraumes in der frühen Neuzeit', *Studia Historiae Oeconomicae* 9 (1974), 95–106.

[39] A. Wyrobisz, 'Functional types of Polish towns in the XVIth–XVIIth centuries', *Journal of European Economic History* 12 (1983), 69–103; J. Ochmański, 'W kwestii agrarnego charakteru miast Wielkiego Księstwa Litewskiego w XVI wieku', in *Studia historica. W 35-lecie pracy naukowej Henryka Łowmiańskiego* (Warsaw, 1958), pp. 279–94.

Craftsmanship in the smaller towns was mainly orientated to the needs of the manorial economy, although there were exceptions to the rule.[40] The pottery, cloth and leather from some small towns was distributed nationwide and acquired a good reputation. Fewer still specialised in activities such as mining.[41] The role of small towns obviously differed from that of the larger towns – Danzig, Cracow, Poznań, Lvov, Lublin, Vilnius and Warsaw, which all happened to be provincial capitals and which acted as centres for manufacture, finance and regional and long-distance trade[42] – and was reflected in the extent of their marketing range. The credit market of Poznań had a radius of 50 to 80 km (for a total area of 8,000–20,000 km^2), while the market of another major centre, Cracow, extended 100–200 km. The main commodities were metals and salt (Lesser Poland), wool (Greater Poland), grain, timber and forest products (Mazovia), cattle, fish and salt (Russia) and furs, leather and forest products (Lithuania). Lesser Poland and Mazovia also traded extensively in grain. As with foreign trade, inter-regional exchange mainly occurred at periodic fairs, the most important of which were held at Poznań, Gniezno, Lublin, Cracow, Sandomierz, Lvov, Jarosław, Torn, Warsaw, Brest, Mohylew, Łuck and Grodno. The growth of inter-regional exchange during the fifteenth and sixteenth centuries set in motion the creation of three large integrated markets, based on cereals in central Poland, forest products in Lithuania and livestock breeding in Ukraine, which, however, only became fully formed during the eighteenth century. A leading role in these developments was played by the nobility and by the city of Danzig, which, although situated at the fringes of these trading systems, constituted the main commercial centre.

By contrast, the sphere of influence of medium-sized towns extended over 1,500 or 2,000 km^2, and that of a small town included just a few hundred square kilometres, no more than a manor's or parish's boundaries.[43] But small towns had other functions besides the economic ones

[40] Wyrobisz, 'Functional types'.
[41] D. Molenda, 'Mining towns in central eastern Europe in feudal times', *Acta Poloniae Historica* 34 (1976), 165–88.
[42] S. Kutrzeba, *Handel Krakowa w wiekach średnich na tle stosunków handlowych Polski* (Cracow, 1903); J. Małecki, *Studia nad rynkiem regionalnym Krakowa w XVI wieku* (Warsaw, 1963); F. W. Carter, *Trade and urban development in Poland. An economic geography of Cracow, from its origins to 1795* (Cambridge, 1994); L. Koczy, *Handel Poznania do połowy wieku XVI* (Poznań, 1930); Ł. Charewiczowa, *Handel średniowiecznego Lwowa* (Lvov, 1925); H. Samsonowicz, 'Handel Lublina na przełomie XV i XVI w.', *Przegląd Historyczny* 59 (1968), 612–27; H. Samsonowicz, 'Warszawa w handlu średniowiecznym', in *Warszawa średniowieczna* (Warsaw, 1975), vol. II, pp. 9–31.
[43] Małecki, *Studia*; H. Samsonowicz, 'Beziehungen zwischen den polnischen Kleinstädten und ihrem Hinterland im 15. Jahrhundert', *Hansische Studien* (Weimar, 1979), vol. IV, pp. 118–26; Wiesiołowski, 'Miasto'.

we have dwelt upon, and it is largely these which explain the nobility's willingness to build new towns despite frequently unfavourable economic conditions. The basic and original function fulfilled by new towns was administrative. All seigniorial towns administered their lords' lands, and royal towns did the same with regard to local government units. The royal towns were a component of the official administration and served as local centres of legal jurisdiction and of self-rule by the nobility. Some of them were directly connected with the central authorities either as official royal residences – Cracow up to the end of the sixteenth century – or as meeting places for the Seym (Piotrków) and for the royal election or coronation.

The link between town and manor implied other functions. The town could become a residence for magnate, nobleman, or bishop, an ancestral home used to establish its owner's reputation, or a military stronghold, especially in the eastern lands of the Commonwealth under persistent nomad threat. It could also be the religious centre of the parish, which usually coincided with the territory of the estate. In the eastern Commonwealth the Catholic parishes, which appeared together with the newly founded towns, coexisted with other religious institutions: Eastern Orthodox churches, Jewish synagogues, sometimes Protestant chapels, or Armenian and Karaitic temples. The presence of religious institutions involved the administration of schools and the establishment and running of religious fraternities.[44]

'Excess' foundations and economic crisis

During the sixteenth century the number of new towns began to exceed the needs of local markets. This was all the more the case because during the same period the proportion of peasants participating in the commodity markets was decreasing. It was common practice to found new seigniorial towns without taking account of the proximity of other settlements and of the need to provide them with a sufficiently large hinterland to supply. But although as a rule only one of two competing centres would survive, the nobility's actions were far from irrational. New towns were located along important trade routes, in the vicinity of river ports, at river crossings, in the middle of landed estates, and in parish centres, all locations with central place functions.[45] Weekly markets and fairs were timed according to events in neighbouring towns

---

[44] Wyrobisz, 'Small towns'; Wyrobisz, 'Functional types'; Wyrobisz, 'Rola miast'; Wyrobisz, 'Townships'.
[45] A. Wyrobisz, 'Polityka Firlejów wobec miast w XVI wieku i założenie Janowca nad Wisłą', *Przegląd Historyczny* 61 (1970), 577–608.

in order either to draw trade away from there or to avoid unnecessary competition.[46] The goal of such foundations was to control local exchange as a source of revenue from stall rents, market fees, tolls and duties, but more especially, to ensure the efficient exchange of manorial produce for imported commodities to improve the profitability of their lands. Paradoxically, therefore, the process of urbanisation in this period was associated with the great landowners' objective to make their estates increasingly self-sufficient. It thus portended the turn of events from the early seventeenth century.

Economic growth in east-central Europe came to an end during the late sixteenth and the first half of the seventeenth century. Poland, Lithuania, Hungary, Bohemia and the Baltic countries experienced economic contraction and the refeudalisation of society. Their economies took on peripheral or quasi-colonial features characterised by specialisation in grain monoculture and the exploitation of natural resources, the use of compulsory (serf) labour, the domination of foreign over domestic trade, an increase in barter and rents paid in kind, a decline in rural demand for urban products, and the expenditure of feudal profits from the export trade on imported luxury goods rather than capital investments. Thus the boom in international trade and the return to an archaic social structure resulted in neo-serfdom and in a related, backward economy.[47] The increased dues imposed on peasants at the end of the sixteenth century led to their pauperisation, which strained market relations. The manorial system lost its efficiency.

Poland's new role in the European market and social involution led to a crisis in the towns. Although urban difficulties had been to some extent anticipated during the sixteenth century, urban decline intensified in the seventeenth and eighteenth centuries as the elements outlined at the beginning of this chapter – customs privileges for the nobility, preferential treatment given to foreign industrial products, price-fixing in favour of manorial industry and trade, and the burghers' inability to take concerted action in self-defence – took increasing effect.

The rise of the manorial serf-based economy and the nobility's policy against towns weakened demand for urban manufactures, eliminated the burghers from the grain market, and concentrated craft production in the villages.[48] The depression was aggravated by the seventeenth-

---

[46] H. Samsonowicz, 'Jarmarki w Polsce na tle sytuacji gospodarczej w Europie w XV–XVI wieku', in *Europa – Słowiańszczyzna – Polska* (Poznań, 1970), pp. 523–32.

[47] J. Topolski, 'La réféodalisation dans l'économie des grands domains en Europe centrale et orientale (XV–XVIIᵉ siècles)', *Studia Historiae Oeconomicae* 6 (1971), 51–63; A. Kamiński, 'Neo-serfdom in Poland-Lithuania', *Slavic Review* 34 (1975), 253–68.

[48] M. Bogucka, 'The towns of east-central Europe from the XIVth to the XVIIth century', in Mączak, Samsonowicz and Burke, *East-central Europe*, pp. 109–27.

century wars which saw the ruin of many towns. Physical destruction, suppression of urban activity, decline of craftsmanship, disappearance of investment capital, and a general ruralisation went hand in hand with legal and political discrimination, anti-urban violence by nobility and clergy, and a deliberate policy of depreciation of the burgher's social status. Where the nobility assumed control, relations between the burghers and the state were eventually severed.

Polish towns failed to serve as islands of capitalist modernisation in the feudal sea. Urban capital fled the towns to be invested in land. Successful townsmen aspired to living in the countryside like great landowners and parroted the nobility's ideals. In contrast, the nobility became increasingly attracted by town life and functions and moved into the urban environment. The broader the range of economic, judiciary, representative, educational and religious functions offered by a town, the more attractive it seemed. The nobility bought urban property on a large scale which was excluded from the town's jurisdiction, thereby diminishing burgher ownership and violating the town's former integrity and separateness, but also strengthening the cultural victory of the feudal way of life.[49]

[49] J. Wiesiołowski, 'The nobility in town. Movements and migration of the nobility between the village and town in Poland during the 15th century', in A. Gąsiorowski (ed.), *The Polish nobility in the middle ages* (Wrocław, 1984), pp. 255–96; M. Bogucka, 'L'attrait de la culture nobiliare? Sarmatisation de la bourgeoise polonaise au XVIIe s.', *Acta Poloniae Historica* 33 (1976), 23–42.

8   Town and country in the Austrian and Czech lands, 1450–1800

Markus Cerman and Herbert Knittler

Introduction

Town–country relations in the Austrian and Czech lands offer a study in contrasts. Urban densities in most regions were high, but towns were on the whole rather small. The legal status of towns was of the utmost importance. Princely towns usually enjoyed a set of privileges *vis-à-vis* the countryside, which they tried to defend against the growing competition of feudal towns and markets. Political and jurisdictional differences mattered. They determined not only the absolute and relative levels of taxation across towns and between town and country, but also the towns' powers over the countryside, including their marketing rights and industrial monopolies, the extent of commercial integration within and between regions, and the central state's ability to negotiate reductions in local privileges. This chapter therefore focuses on the economic consequences of political and institutional relations between towns, feudal lords and the central state from a regional perspective under three headings.

After an introductory section describing urban size and networks in the area, the first main part discusses the long-term characteristics of town–country relations in the context of the struggle between feudal lords and the expansionary state, in which town and countryside participated as secondary actors. The second section examines the long period of demographic and economic expansion between the late medieval and seventeenth-century crises. The most salient feature of the period was the growth of industrial activities, particularly in the textile and mining sectors, in which both town and country played active roles. Town–country conflicts over the distribution of the spoils of industry, though always present, intensified sharply during the seventeenth-century downturn, the topic of the third section. Towns and feudal lords responded to economic crisis by intensifying rent-seeking activities, attempting to divert or raise taxes on trade, and enforcing industrial monopolies; increasing conflict between princely and feudal towns

Figure 8.1   Styria, Upper and Lower Austria, and the Bohemian lands in the early modern period

caused regional trade to dry up and produced urban stagnation or decline in Austria. The major beneficiary of the crisis in demographic terms was Vienna, which reinforced its status as imperial capital. On the positive side, the seventeenth-century crisis weakened the 'traditional' urban and feudal sectors. Rural proto-industries helped further to undermine regulations favouring town crafts. Towns, however, could participate in industrial expansion if they adapted to innovations in production and distribution, such as the woolen industry in the Czech lands and silk weaving in Vienna.

Table 8.1. *Population distribution of Austrian towns, end of the sixteenth to end of the eighteenth century*

	Lower Austria		Upper Austria		Styria	
	1600	1800	1600	1800	1600	1800
20,000 +	1[a]	1[a]	–	–	–	1[b]
5,000–20,000	–	1[c]	1[d]	2[e]	1[b]	–
2,000–5,000	6	8	4	3	–	3
1,000–2,000	6	13	2	4	4	8
<1,000	22	12	4	3	16	8
Total	35	35	11	12	21	20

Notes: Upper Austria does not include Braunau and Schärding; Styria (1800) does not include Schladming.
[a]Vienna   [b] Graz   [c] Wiener Neustadt   [d] Steyr   [e] Linz, Steyr
Source: Sandgruber, *Ökonomie*, p. 107.

Urban size and networks

Austria and Styria

On the common definition of towns as centres with a minimum number of 5,000 to 10,000 inhabitants, the area which is now Austria would appear to be nearly entirely lacking in urban centres for much of the period under consideration.[1] This applies both to the eastern lands of Upper and Lower Austria and Styria, which shared many other structural features, and to Tyrol, Carinthia and the episcopate of Salzburg, which have been excluded from this study because they display quite different institutional characteristics.

Small towns dominated Austria's urban landscape throughout the early modern period (Table 8.1). Although there are few reliable data on urban populations in the Austrian territories, we can estimate that in Lower Austria the number of towns with over 2,000 inhabitants increased from only seven to ten between the sixteenth and the eighteenth century. The pronounced growth of Vienna from the seventeenth

[1] For definitions of the urban threshold, see J. de Vries, *European urbanization* (Cambridge, MA, 1984), p. 58; P. Bairoch, J. Batou and P. Chèvre, *La Population des villes européennes* (Geneva, 1988), p. 255. See also P. M. Hohenberg and L. H. Lees, *The making of urban Europe, 1000–1950* (Cambridge, MA–London, 1985); V. Bácskai, 'Small towns in eastern central Europe', in P. Clark (ed.), *Small towns in early modern Europe* (Cambridge, 1995), pp. 77–89. For Austrian urbanisation, see K. Klein, *Daten zur Siedlungsgeschichte der österreichischen Länder bis zum 16. Jahrhundert* (Vienna, 1980); M. Straka, *Verwaltungsgrenzen und Bevölkerungsentwicklung in der Steiermark 1770–1850* (Graz, 1978), Table I, pp. 95–319; R. Sandgruber, *Ökonomie und Politik. Österreichische Wirtschaftsgeschichte vom Mittelalter bis zur Gegenwart* (Vienna, 1995), p. 107.

century exhausted the country's potential for demographic growth, even though its development as the capital of the Habsburg Empire corresponded to a pattern of growth common to national capitals across western and southern Europe, from London to Naples, from Madrid to Berlin.[2] *Mutatis mutandis*, even the comparatively small Graz benefited strongly from being a major administrative centre in the province of Styria, with its population growing fivefold between the sixteenth century and 1800. Although Upper Austria featured bycontrast a poly-nuclear network of towns, Linz also gained considerably from becoming the provincial capital in 1490, and in the longer run it even overtook the economically more dynamic Steyr, which as the production and commercial centre of the iron industry stagnated after the crisis of the seventeenth century. In 1800, Linz was clearly the leading town with 19,000 inhabitants (Steyr had only 8,000); a few decades before, in 1754, Linz had been assigned 40 per cent of the tax quota of Upper Austrian towns, Steyr only 22 per cent.[3]

To state, however, that at the outset of the early modern period in the three Austrian provinces the proportion of inhabitants in towns with over 2,000 inhabitants was 19 per cent and had risen to only 29 per cent by 1800 does not adequately characterise the region's urban landscape, for it ignores the considerable grey area between town and country which from high medieval times had become increasingly populated by quasi-urban market settlements and market townships. These settlements included both minor towns (*Minderstädte*) as well as urban foundations that never developed into proper towns.[4] Such foundations were aspiring central places under noble or ecclesiastical rule that proliferated particularly during the fifteenth century following a process of jurisdictional fragmentation. Between the sixteenth and eighteenth centuries the number of these market centres increased from *c.*62–72 to 94 in Upper Austria, from 86 to 98 in Styria and from 157 to 210 in

---

[2] F. Baltzarek, 'Das territoriale und bevölkerungsmäßige Wachstum der Großstadt Wien im 17., 18. und 19. Jahrhundert', *Wiener Geschichtsblätter* 35 (1980), 1–30; P. Clark and B. Lepetit (eds.), *Capital cities and their hinterlands in early modern Europe* (Aldershot, 1996), p. 1.

[3] B. Hackl, 'Die Rektifikation des Vierten Standes', unpublished MS, University of Vienna 1998, p. 36; data for Styria in F. Mensi, *Geschichte der direkten Steuern in Steiermark bis zum Regierungsantritte Maria Theresias*, 3 vols. (Graz–Vienna, 1921), vol. III, pp. 76–81, Table IV A.

[4] H. Stoob, 'Minderstädte. Formen der Stadtentstehung im Spätmittelalter', *Vierteljahrschrift für Sozial- und Wirtschaftsgeschichte* 46 (1959), 1–28. For the Czech lands, see J. Kejř, 'Městské zřízení v českém státě ve 13. století', *Československý časopis historický* 27 (1979), 226–52; J. Kejř, 'Trhy a trhové vsi v Čechách a na Moravě', *Právněhistorické studie* 28 (1987), 9–44.

Lower Austria.[5] In Lower Austria, the size of these settlements towards 1600 ranged from just a few houses (Edlitz had only 9) to several hundred (Langenlois counted 330), corresponding to populations between 50 and 2,000 inhabitants. Their existence casts doubt on drawing a purely demographic demarcation between town and country in the Austrian lands; a more plausible definition must take account of a centre's economic functions and legal status.

The Czech lands

Relations between town and country in the Czech lands – here defined within their pre-1635 borders in the case of Upper Lusatia and within their pre-1740 borders in the case of Silesia – differed across the main territories of Bohemia, Moravia, Silesia and Upper Lusatia.[6] Bohemia and Moravia had a network of privileged royal towns (35 in Bohemia and 6 in Moravia), but the total number of settlements equipped with town or market rights was much larger, amounting to about 700 towns and townships of different kinds and sizes. Nevertheless, despite the significant number of partly privileged towns, only 10 to 12 of these had more than 5,000 inhabitants by 1500, and only one, Prague, was considerably larger than this.[7] Urban distribution was very similar in Silesia, with Wrocław accounting for about 20,000 inhabitants by 1500 and only a few more urban centres having anything close to 5,000 residents. In Upper Lusatia, Görlitz and Zittau were the largest; a few other towns hovered around the 5,000 mark towards 1500. Thus, barely six cities in the Czech lands numbered more than 10,000 inhabitants at the dawn of the early modern period. The entire Habsburg monarchy

---

[5] H. Knittler, 'Österreichs Städte in der frühen Neuzeit', in E. Zöllner (ed.), *Österreichs Städte und Märkte in ihrer Geschichte* (Vienna, 1985), p. 47.

[6] The period between the twelfth and the fourteenth century witnessed the formation of the urban network in this area. See K. H. Blaschke, 'Städte und Stadtherren im meissnisch-lausitzischen Raum während des 14. Jahrhunderts', in W. Rausch (ed.), *Stadt und Stadtherr im 14. Jahrhundert* (Linz, 1972), pp. 55ff.; *Dějiny obyvatelstva českých zemí* (Prague, 1996), pp. 49ff., 68ff.; J. Janáček, 'Die Städte in den böhmischen Ländern im 16. Jahrhundert', in W. Rausch (ed.), *Die Stadt an der Schwelle zur Neuzeit* (Linz, 1980), pp. 293–310; F. Kavka, 'Die Städte Böhmens und Mährens zur Zeit des Přemysliden-Staates', in W. Rausch (ed.), *Die Städte Mitteleuropas im 12. und 13. Jahrhundert* (Linz, 1963), pp. 137–53; J. J. Menzel, 'Die schlesischen Städte am Ausgang des Mittelalters', in W. Rausch (ed.), *Die Stadt am Ausgang des Mittelalters* (Linz, 1974), pp. 258f.; Bácskai, 'Small towns', p. 81.

[7] J. Macek, *Jagellonský věk v českých zemích (1471–1526)*, 4 vols. (Prague, 1992–99), vol. III, pp. 19ff., estimates that there were about 400 settlements with town and market privileges in Bohemia alone at the beginning of the sixteenth century. See more generally Bácskai, 'Small towns', p. 77, and M. Bogucka, 'The towns of east-central Europe from the fourteenth to the seventeenth century', in A. Maczak, H. Samsonowicz and P. Burke (eds.), *East-central Europe in transition* (Cambridge, 1985), pp. 97–108.

Table 8.2. *Town size in the Austrian and Czech lands, c.1500–1750 (in thousands)*

	1500	1600	1750
Austria/Styria			
Graz	6	8	20
Krems	–	4	4
Linz	2.5	3	10
Steyr	6	9	7
Wr. Neustadt	7	3.5	4.5
Vienna	20	50	175
Bohemia			
Cheb	5	7–8	–
Kutná Hora	5	4	12[a]
Prague	30	60	59
Moravia			
Brno	4–5	5	15
Olomouc	5–8	6–8	9[b]
Silesia			
Jelenia Góra	–	3	6
Legnica	2	8	6
Świdnica	–	6–11	7
Wrocław	20	30–40	55
Upper Lusatia			
Bautzen	5	5	8
Görlitz	9	10	11
Lubań	–	–	7
Zittau	5	6	7–8

Notes: [a]1700.   [b]1800.
Sources: Bairoch et al., *Population*; K. Blaschke, *Bevölkerungsgeschichte von Sachsen* (Weimar, 1967), pp. 138ff. de Vries, *European urbanization*; Bogucka, 'Towns'; *Dějiny obyvatelstva*; Dugoborski et al., *Dzieje Wrocławia*; Hroch and Petráň, 'Länder'; Jančárek, 'Populáční vývoj'; Macek, *Jagellonský věk*, p. 27; Sandgruber, *Ökonomie*, p. 107.

including the Hungarian lands (but excluding Upper Lusatia and Silesia) counted no more than eight cities over 10,000 and only ten over 5,000 in the same years.[8]

By eastern European standards, however, the urban population in the Czech lands was large and the urban network was reasonably dense. During the sixteenth century the rate of urbanisation – that is, the proportion of the population living in chartered towns – was at least 25

---

[8] de Vries, *European urbanization*, pp. 273ff.; Bácskai, 'Small towns', p. 79; Bairoch et al., *Population*.

per cent in Bohemia and 20 per cent in Moravia.[9] The political and economic status of towns was strongest in the margraviate of Upper Lusatia, where the six princely towns were closely linked in a league (*Sechsstädtebund*) formed during the later middle ages to protect themselves against the feudal and ecclesiastical estates. Of these, Görlitz and Zittau were important trade and industrial centres, and all had held important jurisdictional rights (*Hochgericht*) over large territories since the thirteenth century.[10]

Between 1210 and 1300, 131 new towns were founded in Silesia and were equipped with *ius theutonicum* (German law); 104 of these foundations originated with the territorial princes.[11] Some of the approximately 20 capital towns of the various duchies in Lower Silesia were important trading centres, such as Świdnica and Jawor, and the capital of Silesia, Wrocław, played an outstanding role in west European trade with Poland and the east. Compared to other east-central and east European territories, Silesia had a high density of smaller towns, most of which possessed territorial rights and were equipped with market and jurisdictional privileges that made them independent of feudal lords.[12]

Town and country: jurisdictional aspects

Taxation and the state

Austrian and Czech towns were central places equipped with minimal administrative and economic functions,[13] which could compete outside

---

9   A. Míka, 'Počet obyvatelstva zvláště městského v českých zemích před třicetiletou válkou', *Demografie* 14 (1972), 193–202. de Vries estimates a share of urban population of 2 per cent in the Habsburg lands by 1600, with a European average of 8.2 per cent and an eastern European average of 1.4 per cent (*Urbanisation*, p. 39). In 1700 about 30 per cent of all taxable houses in Bohemia were situated in towns.

10   Blaschke, 'Städte', pp. 65–8.

11   Menzel, 'Schlesische Städte', p. 253; H. Weczerka, 'Entwicklungslinien der schlesischen Städte im 17. und 18. Jahrhundert', in W. Rausch (ed.), *Die Städte Mitteleuropas im 17. und 18. Jahrhundert* (Linz, 1981), pp. 119–42. The term 'German law' refers to a set of favourable settlement laws which applied to the territories of east-central Europe.

12   H. Aubin, 'Die Wirtschaft im Mittelalter', in H. Aubin, L. Petry and H. Schlesinger (eds.), *Geschichte Schlesiens*, 2 vols. (Stuttgart, 1961), vol. I, pp. 401–83; W. Długoborski, J. Gierowski and K. Maleczyński, *Dzieje Wrocławia do roku 1807* (Warsaw, 1958), pp. 88ff., 210ff.; L. Petry, 'Breslau in der schlesischen Städtelandschaft des 16. Jahrhunderts', in Rausch, *Die Stadt an der Schwelle*, pp. 259–74; H. Loesch, 'Die schlesische Weichbildverfassung der Kolonisationszeit', *Zeitschrift der Savigny-Stiftung für Rechtsgeschichte, Germ. Abt.* 58 (1938), 311–36; Menzel, 'Schlesische Städte', pp. 254ff.; Weczerka, 'Entwicklungslinien', p. 126.

13   M. Mitterauer, 'Das Problem der zentralen Orte als sozial- und wirtschaftshistorische Forschungsaufgabe', *Vierteljahrschrift für Sozial- und Wirtschaftsgeschichte* 58 (1971), 433–67.

their immediate boundaries (*Stadtgemarkung* or *Burgfried*) with a land-lord estate or a territorial or jurisdictional court district (*Amt* or *Gericht*). The majority of the bigger Austrian towns had 'territorial' status, that is, they came under the direct authority of the territorial prince and exercised limited autonomy. To claim commercial and industrial privileges, they had to gain the political and legal support of the prince and of his territorial administrators, whose task it was to protect the territorial towns' prerogatives against landlords and jurisdic-tional lords (*Gerichtsherren*). That, for example, was the purpose of Maximilian I's letter to the governor of Upper Austria in 1496, in which he ordered him to publicly ban trade at unchartered rural markets and fairs and to force peasants to sell their produce on the towns' official weekly markets, an order that was frequently repeated during the sixteenth century.[14]

The legal distinction between towns privileged by the territorial prince (*landesfürstliche Städte*) and feudal, tributary or subject towns ruled by a feudal lord (*untertänige Städte*) also had economic impli-cations. In the Austrian lands, the political and jurisdictional influence of noble or ecclesiastical lords was limited to their estates, which were mostly rather small geographical entities, whereas the influence of the prince extended to the whole territory. In theory, therefore, the privi-leges of princely towns could be very far-reaching, but in reality the competitive co-existence of several princely towns resulted in individual towns gaining only very small urban franchises (*Bannbezirke*), and these constraints applied also to the kinds of jurisdictional rights exerted by chartered towns over their hinterland.[15]

The distinction between princely and feudal or subject towns was also important in the Czech lands. Royal and princely towns were generally equipped with charters by the territorial prince that conveyed quasi-independent status, market franchises and sometimes more extensive trading privileges, and jurisdictional powers over their hinterlands (that often included neighbouring secular or spiritual domains) and com-prised rights of high justice (*Hochgericht*). This arrangement derived from the traditional role of castle centres in early and high medieval Bohemia, many of which grew subsequently into royal towns.[16] By

---

[14] A. Hoffmann, *Wirtschaftsgeschichte des Landes Oberösterreich* (Salzburg, 1952), vol. I, p. 156.

[15] H. Fischer, *Burgbezirk und Stadtgebiet im deutschen Süden* (Vienna–Munich, 1954), pp. 50–65.

[16] See J. Žemlička, 'Přemyslovská hradská centra a počátky měst v Čechách', *Českoslo-venský časopis historický* 26 (1978), 559–86; J. Huth, 'Siedlungsgeschichtliche Grund-lagen und Voraussetzungen für die Stadtwerdung von Görlitz und Löbau', *Lětopis*, ser. B, 18 (1971), 189–220; Kavka, 'Die Städte'; J. Kejř, 'Organisation und Verwaltung des

contrast with royal and princely towns, the position of feudal or subject towns was considerably weaker; their inhabitants were feudal subjects who had to pay feudal dues and the town council had only limited rights and jurisdictional powers.[17]

Similar contrasts arose in Austria with the early modern growth of a 'tax state'. Since feudal market settlements were not included in rural tax obligations, they enjoyed considerable fiscal advantages over their urban competitors. Chartered towns responded by trying to integrate market settlements into the tax quotas of the feudal estates. The strategy was particularly successful in Styria, where in 1537 the majority of privileged markets lost their special status and had their tax dues brought into line with those of privileged towns.[18] In Upper Austria, on the other hand, the equal taxation of towns and market settlements lasted for only a brief period around 1500, whereas in Lower Austria the number of chartered towns with a higher tax charge decreased because they were mortgaged to feudal lords to pay for the territorial prince's fiscal needs.[19] By and large, the conflict over modes of taxation was won by the feudal aristocracy, particularly because the contemporaneous push by the noble estates into provincial government allowed them to undermine traditional town privileges further from within the state apparatus.

Initially, therefore, the estates rather than the prince set the para-meters for the development of the state and for the role of the towns within it. This victory is most apparent in Upper Austria, where during the later middle ages the princely towns had joined in a coalition with shared privileges and clearly defined objectives.[20] As late as 1510, the towns successfully lobbied for a princely ban on all competing trade in the countryside. However, the estates were able to reduce the ban's

königlichen Städtewesens in Böhmen zur Zeit der Luxemburger', in W. Rausch (ed.), *Stadt und Stadtherr im 14. Jahrhundert* (Linz, 1972), pp. 79–90; Macek, *Jagellonský věk*, pp. 30ff. On constitutional issues in Czech towns, including the widely used Magde-burg law codes, see Kejř, 'Zřízení'. More generally, see F. Hoffmann, *České město ve středověku* (Prague, 1989), pp. 247ff.

[17] On medieval and early modern 'subject' towns, see Macek, *Jagellonský věk*, pp. 66ff.; R. Nový, 'Poddanská města a městečka v předhusitských Čechách', *Československý časopis historický* 21 (1973), 73–109. Revenues from subject towns formed the main income from the large complex of domains owned by the powerful family of the Rožmberk in the fourteenth century. See U. Henningsen, *Besitz und Einkünfte der Herren von Rosenberg in Böhmen nach dem Urbar von 1379–84* (Marburg an der Lahn, 1989).

[18] H. Knittler, *Herrschaftsstruktur und Ständebildung*, vol. II: *Städte und Märkte* (Vienna, 1973), pp. 86ff.

[19] Ibid., pp. 42–4; F. Baltzarek, 'Beiträge zur Geschichte des vierten Standes in Niederösterreich', *Mitteilungen des österreichischen Staatsarchivs* 23 (1971), 75.

[20] A. Hoffmann, 'Der oberösterreichische Städtebund im Mittelalter', *Jahrbuch des Oberösterreichischen Musealvereines* 93 (1948), 107–45.

impact by introducing allowances for such 'traditional' rural customs as the free sale of grain, cattle, cheese and lard.[21] Indeed, the constant reiteration of rural trading bans is a clear sign that they were generally ineffective.

In the Czech lands, towns bore considerably higher fiscal burdens than the countryside. For instance in Upper Lusatia, in the fourteenth and early fifteenth centuries three-quarters of the tax assessments had to be provided by the six princely towns. When the towns tried to raise the countryside's share to one-third, they met with strong resistance by the estates.[22] Taxation continued to be a key source of tension between princely towns and estates, and it was only during the late seventeenth and early eighteenth centuries that the unequal burden on towns was gradually lifted, at the same time that the overall level of taxation was increased.[23] Princely towns were more vulnerable in this respect since they interacted directly with the prince, whereas subject towns and villages were buffered by the landlords, who saw state taxation cut into their personal incomes.[24] Above all, the push by the Habsburg rulers to consolidate their power after taking over the Bohemian throne in 1526 led to a clash with the princely towns of Bohemia and Upper Lusatia that resulted in the towns' political defeat.[25]

Market rights and franchises

Concessions of market franchises in the Austrian and Czech lands, the earliest of which date to the thirteenth century, responded to a range of needs that included political imitation and competition besides strictly economic factors; thus, all the liberties granted *en bloc* to the towns and markets of Styria in 1377 appear to have been directed mainly against the aristocratic and ecclesiastical estates.[26] However, the main spur in

---

[21] Hoffmann, *Wirtschaftsgeschichte*, p. 258.

[22] R. Jecht, *Geschichte der Stadt Görlitz*, 2 vols. (Görlitz, 1926), vol. I, pp. 282ff.; for Bohemia see O. Placht, *České daně 1517–1652* (Prague, 1924), pp. 12ff.

[23] A. Míka, 'On the economic status of Czech towns in the period of late feudalism', *Hospodářské dějiny – Economic History* 2 (1978), 225–57; J. Novotný, *Zdanění českých měst podle katastrů z r. 1654–1757* (Prague, 1929); J. Pekař, *České katastry* (Prague, 1932); Weczerka, 'Entwicklungslinien', 129.

[24] See Janáček, 'Städte', pp. 297ff.; Kejř, 'Organisation', p. 81; Petry, 'Breslau', pp. 267ff. There were also credit links between territorial towns and the state.

[25] See Janáček, 'Städte', pp. 294ff.; J. Janáček, *České dějiny. Doba předbělohorská*, 2 vols. (Prague, 1984), vol. I:2, pp. 153ff.; Jecht, *Geschichte*, pp. 279ff.; J. Pánek, 'Města v politickém systému předbělohorského Českého státu', in J. Pánek (ed.), *Česká mesta v 16.–18. století* (Prague, 1991), pp. 15–39; *Přehled dějin Československa*, 2 vols. (Prague, 1980), vol. I:1, pp. 535ff.; E. A. Seeliger, 'Zur Verwaltungs- und Verfassungsgeschichte Löbaus bis zum Pönfalle', *Neues Lausitzisches Magazin* 79 (1903), 83–6.

[26] F. Popelka, *Schriftdenkmäler des steirischen Gewerbes* (Graz, 1950), pp. 10–12.

lobbying for a concession seems to have been economic. The attempt by rural inhabitants to engage in trade and manufacturing must be seen in the context of the late medieval agrarian crisis and of the decline in feudal rents it engendered. Complaints made in 1585 concerning villages that consisted of only a few houses but which applied for market privileges either directly or through their feudal lords were not just wild exaggerations. Feudal lords used privileged market settlements to deflect trade and resources from the chartered towns to the agrarian hinterland, thus turning the concession of market privileges into a source of conflict with princely towns.

The main purpose of urban market franchises was to limit trade outside towns.[27] The unchecked proliferation of rural exemptions is thus one of the main reasons why attempts by prince and towns to eliminate rural competition ultimately failed. During the late fifteenth and early sixteenth centuries the expanding seigniorial economy and princely towns in the Czech lands competed for market privileges and for the exclusive right to brew beer. Brewing for rural consumption represented a major source of revenue for princely towns; conversely, landlords were eager to secure supply privileges for their own towns and villages. Feudal competition over brewing rights continued for a long time to be a source of contention at territorial diets.[28]

Until the late fourteenth century, measures to prohibit rural crafts remained limited because of the reduced productive capacities of town artisans. Rural bakers and butchers were allowed to sell their products at town markets and fairs on certain dates, and towns relied on rural wage workers and craftsmen to build urban walls and to provide transport services, building materials and carpentry. From the second half of the fifteenth century onwards, rural crafts exploited the political weakness of princely towns in Austria and Styria to expand strongly. The new marketplaces, which mostly included the main food-processing crafts and frequently also textile trades, seldom respected any limitations to their range of activity established by their founding charters. Privileged *Bannmärkte* set up by the territorial prince in the Austrian lands also competed in manufacturing and trading activities previously reserved

---

[27] See W. Küchler, *Das Bannmeilenrecht* (Würzburg, 1964).

[28] Janáček, 'Städte', p. 295; V. Ledvinka, 'Feudální velkostatek a poddanská města v předbělohorských Čechách', in J. Pánek (ed.), *Česká města v 16.–18. století* (Prague, 1991), pp. 95–120; Macek, *Jagellonský věk*, pp. 322ff.; Pánek, 'Města'; *Přehled dějin*, pp. 538–40; P. Vorel, 'Poddanská residenční města v českých zemích', in *Měšťané, šlechta, a duchovenstvo v rezidenčních městech raného novověku* (Prostějov, 1997), pp. 38–48. Brewing in royal towns declined considerably in the second half of the sixteenth century; see J. Janáček, *Pivovarnictví v českých královských městech v 16. století* (Prague, 1959).

for princely towns.[29] However, it is clear that during the sixteenth century the medium-sized and small princely towns were mainly concerned to protect commercial rights, and that the fight against rural manufacture held a distinctly secondary place.[30]

In Austria and Styria the growing trading activities of feudal and ecclesiastical landlords were a major source of grievance. By the 1530s previous prohibitions began to be replaced by agreements between princely towns and feudal lords concerning the storing and selling of grain, wine and meat products. Initially concessions were restricted to trade in the produce of feudal rent and from restricted demesne activities, but the landlords tended in the longer run to extend their rights so as to establish their own marketing monopolies and exclude their subjects from independent markets (*Anfeilzwang*). The establishment during the second half of the sixteenth century of demesne farms and workshops that resold products bought on monopolistic markets, that produced goods, particularly beer, for sale, and that monopolised services like grain milling, seriously distorted the economic system in favour of the feudal landlords.[31]

Such developments mainly affected the position of the smaller towns. Medium-sized towns like Krems, Wiener Neustadt, Wels, Linz, Freistadt and Judenburg, which were more deeply embedded in supraregional trade networks, found it easier to maintain control over their surrounding countryside, even when they were hit by major shifts in patterns of trade like the withdrawal of German merchant capital during the second half of the sixteenth century.[32] Alternatively, rural areas with strong export-oriented industries like the Styrian–Austrian iron region, and to a smaller degree the Upper Austrian linen-weaving region, could respond to commercial contraction by becoming disengaged from neighbouring towns.

By contrast, the more powerful royal towns of Bohemia and Moravia and the princely towns of Upper Lusatia defended their market and trade privileges to considerable effect. In the first half of the sixteenth century, the towns of Upper Lusatia and Silesia signed treaties with the

---

[29] Knittler, *Herrschaftsstruktur*, pp. 60–2.

[30] Cf. E. Landsteiner, 'Weinbau und Gesellschaft in Ostmitteleuropa', Ph.D. dissertation, University of Vienna, 1992, pp. 243–7.

[31] G. Winner, ' "Adeliger Stand und bürgerliche Hantierung". Die sieben landesfürstlichen Städte und die ständischen Gegensätze in Oberösterreich während des 16. Jahrhunderts', *Historisches Jahrbuch der Stadt Linz 1959*, pp. 57–92.

[32] O. Pickl, 'Die wirtschaftliche Lage der Städte und Märkte der Steiermark im 16. Jahrhundert', in Rausch, *Die Stadt an der Schwelle*, pp. 93–128; E. Landsteiner, 'Wirtschaftliche Integration und frühneuzeitliche Staatsbildung im mittel- und südostmitteleuropäischen Raum, 1450–1650', paper presented to the Twelfth International Economic History Congress, Madrid 1998.

estates allowing feudal lords to establish textile production on their rural lands. Although the previous monopolies of princely towns were undermined by the promotion of new feudal towns and of rural manufacture, their strong institutional position and the buoyant economy enabled territorial towns to stave off the worst effects of feudal competition until the second half of the sixteenth century.[33]

Urban property in the countryside

As a rule, the jurisdictional and fiscal rights of a town administration were restricted to its own district (*Stadtgemarkung*). Late medieval and early modern Austrian towns did not control large swaths of rural property, as occurred elsewhere in the German-speaking lands.[34] Whatever land the towns had was administered to extract feudal cash rents rather than as a source of jurisdictional and marketing power.[35] The main exceptions to this rule were situated in Upper Austria, where at the end of the sixteenth century the seven princely towns had jurisdiction over 2,609 rural holdings.[36] Although a tendency to consolidate the feudal rights of Austrian towns can be discerned during the Reformation when municipalities gained control over the property and seigniorial powers of religious foundations, the results were less imposing than the property that came under the control of some royal and princely towns in the Czech lands.[37] In this sense the ownership of vineyards by burghers, urban communities and hospitals, which reached its climax in the fifteenth and sixteenth centuries and which in the case of some towns in eastern Lower Austria (Wiener Neustadt, Bruck an der Leitha and Hainburg) and Styria extended into Hungary, was unusual. Although they provided an important base for townspeople and for the urban wine trade, they did not support the extension of the town's market franchise because there were no seigniorial powers attached to vineyards.[38]

Princely towns and townsmen in the Czech lands commonly held

[33] Janáček, 'Städte'.
[34] See chapter 10 below.
[35] The question of rural property owned by Austrian townspeople has not yet been analysed systematically; but see L. Sailer, *Die Wiener Ratsbürger des 14. Jahrhunderts* (Vienna, 1931), pp. 69–99.
[36] G. Grüll, *Der Bauer im Lande ob der Enns am Ausgang des 16. Jahrhunderts* (Linz, 1969), p. 60.
[37] Knittler, 'Österreichs Städte', pp. 61ff. In the Czech lands, royal and princely towns maintained jurisdictional rights over neighbouring noble estates until the fifteenth century.
[38] E. Landsteiner, 'Weinbau und bürgerliche Hantierung', in F. Opll (ed.), *Stadt und Wein* (Linz, 1996), pp. 17–50.

rural property, and even the inhabitants of feudal towns could own rural estates. For some towns, the seigniorial rent from communal property represented an important source of municipal revenue, which provided stable incomes and a source of collateral on the credit market. Larger towns could be feudal lords of several neighbouring villages and pose a threat to aristocratic landlords.[39] Towns profited especially from the dissolution of ecclesiastical estates during the Hussite Wars in Bohemia and Moravia, when the property of individual town citizens who had not supported the Hussite movement was also confiscated. At times of peasant unrest, as in the second half of the sixteenth century, towns strongly supported the policy of the estates and of the state to suppress protests, if necessary with violence.[40]

In the seventeenth and eighteenth centuries, the rural possessions of townspeople were a significant factor in town–country relations. In the first half of the eighteenth century about 10 per cent of the total agricultural area was owned by inhabitants of towns other than Prague.[41] They were often involved in specialised crops like vines and hops; in the first half of the eighteenth century, nearly 50 per cent of all vineyards and 43 per cent of all hop fields in the Czech lands were owned by burghers.[42]

---

[39] In 1537, the council of the city of Görlitz owned about fifty villages; twenty-nine more were the property of individual citizens (P. Wenzel, 'Die wirtschaftliche und soziale Struktur der Stadt Görlitz im 15. und 16. Jh. (1437–1547)', M.A. thesis, University of Leipzig, 1963, p. 56). For Löbau, see Seeliger, 'Zur Verwaltungs- und Verfassungs-geschichte', pp. 54ff., 74ff.; for Bautzen, see J. Schneider, 'Materialien zur Geschichte des Bautzener Weichbildes und seiner Ratsdörfer', Lětopis, ser. B, 6 (1959), 353–71, 8 (1961), 183–99; for Wrocław, see R. C. Hoffmann, Land, liberties, and lordship in a late medieval countryside (Philadelphia, 1989); Petry, 'Breslau', pp. 265, 267; H. Wendt, 'Breslaus Streben nach Landbesitz im 16. Jahrhundert', Zeitschrift des Vereins für Geschichte Schlesiens 32 (1898), 215–28. By 1600, 20 per cent of the annual income of the city of Wrocław came from her rural possessions.

[40] Janáček, 'Städte', pp. 293, 298; J. Janáček, 'Městské finance a investice: Praha 1420–1547', Československý časopis historický 25 (1977), 408–26; Macek, Jagellonský věk, pp. 86ff., 373–5; J. Mezník, Venkovské statky pražských měšťanů (Prague, 1965); M. Weber, 'Bauernkrieg und sozialer Widerstand in den östlichen Reichsterritorien bis zum Beginn des 30jährigen Krieges', Jahrbuch des Bundesinstituts für ostdeutsche Kultur und Geschichte 2 (1994), 7–57. For Brno, see J. Mezník, 'Venkovské statky brněnských měšťanů ve 14. a 15. století', Sborník matice moravské 79 (1960), 129–47; for České Budějovice, see J. Čechura, Die Struktur der Grundherrschaften im mittelalterlichen Böhmen (Stuttgart, 1994), pp. 102ff.; for Louny, see J. Vaniš, Hospodaření královského města Loun v druhé polovině 15. století (Prague, 1979), pp. 8ff., 83ff., 110ff.

[41] The leading towns controlling communal rural property in Bohemia towards 1750 were Turnov (15 villages), Cheb (80 villages), České Budějovice (36 villages), and Plzeň (26 villages). See Míka, 'Economic status'.

[42] J. Křivka, Výrobní a peněžní výsledky měšťanského zemědělství v 18. století v severních Čechách (Prague, 1975), suggests that at least 30 per cent of the agricultural product received by townspeople was marketed. See also Míka, 'Economic status', pp. 238ff.

Patterns of development, 1450–1650

The climax of the late medieval crisis in the Czech lands was reached in the course of the fifteenth century, when the agrarian depression was exacerbated by the destruction caused by the Hussite Wars and by the reorientation towards the north of the Czech lands of trade routes leading from German merchant centres via Saxony and Upper Lusatia to Silesia and the east.[43] The crisis marked a watershed in the development of the agrarian system in eastern and east-central Europe and changed town–country relations in the Czech lands. Confronted with declining feudal rents, landlords tried from the late fifteenth century onwards to rebuild their revenues by creating a demesne economy that included the foundation of new subject towns which affected princely towns negatively.[44] Thus, apart from the growth of mining towns, especially in the Krušné Hory, from the second half of the fifteenth century onwards economic recovery in the Czech lands was fuelled mainly by the recovery of agriculture and by rural industry, in particular by textile and glass production.[45]

Mining and metalworking

The increased use from the thirteenth century of the water-wheel, a rising scarcity of fuel timber and a strong demand for foodstuffs in the mining districts of Austria and Styria initiated a process of decentralisation in iron production during the late middle ages. Production, financial and distribution activities were disseminated across an area of several hundred square kilometres which turned into a major industrial region. The main centre of production in the north was the town of Steyr. The organisational and distributive functions of Steyr's southern counterpart, the town of Leoben, were less developed, as were those of secondary centres such as Waidhofen an der Ybbs and Scheibbs. The rise of these industrial poles stimulated inter-regional trade in basic foodstuffs; regions producing an agricultural surplus ('dedicated

---

[43] The best recent accounts of the crisis are A. Kostláň, 'Feudální zatížení českého venkova po husitské revoluci', Ph.D. dissertation, University of Prague, 1988; Hoffmann, *Land*. See also the surveys in Aubin, 'Wirtschaft im Mittelalter'; Janáček, 'Städte'; *Přehled dějin*.

[44] See Janáček, 'Städte', pp. 294ff.; Janáček, *České dějiny*, pp. 153ff.; Ledvinka, 'Velkostatek'; Macek, *Jagellonský věk*; *Přehled dějin*; Vorel, 'Poddanská residenční města'.

[45] See M. Hroch and J. Petráň, 'Die Länder der böhmischen Krone', in H. Kellenbenz (ed.), *Handbuch der europäischen Wirtschafts- und Sozialgeschichte*, 5 vols. (Stuttgart, 1986), vol. III, pp. 968–1005.

districts', *Widmungsbezirke*) were compelled by law to sell their produce to the mining and iron-processing districts.[46]

The huge demand for iron goods provided the main impetus for the diffusion of the iron and steel crafts from the towns to rural market settlements during the first half of the sixteenth century. Rural expansion led to attempts by urban cutlers to subsume rural competitors formally, through regional guild ordinances.[47] The spread of water-driven forge hammers for scythe-making caused a further shift of production to the countryside and stimulated the rise of a new rural centre, Kirchdorf-Micheldorf.[48] The settlement of new scythe smiths provided increased work opportunities for the rural population and increased the rental income for feudal lords. Both factors helped stabilise the feudal system after the late medieval depression.[49] In Austria, the highly dispersed structure of production created a need for greater co-ordination and underpinned the rise of more elaborate administrative structures at the territorial level. Local town guild ordinances were replaced by statutes that applied to whole regions or even to the entire territory. The state increasingly regulated production and trade and interfered in industrial matters.

In the Czech lands, principally to the north, the expansion of iron mining gave rise from the late fifteenth century to intensified settlement.[50] Although several new mining towns soon disappeared, others, like Jachymov, a silver-mining centre, expanded strongly over a relatively brief time. Nevertheless, iron production in the Czech lands did not achieve the same significance as in early modern Austria. Iron forges, which were first established by independent master artisans in the countryside, were granted feudal privileges related to baking and brewing and exemptions from seigniorial dues. In some cases, noble landlords took the initiative in establishing forges on their estates. Later, towards the end of the sixteenth and especially during the seventeenth century, many feudal lords integrated metal forges into their demesne economy and transformed master craftsmen into wage workers. This

---

[46] See H. Knittler, 'Eisenbergbau und Eisenverhüttung in den österreichischen Ländern bis ins 18. Jahrhundert', in H. Matis (ed.), *Historische Betriebsanalyse und Unternehmer* (Vienna, 1997), pp. 119–42.

[47] I. Hack, 'Eisenhandel und Messerhandwerk der Stadt Steyr bis zum Ende des 17. Jahrhunderts', Ph.D. dissertation, University of Graz, 1949.

[48] F. Fischer, *Die blauen Sensen. Sozial- und Wirtschaftsgeschichte der Sensenschmiedezunft zu Kirchdorf-Micheldorf bis zur Mitte des 18. Jahrhunderts* (Graz–Cologne, 1966).

[49] M. Cerman, 'Proto-industrial development in Austria', in S. C. Ogilvie and M. Cerman (eds.), *European proto-industrialization* (Cambridge, 1996), p. 180.

[50] For the settlement process see W. Kuhn, *Geschichte der deutschen Ostsiedlung in der Neuzeit*, 2 vols. (Cologne and Graz, 1955–7); J. Petráň, *Poddaný lid v Čechách na prahu třicetileté války* (Prague, 1964), pp. 109ff.

new system of ownership dominated Czech and Moravian iron production until the late eighteenth century.[51]

Linen

Like the iron industry, the growth of linen production in the Austrian lands can be dated to the later middle ages. The main area of production was the Upper Austrian Mühlviertel north of Linz, which during the sixteenth century was not yet orientated towards a single dominant urban centre. Production relied on a dense network of small market settlements whose 'town' weavers were flanked by rural weavers protected or even directed by their landlords. In 1578, the territorial prince published a territorial guild ordinance for linen weavers, underlining the co-ordinating function of the state. The establishment of a rural putting-out system at a time when production was still dominated by guilds casts doubt on there having been a clear-cut distinction between the two kinds of production. A combination of the two formed the basis for the growing integration of rural weavers into a pattern of supraregional production during the seventeenth and eighteenth centuries.[52]

After 1500, international demand for woollen cloth and especially for linens increased considerably also in the Czech lands. Although it is likely that production for export of linen textiles pre-dated the midsixteenth century, the first surviving contracts between German merchants and producers in the towns of Upper Lusatia, Silesia and Bohemia date from about 1550. Urban linen weavers' guilds grew considerably in both number and size between 1500 and 1620. Although urban producers tried to establish a monopoly over yarn production in the countryside and to prevent rural spinners from exporting elsewhere, the large number of complaints against infringements of export bans shows that guilds and town councils were only partially successful. Rural weaving expanded considerably between 1550 and 1620 and in several regions came to outgrow urban production, thus providing a further source of conflict between urban guilded

[51] Cf. P. Jančárek, 'Populační vývoj českých zemí v předbělohorském období a problematika jeho studia', *Historická demografie* 12 (1987), 125–36; J. Kořan, 'Období přímé výroby železa v českých zemích (polovině 14. – do 30. let 19. stol.)', in R. Pleina (ed.), *Dějiny hutnictví železa v Československu*, vol. I: *Od nejstarších dob do průmyslové revoluce* (Prague, 1984), pp. 47–165; E. Maur, *Český komorní velkostatek* (Prague, 1976); M. Myška, 'Pre-industrial iron-making in the Czech lands: the labour force and production relations circa 1350–circa 1840', *Past and Present* 82 (1979), 44–72; M. Myška, *Proto-industriální železářství v českých zemích* (Ostrava, 1992).

[52] A. Marks, 'Das Leinengewerbe und der Leinenhandel im Lande ob der Enns von den Anfängen bis in die Zeit Maria Theresias', *Jahrbuch des oberösterreichischen Musealvereines* 95 (1950), 169–286; Hoffmann, *Wirtschaftsgeschichte*, pp. 181–96.

and rural non-guilded producers. Even as late as 1627, the linen weavers of Zittau set out to destroy rural looms in the council villages.[53] However, there was little they could do against weavers on other estates who were protected by their landlords and by the agreements between princely towns and estates. Although guilds of smaller subject towns in northern Bohemia like Rumburk, Šluknov, Frýdlant, Liberec and Vrchlabí participated successfully in the linen boom, their protest against rural competitors was useless against the will of the feudal landlords. The boom in guild-based export production lasted until c.1620, marking a period of expansion through proto-industrial towns whose co-operation with the countryside was just as distinctive as that between rural proto-industry and the towns at a later date.[54]

Unlike most Upper Lusatian and several Bohemian and Moravian towns, Silesian towns acted more as centres of trade than production with regard to the linen industry. Although Silesian merchants tried to prevent foreigners from exporting linen without Silesian intermediaries, most towns had local representatives of German, Dutch and English merchant companies. Many Silesian towns were also renowned for their woollen production for export, which once again had its roots in the later middle ages and which remained entirely urban in character until the eighteenth century.[55] The origins of the woollen industry in Upper Lusatia,[56] Bohemia and Moravia were also late medieval; leading Bohemian and Moravian centres in the sixteenth century were Broumov, Jindřichův Hradec and Jihlava.

Production of cloth for export in Bohemian princely towns was rather limited. This fits the general description of craft production in sixteenth-century Bohemian towns as being 'stagnant' and geared mainly to local

[53] G. Aubin and A. Kunze, *Leinenerzeugung und Leinenabsatz im östlichen Mitteldeutschland zur Zeit der Zunftkäufe* (Stuttgart, 1940).

[54] Ibid.; Bogucka, 'Towns'; J. Janáček, *Dějiny obchodu v předbělohorské Praze* (Prague, 1955); J. Janáček, *Řemeslná výroba v českých městech v 16. století* (Prague, 1961); J. Marek, 'Řemeslná výroba v moravských městech v 16. století', *Sborník matice moravské 81* (1962), 124ff.; A. Klíma, *Manufakturní obdobi v Čechách* (Prague, 1955); F. Graus, *Český obchod se suknem ve 14. a počátkem 15. století* (Prague, 1950), pp. 108–11; Janáček, 'Städte', p. 305; Ledvinka, 'Velkostatek'. On proto-industrial cities see Hohenberg and Lees, *Making*, pp. 125ff.

[55] See H. Aubin, 'Die Wirtschaft', in L. Petry and J. J. Menzel (eds.), *Geschichte Schlesiens* (Sigmaringen, 1988), vol. II, pp. 100–32; Aubin and Kunze, *Leinenerzeugung*; Menzel, 'Schlesische Städte', pp. 259f.; K. Maleczyński (ed.), *Historia Śląska* (Wrocław, 1961); M. Wolański, 'Schlesiens Stellung im Ostseehandel vom 15. bis zum 17. Jahrhundert', in I. Bog (ed.), *Der Außenhandel Ostmitteleuropas 1450–1650* (Cologne, 1971), pp. 120–46.

[56] H. Jecht, 'Beiträge zur Geschichte des ostdeutschen Waidhandels und Tuchmachergewerbes', *Neues Lausitzisches Magazin 99* (1923), 55–98; 100 (1924), 57–134; H. Knothe, 'Geschichte des Tuchmacherhandwerks in der Oberlausitz bis Anfang des siebzehnten Jahrhunderts', *Neues Lausitzisches Magazin 58* (1882), 241–380.

rather than export markets. On the other hand, royal towns were still important trade centres. The leading centre, Prague, had major commercial functions, although its international role has been somewhat exaggerated by Czech historiography.[57] The merchants of Prague, many of whom were representatives of larger merchant companies in Germany and elsewhere, organised Bohemia's international trade flows through the city. However, at least since the major upheavals in Bohemia and Moravia caused by the Hussite Wars, it was Wrocław that acted as the main emporium along the principal route of east–west trade which passed through Upper Lusatia and Silesia. As a result, in the sixteenth century northern Bohemian and Moravian textile centres exported their produce with the help of Silesian and Upper Lusatian merchants, who organised the finishing process and distributed the cloth to German, other European and overseas markets.

The seventeenth-century crisis and its aftermath

By the 1590s at the latest, however, signs of incipient economic crisis intensified in both the Czech and the Austrian lands, and by the 1620s a long-lasting depression set in across much of the economy.[58] The first signs of a revival from the economic depression of the seventeenth century can be dated to the 1680s, but the crisis was really only fully overcome some sixty years later. External factors, including the long wars against the Ottoman Empire, the Thirty Years War (especially in northern Austria and the Czech lands), Bavaria's occupation of Upper Austria and the devastation caused by the second siege of Vienna in 1683, increased the length and intensity of the downswing. A temporary upswing in the rural economy and the stabilisation of export-oriented proto-industries up to the 1720s, particularly in the Czech lands, were followed by renewed stagnation during the 1740s when the wars with Prussia disrupted the monarchy's economy, and important trade links with Silesia and the German export towns, especially with reference to textile production, were interrupted.

---

[57] Janáček, *Dějiny obchodu*; Janáček, *Řemeslná výroba*, pp. 130ff., 167ff.; Janáček, 'Städte', pp. 294–7; Ledvinka, 'Velkostatek'; *Přehled dějin*, pp. 535ff.

[58] A general overview of Lower Austria in this period can be found in E. Landsteiner, 'Wiederaufbau oder Transformation? Niederösterreich vor, während und nach dem Dreißigjährigen Krieg', in W. Leitsch and St. Trawkowski (eds.), *Polen and Österreich in 17. Jahrhundert* (Vienna–Cologne–Weimar, 1999), pp. 133–203, and E. Maur, 'Wirtschaftliche, soziale und demographische Entwicklung Böhmens 1648–1740', in Leitsch and Trawkowski, *Polen and Österreich*, pp. 68–108; M. Hroch and J. Petráň, *Das 17. Jahrhundert. Krise der Feudalgesellschaft?* (Hamburg, 1981).

Population

The reaction of Austrian towns to the problems of the seventeenth and early eighteenth centuries is best illustrated by contrasting developments in industrial and agrarian towns and in the capital, Vienna. In the case of the small number of trading towns and of centres geared to industrial production for export, the collapse of German merchant capital and the resulting loss of commercial outlets during the seventeenth century led to the disintegration of their pre-existing trading networks, to a decline in economic dynamism, and to a retreat into simplified relations with their immediate hinterland. Consequently the urban population stagnated at pre-1600 levels until 1750. The population of Steyr decreased from 9,000 to 7,000, that of Wels from 4,500 to 3,000, the wine-trading towns of Klosterneuburg and Krems stagnated at a mere 3,000–4,000 inhabitants. Only a few centres, like Leoben, which grew from 1,900 to 2,100, and Wiener Neustadt, which expanded from 3,500 to 4,500, made small-sized gains. If one also considers the eighteen princely towns and market towns of Lower Austria, which were particularly badly hit by warfare, the picture of stagnation and decline becomes even more pronounced. The number of tax units in those towns decreased by at least a quarter between 1560 and 1665, and the wealth of town citizens was reduced by more than half.[59] Economic hardship was exacerbated by the high debts incurred by municipal administrations and by the fact that state taxes were not reduced in line with demographic and economic contraction. In Styria the tax contribution of towns remained at the same level between 1572 and 1699, while the overall tax burden increased.[60]

Thus, the rise of the Austrian population living in centres of over 2,000 inhabitants from 7–8 per cent to 11 per cent between 1650 and 1750 can mainly be attributed to the growth of the provincial and national capitals, in particular of Vienna.[61] Indeed, the demographic stagnation of Austrian towns in the seventeenth and eighteenth centuries is in some respects a consequence of the astonishing rise of the capital city. Between 1600 and 1750, the population of Vienna rose from 50,000 to 175,000, and it grew by a further 57,000 up to 1800, for a nearly five-fold gain over two centuries. Graz and Linz followed similar trends, although estimations based on the tax quota suggest that Linz, whose tax quota as the administrative capital of Upper Austria rose from 19 to 40 per cent of the regional total between 1575 and 1754, was rather more

[59] Landsteiner, 'Wiederaufbau', Table 2.
[60] Mensi, *Geschichte*, pp. 74ff., Table IIIB.
[61] Sandgruber, *Ökonomie*, p. 107.

dynamic than the capital of Styria, Graz, whose relative tax assessment between 1572 and 1742 increased only from 21 to 30 per cent.[62]

The rise of Vienna corresponded in several respects to patterns of development in other European capital cities. The establishment during the sixteenth and seventeenth centuries of the imperial court and of the central state administration drew in the country's rural elites and led to a rising concentration of feudal and fiscal revenues and to increased luxury consumption and building activities. The growth of the bureaucracy and the expanding number of domestic servants lowered the proportion of rightful citizens in the population and pushed craftsmen and master artisans into the suburbs.[63] The city's catchment radius for in-migration extended far beyond its immediate hinterland: three-quarters of the master artisans working in Vienna in 1742 had not been born in the capital.[64]

The relationship between Vienna's inner precinct and the ring of feudal estates surrounding it was very unusual for Austria. Thus, in 1779 Vienna's area of legal and fiscal jurisdiction included eleven separate local districts governed by forty-six local landlords.[65] Whereas the feudal landholdings established around Vienna after the second Turkish siege in 1683 provided the traditional combination of land and feudal rents, the situation changed following the erection of a new defence line (*Linienwall*) in 1704 that cut through the seigniorial demesnes. Thenceforth, demesne produce that crossed the new defence line into the suburbs had to pay a toll, and the profitability of feudal estates declined.

While the larger royal towns in Bohemia and Moravia generally saw little growth during the seventeenth and eighteenth centuries, several feudal ('subject') towns with strong textile activities experienced rapid expansion. By the mid-eighteenth century the five largest towns in Bohemia included two subject towns, Jindřichův Hradec and Liberec (the other three were Prague, Cheb and Kutná Hora).[66] By contrast, some of the earlier trade and industrial centres like Jawor in Lower

---

[62] Cf. Hackl, 'Rektifikation'; Mensi, *Geschichte*.

[63] W. Pircher, *Verwüstung und Verschwendung. Adeliges Bauen nach der Zweiten Türkenbelagerung* (Vienna, 1984), p. 84; E. Lichtenberger, *Die Wiener Altstadt* (Vienna, 1977), p. 101.

[64] M. Mitterauer, 'Zur familienbetrieblichen Struktur im zünftischen Handwerk', in H. Knittler (ed.), *Wirtschafts- und sozialhistorische Beiträge* (Vienna, 1979), pp. 197ff.

[65] W. Sauer, *Grund-Herrschaft in Wien 1700–1848* (Vienna, 1993).

[66] See *Dějiny obyvatelstva*, pp. 127–31; Míka, 'Status', pp. 245ff.; Novotný, *Zdaněni*; *Přehled dějin*, vol. I:2, pp. 229–31; E. Maur, 'Velikost českých městských obcí podle tereziánského katastru', *Historická demografie* 19 (1995), 169–206. Other data on Czech towns in A. Klíma, 'Die Länder der böhmischen Krone 1648–1850', in I. Mieck (ed.), *Handbuch der europäischen Wirtschafts- und Sozialgeschichte*, 5 vols. (Stuttgart,

Silesia decayed or stagnated, and others such as Görlitz and Zittau in Upper Lusatia underwent serious decline during the seventeenth-century crisis but recovered thereafter.[67]

Marketing functions

During the seventeenth century the structural antagonism between privileged towns and feudal estates in Austria and Styria persisted in response to the continued growth of feudal markets and of rural craft activities. However, the expansion of activities directly controlled by feudal lords and the imposition of compulsory purchases and sales had already reached a climax before 1620.

At the nadir of the crisis during the first half of the seventeenth century the traditional institutions organising town–country trade, like weekly markets and fairs, were showing clear signs of distress. On the other hand, since the total arable area available to fourteen Lower Austrian towns was on average insufficient to provide for the towns' grain requirements, it is clear that supply relations with the countryside were never entirely interrupted even during the worst phase of the recession.[68] Similar conclusions apply to craft and industrial activities. New guilds were established in some very small, quasi-rural centres and rural craftsmen living within town districts were integrated through territorial guild ordinances.[69] Town–country relations were not, and perhaps could not be, entirely broken.

In the Czech lands, as we have seen, small and medium-sized towns, especially feudal foundations practising administrative and market functions for the surrounding countryside, experienced quite significant growth during the seventeenth and eighteenth centuries. These centres, which were usually where the feudal landlords or their representatives lived, peaked after 1650 when the demesne economy experienced its golden age. Most demesne products – grain, fish, beer and cattle, as well as industrial materials such as flax, hemp and wool – were geared to the local market. Only a minority of estates, mainly situated in the central

1993), vol. IV, pp. 688–719. On 'subject' towns see L. Dědková, 'Ochranná municipální města v Čechách', *Sborník archivních prací* 28 (1978), 292–355, and the contributions in M. Macková (ed.), *Poddanská města v systému patrimoniální správy* (Ústí n. O., 1996).

[67] C. Wenzel, *Beiträge zur Wirtschafts- und Sozialgeschichte der Stadt Görlitz im 17. Jahrhundert* (Görlitz, 1993).

[68] R. Sandgruber, *Die Anfänge der Konsumgesellschaft* (Vienna, 1982), pp. 134ff. See S. Lilja, 'Small towns in the periphery: population and economy of small towns in Sweden and Finland during the early modern period', in Clark, *Small towns*, p. 59.

[69] G. Otruba, *Gewerbe und Zünfte in Niederösterreich* (St Pölten, 1989), pp. 17ff.

Elbe basin of Bohemia, produced actively for supraregional markets like Prague or for international export.

The landlords' support for the commercial functions of their towns was also an aspect of their antagonism towards the princely towns, whose economic and political powers were fading after 1650, particularly in Bohemia and Moravia.[70] It would nevertheless be misleading to suggest that the growing power of the landlords was an unmitigated blessing for feudal towns. When it came to defending their economic interests, landlords did not hesitate to deprive subject towns of their rights. From 1550 onwards, subject towns throughout Bohemia lost the privilege to brew beer and to sell it to the surrounding countryside to the benefit of the demesne breweries, and lords established staple rights forcing towns and villages to buy goods from the demesne economy at fixed prices.[71]

Urban and rural manufacture

In Vienna, the authority of landlords over rural crafts and proto-industries tended to increase over time, particularly during the latter half of the eighteenth century. On the one hand, lords had vast land resources at their disposal to settle craftsmen on; on the other hand, the state increasingly applied a more liberal economic policy to exempt territorial niches and sectors from the jurisdiction of the guilds. These conditions provide the institutional background for the rise in the Viennese suburbs of a partially export-oriented proto-industrial production, especially in the suburbs of Schottenfeld and Gumpendorf in textiles. There was in any case room to establish new manufactories and workshops because guild restrictions were mostly ineffective.[72] Elsewhere in Austria, state privileges were more significant than feudal intervention in creating institutional niches for non-guilded industrial production. In the Czech lands, by contrast, the state found it hard to overcome the regulatory powers of the feudal landlords over commercial and industrial matters and their extensive jurisdictional authority before the mid-eighteenth century.

[70] See Janáček, 'Städte'; Ledvinka, 'Velkostatek'; V. Ledvinka, 'Poddanská města a městečka na panstvích jihočeských Vítkovců v 16. a počátkem 17. století', in M. Macková (ed.), *Poddanská města v systému patrimoniální správy* (Ústí n. O., 1996), esp. pp. 175ff.; F. Matějek, 'Postavení města v rámci panství', in *Měšťané, šlechta, a duchovenstvo v rezidenčních městech raného novověku* (Prostějov, 1997), pp. 73–85.

[71] J. Procházka, 'Města a společnost na konci 18. století', in *Měšťané*, pp. 49–57. See more generally Klíma, *Manufakturní období*; Klíma, 'Länder'.

[72] M. Cerman, 'Proto-industrialization in an urban environment: Vienna, 1750–1857', *Continuity and Change* 8 (1993), 281–320.

The early phase of industrialisation in Vienna's main textile industry, silk, featured a difficult coexistence between guild and non-guild producers that followed traditional town–country divisions. This was to a lesser extent also the case for other proto-industrial regions in Austria. The distribution of production across a network of small and half-agrarian settlements and townships in the linen industry of the Upper Austrian Mühlviertel, which expanded after the loss of Silesia in 1763, was discussed earlier. The manufactories established during the eighteenth century on the basis of state privileges reflected a policy that aimed to abolish any remaining legal differences over industrial production in town and country.[73] The policy's high point in terms of industrial privileges was reached between 1740 and 1760. Most grants were made to manufactories in Lower Austria, whose main activities were cloth-, iron- and metal-processing as well as chemical and food production.

The spread in Austria of rural domestic industries in poor agricultural areas was a major feature of the eighteenth century. Initially, the Linz woollen manufactory (founded in 1672) and the two big cotton manufactories in Schwechat (1724) and Fridau (1752) determined the organisation and dimensions of the main rural industrial activities. Up to the late eighteenth century, when domestic weaving and spinning intensified, the industries relied on part-time by-employment of the peasant, cottar and landless population, and domestic industries therefore remained bounded by traditional social structures under the control of communal and feudal institutions.[74] The expansion of rural proto-industries took place at the same time that most traditional industrial and commercial privileges were abolished. Those measures marked a new era in town–country relations, in which medium-sized and small towns which saw themselves deprived of their ancient rights took on a largely passive, spectator role.

In the Czech lands, the development of rural industries, particularly textiles, in the late seventeenth and eighteenth centuries did not cause the deindustrialisation of towns.[75] Several towns (Zittau in Upper Lusatia, Jelenia Góra in Silesia, Rumburk, Šluknov and Trutnov in Bohemia) became the centres of strong rural manufactures and the hubs

---

[73] F. Mathis, 'Städte und Märkte zur Zeit der Frühindustrialisierung', in Zöllner, *Städte*, pp. 69–84; G. Otruba, 'Manufaktur und Stadt – bzw. deren Bedeutung für die Entstehung 'zentraler Orte' im Alpen- und Donauraum', in G. Frühsorge et al. (eds.), *Stadt und Bürger im 18. Jahrhundert* (Marburg, 1993), pp. 178–207.

[74] Cerman, 'Proto-industrial development', pp. 174ff.; A. Komlosy, *An den Rand gedrängt. Wirtschafts- und Sozialgeschichte des Oberen Waldviertels* (Vienna, 1988), pp. 26–32.

[75] In some subject towns, market-oriented textile production lost in importance after 1650 compared to the sixteenth century. See L. Lancinger, 'Výrobní a majetková struktura Nového Města nad Metují po jeho založení a po třicetileté válce', *Acta Musei Reginahradecensis*, ser. B, 12 (1970), 29–64.

of complex patterns of industrial co-operation, in which labour-intensive production was concentrated mainly, though by no means exclusively, in the countryside and cloth finishing and marketing was situated in towns. In contrast to the linen industry, which saw widespread production in the countryside, woollen cloth continued to be woven mainly in towns under guild supervision because of the greater skills required. However, in this case also town and country co-operated closely, since spinning was a pre-eminently rural affair.[76]

Proto-industrial production lay at the heart of the dynamic town–country relationship in the Czech industrial regions. Though urban productive capacities were limited compared to the huge number of domestic producers in the countryside, each of the main town centres of northern Bohemia, northern Moravia, Upper Lusatia and Silesia had hundreds of woollen and linen weavers until the early nineteenth century.[77] Instead, in the agricultural regions of central Bohemia the lack of commercial opportunities, harsh feudal rule over subject towns and the economic decline of royal towns engendered patterns of stagnation similar to those in much of Austria.

Conclusion

A discussion of urbanisation in the Austrian and Czech lands based purely on demographic measures has been shown to be inappropriate. Although rates of urbanisation as defined by urban size were low, there was a considerable number of towns and urban settlements with legal rights, endowed with administrative and commercial (central place) functions, and of a size just below the customary cut-off point of 5,000

[76] For individual linen- and woollen-producing centres after 1650, see J. Čechura, 'Broumov 1615–1754: ein Kapitel des proto-industriellen Stadiums in Europa', *Frühneuzeit-Info* 7 (1996), 195–214; W. Hawelka, *Geschichte des Kleingewerbes und des Verlages in der Reichenberger Tucherzeugung* (Liberec, 1932); J. Joza, *Z minulosti textilního průmysl v Libereckém kraji* (Liberec, 1958); Klíma, *Manufakturní období* (n. 31); Míka, 'Status', pp. 232ff., 248–51; J. Janáček, *Přehled vývoje řemeslné výroby v českých zemích za feudalismu* (Prague, 1963); F. Mainuš, *Plátenictví na Moravě a ve Slezsku v 17. a 18. století* (Ostrava, 1959); F. Mainuš, *Vlnařství a bavlnařství na Moravě a ve Slezsku v XVII a XVIII století* (Ostrava, 1960); M. Myška, 'Proto-industrialization in Bohemia, Moravia and Silesia', in Ogilvie and Cerman, *European proto-industrialization*, pp. 188–207; A. Kunze, 'Vom Bauerndorf zum Weberdorf. Zur sozialen und wirtschaftlichen Struktur der Waldhufendörfer der südlichen Oberlausitz im 16., 17. und 18. Jahrhundert', in M. Reuther (ed.), *Oberlausitzer Forschungen* (Leipzig, 1961), pp. 165–92; W. Rusiński, 'Tkactwo lniane na Śląsku do 1850 roku', *Przegląd Zachodni* 5 (1949), 369–419, 639–66. See more generally Bogucka, 'Towns'; Procházka, 'Města'.

[77] The number of woollen weavers in Görlitz declined from 489 to 300 between 1720 and 1800, but grew from 330 to 820 in Liberec in the same period. Cf. Jecht, 'Beiträge'; Hawelka, *Geschichte*.

inhabitants. The concentration of population in small towns can be explained by the absorption of much of Austria's urban growth potential by the capital city, Vienna, and by the significant expansion after the sixteenth century of smaller feudal towns in Bohemia, which modified the previous balance of power in which princely towns played the dominant role, but which did little to energise the middle-ranking towns with 5,000 or so inhabitants.

One of the reasons for mid-range urban stagnation in the Czech lands was the absence of strong industrial or trading cities with regional or supraregional functions, the only exceptions being Zittau and Görlitz in Upper Lusatia and Wrocław in Silesia. Most of the new industrial centres which arose during the second half of the sixteenth century and expanded after 1650 were smaller subject towns. They were economically successful but politically weak, as were the princely towns after 1650 when the state administration began to rely entirely on the feudal estates as local administrators. Therefore, with the partial exception of Silesia, the political and administrative roles of early modern towns in the Czech lands were limited.

Through much of the early modern period, the mercantilistic ideology of the state combined with the strong powers of feudal lords helped to undermine the remaining medieval privileges of towns in Austria and in the Czech lands. The trading and production monopolies of towns were lost or modified. The towns that adapted more successfully than others to the new conditions were situated at the heart of the industrial regions which emerged in the Austrian and Czech lands at the turn of the nineteenth century.

9   Town and country in Germany, 1350–1600

Tom Scott

Introduction

The pattern of town–country relations in the German-speaking lands from the Alps to the North Sea from the fourteenth to the seventeenth centuries displayed a greater variety than in any other part of Europe. It ranged from fully-fledged city-states in the Swiss Confederation, sovereign principalities in their own right, to spheres of regional economic influence in the southern Low Countries, where the leading cities dominated the economy of their hinterlands without achieving exclusive jurisdiction. Across this spectrum the cities of Germany were located at intermediate points. Some, such as Nuremberg, attempted to acquire land which would directly serve their commercial interests as a source of labour or raw materials; others, such as Augsburg or Cologne, came to dominate the economies of their hinterlands in the organisation of production and distribution without ever amassing a landed territory of any size. Nuremberg was a city-state in all but name; Augsburg and Cologne echoed the regional economic sway exercised by the Flemish cities.

In either dimension, cities were concerned to extend their centrality – whether jurisdictional, political, economic, or social – over their surrounding countryside, in other words to establish a hierarchy of influence or dependence. But it should not be forgotten that relations between town and country were shaped by co-operation between cities as well as by competition. This, too, was a particular feature of the German-speaking lands, reflected in both political and commercial alliances. The fourteenth and fifteenth centuries were the heyday of urban leagues of mutual defence and protection against the pretensions of both emperor and princes, all of which saw their function as essentially regional. Commercial alliances, by contrast, were less circumscribed: Germany gave rise to the largest association of merchant venturers in European history, the Hanseatic League, numbering over eighty cities at its peak, strewn across the map of northern Germany.

Figure 9.1   German-speaking lands in the early modern period

The Hansa might have developed as an integrated commercial network, especially once its character had evolved from a looser 'merchant' to a tighter 'city' Hansa by the fifteenth century, but regional tensions bedevilled Hanseatic history. Those Hanseatic cities which saw themselves primarily as entrepôts in the carrying trade, rather than as outlets for the economy of their hinterlands, developed a different pattern of town–country relations from that of those members which were partly engaged in local industry and in putting-out.

The following analysis begins by tracing the varieties of urban territorial expansion, before turning to the rise of regional economic systems in which a metropolis and its hinterland of lesser towns and villages were

202 *Tom Scott*

integrated in a complementary network of economic functions or 'economic unit' (*Wirtschaftseinheit*).[1] Though this distinction is in some respects artificial, it offers a reasonable way of uncovering underlying patterns in the otherwise irreducible complexity of town–country relations in pre-modern Germany.

Institutional patterns

Stages of expansion

Urban territorial expansion has traditionally been seen as unfolding through three distinct stages: (1) the acquisition by individual citizens of property rights and revenues (which might include jurisdictions or markets) in the countryside; (2) the development of personal or corporate ties between country dwellers and cities in the form either of outburghership, that is, the extension of the legal privileges of citizenship to nobles, ecclesiastical foundations, or even peasants, without requiring them to take up urban residence, or else of protective agreements which afforded the cities access to strategic strongholds in times of military emergency or more continuous supervision of turnpikes and bridges in peacetime; (3) the acquisition of lands and subjects by the city as a corporation, either as a mortgage which might later be redeemed, or as the launching-pad for consolidation into a dependent territory, over which the magistracy possessed exclusive jurisdiction. These stages are not always clearly distinguishable, let alone chronologically successive, and in certain circumstances an informal hinterland policy (*Umlandpolitik*) might go much further towards securing a city's domination of its surrounding countryside than the formal construction of a rural territory. Indeed, some historians have argued that it is quite misleading to talk of a territorial policy at all; they would prefer the more neutral term *Landgebietspolitik* (that is, the acquisition of rural estates), since a deliberate territorial policy with anti-feudal overtones can rarely be ascribed to the ruling elites of German cities.[2]

---

[1] H. Ammann, *Die wirtschaftliche Stellung der Reichsstadt Nürnberg im Spätmittelalter* (Nuremberg, 1970), pp. 194ff.

[2] Cf. H.-J. Behr, 'Die Landgebietspolitik nordwestdeutscher Hansestädte', *Hansische Geschichtsblätter* 94 (1976), 18; W. Rösener, 'Aspekte der Stadt–Land-Beziehungen im spätmittelalterlichen Deutschland', in J.-M. Duvosquel and E. Thoen (eds.), *Peasants and townsmen in medieval Europe. Studia in honorem Adriaan Verhulst* (Ghent, 1995), pp. 668–9. For Brunswick, see H. Germer, *Die Landgebietspolitik der Stadt Braunschweig bis zum Ausgang des 15. Jahrhunderts* (Göttingen, 1937). For tacit co-operation between city and ecclesiastical prince, and cathedral chapter, see M. Wilmanns, *Die Landgebietspolitik der Stadt Bremen um 1400 unter besonderer Berücksichtigung der Burgenpolitik des Rates im Erzstift und in Friesland* (Hildesheim, 1973), pp. 11, 265.

A closer examination of these various stages will help to reveal the mixture of motives which informed the cities' actions. For a string of south German imperial cities in Swabia the acquisition of rural property by individual burghers was the necessary – though not always the sufficient – precondition of any subsequent territorial consolidation. The range of such acquisitions corresponded closely to the size of the city itself. For Augsburg, the regional metropolis, the radius of bourgeois property extended for as much as 40 or even 60 km; for sub-regional centres such as Memmingen, Nördlingen, or Kaufbeuren it was no more than 20 km; but for local market towns such as Kempten, Donauwörth, or Lauingen a mere 10 to 15 km.[3] Augsburg citizens invested in land for a variety of reasons: status and privilege – to assemble over time a congeries of estates as the nucleus of a dynastic lordship upon which a patent of nobility might be conferred; financial insurance – to use estates as a security or cash reserve to offset risks incurred in long-distance trade; commercial exploitation – to view land as the vehicle for agricultural improvement, as the famous merchant house of Fugger did with its lordship of Mickhausen.[4] This differentiated picture is confirmed for the Wendish cities of the Hanseatic League along the Baltic coast. Here, too, burghers bought up estates as a capital reserve or substitute bank. This somewhat conservative stance contrasted with the aggressive intervention of certain Stralsund merchants in the grain and wool production of the island of Rügen in the early fifteenth century, where they established a purchasing monopoly and made substantial profits.[5]

[3] R. Kiessling, 'Bürgerlicher Besitz auf dem Land – ein Schlüssel zu den Stadt–Land-Beziehungen im Spätmittelalter, aufgezeigt am Beispiel Augsburgs und anderer ostschwäbischer Städte', in P. Fried (ed.), *Bayerisch–schwäbische Landesgeschichte an der Universität Augsburg 1975–1977* (Sigmaringen, 1979), pp. 130–2.

[4] R. Kiessling, 'Herrschaft – Markt – Landbesitz: Aspekte der Zentralität und der Stadt–Land-Beziehungen spätmittelalterlicher Städte an ostschwäbischen Beispielen', in E. Meynen (ed.), *Zentralität als Problem der mittelalterlichen Stadtgeschichtsforschung* (Cologne-Vienna, 1979), pp. 211–12. Augsburg, by virtue of its size, was perhaps exceptional, but even in the smaller Swabian cities the spectrum of motives for bourgeois land purchases was considerable. For Memmingen, see R. Kiessling, *Die Stadt und ihr Land: Umlandpolitik, Bürgerbesitz und Wirtschaftsgefüge in Ostschwaben vom 14. bis ins 16. Jahrhundert* (Cologne–Vienna, 1989), pp. 353–4.

[5] K. Fritze, *Am Wendepunkt der Hanse: Untersuchungen zur Wirtschafts- und Sozialgeschichte wendischer Hansestädte in der ersten Hälfte des 15. Jahrhunderts* (Berlin, 1967), pp. 109–11; K. Fritze, *Bürger und Bauern zur Hansezeit: Studien zu den Stadt–Land-Beziehungen an der südwestlichen Ostseeküste vom 13. bis zum 16. Jahrhundert* (Weimar, 1976), pp. 91–2; K. Fritze, 'Soziale Aspekte der Stadt–Land-Beziehungen im Bereich der wendischen Hansestädte (13. bis 16. Jahrhundert)', in H. K. Schulze (ed.), *Städtisches Um-und Hinterland in vorindustrieller Zeit* (Cologne–Vienna, 1985), p. 29; K. Fritze, 'Stadt–Land-Beziehungen im hansischen Bereich im Mittelalter', in K. Fritze, E. Müller-Mertens and J. Schildhauer (eds.), *Gewerbliche Produktion und Stadt–Land-Beziehungen* (Weimar, 1979), pp. 111–14. For Nuremberg see K. F. Krieger, 'Bürgerli-

Elsewhere, however, agricultural investment by burghers could invigorate the rural economy. In Thuringia, another region where pastureland was being bought up to create sheep-farms, burghers of Erfurt were acquiring land for the cultivation of woad as an industrial crop; a similar development can be traced in Cologne's hinterland. As early as the fourteenth century Cologne's bourgeois investors were sowing vetches and clover as catch-crops to improve the nitrogen content of the soil on their rural estates, while in the same period in the environs of Nuremberg pine trees were being planted on sandy soil ill-suited to tillage, until in the sixteenth century council and citizens combined to promote irrigation by means of bucket-wheels which could turn dry land into lush meadows.[6]

Where urban ecclesiastical and charitable foundations, rather than individual citizens, acquired rural property, the opportunities accruing to city magistracies were all the greater, since they frequently held the stewardships of such corporations. Smaller and less powerful cities in Swabia, for instance, faced with hostility from the surrounding nobility, were particularly adept at gaining control of their hinterlands by stealthily appropriating their hospitals' rural holdings. This could occur in the larger cities as well: Memmingen's Lower Hospital played a crucial role in enabling the city to carve out a rural territory, while even Augsburg initially acquired indirect domination over its hinterland through stewardship of the city's hospitals, parish funds and friaries.[7]

Outburghership

Such a conflation of landlordship and jurisdictional lordship encouraged cities to extend rights of citizenship to their allies and dependants in the

cher Landbesitz im Spätmittelalter: das Beispiel der Reichsstadt Nürnberg', in Schulze, *Städtisches Um- und Hinterland*, p. 92.

[6] W. Held, *Zwischen Marktplatz und Anger: Stadt–Land-Beziehungen im 16. Jahrhundert in Thüringen* (Weimar, 1988), pp. 86–7, 108–9; F. Irsigler, 'Kölner Wirtschaft im Spätmittelalter', in H. Kellenbenz (ed.), *Zwei Tausend Jahre Kölner Wirtschaft*, 2 vols. (Cologne, 1975), vol. I, pp. 237–8; F. Irsigler, 'Stadt und Umland im Spätmittelalter: Zur zentralitätsfördernden Kraft von Fernhandel und Exportgewerbe', in Meynen, *Zentralität*, p. 5; F. Schnelbögl, 'Die wirtschaftliche Bedeutung ihres Landgebiets für die Reichsstadt Nürnberg', in Stadtarchiv Nürnberg (ed.), *Beiträge zur Wirtschaftsgeschichte Nürnbergs*, 2 vols. (Nuremberg, 1967), vol. I, pp. 62–3, 67–8.

[7] R. Kiessling, 'Das Umlandgefüge ostschwäbischer Städte vom 14. bis zur Mitte des 16. Jahrhunderts', in Schulze, *Städtisches Um- und Hinterland*, pp. 36–7; W. Leiser, 'Territorien süddeutscher Reichsstädte', *Zeitschrift für bayerische Landesgeschichte* 38 (1975), 971; P. Blickle, 'Zur Territorialpolitik der oberschwäbischen Reichsstädte', in E. Maschke and J. Sydow (eds.), *Stadt und Umland* (Stuttgart, 1974), pp. 54–71; Kiessling, *Die Stadt*, pp. 278ff.; Kiessling, 'Herrschaft – Markt – Landbesitz', p. 189. See fundamentally R. Kiessling, *Bürgerliche Gesellschaft und Kirche in Augsburg im Spätmittelalter* (Augsburg, 1971).

countryside. Outburghership (as it may conveniently be termed in English) was a pervasive institution in the German-speaking lands, though its significance has been overshadowed by the cities' territorial expansion. Only in the Swiss Confederation and in the southern Low Countries has outburghership been accorded its due weight, but a comparison between these two areas highlights the very different purposes which it might serve. There is now broad agreement that the Swiss Confederation consolidated in the fourteenth century as the rural cantons entered into a series of protective alliances with the leading cities of northern Switzerland.[8] What undergirded this remarkable development was the large-scale manumission of serfs, who then acquired burgher's rights, in some cases by the thousands, in such cities as Lucerne, Berne, and Zurich. Outburghership was also the principal means whereby Berne undermined the power of the local nobility and so constructed a vast rural territory which became the largest city-state north of the Alps.[9]

In the southern Low Countries, by contrast, outburghership never became the instrument of state-building. Although the dominant cities of Flanders – the *drie steden* of Ghent, Bruges and (with some reluctance) Ypres – all held outburghers (including members of the local nobility), it was the lesser towns which most assiduously granted citizen's rights to the rural population, not least as a demographic and economic insurance policy against being swallowed up by the *drie steden*, which by the early fourteenth century had succeeded in dividing Flanders among themselves into separate spheres of influence known as 'quarters'. Indeed, there is some evidence that the counts of Flanders themselves encouraged the lesser towns to acquire outburghers (*buitenpoorters*) as a political counterweight to their arch-rivals, the *drie steden*. Whereas the latter sought to regulate outburghership strictly, the former often found themselves faced with the problem of double citizenship, as their *buitenpoorters* took out burgher's rights in other small towns or in the larger cities. This underscores the primarily commercial benefits which *buitenpoorterij* was perceived as offering those who required ready access to urban markets; politically, it worked to thwart, not to abet, any territorial consolidation in the form of city-states.[10]

---

[8] Cf. T. Scott, 'Liberty and community in medieval Switzerland', *German History* 13 (1995), 98–113, esp. 110. On this point see fundamentally H. C. Peyer, *Verfassungsgeschichte der alten Schweiz* (Zurich, 1978).

[9] Scott, 'Liberty and community', pp. 110–11, with detailed references. For Zurich see also A. Largiadère, 'Die Anfänge des Zürcherischen Stadtstaates', in *Festgabe Paul Schweizer* (Zurich, 1922), pp. 1–92, esp. 20ff.

[10] D. Nicholas, *Town and countryside: social, economic, and political tensions in fourteenth-century Flanders* (Bruges, 1971), pp. 235–49 and *passim*. But see now P. Stabel, *Dwarfs*

The function of outburghers for the German cities fell variously between the two poles of Switzerland and Flanders. Up to the mid-fourteenth century, many free and imperial cities, particularly in southern Germany, had acquired outburghers under several headings: individual noblemen, convents as corporate citizens, even peasants (the latter usually called paleburghers). Once Emperor Charles IV's Golden Bull of 1356 had outlawed the acceptance of paleburghers by cities, however, the number of peasant outburghers generally declined, though they rarely disappeared altogether. Only Nuremberg, with its strong imperial connections, seems to have observed the ban on paleburghers rigorously.[11] In Frankfurt, the institution of paleburghership was super-seded by the assertion of judicial authority over all its rural dependants, while noble outburghership was replaced in the later fifteenth century by a series of service and protective alliances, including access to castles (*Öffnungsrecht*).[12] But a string of Swabian cities managed to retain both noble and peasant outburghers,[13] while in Alsace the number of Stras-burg's peasant outburghers may even have increased. Many more towns and cities than is commonly believed possessed outburghers, and they included territorial towns, whose subordination to princely overlordship should have rendered such a policy virtually impossible to sustain. That, in turn, helps to throw light upon the reasons for acquiring and retaining outburghers. For a city such as Cologne, caught between powerful ecclesiastical and secular princes (just as Augsburg was), the many treaties of outburghership concluded with leading noble families in its environs may be regarded as the specific substitute for the city's inability to construct a rural territory.[14] Elsewhere, binding wealthy rural con-vents to civic interests by obliging them to take out corporate citizen-ship, as practised by Augsburg, was a useful means of harnessing and channelling their economic clout.[15]

In general, no doubt, outburghership satisfied essentially defensive

among giants: the Flemish urban network in the late Middle Ages (Leuven–Apeldoorn, 1997), pp. 94–106, esp. 95–7, 99.

[11] W. Leiser, 'Das Landgebiet der Reichsstadt Nürnberg', in R. Endres (ed.), *Nürnberg und Bern: zwei Reichsstädte und ihre Landgebiete* (Erlangen, 1990), p. 246.

[12] E. Orth, 'Stadtherrschaft und auswärtiger Bürgerbesitz: die territorialpolitischen Konzeptionen der Reichsstadt Frankfurt im späten Mittelalter', in Schulze, *Städtisches Um- und Hinterland*, pp. 149–50; B. Schneidmüller, 'Städtische Territorialpolitik und spätmittelalterliche Feudalgesellschaft am Beispiel von Frankfurt am Main', *Blätter für deutsche Landeskunde* 118 (1982), 131.

[13] Kiessling, *Die Stadt*, pp. 36, 300, 553, 695; Kiessling, 'Herrschaft – Markt – Landbesitz', p. 192. Even before the Golden Bull, a group of Swabian cities had reached a compact in 1298 not to accept further paleburghers (*Die Stadt*, p. 300).

[14] H. J. Domsta, *Die Kölner Aussenbürger: Untersuchungen zur Politik und Verfassung der Stadt Köln von der Mitte des 13. bis zur Mitte des 16. Jahrhunderts* (Bonn, 1973).

[15] Kiessling, 'Herrschaft – Markt – Landbesitz', p. 190.

purposes: to secure a demographic and fiscal reservoir which would buttress the oppidan population and finances, and reinforce the civic militia in time of war. In Freiburg im Breisgau, for instance, an Outer Austrian territorial town on the upper Rhine, which clung tenaciously to its peasant outburghers until the sixteenth century, its rural citizens may have added another 10 per cent to the population of a commune which was undergoing a severe demographic and economic crisis.[16] But hitherto overlooked sources for Swabia provide a hint that outburghership may on occasion have operated in tandem with the cities' efforts to control the manufacturing output of their hinterlands. Towards the end of the fifteenth century in Kempten, the centre of the Allgäu linen industry, 400 urban weavers with 300 apprentices were matched by 600 outburghers who, the context implies, were almost certainly linen-weavers, too, employed as outworkers.[17] Its close neighbour Isny, moreover, which sheltered 250 linen-weavers within its walls, also recorded an unspecified number of outburghers accountable to the city but residing in the surrounding villages under feudal lords.[18] This evidence must not be pressed too far, but it does suggest an echo of the experience of the lesser Flemish cities.

The construction of landed territories

When we turn to the construction of landed territories as such, an immediate difference between north and south Germany becomes apparent. While many south German imperial cities, including quite small ones, and even some territorial towns, were able to transform a miscellany of estates, jurisdictions and protective agreements into consolidated dependencies, in the north only a handful of larger cities succeeded, and even then mainly by means of mortgages rather than outright purchases (with Erfurt as a prominent exception). That was particularly true of the leading Hanseatic cities: Brunswick and Lüneburg as inland members almost exclusively, and the major ports of Bremen, Hamburg and Lübeck to a large degree, relied upon acquisitions by mortgage.[19] Despite the political constraints which stood in the

[16] T. Scott, *Freiburg and the Breisgau: town-country relations in the age of Reformation and Peasants' War* (Oxford, 1986), pp. 78–98.

[17] T. Scott, 'Economic landscapes', in B. Scribner (ed.), *Germany. A new social and economic history*, vol. I: *1450–1630* (London–New York, 1995), p. 15; T. Scott (ed.), *Die Freiburger Enquete von 1476* (Freiburg im Breisgau, 1986), p. 13. See R. Kiessling, 'Handel und Gewerbe, Stadt–Land-Beziehungen', in V. Dotterweich et al. (eds.), *Geschichte der Stadt Kempten* (Kempten, 1989), p. 131.

[18] Scott, *Enquete*, p. 11.

[19] Behr, 'Landgebietspolitik', pp. 26–8. This applies also to Bremen as a territorial town; its active mortgage policy coincided with its membership of the Hanseatic League from

way of a concerted territorial policy in northern Germany, the recourse
to mortgages was determined in the end by commercial considerations.
For the Hanseatic cities peace, the protection of trade routes, and the
maintenance of commercial privileges were much more important than
the acquisition of rural territories for their own sake.[20] This can readily
be illustrated by Lüneburg's behaviour in 1392, when it handed back a
string of mortgaged lordships to the dukes of Brunswick in return for
the proclamation of a regional public peace (*Landfriede*), enshrined in a
treaty known as the *Sate*.[21]

The drawback to mortgages was that they could so easily be redeemed. Lübeck's one attempt to construct a territorial buffer (as
opposed to a commercial vantage-point) by acquiring in mortgage the
sizeable bailiwick of Segeberg to the west from the counts of Holstein in
the mid-fourteenth century lasted no more than a generation.[22] All told,
many Hanseatic and north German cities lost territory over time from
their heyday in the fourteenth century.[23] That was also true of the one
imperial city in central Germany which had resorted to a mortgage
policy, namely Frankfurt am Main, only thirteen of whose nineteen
acquisitions by mortgage during the fourteenth and fifteenth centuries
remained by 1500.[24]

It would be quite wrong to leave the impression, however, that north
German cities acquired territories only by mortgage, or that their
motives were exclusively commercial. Of the Wendish cities of the
Hanseatic League, Rostock, Greifswald and Stralsund all built up
modest territories in the fifteenth century, with around a score of villages
each, which they controlled outright; only Wismar had almost none. To
protect its trade routes, Stralsund constructed a rampart-cum-ditch
(*Landwehr*), as did other Hanseatic cities,[25] though the best-known
Landwehren were those of Rothenburg ob der Tauber and Schwäbisch
Hall in the south. The few imperial cities in northern Germany all
managed to acquire dependent territories – Dortmund, Soest, Goslar

1358 (Bremen only became an imperial city in 1646). Wilmanns, *Landgebietspolitik*,
pp. 13, 15, 36, and *passim*.
[20] E. Raiser, *Städtische Territorialpolitik im Mittelalter: eine vergleichende Untersuchung über
verschiedene Formen am Beispiel Lübecks und Zürichs* (Lübeck/Hamburg, 1969), p. 27.
[21] Ibid., p. 28.
[22] G. Fink, 'Lübecks Stadtgebiet (Geschichte und Rechtsverhältnisse im Überblick)', in
A. von Brandt and W. Koppe (eds.), *Städtewesen und Bürgertum als geschichtliche Kräfte*
(Lübeck, 1953), pp. 274–5.
[23] Raiser, *Städtische Territorialpolitik*, p. 18; Behr, 'Landgebietspolitik', p. 35.
[24] Orth, 'Stadtherrschaft', pp. 115–16. Mortgages were by no means unknown in south
German cities, either. Nördlingen pursued an active territorial policy in the fifteenth
century, buying up lordships from the counts of Oettingen – but always with the latter
reserving the right of redemption; see Kiessling, *Die Stadt*, pp. 56–7.
[25] Behr, 'Landgebietspolitik', p. 19.

and Mühlhausen.[26] But the most remarkable instance was that of Erfurt which, despite being effectively shorn of its imperial status during the fifteenth century, could boast in 1500 a territory of at least 610 km^2 comprising over sixty villages and the small town of Sömmerda.[27]

It remains true, nevertheless, that the greatest concentration of civic territories was to be found among the ranks of the south German imperial cities (see Table 9.1). Leading the way, and half as large again as its nearest rival, was Nuremberg, once it had acquired the Neue Landschaft from the Palatinate in 1504.[28] Then came Ulm, which began buying up lordships in western Swabia from its surrounding secular and ecclesiastical nobility in the late fourteenth century. By the sixteenth, its territory encompassed three towns, fifty-five villages and twenty-two other dependencies.[29] After Erfurt, in third place, came the Franconian city of Rothenburg,[30] Schwäbisch Hall in northern Württemberg, Rottweil on the eastern fringes of the Black Forest, and Strasburg, the metropolis of Alsace.[31] Apart from their imperial or free status, these cities had no common denominator. They were, however, only the tip of the iceberg. In Upper Swabia alone, apart from Ulm, and Biberach's very scattered possessions, two further groups of cities can be distinguished: those with medium-sized territories of some influence, among them Memmingen and Lindau, and others whose territory barely extended beyond the immediate urban precinct, such as Kempten and Isny.[32]

But size, of itself, is not an adequate criterion for measuring the economic and demographic significance of these territories. For the

[26] Rösener, 'Aspekte', p. 668; Held, *Zwischen Marktplatz und Anger*, p. 92.
[27] Held, *Zwischen Marktplatz und Anger*, p. 92. Held gives a figure of eighty-three villages and 610 km^2. S. Tode, *Stadt im Bauernkrieg 1525: Strukturgeschichtliche Untersuchungen zur Stadt im Raum anhand der Beispiele Erfurt, Mühlhausen/Thür., Langensalza und Thamsbrück* (Frankfurt am Main, 1994), pp. 77, 80, gives a more cautious figure of around sixty villages, but reckons the territory at 900 km^2, surely much too large.
[28] Leiser, 'Landgebiet', pp. 227, 232, 235, revising downwards the area of 1,500 km^2 given by G. Wunder, 'Reichsstädte als Landesherren', in Meynen, *Zentralität*, p. 79, for the beginning of the nineteenth century. The view propounded by several modern English-language scholars that Nuremberg's territory amounted to no more than 80 km^2 (25 sq. miles) appears to be based on a confusion between German miles and English statute miles (1 German mile = 4.6 statute miles).
[29] H. Schmolz, 'Herrschaft und Dorf im Gebiet der Reichsstadt Ulm', in Maschke and Sydow, *Stadt und Umland*, p. 168.
[30] L. Schnurrer, 'Der Bürger als Grundherr: die Grundherrschaft Heinrich Topplers aus Rothenburg (†1408)', in Schulze, *Städtisches Um- und Hinterland*, p. 62. On Rothenburg see H. Woltering, *Die Reichsstadt Rothenburg o. T. und ihre Herrschaft über die Landwehr*, 2 vols. (Rothenburg ob der Tauber, 1965/6–1971/2).
[31] G. Wunder, *Das Strassburger Gebiet: ein Beitrag zur rechtlichen und politischen Geschichte des gesamten städtischen Territoriums vom 10. bis zum 20. Jahrhundert* (Berlin, 1965), p. 105.
[32] Blickle, 'Territorialpolitik', p. 56.

Table 9.1. *Territories of German and Swiss cities in the early sixteenth century* (km^2)

Rank	German cities	Size	Rank	Swiss cantons	Size
1	Nuremberg[a]	1,200[a]	1	Berne[b]	9,000[b]
2	Ulm	830	2	Zurich	1,700
3	Erfurt[c]	610	3	Lucerne	1,485
4	Rothenburg ob der Tauber	400	4	Solothurn	780
5	Schwäbisch Hall	330	5	Basle	460
6=	Strasburg	220	6	Schaffhausen	295
	Rottweil		7	Zug	240

Notes:
[a] Includes the Neue Landschaft (1504).
[b] Includes the Vaud (acquired 1536)
[c] See n. 27.

largest city territories, those of Nuremberg and Ulm, the rural population added another 40 per cent and 60 per cent respectively to the urban
total; in Rothenburg and Schwäbisch Hall, by contrast, each with a
population of 5,000 or just over, their territories added as much as 150
per cent or 220 per cent respectively.[33] Beyond Swabia, the population
of Strasburg's direct territory came to 10,000, that is, just under half the
number living within the city walls, but if the lands indirectly under civic
control (bourgeois estates and the properties of convents and foundations) are taken into account, they add another 13,000 persons (and 500
km^2!) to the previous total.[34] Even Frankfurt's territory, though diminutive (a mere 110 km^2), was densely populated, with 5,000 subjects at
the end of the *ancien régime*.[35]

However impressive these figures may be, the fact remains that
German city territories rarely rivalled their Swiss counterparts (see
Table 9.1). Even a relatively insignificant canton such as Solothurn was
larger than any German city-state except Nuremberg and Ulm. And
indeed, the comparison shows how poorly size correlates with economic
clout. In the course of the sixteenth century, Basle became the financial
nerve-centre of the Confederation, with almost 59 per cent of finance
for public loans being raised on the city's capital market,[36] yet its
territory, hemmed in by topography (the Jura Alps to the south) and by

[33] Wunder, 'Reichsstädte', p. 79.
[34] Wunder, *Strassburger Gebiet*, p. 105. In the seventeenth century, Strasburg's indirect
territory shrank appreciably, but its direct territory remained unaltered.
[35] Orth, 'Stadtherrschaft', p. 117.
[36] M. H. Körner, *Solidarités financières suisses au seizième siècle* (Lausanne, 1980), p. 440.

political geography (the block of Outer Austrian lands in Upper Alsace), remained relatively modest in size. In terms of manufacturing and commerce, moreover, it is arguable that Zurich was much more important than the essentially agricultural Berne, more than five times its extent. Much the same applies to Germany, where only the first three cities had territories commensurate with their economic ranking.

The purposes of territorial expansion

Such discrepancies should counsel us against assuming too uniform or consistent a purpose in the territorial policy of the south German cities. As often as not, territorial expansion was opportunistic and piecemeal, beset by hesitations and reversals.[37] Both Nuremberg and Ulm on occasion spurned the chance of acquiring yet more territory, reckoning that it would bring more trouble than it was worth.[38] And yet the fact that so many cities chose to pursue a territorial policy at all suggests (apart from the objective possibility of doing so) some underlying common strands.

At the outset we may posit the cities' need to secure their own subsistence: protecting supplies of essential foodstuffs, above all grain, was a constant preoccupation.[39] From the fifteenth century, it is true, the larger cities were obliged to go well beyond their hinterlands, especially in times of dearth, to secure essential grain supplies; after 1500 an extensive regional grain trade developed in southern Germany, which led ultimately to the formation of genuinely complementary economic regions – a grain-exporting Swabia, for instance, linked symbiotically to a dairy-products- and meat-exporting northern Switzerland.[40] Beyond that, the southern cities regarded their rural dependencies as a useful source of income – unlike the Hanseatic cities, less concerned with the economic potential of their hinterlands. Rothenburg ob der Tauber, for instance, derived just under 5 per cent of its annual civic revenues from its territory,[41] a rate of return that may be regarded as broadly typical. But in some instances the figure could be much higher: around 10 per cent of Frankfurt's civic taxes came from just ten

---

[37] Schneidmüller, 'Städtische Territorialpolitik', p. 117.
[38] Wunder, 'Reichsstädte', p. 82.
[39] Leiser, 'Territorien', p. 967.
[40] R. Kiessling, 'Markets and marketing, town and country', in Scribner, Germany, pp. 151–2; F. Göttmann, Getreidemarkt am Bodensee: Raum – Wirtschaft – Politik – Gesellschaft (1650–1810) (St Katharinen, 1991). See in general W. Habermann and H. Schlotmann, 'Der Getreidehandel in Deutschland im 14. und 15. Jahrhundert: ein Literaturbericht', Scripta Mercaturae 11/2 (1977), 27–55.
[41] Wunder, 'Reichsstädte', p. 87.

of its villages,[42] while in years of good harvest a startling 22 per cent of Ulm's income derived from its extensive rural territory.[43]

The cities undoubtedly saw their territories as demographic reservoirs, compensating for the notorious inability of pre-industrial towns to reproduce their populations without immigration. But that in no sense betokened a willingness on the part of the south German cities to confer upon their rural subjects any preferential status, let alone citizenship. Almost without exception, the latter were, and remained, serfs throughout the early modern period,[44] though the inhabitants of dependent towns, as with Geislingen, Albeck, and Leipheim under Ulm's sovereignty, lived under a lighter form of residential serfdom, whereas its villagers were bound by a heavier personal serfdom.[45] By contrast, where cities and towns already held peasant outburghers, it is not at all clear – if Freiburg im Breisgau is anything to go by – that in the constant friction with local feudal lords they were able to prevent them being treated functionally as serfs.[46]

Can these findings, in conclusion, yield a typology of cities and their motives for pursuing a territorial policy? A tentative scheme has been put forward by Elisabeth Raiser, who distinguishes between policies embraced by: (1) the *Aristokratenstadt*, the city dominated by a patriciate deriving much of its prestige and wealth from feudal landholding; (2) the *Fernhandelsstadt*, the long-distance trading town; (3) the *Gewerbestadt*, or artisanal town, engaged in crafts and manufactures. From the outset, she emphasises that these three categories frequently overlap. The pre-eminent example of a feudal-patrician city north of the Alps is Berne, whose magistrates, the *Twingherren*, were primarily concerned to buttress their rural power, rather than to invest in trade, with the result that the pursuit of territorial aggrandisement became the city's *raison d'être*, in which endeavour it was extraordinarily successful, yet left the agricultural economy of its hinterland largely untouched.[47] It has to be

---

[42] Schneidmüller, 'Städtische Territorialpolitik', p. 134.
[43] Wunder, 'Reichsstädte', p. 87.
[44] Ibid., p. 88 (Ulm, Schwäbisch Hall, Heilbronn, Rothenburg); Schneidmüller, 'Städtische Territorialpolitik', pp. 133, 135 (Frankfurt am Main).
[45] Schmolz, 'Herrschaft und Dorf', p. 173.
[46] Scott, *Freiburg and the Breisgau*, pp. 78ff.
[47] Raiser, *Städtische Territorialpolitik*, pp. 23–4. In the fourteenth century Berne was famously described as 'in a certain sense the fortified headquarters of a corporation of aristocratic seigneurs' (A. Gasser, *Entstehung und Ausbildung der Landeshoheit im Gebiete der Schweizerischen Eidgenossenschaft* (Aarau–Leipzig, 1930), p. 394), but that was less true by the later fifteenth century, especially after the *Twingherrenstreit* of 1470, as patricians began to withdraw from civic office, acquire patents of nobility, and retire to stewardships of rural bailiwicks. See F. de Capitani, 'Sozialstruktur und Mechanismen der Herrschaft in der spätmittelalterlichen Stadt Bern', in Endres, *Nürnberg und Bern*, pp. 43–4.

said, though, that Berne was highly unusual, even among Swiss cities. Its rival Zurich was also a city of textile manufacturers and merchants, who were likewise represented on the council.[48] Zurich's territorial policy, therefore, was driven not only by the need to protect its patricians' landed interests but also by commercial imperatives, above all control of the rivers which bore Zurich's trade northwards to the Rhine and southwards on the upland routes over the alpine passes to Italy. Perhaps the only true comparison is with Metz, which over the centuries did everything in its power to entrench the rural lordships of its patricians, to the point where, in 1550, five Messin families owned two-thirds of all the city's rural property.[49]

About Raiser's second category there is general agreement. Long-distance trading cities were more concerned with safeguarding trade routes and commercial privileges than with acquiring territory for its own sake. Hence, where lands were acquired (often by mortgage), they lay axially along arteries of trade, rather than radially as the market area of a central place.[50] This is primarily the case with the cities of the Hansa,[51] but it might apply elsewhere, as with Frankfurt am Main. However, there were many more cities throughout Germany which *combined* the roles of entrepôt and central place, Erfurt and Ulm being classic examples. Yet we should also recall that two of Germany's foremost centres of manufacturing and commerce, Augsburg and Cologne, prospered without recourse to any rural territory at all.[52]

For Raiser's third category, the artisanal town, a rural territory fulfilled an essential function as a supplier of produce and raw materials, and as a consumer of urban goods and services. Hence, these towns were particularly keen to enforce exclusive buying and selling at the town's market (the *Marktzwang*) and, as a corollary, to suppress any marketing or forestalling within their own territory, or at least within their market franchise (*Bannmeile*).[53] The merit of this category is that it can encompass a span from large cities to small towns. The problems with it, however, are twofold. In the first place, it fails to recognise that some towns and cities secured control of their market area, not by

[48] N. Birnbaum, 'The Zwinglian Reformation in Zurich', *Past and Present* 15 (1959), 28–32.
[49] Raiser, *Städtische Territorialpolitik*, p. 26; J. Schneider, *La Ville de Metz aux XIIIe et XIVe siècles* (Nancy, 1950), pp. 406–7, 412, 424, 448. His argument is misunderstood by D. Nicholas, *The later medieval city 1300–1500* (London–New York, 1997), pp. 93–4.
[50] Raiser, *Städtische Territorialpolitik*, pp. 27–8; Nicholas, *Later medieval city*, p. 98.
[51] Behr, 'Landgebietspolitik', pp. 23, 25; Fritze, 'Stadt–Land-Beziehungen', p. 110.
[52] Augsburg did possess a very small territory to the north of the city, the Lower Bailiwick; see Kiessling, 'Herrschaft – Markt – Landbesitz', p. 187.
[53] Raiser, *Städtische Territorialpolitik*, pp. 30–1.

acquiring a dependent territory, but by extending their urban precinct (*Stadtmark*) into the countryside. The most striking example is the small imperial city of Wimpfen on the river Neckar, which extended its so-called *Markung* to embrace an area of around 30 km², which it equated with the ambit of its market franchise. This area was quite distinct from Wimpfen's rural territory (very modest in size), which was centred upon the Forest of Wimpfen, 11 km to the north-west, together with a few odd villages elsewhere.[54] Several north German cities pursued a similar strategy of extending their *Stadtmark* and protecting it by a series of ramparts-cum-ditches.[55]

The second objection is more serious. The response of German cities to those who defied their market rights was far from uniform. Reactions to the rise of country crafts, rural guilds and village markets ranged from suppression through supervision to integration – or even calm indifference. This variety of responses can hardly be explained by differences of territorial policy, predicated upon Raiser's threefold typology of towns and cities. Rather, it can only be understood in the light of the cities' wider relations with their surrounding countryside in terms of centrality within a regional economic system. To that we must now turn.

Economic relations

Urban hierarchies and networks

In Germany, the work of historical geographers has been particularly influential in analysing the economic relations between town and country. Taking the town's primary function to be a market, Hektor Ammann argued that around any town three zones of centrality might be discerned: the immediate marketing area; a wider marketing space which might encompass the narrower market areas of smaller towns; and a third area of economic influence determined by the intensity of long-distance trade. Subsequent research has refined the radii of his circles to suggest that the immediate market area (*Umland*) may range from 10 to 30 km, depending on the pull of the urban centre; the wider market area (*Hinterland*) may stretch up to 50 or 60 km, but rarely further; while the outer sphere of influence (*Einflußbereich*), from which visitors to the annual fair might be drawn or migrants attracted to the

---

[54] A. Hafer, *Wimpfen: Stadt–Raum-Beziehungen im späten Mittelalter* (Stuttgart, 1993), pp. 132–5, 174 (map), 268ff.; T. Scott and B. Scribner, 'Urban networks', in Scribner, *Germany*, pp. 117–18.

[55] J. Köppke, *Hildesheim, Einbeck, Göttingen und ihre Stadtmark im Mittelalter* (Hildesheim, 1967), pp. 103–6, 140–2, 145–6, and *passim*; Rösener, 'Aspekte', p. 670.

city's labour market, could extend to 100 km (in the case of true metropolises even further).[56] Centrality was not purely radial, however, and could be shaped by a network system, which is axial, linking towns as 'nodes, junctions, outposts or relays' of a trading network.[57] This axial principle has already been detected in the territorial policies of many Hanseatic cities. But it has a much wider application throughout the German lands, where the arteries of trade so strongly followed the country's extensive river system. On the upper Rhine, for instance, the wine-exporting communes of Alsace were located along the river Ill at regular intervals 'like pearls on a string', with elliptical market areas.[58] Again, topography and natural endowment might ensure that centrality was dendritic, with a metropolis as the gateway of an elongated hinterland, shaped like the trunk of a tree with branches emanating from it.[59] These varieties of centrality, moreover, were neither mutually exclusive nor immutable: they might complement each other and shift over time. By the mid-sixteenth century, for instance, Nördlingen in northern Swabia had lost much of its significance as a long-distance trading city, boasting an international fair, to become the market centre for its hinterland. Its economic centrality, in other words, was by then more radial than axial, as the city cautiously sought to dominate its immediate market area.[60]

Market franchises

In this sense, the term *Umlandpolitik* may be preferable to the more narrowly defined concept of *Territorialpolitik*, provided that we recognise that control of the immediate market area alone was often only the launching-pad for a much more ambitious policy of regional economic

[56] H. Ammann, 'Vom Lebensraum der mittelalterlichen Stadt', *Blätter für deutsche Landeskunde* 31 (1963), 290–3; P. Schöller, 'Der Markt als Zentralisationsphänomen: das Grundprinzip und seine Wandlung in Zeit und Raum', *Westfälische Forschungen* 15 (1962), 85–92. For a recent critique, see D. Rippmann, *Bauern und Städter: Stadt-Land-Beziehungen im 15. Jahrhundert. Das Beispiel Basel* (Basle–Frankfurt am Main, 1990), pp. 47–8. Ammann's typology is clearly indebted to W. Christaller, *Central places in southern Germany*, transl. C. W. Baskin (Englewood Cliffs, NJ, 1966) (German orig. Jena, 1933).

[57] P. M. Hohenberg and L. Hollen Lees, *The making of urban Europe 1000–1950* (Cambridge, MA–London, 1985), p. 62.

[58] Scott and Scribner, 'Urban networks', pp. 131–7; Christaller, *Central places*, pp. 57–8; T. Scott, *Regional identity and economic change: the upper Rhine, 1450–1600* (Oxford, 1997), p. 79.

[59] C. A. Smith, 'Exchange systems and the spatial distribution of elites: the organisation of stratification in agrarian society', in C. A. Smith (ed.), *Regional analysis*, 2 vols. (New York–San Francisco–London, 1976), vol. I, pp. 309–74.

[60] Kiessling, *Die Stadt*, p. 259.

hegemony. That is particularly evident where the cities' market franchises were concerned. Most German towns and cities sought to uphold a franchise with a radius of at least 1 or 2 German miles (7.4–14.7 km) (see n. 28), within which no other market might be held, any attempts to evade or pre-empt the urban market by forestalling or hawking were forbidden, and foreign lords prohibited from levying tolls or turnpike charges.[61] In the period from 1350 to 1600 such franchises were proclaimed – to take evidence from Swabia – by Nördlingen and Lauingen. What stands out, however, is that these ordinances often applied only to certain commodities and that they were frequently extended. In the mid-sixteenth century Lauingen doubled its general franchise from 1 to 2 miles in an effort to ward off Augsburg's commercial penetration, but imposed a 4-mile (29.5 km) franchise for loden cloth subject to its quality control (*Schau*), since the town could not obtain sufficient supplies of wool in the locality.[62] Larger metropolises were noticeably more aggressive in extending their *Bannmeilen*. Augsburg began in the fifteenth century with a modest 1-mile franchise, but by 1500 this had risen to 3 miles, and thereafter was extended to 6 or even 10 miles (73.6 km) on occasion.[63] By this means Augsburg contrived to subordinate much of the textile production of eastern Swabia to its *Schau*, and thereby was able to dominate its marketing and distribution. By contrast, a small Swabian territorial town, such as Mindelheim, had no need to impose a market franchise at all, since its overlords, the Frundsbergs, ensured that it functioned as the principal central place for their territory as a whole, so that its boundaries constituted the market franchise. By the sixteenth century the franchise area for most medium-sized towns in Swabia had reached 2 or 3 miles, for the larger cities 6 to 8 miles.[64]

The subordination of the hinterland

The extension of market franchises went hand in hand with increasing efforts to subordinate the economy of their hinterlands to the cities' needs. Several areas of late medieval Germany witnessed the rapid spread of rural crafts and manufacturing, whose output in many cases

---

[61] Kiessling, 'Umlandgefüge', pp. 38, 40–1; Kiessling, *Die Stadt*, p. 91.
[62] Kiessling, *Die Stadt*, pp. 194, 617.
[63] Kiessling, 'Umlandgefüge', pp. 40–1; Kiessling, 'Herrschaft – Markt – Landbesitz', p. 195.
[64] Kiessling, *Die Stadt*, pp. 635–6, 670, 706; Kiessling, 'Die "Nachbarschaft" und die "Regionalisierung" der Politik: Städte, Klöster und Adel in Ostschwaben um 1500', in F. Seibt and W. Eberhardt (eds.), *Europa 1500: Integrationsprozesse im Widerstreit. Staaten, Regionen, Personenverbände, Christenheit* (Stuttgart, 1987), pp. 265, 271.

was organised along early capitalist lines through the putting-out system (*Verlagssystem*). But however much the transformation of the rural economy was ultimately the consequence of urban investment and labour recruitment, its preconditions lay within the countryside itself. Swabia once again may serve as an example.

Chronologically, the rise of linen manufacturing on the northern littoral of Lake Constance can be traced back to the thirteenth century.[65] Here, growing population, in an area largely of partible inheritance at the western end of the lake, created pressure within the agrarian economy for by-employment, yet the linen industry was firmly established from an equally early date in the much less populous eastern Swabia and Allgäu, areas of impartible inheritance, somewhat wetter and colder than along Lake Constance, which were largely given over to dairying. This suggests that climate and topography could be as important as population pressure. For the low-lying marshy tracts along the rivers Iller and Lech, together with high rainfall on the northern slopes of the Alps, clearly created ideal conditions for flax-growing,[66] but after spinning and weaving the cloth still had to be bleached. Although various processes were employed, they all at one stage or another used milk before the cloths were finally crofted on bleaching-grounds. The coexistence of dairying and linen manufacture in eastern Swabia, therefore, was not accidental: the former functionally determined the latter.[67] Self-evidently, too, the availability of natural resources determined the spread and location of rural fulling plants or mills, foundries or glassworks, and metallurgical industries.

Yet the cities' attempts to harness the small towns and villages of their hinterlands as an economic and demographic reservoir, evident from the mid-fourteenth century onwards, were fraught with contradiction, for they sought at once to stimulate *and* to regulate rural production. Rural crafts and manufactures were encouraged – so long as they did not compete with the cities' domestic output. But this was easier said than done, especially if individual entrepreneurs deliberately disregarded civic ordinances to corner a particular market and to distribute its output to domestic and international customers directly, bypassing the urban exchanges and staples. Ideally, the countryside was to be restricted to working up raw materials or to the first stages of the

---

[65] H. Ammann, 'Die Anfänge der Leinenindustrie des Bodenseegebiets', *Alemannisches Jahrbuch* (1953), pp. 251–313; W. von Stromer, 'Gewerbereviere und Protoindustrien in Spätmittelalter und Frühneuzeit', in H. Pohl (ed.), *Gewerbe- und Industrielandschaften vom Spätmittelalter bis ins 20. Jahrhundert* (Stuttgart, 1986), pp. 47, 57.

[66] Kiessling, *Die Stadt*, p. 448.

[67] Scott, 'Economic landscapes', pp. 2–3.

manufacturing process itself. This can be illustrated by the development of the textile industry in Upper Germany.

As well as cultivating flax and spinning it into yarn, rural linen-weavers had originally produced lesser cloths of their own. But with the rise of fustian manufacture (cloth with a linen warp and cotton weft) the social relations of production altered. Because cotton was not an indigenous crop, but had to be imported from the Mediterranean, fustian-weaving came to be organised by urban merchants with long-distance trading connections. These entrepreneurs preferred to restrict the manufacture of the more profitable fustian to the urban guilds, where quality control was easier to enforce, but after some initial resistance rural weavers were allowed to make warps, which would then be sold to urban weavers or merchants for weaving with a cotton weft.[68] This division of labour came to prevail throughout Middle Swabia, and even spread to the manufacture of purely linen cloths such as *Golschen*. In this fashion, many smaller towns and markets, together with their catchment areas, became contracted suppliers of warps to the larger mercantile cities.[69] The pattern which typically developed was for the cities to ban weaving in their immediate *Umland* or market franchise area, to regulate the production of warps in their hinterland, and, should further supplies be required from their wider sphere of influence, to enter into collective guild purchase agreements with brokers at a fixed price.[70]

This division of labour was largely specific to the fustian industry. In northern Swabia, which by 1500 had become predominantly an area of wool production, few rural craftsmen wove woollen cloth. Production of loden, the heavy, felted, short-pile woollen cloth used for coats and blankets, remained an essentially urban trade, with countryfolk reduced to spinning yarn, which was often, though not exclusively, women's work. Even in thoroughgoing fustian regions, moreover, the pattern of concentric circles of differential activity might be subverted by buccaneering merchant houses, such as the Fuggers, who lured rural spinners

---

[68] R. Kiessling, 'Stadt und Land im Textilgewerbe Ostschwabens vom 14. bis zur Mitte des 16. Jahrhunderts', in N. Bulst, J. Hoock and F. Irsigler (eds.), *Bevölkerung, Wirtschaft und Gesellschaft: Stadt–Land-Beziehungen in Deutschland und Frankreich 14. bis 19. Jahrhundert* (Trier, 1983), p. 124; Kiessling, 'Umlandgefüge', pp. 42–3; Kiessling, 'Herrschaft – Markt – Landbesitz', pp. 200–1.

[69] Kiessling, 'Stadt und Land', pp. 125–6. *Golschen* is normally understood to be coarse linen (Kiessling, 'Umlandgefüge', p. 49; Kiessling, *Die Stadt*, p. 484), but elsewhere Kiessling takes it as high-quality linen (i.e. lawn): Kiessling, 'Stadt und Land', pp. 125, 127.

[70] Kiessling, *Die Stadt*, p. 482; Kiessling, 'Umlandgefüge', p. 42; Kiessling, 'Entwicklungstendenzen im ostschwäbischen Textilrevier während der Frühen Neuzeit', in J. Jahn and W. Hartung (eds.), *Gewerbe und Handel vor der Industrialisierung* (Sigmaringendorf, 1991), p. 30; R. Holbach, *Frühformen von Verlag und Grossbetrieb in der gewerblichen Produktion (13.–16. Jahrhundert)* (Stuttgart, 1994), p. 165.

and weavers in Ulm's hinterland away from civic supervision and into their employ, setting up rival enterprises under their own control in the small towns of Weissenhorn and Pfaffenhofen.[71] Here the Fuggers were able to capitalise on the fact that Ulm had permitted many more full-time fustian-weavers – anywhere between 300 and 600 – to ply their trade in its hinterland and to supply the city's market with finished cloths than its more restrictive east Swabian counterparts.[72]

The characteristic rise of semi-finished products in the countryside was echoed in other branches of manufacturing, particularly the wood-working and iron industries, where rural craftsmen would make wooden wheels, barrel-staves or bed-frames, ready to be finished by urban masters who clad them with iron. This applied in other areas of Germany as well. In the course of the fifteenth century, a wide range of semi-finished ironware was produced in Cologne's hinterland – knives, swords, armour, pots and pans – which were delivered to urban craftsmen for polishing, trimming, embellishing, or undergoing the later and more skilled stages of production (such as attaching handles).[73]

Rural putting-out

What impelled these developments was, above all, recourse to putting-out. Evidence for supplying raw materials or the tools of trade, or else for advancing the necessary capital, to dependent pieceworkers can be traced in the textile industry of the cities of Upper Swabia, the Lake Constance area, and northern Switzerland for linen and fustian, and in the Cologne region for woollen cloth, as far back as the late thirteenth century.[74] Less certain, however, is when merchants and richer craft-masters began to put out work to rural wage-labourers beyond the city

[71] Kiessling, *Die Stadt*, pp. 214–15; Kiessling, 'Umlandgefüge', pp. 48–9; Kiessling, 'Stadt und Land', pp. 119, 127; Kiessling, 'Herrschaft – Markt – Landbesitz', pp. 202–3.
[72] H. Kellenbenz, 'The fustian industry of the Ulm region in the fifteenth and early sixteenth centuries', in N. B. Harte and K. G. Ponting (eds.), *Cloth and clothing in medieval Europe: essays in memory of Professor E. M. Carus-Wilson* (London, 1983), pp. 261–4; B. Kirchgässner, 'Der Verlag im Spannungsfeld von Stadt und Umland', in Maschke and Sydow, *Stadt und Umland*, p. 86; Kiessling, 'Stadt und Land', p. 120; Holbach, *Frühformen*, p. 186.
[73] Kiessling, 'Stadt und Land', p. 131; Kiessling, 'Umlandgefüge', p. 43; Irsigler, 'Stadt und Umland', pp. 5–6.
[74] R. Kiessling, 'Frühe Verlagsverträge im ostschwäbischen Textilrevier', in H. Mordek (ed.), *Aus Archiven und Bibliotheken: Festschrift für Raymund Kottje zum 65. Geburtstag* (Frankfurt am Main, 1992), p. 443, following Ammann, 'Anfänge', pp. 251–313; F. Irsigler, 'Frühe Verlagsbeziehungen in der gewerblichen Produktion des westlichen Hanseraumes', in K. Fritze, E. Müller-Mertens and J. Schildhauer (eds.), *Zins – Profit – ursprüngliche Akkumulation* (Weimar, 1981), pp. 176, 181.

walls. Territorially organised putting-out did make its appearance in the first half of the fourteenth century around Constance, Ulm, Augsburg, Memmingen and in the Allgäu, but in Nördlingen and northern Swabia there was no sign of outwork as late as 1400.[75] In the case of Cologne, weavers in the city's guilds were already complaining about competition from rural wool-workers before 1300, but on closer inspection it turns out that cloth was being manufactured in a string of smaller towns around Cologne, rather than in villages. Once such cloth had received the city's quality seal, it was sold on by Cologne's merchants as a 'domestic' product.[76]

The chief stimulus to the spread of putting-out to the countryside was the desire on the part of urban merchants to avoid irksome civic or guild restrictions on production and employment within the cities. But it was not long before feudal lords espied the economic advantage in promoting rural textiles themselves. In the countryside such lords stepped into the merchants' shoes by offering to buy up and distribute the output of their peasants' by-employment.[77] All the principal textile areas of Germany, from Thuringia and Westphalia in the north to the regions already discussed further south, were penetrated to some degree by the putting-out system, but its deployment varied according to the type of cloth produced. A comparison between linen and fustian manufacture will make this point clear.[78] Where fustian-weaving came to predominate, the cost of importing raw cotton from abroad ensured that production required the injection of merchant capital; the first major putter-out around the city of Constance, for instance, was a financier and speculator, Ulrich Imholz, active in the early 1400s. But where fustian manufacturing failed to supplant linen-weaving – as with St Gallen, the tiny city-state which dominated the textile industry of eastern Switzerland – putting-out was hardly deployed until the early sixteenth century.[79]

The other branches of industry in which the putting-out system was

[75] Kiessling, 'Frühe Verlagsverträge', pp. 444–5, which revises his more cautious dating to the early fifteenth century expressed in 'Stadt und Land', pp. 117–19. For Memmingen, see also Kiessling, *Die Stadt*, p. 482.
[76] Irsigler, 'Frühe Verlagsbeziehungen', pp. 181–2. See Holbach, *Frühformen*, pp. 97–8.
[77] Kiessling, 'Frühe Verlagsverträge', p. 456.
[78] Held, *Zwischen Marktplatz und Anger*, p. 173; Holbach, *Frühformen*, p. 114, who notes the case of Gera where, characteristically, the preparation of wool and its weaving were organised by outwork in *Verlag*, but dyeing and finishing were undertaken centrally in the town. Ibid., pp. 167–9 for Westphalia's linen industry.
[79] Kirchgässner, 'Verlag', pp. 93–7. Linen *Verlag* did occur in Swabia, however, before the sixteenth century, though it was never prevalent (Kiessling, 'Frühe Verlagsverträge', pp. 451–2). On St Gallen's linen industry see H. C. Peyer, *Leinwandgewerbe und Fernhandel der Stadt St. Gallen von den Anfängen bis 1520*, 2 vols. (St Gallen, 1959–60).

commonplace were metal-, wood- and leather-working. Just as with wool-weaving, though a century later, Cologne's merchants used putting-out to employ iron-workers in a vast swath of countryside from the Eifel through Berg and Mark to the Sauerland to make semi-finished metalwares, not least for the city's weapons industry; to that end the city established stamping- and grinding-mills in its subsidiary towns.[80] But the production of the main centres east of the Rhine was never monopolised by Cologne; indeed, Solingen enjoyed a flourishing independent trade with Antwerp and the Low Countries in the sixteenth century.[81] This somewhat looser network of town–country relations in metallurgical putting-out can also be observed in the area of greatest technological advance in late medieval Germany, Nuremberg with the district of the Upper Palatinate to the east. Nuremberg never organised its hinterland as an industrial zone for the mass production of metal goods in the way that the Upper Swabian cities did with linen- and fustian-weaving. In 1534 the city's iron merchants were even prepared to cede all production by putting-out to a single merchant house, the Ambergers, in order to concentrate on distribution. It was as long-distance traders and investors that they used putting-out to secure supplies of copper, silver and lead from the mines of Bohemia, the Erzgebirge and Thuringia, rather than as putters-out controlling the production of Nuremberg's hinterland. Along the trade routes to these mining regions villagers were employed on piecework to fashion wooden goods from the forests of the Fichtelgebirge and Thuringia. This axial putting-out was the origin of the city's fame as a producer of wooden toys, gewgaws and carved objects, the so-called *Nürnberger Tand*.[82] Moreover, unlike textiles, in those cases where putting-out was used in metal production, especially in Nuremberg's pioneering wire-drawing sector (fully automated by 1590), it dominated the later, rather than the preliminary, stages of manufacture.[83]

The variations in the forms of putting-out which this brief survey has revealed should make us cautious about attributing to it a pivotal significance in the rise of early capitalism or the spread of proto-industrialisation. Hermann Aubin's researches on Nuremberg – the test-case, *par excellence* – led him firmly to the conclusion that early capitalist business practices postdate the emergence of putting-out, whose origins he identifies instead in the prevailing shortage of the means of produc-

---

[80] Irsigler, 'Frühe Verlagsbeziehungen', pp. 181–2; Holbach, *Frühformen*, pp. 309–10.
[81] Holbach, *Frühformen*, p. 252.
[82] H. Aubin, 'Formen und Verbreitung des Verlagswesens in der Altnürnberger Wirtschaft', in Stadtarchiv Nürnberg, *Beiträge*, vol. II, pp. 641, 645, 649–53, 646; Holbach, *Frühformen*, p. 533.
[83] von Stromer, 'Gewerbereviere', pp. 87–9.

tion in the middle ages.[84] With the exception of liquation plants in the mining industry, it is in fact very hard to point to capitalist investment which might have led to the establishment of factory production on an industrial scale. Where such proto-factories or industries did emerge before 1500 – and Nuremberg's metallurgy is the prime example – they could survive for centuries without prompting any epochal shift to industrialisation.[85] That was true of textiles as well. In the district of Altenburg in the Siegerland south-east of Cologne, to take a particularly telling example, a large textile enterprise (*Zeugwirkerei*) was founded in the sixteenth century by Heinrich Cramer, who employed Netherlandish cloth-workers equipped with the latest technology of yarn-spinning wheels in 100 weaving sheds, complete with a fulling-mill and a dyeing plant. As well as production in this manufactory, piecework was also put out to weavers in the surrounding villages, and Cramer also invested in extensive sheep farms to maintain the supply of raw wool.[86] Yet even this classic instance of vertical integration never gave any sign that Cramer's enterprise might be the prelude to full-scale industrialisation of the region.

Rural competition

The increasing economic domination of hinterlands by their cities in the period from 1350 to 1600, of which the putting-out system was the most striking manifestation, was not accepted without resistance; indeed, the activity of entrepreneurs who employed outworkers in the countryside in order to circumvent urban ceilings on production served to create competition for the cities' guilds and markets. That was especially true of textiles, where complaints about rural weavers (*Gäuweber*), who wove to lesser standards, undercut urban price tariffs, and shunned the civic cloth exchanges, were legion across the breadth of Upper Germany from Lake Constance to the Allgäu.[87] The problem of the rural weavers, however, was certainly not caused by putting-out

---

[84] Aubin, 'Formen', pp. 663, 666. *Verlag* hardly penetrated the overseas trading cities of the Hanseatic League; as entrepôts, small-scale commodity production was their hallmark. See E. Pitz, 'Wirtschaftliche und soziale Probleme der gewerblichen Entwicklung im 15./16. Jahrhundert nach hansisch-niederdeutschen Quellen', in F. Lütge (ed.), *Wirtschaftliche und soziale Probleme der gewerblichen Entwicklung im 15.–16. und 19. Jahrhundert* (Stuttgart, 1968), p. 37. Ship-building provides a partial exception (ibid., p. 39). For other scattered references see Holbach, *Frühformen*, pp. 370, 425.
[85] von Stromer, 'Gewerbereviere', pp. 42ff.
[86] Holbach, *Frühformen*, pp. 113–14.
[87] Kirchgässner, 'Verlag', p. 86; Kiessling, 'Herrschaft – Markt – Landbesitz', pp. 202–3; Kiessling, 'Stadt und Land', pp. 118–20.

alone. Wherever the need for supplementary income arose, peasants might resort to weaving as a by-employment – indeed, the rise of an entire cottar class in Swabia has been attributed to the spread of rural weaving.[88] Memmingen's urban textile guilds fought a running battle around 1500 against the rural weavers, many of them resident within the city's own territory, while Nördlingen's cloth industry was threatened by rural textiles deliberately promoted by the city's princely neighbours, the counts of Oettingen. These issues surfaced once again during the German Peasants' War of 1525, when territorial dependants of the Swabian imperial cities, many engaged in rural manufacturing, failed to forge alliances of solidarity with urban wage-earning weavers.[89]

Yet the textile cities of Upper Germany faced competition on a much broader front than that. Quite apart from the threat posed by rural industries, their artisans were exposed to competition from a wide variety of everyday craft goods produced in the countryside – Memmingen's cobblers and leather-workers are just two examples – which owed nothing whatever to the impact of early capitalism or the use of the putting-out system. Moreover, notwithstanding the recourse to *Marktzwang*, their chartered markets were being challenged by rival foundations in their hinterlands – as Nördlingen, Memmingen and Kempten all complained. Even the territorial town of Mindelheim, despite being isolated from any immediate threat by the *cordon sanitaire* of Frundsberg lordship, found itself confronted with market competition from beyond its borders.[90]

The proliferation of country crafts and village markets was by no means confined to Swabia – or even to Germany: it was a pan-European phenomenon in this period,[91] whose aetiology can barely be explored here. Within Germany itself there was scarcely a region, from Mecklenburg or Saxony in the north to Bavaria and Swabia in the south, where the threat of rural competition did not exercise urban magistrates (or territorial rulers, for that matter), though the coastal cities of the

---

[88] H. Grees, *Ländliche Unterschichten und ländliche Siedlung in Ostschwaben* (Tübingen, 1975).

[89] R. Kiessling, 'Umlandpolitik, wirtschaftliche Verflechtung und innerstädtischer Konflikt in den schwäbischen Reichsstädten an der Wende vom Mittelalter zur Frühen Neuzeit', in J. Jahn, W. Hartung and I. Eberl (eds.), *Oberdeutsche Städte im Vergleich: Mittelalter und Frühe Neuzeit* (Sigmaringendorf, 1989), pp. 115, 120; Kiessling, *Die Stadt*, pp. 224, 483–90, 775–84.

[90] Kiessling, *Die Stadt*, pp. 180–5, 443–7, 508–9, 690; Kiessling, '"Nachbarschaft"', pp. 266, 270.

[91] H. Kellenbenz, 'Rural industries in the West from the end of the middle ages to the eighteenth century', in P. Earle (ed.), *Essays in European economic history* (Oxford, 1974), pp. 45–88. Kellenbenz's main emphasis, however, is on crafts from the later sixteenth century onwards.

Hanseatic League seem to have remained relatively unscathed – or indifferent.[92] But it is generally agreed that the greatest concentration was in south-west Germany and Switzerland, areas of relatively dense population but with few obvious signs, at least until the later sixteenth century, of rural immiseration.[93] On the upper Rhine the middling territorial towns with populations up to 5,000, rather than the larger independent imperial cities, seem to have been worst affected,[94] which might suggest that the pursuit of a territorial policy offered some protection against economic competition from the countryside. That is exactly what some have argued for the Swabian imperial cities, and, in northern Germany, for the city of Soest in Westphalia, which used its territorial sovereignty to enforce market rights and to suppress artisan activity in the surrounding countryside.[95] As a general statement, however, this explanation does not hold water. It does not apply, as we have seen, to several important Swabian cities, and above all it ignores the experience of the powerful Swiss city-states, whose metropolises without exception were exposed to burgeoning crafts and informal marketing in their cantonal hinterlands. In the long run, for the territorial towns of Germany the issue was resolved by their princely rulers 'territorialising' crafts and manufacturing, that is to say, integrating rural crafts into a common structure embracing town and country, Bavaria being the classic example.[96] But that solution was only achieved at the price of eroding or destroying the traditional liberties and ancient market privileges of the territorial towns.[97] For their part, the imperial and free cities had to survive as best they could.

Patterns of integration and subordination

The pattern of town–country relations in the German-speaking lands between 1350 and 1600, therefore, admits of no easy generalisations. The size of a city's territory was no sure guide either to that city's economic clout[98] or to its ability to absorb or suppress competition from

---

[92] Fritze, *Wendepunkt*, p. 108; Fritze, *Bürger*, pp. 46–51; Fritze, 'Stadt–Land-Beziehungen', p. 111. The threat from rural crafts is put somewhat higher by Pitz, 'Wirtschaftliche und soziale Probleme', p. 34.

[93] W. Reininghaus, *Gewerbe in der Frühen Neuzeit* (Munich, 1990), pp. 65ff., 70.

[94] Scott, *Freiburg and the Breisgau*, pp. 116–18, 157–60; Scott, *Regional identity*, pp. 102–72.

[95] Wunder, 'Reichsstädte', p. 88; K. Diekmann, 'Die Herrschaft der Stadt Soest über ihre Börde', Diss. jur. Münster, 1962, pp. 133–7; Raiser, *Städtische Territorialpolitik*, p. 31.

[96] Kiessling, *Die Stadt*, pp. 749–50.

[97] For the territorial ordinance of 1495 in the margraviate of Baden, see Scott, *Regional identity*, p. 108.

[98] See C. R. Friedrichs, 'The Swiss and German city-states', in R. Griffith and C. G.

its hinterland. More fundamentally, however, a city's economic influence could lead to diametrically opposing patterns of town–country
relations. To test this point, let us, in conclusion, survey the contrasting
fortunes of three leading cities, Nuremberg, Cologne and Augsburg.
Nuremberg, with the largest territory of any German city, brought
neighbouring towns and villages beyond its immediate hinterland into
the orbit of its cloth- and metal-working industries. This was more than
an act of economic imperialism: the communities themselves were eager
to grab a share of Nuremberg's industrial prosperity and marketing
power. Beyond this hinterland lay an arc of cloth-producing towns to
the south-west and another of metallurgical centres to the east, both
possessing sufficient economic centrality to set bounds on Nuremberg's
influence. Within these arcs lay Nuremberg's 'economic unit', in which
metropolis and subaltern central places combined in a mutually reinforcing integrated regional economic system.[99] Beyond that lay, of course,
a wider sphere of influence, but once the levers of economic power were
no longer direct but indirect, with the city reliant upon middlemen, then
this outer third circle or wider sphere of influence was clearly no longer
part of the city's 'economic unit'.[100]

In the case of Cologne, a city without a landed territory, the economic
unit was not only somewhat larger than Nuremberg's, with a maximum
radius of around 70 km as opposed to the latter's 50 km; it was, as we
have seen, less thoroughly integrated, too. What stands out, above all, is
the highly fluctuating size of its trade-specific areas of supply and
putting-out. These range from a tightly drawn ellipse for hops, through
a somewhat larger oval for cloth, to a circle of steel suppliers lying
entirely eccentric of the city east of the Rhine, with a yet larger, irregular
circle of copper and iron suppliers concentric around the city, to the
largest circle of all, that of suppliers of peltry.[101] It would be hazardous
simply to equate Cologne's economic unit with the largest circle *tout
court*, not least because peltry was of much less importance to the city's
economy than metal goods or cloth. Rather, we should conceive of the
city's economic unit in terms of variable geometry, with different configurations and levels of intensity.

With Augsburg, by contrast, Cologne's direct counterpart as an overseas manufacturing and trading city without a dependent territory, an
entirely different situation confronts us. Its economic unit, it is true, had

Thomas (eds.), *The city-state in five cultures* (Santa Barbara, CA–London, 1981),
p. 124.
[99] Ammann, *Wirtschaftliche Stellung*, pp. 194–223.
[100] See the general observations in Kiessling, 'Umlandgefüge', p. 45.
[101] Irsigler, 'Stadt und Umland', pp. 7, 14 (map).

a radius of around 60 to 70 km; by 1550 its active textile hinterland, in terms of weavers under civic control or of migrants to the city, may even have been no more than 40 km in radius, with the small and medium-sized towns therein fulfilling the role of sub-central collection-points or intermediate markets in a smoothly integrated system. But on the fringes of its economic sphere, where its influence should have been weakest, Augsburg began to act as a commercial predator with overt monopolistic tendencies. The city's fustian merchants and putters-out began to throttle the textile industry of such centres as Lauingen (just within the 70-km radius), Nördlingen and Memmingen (just outside), and even threatened the western Swabian metropolis of Ulm. This in large measure accounts for Nördlingen's switch to loden production, and Lauingen's turn towards both wool and *Golschen*; while, for its part, one of Memmingen's leading merchant dynasties, the Vöhlin, upped sticks and decamped to Augsburg early in the sixteenth century.[102] In the long run, the middling cities of eastern Swabia found their economic vitality stunted in the shade of Augsburg's commercial upas-tree – a contradictory result of market integration and the intensification of town–country relations which in the German context was exceptional, but which seems to reflect a general pattern in the economy of early modern Europe as a whole.[103]

[102] Kiessling, 'Herrschaft – Markt – Landbesitz', p. 202; Kiessling, *Die Stadt*, pp. 224, 391, 499, 525, 617, 738–9; Kiessling, 'Umlandgefüge', pp. 48–9.

[103] M. Prak, 'Le regioni nella prima Europa moderna', *Proposte e ricerche: economia e società nella storia dell'Italia centrale* 35 (1995), 21.

10 Town and country in Switzerland, 1450–1750

Martin Körner

Translated by R. Morris and S. R. Epstein

It was not until the 1970s and 1980s that Swiss historians began to turn their attention to the relationship between town and country.[1] The first systematic studies by Frantisek Graus on the late middle ages and Jean-François Bergier on the early modern period focused on the ambivalence of the concept of a 'town', the demographic differences between town and country, the shifting legal relationships between town- and country-dwellers, the economic dependence of farmers and handicraft workers on town markets, and urban territorial policy.[2] Whereas Graus stressed the underlying persistence of the feudal hierarchy, the development of rural resistance to urban domination and the unstable anti-dynastic alliances between peasants and townsmen, Bergier set out a series of analytical contrasts – *espace rural* versus *tissu urbain*, symbiosis versus dependence – to express the townsmen's economic domination of rural areas through control over the labour market and over foreign mercenary services, over the putting-out system and rural credit, and, more generally, their legal and administrative centrality. Both authors drew attention to the fact that the sources tend to show us the countryside through urban eyes rather than vice versa. Late medieval observers tended either to idealise or to demonise the urban environment, while descriptions of Switzerland by early modern travellers often failed to distinguish clearly between town and country.

[1] *Villes et campagnes XVᵉ–XXᵉ siècle* (Lyons, 1977); G. Gaudard, C. Pfaff and R. Ruffieux (eds.), *Freiburg: Die Stadt und ihr Territorium. Politische, soziale und kulturelle Aspekte des Verhältnisses Stadt-Land seit dem Spätmittelalter* (Fribourg, 1981); M. Svilar (ed.), *Stadt und Land. Die Geschichte einer gegenseitigen Abhängigkeit* (Berne, 1988).

[2] F. Graus, 'Tendenzen der Stadt–Land Beziehungen im ausgehenden Mittelalter', in Gaudard, Pfaff and Ruffieux, *Freiburg*, pp. 26–41; J. -F. Bergier, 'Les rapports économiques et sociaux entre les villes et la campagne en Suisse au cours des temps modernes', ibid., pp. 42–59. Bergier's essay has also appeared as 'Villes et campagnes en Suisse sous l'ancien régime. Quelques variations', *Schweizerische Zeitschrift für Geschichte* 31 (1991), 391–402.

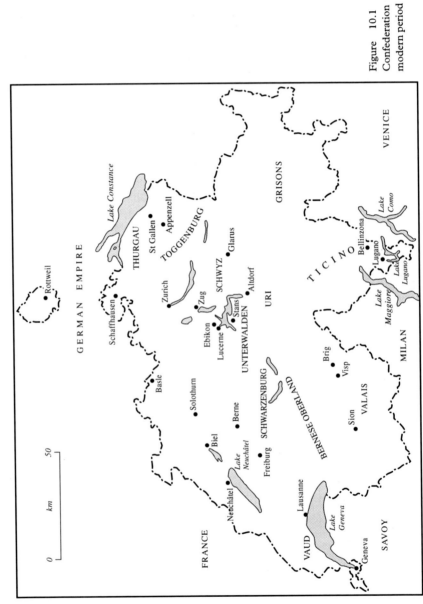

Figure 10.1 The Swiss Confederation in the early modern period

Institutional structures

What meaning should be assigned to the words 'town' and 'country'?[3] Medieval historians have established certain criteria for a 'town', which include autonomous government by a local authority, a charter of rights and liberties, concentration of trade and industry, and a system of defence. To centres which met these criteria we must add, in the early modern period, a growing number of rural settlements which increasingly became a focus for their immediate hinterland and whose inhabitants aspired to a distinctly 'urban' way of life.[4] An analogous distinction can be made between the constitutional identities of different rural areas of Switzerland during our period: rural republics; territories subject to the city-states; the Common Territories, which were ruled by a variety of governing councils attended by representatives of both urban and rural areas; and rural populations focusing on a progressively more 'urban' local centre.

Thus, although a typology based only on data from the old Swiss Confederacy would be too restrictive, we must certainly retain the traditional differentiation between urban and peasant republics, small member 'states' of the Swiss Confederation. We will therefore distinguish on the one hand the hierarchy of relations between the political centres in some typical city-states (Zurich, Berne, Lucerne, Freiburg, Solothurn, Basle, Schaffhausen and Geneva) and their rural hinterland, and on the other hand the rather more vague distinction between town and country in the fiefdoms and predominantly rural states. In monarchic areas such as St Gallen (ruled by its abbot), the dukedom of Neuenburg and the old prince-bishopric of Basle, the political and economic dominance of the chief cities – St Gallen, Neuenburg and Pruntrut – was still evident. Things are less clear in the Valais: the influence of the chief towns of the upper Zenden – Brig, Visp, Raron, Siders and Sitten – on the valley communities, and the interaction between this town–country relationship and the Great Council of Sitten, which was presided over by the bishop up to the 1630s, have still to be examined in detail.[5] In Graubünden and the peasant republics the situation was different again. In seventeenth-century Uri, the 'capital',

---

[3] W. Bickel, *Bevölkerungsgeschichte und Bevölkerungspolitik der Schweiz seit dem Ausgang des Mittelalters* (Zurich, 1947), pp. 56–65; J.-F. Bergier, *Wirtschaftsgeschichte der Schweiz von den Anfängen bis zur Gegenwart* (Zurich, 1990), pp. 40–7; M. Mattmüller, *Bevölkerungsgeschichte der Schweiz*, vol. I: *Die frühe Neuzeit 1500–1700* (Basle, 1987), pp. 196–227; F. Walter, *La Suisse urbaine 1750–1950* (Geneva, 1993), pp. 21–2. See also Graus, 'Tendenzen', p. 17; Bergier, 'Rapports', 393.

[4] See also K. Gerteis, *Die deutschen Städte in der Frühen Neuzeit. Zur Vorgeschichte der 'bürgerlichen Welt'* (Darmstadt, 1986), pp. 13–17.

[5] In this connection a study of the resolutions of the Council of the Valais would be very

Altdorf, exerted an irresistible attraction over the elite elements in the population, and this created a degree of antagonism between the dominant centre and the surrounding countryside.[6]

Agrarian historians tend to categorise rural areas according to their dominant agricultural activity: into lowlands producing grain and uplands devoted to pasture, with a third mixed zone combining the two, and a fourth constituted by the self-sufficient communities of the Alps.[7] But we can also distinguish between regions whose products were almost entirely agricultural and those which were increasingly active in commerce and industry.[8] How are we to describe the nexus of inter-action, solidarity and dependence which connected the rural areas, with their widely differing constitutional and economic structures, and the hierarchy of the network of towns? There have been a few preliminary studies, but there is little theoretical work on the subject and few attempts at empirical study based on any particular model.[9]

In the late fourteenth and fifteenth centuries there were frequent conflicts among the confederal republics and between urban and rural areas on the basis of contrasting interpretations of the alliances and treaties that bound them.[10] However, the covenant drawn up at the Diet of Stans in 1481, which regulated federal relations until 1798, consolidated the position of the peasant republics in Switzerland's federal and social structure and thereafter frequently acted as a brake on the centralising endeavours of the city-states. The Reformation, which split the Confederation along confessional lines, also weakened the traditional opposition between town and country and produced a new system of alliances.[11]

In the second half of the sixteenth century, 35 per cent of the items

---

worth while. Nine volumes, covering the period up to 1613, have been published to date (*Walliser Landratsabschiede seit dem Jahre 1500* (Brig, 1916–)).

[6] U. Kälin, *Die Urner Magistraten-Familien. Herrschaft, ökonomische Lage und Lebensstil einer ländlichen Oberschicht, 1700–1850* (Zurich, 1991), p. 14.

[7] Mattmüller, *Bevölkerungsgeschichte*, vol. I, pp. 409–10; J. Mathieu, *Eine Agrargeschichte der inneren Alpen. Graubünden, Tessin, Wallis 1500–1800* (Zurich, 1992), pp. 19–41.

[8] R. Braun, *Das ausgehende Ancien Régime in der Schweiz. Aufriss einer Sozial- und Wirtschaftsgeschichte des 18. Jahrhunderts* (Göttingen–Zurich, 1984), esp. pp. 58–142. See also T. Meyer, *Handwerk, Hauswerk, Heimarbeit: nicht-agrarische Tätigkeiten und Erwerbsformen in einem traditionellen Ackerbaugebiet des 18. Jahrhunderts (Zürcher Unter-land)* (Zurich, 1986); and for a contrasting view U. Pfister, *Die Zürcher Fabriques. Proto-industrielles Wachstum vom 16. zum 18. Jahrhundert* (Zurich, 1992).

[9] A. Radeff, 'Cercles ou noyaux? Les espaces lausannois au XVIIᵉ siècle', *Schweizerische Zeitschrift für Geschichte* 34 (1984), 69–86.

[10] *Handbuch der Schweizergeschichte* (Zurich, 1972), vol. I, pp. 232–3, 268–70, 304, 326–8; H. C. Peyer, *Verfassungsgeschichte der alten Schweiz* (Zurich, 1978), pp. 39–41, 84–5; E. Walder, *Das Stanser Verkommnis. Ein Kapitel eidgenössischer Geschichte* (Stans, 1994).

[11] Peyer, *Verfassungsgeschichte*, esp. pp. 40–4, 86–7; see also *Geschichte der Schweiz und der*

discussed at the meetings of the thirteen members of the Confederation were tabled by representatives of the five peasant republics of Uri, Schwyz, Unterwalden, Glarus and Appenzell – an adequate representation of their relative political weight.[12] Between 1618 and 1648 there were well over 660 items relating to the external economy, but not all of these were of equal interest to the five republics, which were practically absent from debates on foreign trade, but made their presence felt in discussions over pensions and the hire of mercenaries. On the other hand, although they were very directly involved in the 670 or so debates relating to the internal economy, it is noticeable that they were seldom able to impose their will on the economically more powerful urban republics in such matters as internal customs duties.[13]

The rural and urban landscape[14]

The economic, social and administrative activities of the towns imposed fundamental changes on their immediate hinterland and on the wider landscape.[15] The towns surrounded themselves with fortifications, extended existing roads and built new ones through their territories that had to be fit for wheeled traffic.[16] This altered the rural landscape and stimulated the development of the smaller towns and communities along the way.[17] As urban entrepreneurs began to organise rural cottage industries, the very look of the villages changed as houses were adapted to fit in with changed working conditions. This was the origin of the

Schweizer (Basle, 1986), pp. 387–8; *Handbuch*, vol. I, pp. 421–2; U. Im Hof, *Die Schweiz. Illustrierte Geschichte der Eidgenossenschaft* (Stuttgart, 1984), p. 79.

[12] The members of the Confederation were as follows (with the date of association in brackets): Uri, Schwyz and Unterwalden (1291), Lucerne (1332), Zurich (1351), Glarus and Zug (1352), Berne (1353), Solothurn and Fribourg (1481), Basle and Schaffhausen (1501), Appenzell (1513). Alliances were established with Neuchâtel (1424), St Gallen (1451), Valais (1473), the Grisons (1497), Geneva (1558).

[13] M. Körner, 'Eidgenössische Wirtschaftspolitik im 17. Jarhundert. Anteil und Gewicht der Bergkantone', in L. Carlen and G. Imboden (eds.), *Wirtschaft des alpinen Raums im 17. Jahrhundert* (Brig, 1988), pp. 75–7. A systematic examination of the aspects of economic policy discussed at the conferences of the four forest cantons (Lucerne, Uri, Schwyz and Unterwalden) and of the five inner republics (the four forest cantons plus Zug) could throw much needed light on relations between the rural republics and their urban counterpart, Lucerne.

[14] This section relies heavily upon *Die Kunstdenkmäler der Schweiz* (Basle, 1933–).

[15] Gerteis, *Städte*, pp. 34–8.

[16] See, for example, the network of roads around Berne as shown in an anonymous watercolour, 'A view of Berne from the Bantigerhubel', *c.*1800 (Berne, private collection, reproduced in C. Menz and B. Weber, *Berneim Bild 1680–1880* (Berne, 1981), p. 57).

[17] A. Hauser, *Was für ein Leben. Schweizer Alltag vom 15. bis 18. Jahrhundert* (Zurich, 1987), p. 35; H. Wicki, *Bevölkerung und Wirtschaft des Kantons Luzern im 18. Jahrhundert* (Lucerne, 1979), pp. 464–5.

ribbon-weavers' houses so typical of the Basle area; the proto-industrial landscape around Zurich was dotted with large houses, subdivided and occupied by numerous families working from home – the typical houses known as *Reihenflarz, Querflarz* and *Längsflarz*.[18]

The business of regional government itself set its mark on the landscape: accommodation for functionaries, tax collectors and customs officials; fortified residences for local governors; state demesnes and granaries; increased exploitation of woodlands and quarries.[19] In places, the countryside assumed a tamer appearance as urban aristocrats acquired country estates and summer residences, surrounded by parkland and approached by well-maintained avenues.[20] The elites of Lucerne set the trend towards land ownership in the sixteenth century, but the idea appealed to imitators elsewhere. A wealthy and politically successful burgher would begin by owning at least one town house. Then he would aspire to a conveniently situated country residence surrounded by gardens, vineyards and meadows; move on to a bigger and better property, with perhaps a fishpond so he could eat his own fish on Fridays; add some summer grazing for his cattle and horses; and finally buy himself a chateau.[21] The urban aristocracy's craze for country estates did not reach Geneva until the seventeenth century; the eighteenth century has been described as the golden age of French-style chateau building.[22]

The nearer to the town, the more perceptible the urban influence. In the surrounding countryside, especially in the roadside villages, the traditional landscape yielded to gardens, pasture and other specialised usage for the benefit of the urban population.[23] Almost all these

---

[18] P. Fink, *Geschichte der Basler Bandindustrie 1550–1800* (Basle, 1983), pp. 86–7; R. Jäger et al., *Baumwollgarn als Schicksalsfaden. Wirtschaftliche und gesellschaftliche Entwicklungen in einem ländlichen Industriegebiet (Zürcher Oberland) 1750–1920* (Zurich, 1986), pp. 37–43.

[19] F. Guex, *Bruchstein, Kalk und Subventionen. Das Zuricher Baumeisterbuch als Quelle zum Bauwesen des 16. Jahrhunderts* (Zurich, 1986), pp. 65, 195; M. Irniger, *Der Sihlwald und sein Umland. Waldnutzung, Viehzucht und Ackerbau im Albisgebiet von 1400–1600* (Zurich, 1991).

[20] J. Schweizer, 'Burgen, Schlösser und Landsitze', in *Illustrierter Berner Enzyklopädie*, vol. III: *Siedlung und Architektur im Kanton Bern* (Wabern and Berne, 1987), pp. 80–109; A. Radeff, *Lausanne et ses campagnes au 17ᵉ siècle* (Lausanne, 1979), pp. 237–51, map on p. 240.

[21] M. Körner, 'Endettement paysan, placements bourgeois et finances urbaines en Suisse au XVI siècle', in *Villes et campagnes*, pp. 76–7; K. Messmer and P. Hoppe, *Luzerner Patriziat. Sozial- und wirtschaftsgeschichtliche Studien zur Entstehung und Entwicklung im 16. und 17. Jahrhundert* (Lucerne, 1974), pp. 132–43.

[22] *Encyclopédie de Genève*, vol. II: *La Campagne genevoise* (Geneva, 1989), pp. 43–4.

[23] A.-M. Piuz, 'Le marché urbain', in her *A Genève et autour de Genève aux XVIIᵉ et XVIIIᵉ siècles. Etudes d'histoire économique* (Lausanne, 1985), pp. 54–5.

villages boasted some property owned by a wealthy burgher.[24] Closer
still to the town, in the lands under its immediate jurisdiction, one could
find a medieval legacy of monasteries (some newly secularised), plague
and leper houses, gallows and mills, to which more recent times had
added bleaching-grounds, brickworks, quarries, vineyards, fairgrounds,
common lands, an ever-increasing number of gardens, and summer-
houses. This area merged almost imperceptibly into the suburbs just
outside the town walls, with their guest-houses, taverns and religious
houses – and their populations of journeymen, artisans, gardeners,
labourers in farm and vineyard, fishermen, beggars and vagabonds, with
here and there a henhouse or sty for the livestock which – like tanning,
smithing, dyeing and (from the end of the seventeenth century) textiles
– was no longer permitted within the town walls.[25] Some maps in the
historical atlas of Swiss towns show the erosion of the countryside
resulting from urban growth during our period.[26]

Sometimes innovations originated from the countryside, and the
matter had to be argued out with the urban government. One example is
the enclosure movement. In the Freiburg mountains it was imposed by
the urban patriciate and governors towards the end of the sixteenth
century, but in the canton of Lucerne the initiative for enclosure, as well
as irrigation and the partition of woodlands, came, both then and later,
from the peasants themselves, who forced their new ideas on the town
council despite the latter's vigorous resistance.[27] In the canton of Schaffhausen, however, the council acted swiftly to prevent vineyards being dug
up.[28] It seems that even in the sixteenth century, these rural–urban
disputes over agricultural innovation were already decisively altering the
agrarian landscape. Villages, too, were significantly affected by another
peasant initiative, the two waves of chapel and church building which
swept the country in the later fifteenth century, and again shortly before
the Reformation.[29] Research in the Lucerne area has shown that many
new parish churches built in the eighteenth century were initiated, and to

[24] W. Maync, *Bernische Wohnschlösser, Bernische Campagnen, Kleine Berner Landsitze* (Berne, 1979–83).
[25] *Siedlungsforschung: Archäologie–Geschichte–Geographie* (Bonn, 1983/4–).
[26] *Historischer Städteatlas der Schweiz*, vol. I: *Frauenfeld*, vol. II: *Neunkirch*, vol. III: *Weesen* (Zurich, 1966).
[27] N. Morard, 'Les premières enclosures dans le canton de Fribourg à la fin du moyen âge et le progrès de l'individualisme agraire', *Schweizerische Zeitschrift für Geschichte* 21 (1971), 249–81; A. Ineichen, *Innovative Bauern. Einhegungen, Bewässerung und Waldteilung im Kanton Luzern im 16. und 17. Jahrhundert* (Lucerne, 1996).
[28] U. Leu, 'Zur Geschichte des Weinbaus in Merishausen', *Schaffhauser Beiträge zur Geschichte* 63 (1986), 153–6.
[29] H. von Rütte, 'Kontinuität und Bruch in der Religionspraxis der Bauern', *Itinera* 8 (1988), 33–4.

a large extent financed, by the villagers themselves with the approval if not the assistance of the urban government.[30]

Demography

How did urbanisation and rural emigration influence relations between town and country? Early modern Switzerland had a low rate of urbanisation of 5 to 8 per cent, comparable to that in Austria, Hungary, Scandinavia and Russia, if we count only towns over 5,000 inhabitants.[31] If we include also the small towns and municipal centres of the rural Republics, the rate of urbanisation climbs to 16–19 per cent, tapering off to about 12 per cent by 1800.[32] The smaller the town, the more its economy and demographic development resembled that of the surrounding countryside. A 'big' town could correspondingly be defined as an extensive, thickly populated settlement which no longer made its living exclusively, or even principally, from farming.

Most of the time the increase in urban population was severely limited by high mortality rates. Until plague ceased to be endemic, demographic growth was largely due to immigration, planned settlement and a higher birth-rate among incomers.[33] Almost all immigrants to the towns came from the surrounding countryside, though some were from further afield.[34] Newcomers to Lucerne were almost all from close by; but it was not until the end of the eighteenth century that the rate of immigration became fast enough to push up the total number of inhabitants.[35] Periods of emigration were not unknown, as from Geneva in the seventeenth and eighteenth century.[36] The towns'

---

[30] H. Horat, *Die Baumeister Singer im schweizerischen Baubetrieb des 18. Jahrhunderts* (Lucerne, 1980); H. Horat, *Das Baubuch von Ruswil 1780–1801* (Lucerne, 1984).

[31] Bergier, *Wirtschaftsgeschichte*, pp. 40–1; P. Bairoch, *De Jéricho à Mexico* (Paris, 1985).

[32] A.-L. Head-König, 'Contrastes ruraux et urbains en Suisse de 1600 au début du XIX siècle: la croissance démographique des villes et des campagnes et ses variables', in *Mélanges d'histoire économique offerts au professeur Anne-Marie Piuz* (Geneva, 1989), pp. 125–36.

[33] Mattmüller, *Bevölkerungsgeschichte*, pp. 196–227. For a general discussion of emigration, see A. Perrenoud, 'Le rôle de la migration dans la régulation démographique et son influence sur les comportements', in *Pour une histoire économique et sociale internationale. Mélanges Paul Bairoch* (Geneva, 1995), pp. 571–93.

[34] A. Perrenoud, *La Population de Genève du seizième au début du dix-neuvième siècle*, vol. I: *Structures et mouvements* (Geneva, 1979), pp. 245–355; J. Fayard Duchene, *Les Origines de la population de Sion à la fin du XVIIIᵉ siècle* (Sion, 1994), pp. 229–337.

[35] H.-R. Burri, *Die Bevölkerung Luzerns im 18. und frühen 19. Jahrhundert* (Lucerne, 1975), pp. 85–9; A. Balthasar, 'Luzern: vom Städtchen zur Stadt. Die langfristige Bevölkerungsentwicklung 1700–1930 unter Anwendung der Generalised Inverse Projection', *Schweizerische Zeitschrift für Geschichte* 38 (1988), 1–29.

[36] A.-M. Puiz and L. Mottu-Weber, *L'Economie genevoise de la Réforme à la fin de l'ancien régime, XVIᵉ–XVIIIᵉ siècles* (Geneva, 1990), p. 55; Balthasar, 'Luzern'.

immigration policies varied according to their economic requirements
and the availability of work. After the middle of the sixteenth century
it became progressively more difficult for immigrants to find a place in
town society, let alone improve their social or legal status. The vast
majority had to be content with a lowly position as unskilled workers,
servants or employees.[37] Geneva even made a habit of sending low-
born orphans back into the country to live with peasant families.[38]
There were even larger numbers of temporary immigrants, either from
the hinterland or (like the Huguenot refugees of the late seventeenth-
century 'Second Refuge' from France) from abroad, who formed a
convenient pool of temporary labour and whose numbers could, if
necessary, be reduced by expulsion.[39] By contrast, temporary emigration from the towns is demographically irrelevant, since it mainly
concerned governors, clergy, patricians and aristocrats paying a brief
visit to their estate, residence or rectory, either on business or just for
the season.[40] On the whole, then, population grew faster in the
country than in the towns. The general decline in the birth rate – the
so-called modern 'demographic transition' – was sharper, and began
earlier, in the towns with a surplus of women, an increasing rate of
singles amongst the lower classes and the beginning of contraception.
During the eighteenth century this pattern spread from town to
country.[41]

Financial relations

Money and finance

During the middle ages, the urban republics and the ruling counts,
dukes, abbots and bishops (who also mostly lived in towns) monopolised
the mints and kept a tight hold on the money supply and the exchange

[37] Perrenoud, *Population*, pp. 191–8. Compare the discrimination against *vavasours* (sub-
vassals) in Schaffhausen, in K. Bächthold, 'Die Hintersassen in der Stadt Schaffhausen', *Schaffhauser Beiträge zur Geschichte* 59 (1982), 18–43.
[38] D. Zumkeller, *Le Paysan et la terre. Agriculture et structure agraire à Genève au XVIII siècle*
(Geneva, 1992), pp. 48–51.
[39] Perrenoud, *Population*, pp. 325–49; M.-J. Ducommun and D. Quadrioni, *Le Refuge
protestant dans le Pays de Vaud (fin XVIF–début XVIIF s.). Aspects d'une migration*
(Geneva, 1991); M. Küng, *Die bernische Asyl- und Flüchtlingspolitik am Ende des 17.
Jahrhunderts* (Geneva, 1993).
[40] See R. Braun, *Ancien Régime*, pp. 211–55; also D. Gugerli, *Zwischen Pfrund und Predigt.
Die protestantische Pfarrfamilie auf der Zürcher Landschaft im ausgehenden 18. Jahrhundert*
(Zurich, 1988).
[41] Head-König, 'Contrastes', pp. 136–41; A. Perrenoud, 'La transition démographique
dans la ville et la campagne genevoises du XVIIe au XIXe siècle', in *Mélanges Anne-
Marie Piuz*, pp. 231–53.

value of the circulating coinage. This domination continued into early modern times. Valley communities like Uri, Schwyz and Nidwalden that were ruled by popular assembly (*Landsgemeinde*) were minting their own coins by the 1500s, but the most important mint of the inner republics was south of the Alps in the town of Bellinzona, where the infrastructure had been inherited from the dukes of Milan. The other peasant republics seldom, if ever, minted their own coins, and all of them accepted the detailed regulations of the urban republics regarding the appearance, quality and value of the coinage and the management of the currency. Any discrepancy was curbed by the combined pressure of urban monetary policies, which also governed all regional conferences on monetary matters.[42] In the urban states decisions on the coinage were monopolised by the central government, and the rural areas had no say in the matter. This goes some way to explain the angry disputes over such things as prices, debts, the inter-regional trade in agricultural products, the value of savings, and finally the outbreak of the Peasant War after the devaluation of the Bernese currency at the end of 1652.[43]

By the end of the middle ages, most of the Swiss towns were struggling under a heavy burden of debt. After 1500 this was gradually reduced and some urban accounts began to show a surplus, initially thanks to the subsidies and profits from hiring mercenaries to allied European powers, particularly France. After the Burgundian Wars (1474–7) a series of internal legal disputes led to agreements (such as the Pensionenbrief of 1503) to curb uncontrolled mercenary expeditions and subject them to the authority of the urban elites. Under these agreements, the republics and allied regions (*Zugewandte*) of the Swiss Confederation received payments which in the sixteenth century constituted between 15 and 66 per cent of the city-states' income and enabled them to pay off their debts.[44] This also had an indirect effect on rural–urban relationships. Swiss burghers, serving in a mercenary regiment abroad in which their town held a share, were entitled to lord it over their rural counterparts who were debarred from high rank in foreign service, though they could act as serving or staff officers in their own local militia.[45]

The mercenary windfall affected all the urban states in the Confederation – a fact that greatly weakens the argument that their finances

[42] J.-P. Divo and E. Tobler, *Die Münzen der Schweiz im 17. Jahrhundert* (Zurich, 1987); N. Furrer, *Das Münzgeld der alten Schweiz: Grundriss* (Zurich, 1995).
[43] See A. Suter, *Der schweizerische Bauernkrieg von 1653. Politische Sozialgeschichte – Sozialgeschichte eines politischen Ereignisses* (Tübingen, 1997).
[44] M. Körner, *Solidarités financières suisses au XVIe siècle. Contribution à l'histoire monétaire, bancaire et financière des cantons suisses et des états voisins* (Lausanne, 1980).
[45] Peyer, *Verfassungsgeschichte*, pp. 40–2, 66–8, 127–33.

were retrieved through the secularisation of church and monastic property during the Reformation.[46] Indeed, the Catholic republics managed to discharge their debts without plundering church property. The Reformed republics, for their part, assumed increased financial obligations towards their churches, not only by paying stipends, maintaining existing churches and building new ones, but also maintaining schools and giving succour to both the urban and the rural poor – activities that in Catholic republics were still largely supported by separate, ecclesiastical foundations.[47] It is nevertheless undeniable that the Reformation enhanced the financial autonomy of the Protestant city-states and greatly increased their disposable assets, and that in the long term (during the sixteenth century and after) this had a positive effect on urban finances.

It is also the case that during and after the sixteenth century, the city-states drew most of their income from indirect taxes, fees and duties; from the late middle ages to the end of the ancien regime they made sporadic, and not always successful, attempts to impose a modest level of direct taxation.[48] In the mid-sixteenth century, for example, Berne conquered an area of land in the Vaud from the duchy of Savoy, a success that entailed an increase in the city's debt which was paid off by means of a special levy imposed on the conquered lands.[49] In the first half of the seventeenth century Basle, Zurich and Berne made sporadic attempts to raise direct taxes, while from 1691 to 1702 the ruling aristocracy of Lucerne exacted additional payments from their burghers and peasant farmers.[50] But no region adopted any permanent system of income tax.

The subject rural areas put up a largely successful resistance against attempts to standardise market and consumer taxes at the highest possible level, impose new import and export levies, abuse state monopolies, tax legal transactions and so on.[51] In the long term, however, the

---

[46] Ibid., pp. 118–19, 122–3.

[47] M. Körner, 'Le financement de l'Eglise dans les états de la Réforme protestante. Le cas de Berne du XVI au XVIII siècle', in M. Pacaud and O. Fatio (eds.), *L'Hostie et le denier. Les finances ecclésiastiques du haut Moyen Age à l'époque moderne* (Geneva, 1991), pp. 213–20.

[48] Excepting St Gallen and Schaffhausen, which regularly raised income tax (which in the latter, however, was abolished in 1688). H.-P. Höhener, *Bevölkerungs und Vermögensstruktur der Stadt St. Gallen im 16. und 17. Jahrhundert* (Zurich, 1966); K. Schmuki, *Steuern und Staatsfinanzen. Die bürgerliche Vemögenssteuer in Schaffhausen im 16. und 17. Jahrhundert* (Zurich, 1988).

[49] Körner, *Solidarités*, p. 278.

[50] On Basle, Berne and Zurich in the seventeenth century see Suter, *Bauernkrieg*, pp. 363ff.; on Lucerne see M. Körner, *Luzerner Staatsfinanzen 1415–1798. Strukturen, Wachstum, Konjunkturen* (Lucerne, 1981), pp. 170–5.

[51] M. Körner, 'Trotz, Hochmuot und Rebellion macht guotte Policeÿ zergon. Ein

urban elites came off best: from the sixteenth century onwards indirect taxation, along with *regalia* (state prerogatives) and entrepreneurial profits, contributed over half the state's total income. On the other hand, between 1500 and 1800 anything from 20 to 60 per cent of the income received by rural governors was ploughed straight back into the rural areas.[52] In Bernese Interlaken, anything between 49 and 80 per cent of income was redistributed in the sixteenth and seventeenth centuries.[53] Moreover, this does not include rural developments centrally financed by the state, such as public works, building or mining.[54] The rural hinterlands also got a share of occasional state income from fines and confiscations imposed by rural governors, and from ingress and exit fees paid by those entering or leaving the district. It is nevertheless likely that this transfer of resources to the countryside, instigated by the urban elites, profited industry at the expense of the agricultural sector.

Credit markets

Credit obligations were also an important part of town–country interactions. The burden of rural debt mounted steadily throughout the sixteenth and seventeenth centuries.[55] Even in the early sixteenth century there were woollen drapers in Geneva whose debtors, both rural and urban, were scattered within a 100 km radius of the town.[56] More-

---

Konflikt um die rechte Ordnung zwischen Stadt und Landschaft Basel im ausgehenden 16. Jahrhundert', in B. Bietenart et al. (eds.), *Ansichten von der rechten Ordnung. Bilder über Normen und Normenverletzungen in der Geschichte. Festschrift Beatrix Mesmer* (Berne, 1991), pp. 115–26; Körner, *Luzerner Staatsfinanzen*, pp. 110–12, 133–4; H. Berner, 'Hinnahme und Ablehnung landesherrlicher Steuern im fürstbischöflichen Birseck', in S. Guex, M. Körner and A. Tanner (eds.), *Staatsfinanzierung und Sozialkonflikte (14.–20. Jh.)* (Zurich, 1994), pp. 159–70; A. Schnyder, 'Ländliche Gesellschaft und öffentliche Finanzen im alten Basel', ibid., pp. 171–83; A. Radeff, 'Des boutiquiers révoltés. Commerce rural et patentes dans l'ancien Etat de Berne à la fin du 18e siècle', ibid., pp. 185–207. Of general significance here are the items relating to transfer of resources in the list of demands made by the peasants at the time of the Peasant War: see Suter, *Bauernkrieg*, pp. 371–81.

[52] M. Körner, 'Steuern und Abgaben in Theorie und Praxis im Mittelalter und in der frühen Neuzeit', in E. Schremmer (ed.), *Steuern, Abgaben und Dienste vom Mittelalter bis zur Gegenwart* (Stuttgart, 1994), pp. 68–70, 75; Körner, *Luzerner Staatsfinanzen*, pp. 263–70.

[53] N. Bartlome and S. Hagnauer, 'Abschöpfung und Umverteilung. Zu den Finanzhaushalten bernischer Ämter im 16. und 17. Jahrhundert', *Itinera* 19 (1997), pp. 157–79.

[54] Körner, *Luzerner Staatsfinanzen*, pp. 333–47.

[55] O. Sigg, 'Bevölkerungs-, agrar- und sozialgeschichtliche Probleme des 16. Jahrhunderts am Beispiel der Zürcher Landschaft', *Schweizerische Zeitschrift für Geschichte* 24 (1974), 1–25.

[56] L. Mottu-Weber, *Economie et refuge à Genève au siècle de la Réforme: la draperie et la soierie (1540–1630)* (Geneva, 1987), pp. 31, 37, 39.

over, the towns were investing more and more of their surplus revenues
in the countryside, and they were willing to accept the transfer of
obligations or mortgages in lieu of taxes. This practice originated in the
sixteenth century and was almost universal within some 30 km of all the
major cities.[57] Towards the end of the seventeenth century, 97 per cent
of mortgage debts owed to Lucerne were from its rural hinterland, 23
per cent by burghers in the small towns and 74 per cent by countrymen.[58] In some country areas (Ebikon, for example) up to 36 per
cent of the people living in a single administrative district were in debt to
townsmen or urban institutions.[59] Between 1685 and 1708, at least
20–26 per cent of the annual income of the town council of Burgdorf
was from country interest payments.[60] In the eighteenth century the
concentration of moneylenders in the great cities slowly decreased in
favour of the smaller towns, although in Lucerne the number of rural
debtors, and their total indebtedness, again increased sharply, especially
after 1750.[61] Right up to the end of the ancien regime, debts kept the
rural areas more or less in thrall to the towns.[62]

It was in real-estate loans that the supply of urban capital most closely
corresponded to rural demand. A large number of individuals from the
wealthy cities, including merchants, provincial governors, aristocrats
and military entrepreneurs, not to mention owners of estates and
country houses, had financial contacts with the peasant population. The
administration of the lands mortgaged to the Lucerne patriciate mainly
devolved to rural offices headed by members of that same patriciate.
Officially, governors were forbidden to seal documents in their own
districts, but they got around this by using subordinates as proxies.
There were also clusters of urban real-estate and small loans around the
patrician country estates.[63] This indebtedness created a kind of patron-

[57] M. Körner, 'Die Kreditgeschäfte der Stadt Schaffhausen im 16. Jahrhundert',
Schaffhauser Beiträge 51 (1974), 62–88; Körner, *Solidarités*, pp. 146–7, 150–5, 160–3,
176–83, 200–3; Körner, *Luzerner Staatsfinanzen*, pp. 304–5; *Geschichte der Schweiz*,
pp. 392–3.
[58] Körner, *Luzerner Staatsfinanzen*, pp. 304–5.
[59] A. Ineichen, 'Bäuerliche Verschuldung im Ancien Régime. Das Beispiel Ebikon (bei
Luzern) um 1690', *Schweizerische Zeitschrift für Geschichte* 42 (1992), 69–93.
[60] J. Scheuermeier-Poglajen, 'Die Rechnungen von Stadt und Schultheissenamt Burgdorf
von den 1680er Jahren bis 1711', MA dissertation, University of Berne, 1992, p. 76.
[61] Wicki, *Bevölkerung*, pp. 260–74; Körner, *Luzerner Staatsfinanzen*, p. 139.
[62] U. Pfister, 'Le petit crédit rural en Suisse aux XVIe–XVIIe siècles', *Annales ESC*
(1974), 1339–57.
[63] M. Körner, 'Luzern als Finanzplatz im 16. Jahrhundert', in *Luzern 1178–1978. Beiträge
zur Geschichte der Stadt* (Lucerne, 1978), p. 231; Körner, 'Kreditformen und
Zahlungsverkehr im spätmittelalterlichen und frühneuzeitlichen Luzern', *Scripta
Mercaturae* (1987), 116–57, esp. 123–9.

client relationship between town and country along the lines of Ulrich Pfister's typology.[64]

Since banking and foreign trade remained the prerogative of the towns up to the end of the ancien regime, I shall pay little attention to them here. While international banking remained almost entirely in urban hands,[65] there were some commercial exceptions in the form of livestock farmers and Jewish horse-dealers, who more or less controlled animal exports; we should also mention the pedlars and chapbook merchants who became more and more prominent in the annual trade fairs of the eighteenth century, and in between hawked their wares around the countryside.[66]

Agricultural markets

At the heart of economic relations between town and country was the local market. For our period, Anne-Marie Piuz has proposed a model based on two concentric circles, within which the urban market controls a variety of products and services.[67] This area can be subdivided into a number of zones associated with urban subsistence, rents (pensions, interest and feudal dues paid to the burghers), the production of energy resources (wood, water and coal) for the town, industry, trade, weights and measures, and culture, all of them under urban control; and government, taxation and demography, which were examined previously. Each of these zones was a separate 'market' with its own institutions, rules, checks and balances. In pre-modern Switzerland, as elsewhere, the subsistence zone producing grain, meat, milk, wine and oil was the largest in terms of both volume and value, followed (in terms of volume) by energy and building materials; the provision of raw materials for handicrafts and nascent industries, along with finished

[64] U. Pfister, 'Politischer Klientelismus in der frühneuzeitlichen Schweiz', *Schweizerische Zeitschrift für Geschichte* 42 (1992), 28–68.
[65] H. Mottet (ed.), *Geschichte der Schweizer Banken* (Zurich, 1987); M. Körner, *Banken und Versicherungen im Kanton Luzern* (Lucerne, 1987), pp. 1–24; Körner, 'Banques publiques et banquiers privés dans la Suisse préindustrielle: administration, fonctionnement et rôle économique', in *Banchi pubblici, banchi privati e monti di pietà nell'Europa preindustriale. Amministrazione, tecniche operative e ruoli economici* (Genoa, 1991), pp. 881–92.
[66] A. Radeff, 'Grandes et petites foires du Moyen Age au 20ᵉ siècle. Conjoncture générale et cas vaudois', *Nuova rivista storica* (1991), 329–48; A. Radeff, 'Faire les foires. Mobilité et commerce périodique dans l'ancien canton de Berne à l'époque moderne', *Bulletin du Centre Pierre Léon d'histoire economique et sociale* (1992), 67–83; A. Radeff, *Economie globale d'Ancien Régime. Commerce de la Suisse occidentale, de Franche-Comté et de Savoie au 18ᵉ siècle* (Lausanne, 1996); R. U. Kaufmann, *Jüdische und christliche Viehhändler in der Schweiz* (Zurich, 1988).
[67] Piuz, *A Genève*, pp. 45–58.

products, was of lesser importance. The urban market was typically
both privileged and threatened: privileged because it was controlled and
supervised by the urban authorities; threatened because, owing to
frequent shortages, it was not always possible to guarantee a supply of
agricultural surpluses, raw materials or energy for a town's inhabitants.

The model divides the subsistence market itself into three concentric
circles. In the innermost one, the town set all the rules: in Geneva,
which Piuz uses as her example, trade with middlemen was forbidden
and the peasants had to sell their produce directly on the town market to
ensure that day-to-day needs were met at moderate prices. However,
property in this zone had been passing into the hands of the bourgeoisie
since the sixteenth century, giving them the opportunity to sell the
produce of their estates at privileged conditions. An increasing proportion of the peasantry became tenants or labourers for the big urban
landowners, but often with a smallholding or small business somewhere
in town or the country.[68]

Piuz's second circle had an inner and an outer ring. The radius of the
former was constrained by two factors. First, its produce included fruit,
vegetables and milk which were perishable and had to be marketed
quickly; secondly, it could be no larger than the distance that could be
covered by a man and his beast of burden in one day. This second ring
was the town's daily supply zone, which produced not only perishable
goods but also grain and meat; we do not know, at present, how much of
this was for home consumption and how much was traded on the
market. It is a safe assumption that, under normal circumstances, the
subsistence needs of most small and medium-sized Swiss towns were
met from within these first two 'rings'. Larger towns also looked to
inter-regional or international trade, to the outer ring of the second
band, where relations would be mediated by professional merchants and
traders.

The town walls were heavily fortified and the gates closed at
sundown, keeping the peasantry outside; the walls also served to keep
out the poorest elements, beggars and vagrants, from the town. At
sunrise the agricultural labourers – vineyard workers, for example – who
lodged in the town would be let out, and country folk bound for the
market would come through the town gates, where they would generally
have to pay tolls on their wine, livestock or meat. The agricultural
season also affected town life: in Geneva, Switzerland's largest town, all
public activity was suspended during the grain and grape harvests so

[68] See A. Radeff, *Lausanne et ses campagnes au 17ᵉ siècle* (Lausanne, 1979); Zumkeller, *Le Paysan*.

that the burghers could see to their rural estates, and the town council never met during the grape harvest.[69]

The peasants, on the other hand, adapted their weekly and seasonal rhythms to fit in with the dates of the weekly and annual markets. Fairs and markets had been held annually in many places since the middle ages, but after 1500 they were becoming larger, more widespread, more specialised and more frequent. Towns which had always had markets held them more frequently; under pressure from the peasants and local economic lobbies, villages which possessed the necessary infrastructure set up new annual markets scarcely more than 10–15 km apart. As the number of village markets grew, the big annual markets tended to become more localised and to some extent more specialised, as in the case of the autumn markets which concentrated exclusively on livestock. And overall, there were simply more, and more regular, markets, because an ever-growing demand was being met by an ever-increasing supply. As annual markets spread even into the mountain valleys, many substantial villages began to look like quasi-towns, though they did not attain the corresponding legal status until the end of the eighteenth century. These developments prepared the ground for the new towns of the nineteenth century.[70]

With the increase in urban landownership, both by burghers and by institutions such as churches, monasteries, hospitals, charitable institutions or the town authorities themselves, the towns produced an outpouring of rules and regulations for agriculture. The urban elites directed the exploitation of woodlands and quarries,[71] the timing of the

[69] A.-M. Piuz, 'Les relations économiques entre les villes et les campagnes dans les sociétés préindustrielles', in *Villes et campagnes*, pp. 1–53; also in her *A Genève*, pp. 9–44.

[70] M. Körner, 'Das System der Jahrmärkte und Messen in der Schweiz im periodischen und permanenten Markt 1500–1800', *Jahrbuch für Regionalgeschichte und Landeskunde* 19 (1993/4), 13–34; see also Radeff, 'Grandes et petites foires'; A. Radeff, 'Des Vaudois trop audacieux pour Leurs Excellences de Berne? Foires et marchés au 18ᵉ siècle', in *Mélanges Colin Martin* (Lausanne, 1992), pp. 275–90; A. Radeff, 'Paysans menacés et menaçants: luttes d'influence autour des foires bernoises d'Ancien Régime', in A. Tanner and A.-L. Head-König (eds.), *Les Paysans dans l'histoire de la Suisse*, in *Société suisse d'histoire économique et marchande* 10 (1992), 129–42; A. Radeff, 'Elevage, commerce et industrie sous l'Ancien Régime: foires et marchés neuchâtelois', *Musée neuchâtelois* (1994), 3–21; F. Häusler, *Die alten Dorfmärkte des Emmentals* (Langnau, 1986).

[71] Guex, *Bruchstein*; Irniger, *Sihlwald*; N. Nöthlin, 'Energieträger–Rohstoff–Weide. Die Bedeutung von Wald und Holz im 16. bis 18. Jahrhundert am Beispiel des Basler Forstwesens', *Basler Zeitschrift für Geschichte und Altertumskunde* 93 (1993), 175–214; N. Nöthlin, 'Die Bedeutung von Wald und Holz für einige Schweizer Städte vom 14. bis 18. Jahrhundert', in S. Cavaciocchi (ed.), *L'uomo e la foresta, secc. XIII–XVIII*, Istituto Internazionale di Storia Economica 'F. Datini', series II/27 (Prato, 1996), pp. 1041–8; R. Gerber, *Öffentliches Bauen im mittelalterlichen Bern. Verwaltungs- und finanzgeschichtliche Untersuchung über das Bauherrenamt der Stadt Bern 1300 bis 1550* (Berne, 1994).

grape harvest,[72] dates for the market,[73] and wage levels for labourers and journeymen.[74] However, in the sixteenth century the peasants won the right to be paid for feudal services.[75] At the same time there was an increase in the transfer of rural income to the urban centres, in the form of surplus ground rents, tithes or profits from the sale of produce. In the Catholic city-state of Lucerne, a third of all tithes were paid to the town.[76] From the sixteenth century onwards, grain which had been delivered to the towns in lieu of tithes and taxes, or bought by the administration on the town market, was stored in increasingly large and numerous public granaries and subsequently put back on the market. This meant that at times of shortage the peasants were forced to buy back seed corn at inflated prices.[77] During the Enlightenment it was again the urban landowners, and members of the towns' economic, scientific and patriotic circles, who led most of the initiatives towards agrarian reform, although there were occasional contributions from enlightened peasant farmers.[78]

Handicrafts and rural industry

At the beginning of the sixteenth century, handicrafts and trade were still part of the general urban privilege system. The vast majority of professions in Switzerland's chief urban centres, especially in the German-speaking areas, were controlled by guilds.[79] Restrictive guild

---

[72] A.-M. Piuz, 'Climat, récoltes et vie des hommes à Genève, XVIᵉ et XVIIᵉ siècles', *Annales ESC* 29 (1974), 599–618, also in Piuz, *A Genève*, pp. 61–81; Radeff, *Lausanne*, pp. 102–6.

[73] Wicki, *Bevölkerung*, pp. 372–3; Piuz and Mottu-Weber, *L'Economie*, pp. 349–50.

[74] Piuz and Mottu-Weber, *L'Economie*, pp. 235–7, 366.

[75] D. Rippmann, 'Der Weiler zu Oberwil (BL) im 16. Jahrhundert: Lohnarbeit und Interessenkonflikte im fürstbischöflichen Amt Birseck', *Geschichte 2001. Mitteilungen der Forschungstelle Baselbieter Geschichte* 9 (June 1922), 1–8.

[76] Wicki, *Bevölkerung*, p. 188.

[77] Körner, *Luzerner Staatsfinanzen*, pp. 348–63; M. Körner, 'Kornhäuser in der städtischen Versorgungspolitik: Berneim Vergleich mit Luzern', in T. Lötscher (ed.), *'währschafft, nuzlich und schön – Bernische Architekturzeichnungen des 18. Jahrhunderts* (Berne, 1994), pp. 25–9; P. Giger, 'Verwaltung der Ernährung. Obrigkeitliche Kontrolle des Zürcher Kornmarktes im 18. Jahrhundert', in S. Brändli (ed.), *Schweiz im Wandel. Studien zur neueren Gesellschaftsgeschichte. Festschrift Rudolf Braun* (Basle, 1990), pp. 317–29; L. Wiedmer, *Pain quotidien et pain de disette. Meuniers, boulangers et Etat nourricier à Genève (XVIIᵉ–XVIIIᵉ siècles)* (Geneva, 1993), pp. 41–96.

[78] E. Erne, *Die schweizerischen Sozietäten. Lexikalische Darstellung der Reformgesellschaften des 18. Jahrhunderts in der Schweiz* (Zurich, 1988), pp. 158–9, 217–18; Braun, *Ancien Régime*, pp. 302–3; Piuz and Mottu-Weber, *L'Economie*, pp. 227–33; C. Pfister, *Geschichte des Kantons Bern seit 1798*, vol. IV: *Im Strom der Modernisierung. Bevölkerung, Wirtschaft und Umwelt 1700–1914* (Berne, 1995), pp. 175–80; Jäger et al., *Baumwollgarn*, pp. 20–6.

[79] On handicrafts, trade and the guilds see A.-M. Dubler, *Handwerk, Gewerbe und Zunft in Stadt und Landschaft Luzern* (Lucerne, 1981); A.-M. Dubler, 'Die Welt des Handwerks.

practices began to appear shortly after 1500, or at the latest during the recession of the 1560s and 1570s: small businesses were strictly regulated and standardised, manufacture and commerce were rigidly separated, and prices and wages were controlled.[80] Guild members were given preference over the competition, training was standardised and production monitored.

In the later middle ages, agriculturally related trades and handicrafts had developed in some of the villages: milling, innkeeping, smithing and so on. Sixteenth-century demographic growth increased the number of artisans in the villages and scattered hamlets throughout German-speaking Switzerland, especially those in trades which required little capital investment: tailors, cobblers, weavers, builders, and subsequently smiths, rope-makers, cartwrights, saddlers, coopers. This development may owe something to the boom years of *c*.1530–60. The subsequent recession sparked conflicts between urban and rural artisans. Where economic management was decentralised, as in the Berne territories (including the city's possessions in the Aargau and the Vaud) and the city-states of Lucerne and Solothurn, and later eastern Switzerland, rural artisans managed to organise themselves in guilds – or associations or brotherhoods of master craftsmen – on the urban model, under the protection of the urban elites, and so survived the recession. Guilds also emerged in the market towns and local centres in the heart of Switzerland, in Schwyz, Altdorf, Stans and Sarnen. By contrast, where economic policy was strongly centralised, as in Basle, Schaffhausen, Zurich and even Zug, the town guilds used their powers to fend off rural competitors; while finally, guilds remained unknown in the Alpine and subalpine districts of Appenzell, Toggenburg, Sargans and Glarus, in the Bernese Oberland and in the Valais. In the city republic of Geneva, the first associations of master craftsmen appeared, in the textile industry, in the last quarter of the sixteenth century; the bakers formed a guild only in 1628, and other trades lagged still further behind.[81] There were, however, some 'free and honourable' trades, such as milling, which managed to win concessions necessary to the practice

Ein historischer Rückblick auf das Handwerk in der Schweiz', in *Handbuch der schweizerischen Volkskultur* (Zurich, 1992), pp. 1039–52; A.-M. Dubler (ed.), *Handwerksgeschichte*, in *Itinera* 14 (1993); Meier, *Handwerk*; K. H. Flatt, 'Kleinstädtische Wirtschaft im Ancien Régime am Beispiel von Wangen a. A.', *Jahrbuch des Oberaargaus* (1984), 175–96.

80 This also applied to work in the countryside: see the exemplary study by K. Schmuki, 'Eine Schaffhauser Taxierordnung aus dem Jahre 1647 – Obrigkeitlich festgelegte Preise und Löhne für Handwerker und Gewerbetreibende um die Mitte des 17. Jahrhunderts', *Schaffhauser Beiträge* 60 (1983), 27–62.

81 Mottu-Weber, *Economie*; Piuz and Mottu-Weber, *L'Economie*, pp. 396–408; Wiedmer, *Pain quotidien*, pp. 265–6.

of their profession, and survived without provoking any particular conflict between town and country.[82]

The textile industries – linen, silk, wool and cotton – which spread through various regions of Switzerland from the earliest years of the sixteenth century were mostly not regulated by guilds, but initiated and controlled by merchants (comparable to the great English clothiers), who dispensed work to be done at home by poor people, and subsequently collected the products for finishing and sale.[83] This system existed as far back as the 1520s in the Ticino towns of Lugano and Locarno, in the 1540s in Geneva, and later on in Zurich and Basle;[84] in eastern Switzerland, around St Gallen, the same system developed on the basis of existing cottage industries.[85] The clothiers were quick to establish a division of labour between the processing, done in the towns, and the weaving, done in the country; auxiliary tasks, such as spinning, were done by women, most of whom lived in the country. The Lugano clothiers were employing home workers by the 1520s, both in the town and in the surrounding country. The industry established itself in Geneva and Zurich in the second half of the sixteenth century; it did not reach Basle until the beginning of the seventeenth century. It soon spread to country regions outside the territories politically dominated by the great cloth towns. The regional distribution of the textile industry was structurally very similar to that of the guilds: the clothiers in the guilded city-state towns of Basle and Zurich had a monopoly over industry in their own territory, whereas elsewhere practices were freer from corporate control and more responsive to economic fluctuations.[86] During the

[82] Wiedmer, *Pain quotidien*, pp. 245–6; A.-M. Dubler, *Müller und Mühlen im alten Staat Luzern. Rechts-, Wirtschafts- und Sozialgeschichte des luzernischen Landmüllergewerbes 14. bis 18. Jahrhundert* (Lucerne, 1978).

[83] On rural industry in general and the organisation of the textile industry in particular, see the overview in Bergier, *Wirtschaftsgeschichte*, pp. 147–87.

[84] J. Wiget, *Wirtschaft und Politik im spätmittelalterlichen Luzern. Die wirtschaftlichen Unternehmungen des Luzerner Schultheissen Heinrich Fleckenstein 1484–1558* (Schwyz, 1978); Mottu-Weber, *Economie*; L. Mottu-Weber, 'Marchands et artisans du second refuge à Genève', in *Genève au temps de la Révocation de l'Edit de Nantes 1680–1705* (Geneva, 1985), pp. 313–97; Fink, *Bandindustrie*; Pfister, *Zürcher Fabriques*.

[85] A. Tanner, *Spulen–Weben–Sticken. Die Industrialisierung in Appenzell Ausserrhoden* (Zurich, 1982); A. Tanner, 'Das ganze Land eine Baumwollenfabrik. Ulrich Bräker als Garnhändler, Weber und kleiner Fabrikant', *Toggenburgenblätter für Heimatkunde* 36 (1985), 23–50; A. Tanner, 'Die Baumwollindustrie in der Ostschweiz 1750–1914: Von der Proto-industrie zur Fabrik- und Hausindustrie', in K. Ditt and S. Pollard (eds.), *Von der Heimarbeit in die Fabrik. Industrialisierung und Arbeiterschaft in Leinen- und Baumwollregionen Westeuropas während des 18. und 19. Jahrhunderts* (Paderborn, 1992), pp. 162–91.

[86] Wicki, *Bevölkerung*, pp. 336–7; F. Kurmann, *Das Luzerner Suhrental im 18. Jahrhundert. Bevölkerung, Wirtschaft und Gesellschaft der Landvogteien Büron/Triengen und Knutwil* (Lucerne, 1985), pp. 203–25; Küng, *Asyl- und Flüchtlingspolitik*, pp. 319–46; Pfister, *Geschichte*, pp. 231–2.

seventeenth and eighteenth centuries, however, when the cloth towns
were in the habit of commissioning piecework from other cantons, the
increased demand for labour was often used by the rural weavers' guilds
to improve their pay and working conditions. By about 1700 it is
possible to distinguish four main regions with strong rural or proto-
industries, namely St Gallen, Zurich, Basle and Geneva, each with its
own organisation and division of labour between town and country.[87]

Around 1670, after many years of struggle, the clothiers in Appenzell-
Innerrhoden finally managed to have some of their textile exports
exempted from compulsory quality control by St Gallen and from the
latter's monopoly over the export market. In the later seventeenth
century rural middlemen, working in the cotton trade on behalf of the
leading Zurich clothiers, succeeded in supplanting some of the small
urban producers.[88] The latter half of the eighteenth century saw a
recession in the linen industry of eastern Switzerland and a corresponding boom in the rural areas of the Oberaargau, in Bernese territory.
During the same century the entrepreneurs of Glarus shook off the
domination of Zurich, whereas in the Jura, the outwork system was
introduced into the cotton-printing and clock-making industries under
the leadership of Geneva, the Vaud and the town of Neuenburg.[89]

Changes in agricultural practice towards a more market-oriented
pastoral economy with emphasis also on potato production, were more
rapid in the areas of rural industry. Unlike traditional agriculture, which
had focused on local urban supply, this was part of a more integrated
economy with different and more complex imperatives and structural
problems.[90] Most historians agree that the system was very fragile and
that proto-industrial areas tended to suffer more from economic crises,
either because the supply of paid work dried up or because there was no
bread to buy even if there were wages to buy it – whereas the towns, with
their larger supply of capital, were able to obtain supplies.[91]

[87] Pfister, *Zürcher Fabriques*, p. 135.
[88] Ibid., pp. 209–56, 503.
[89] P. Caspard, *La Fabrique-Neuve de Cortaillod 1752–1854. Entreprise et profit pendant la Révolution industrielle* (Fribourg, 1979); *Histoire du Pays de Neuchâtel*, vol. II: *De la Réforme à 1815* (Hauterive, 1991), pp. 197–215; Piuz and Mottu-Weber, *L'Economie*, pp. 409–99. On the Geneva region in the late eighteenth century see Zumkeller, *Le Paysan*, pp. 56–61.
[90] Pfister, *Zürcher Fabriques*, pp. 393–511.
[91] M. Mattmüller, 'Kleinlandwirtschaft und Heimindustrie in proto-industriellen Gebieten der Schweiz', in *Studia polono-helvetica* (Basle, 1989), pp. 79–94; F. Göttmann, 'Aspekte der Tragfähigkeit in der Ostschweiz um 1700: Nahrungsmittelversor-
gung, Bevölkerung, Heimarbeit', in J. Jahn and W. Hartung (eds.), *Gewerbe und Handel vor der Industrialisierung* (Sigmaringendorf, 1991), pp. 153–82; F. Göttmann, 'Bevölk-
erungswachstum und Landwirtschaft. Wie ernährt man eine angewachstene Bevölk-
erung mit den selben landwirtschaftlichen Ressourcen?', *Schweizerische Zeitschrift für*

Conclusion

When pre-modern Switzerland is being compared with other European states it is important to remember that the former was not a centralised monarchy but mainly a confederation of sovereign city-states and peasant republics. Hence there was no truly centralised or mercantilised economic policy. Just as importantly, cottage industries, proto-industrialisation, markets and (to a large extent) foreign trade were directed and controlled by the 'capitals' of the major city-states. The further these 'capitals' were from the centre of Switzerland, the greater their economic dominance. There was a considerable variety of rural–urban relationships between individual city-states. In the secondary and tertiary sector, for example, Basle, Zurich, Schaffhausen and Geneva pursued a consistent economic policy which favoured entrepreneurs and merchants living in the capital. The policies of the old state of Berne, on the other hand, encouraged the economic activities which had developed in the towns and larger rural centres. In the peasant republics and the city-states of central Switzerland, the dominant economic activities of milk and livestock production, mercenary service and the corresponding foreign trade had always been under the control of the socio-politically dominant families in the capital or the rural centres. For banking and exchange facilities, in particular international payment transactions and capital investment, they were wholly dependent on the commercial bankers of Geneva, Lausanne, Berne, Basle and Zurich. In the central region between Geneva and Lake Constance, where proto-industrialisation and the outwork system were solidly established, the division of labour between town and country, still perceptible in the late middle ages and the sixteenth century, became progressively blurred: by the end of the ancien regime, a more or less unified economic area had been created which was able to adapt to the economic liberalism of the nineteenth century with a considerable degree of flexibility.[92]

Geschichte 45 (1995), 205–13; W. Frey and M. Stampfli, *Das Janusgesicht der Agrarmodernisierung. Der demographische, ökonomische und soziale Transformationsprozess der bernischen Amtsbezirke Büren und Konolfingen zwischen 1760 und 1880* (Berne, 1991).

[92] For a more extended version of this chapter see M. Körner, 'Stadt und Land in der frühen Neuzeit', *Itinera* 19 (1997), 49–88.

11   Town and country in France, 1550–1750

Thomas Brennan

Hierarchies and distinctions

Walls separated town and country through much of the early modern period. Walls not only protected towns, they also helped give them a sense of autonomy and identity. By the eighteenth century, when many French cities had lost their walls and all had lost their autonomy, the town walls do not seem to have much relevance. But an important study of late medieval towns argues for the distinctive social and political roles that walls gave the *bonnes villes* in an age of endemic war and political chaos.[1] Walls made a town into a military force, at a time when the monarchy could often barely assemble an army. Towns used their walls to divide the world up between what was 'polite', 'policed', 'civilised', 'urbane' – all words etymologically linked to towns – and what was not.[2] Towns used their walls to order themselves internally – into guilds and confraternities, but also into a political and civic unity. The town walls, and the *bonnes villes* they created, did not last through the early modern period. A study of Toulouse, for example, charts the slow death of this civic identity, as power and public ritual were gradually usurped by royal officials in the seventeenth and eighteenth centuries.[3] At the same time, the decline of town walls through the early modern period coincided with the increasing integration of town and countryside, as towns exerted greater influence over their hinterlands economically, judicially and culturally.

The number of walled communities in the fifteenth century has been estimated at over one thousand, which means that walls did not

[1] B. Chevalier, *Les Bonnes Villes de France du XIVe au XVIe siècle* (Paris, 1982).
[2] J.-C. Perrot, *Genèse d'une ville moderne: Caen au XVIIIe siècle* (Paris, 1975), pp. 15–27; B. Lepetit, *The pre-industrial urban system: France, 1740–1840*, transl. G. Rogers (Cambridge, 1994), pp. 53–63, show how this vocabulary disappeared in the eighteenth century.
[3] R. A. Schneider, *Public life in Toulouse 1463–1789: from municipal republic to cosmopolitan city* (Ithaca, 1989).

Figure 11.1   Early modern France

distinguish small towns from villages.[4] Indeed, the lower limits of towns
in early modern France are notoriously difficult to define. A simple
demographic criterion misses subtle distinctions that mattered deeply to
contemporaries, such as town walls and charters, the number of religious and administrative institutions and differences in economic function. Of the 64 communes in the Dauphiné identified as cities or market
towns by contemporaries in the eighteenth century, barely half had
more than 2,000 inhabitants and 6 had less than 1,000.[5] And yet there

---

[4] Chevalier, *Bonnes Villes*, p. 53.
[5] J. Favier, 'Economic change, demographic growth and the fate of Dauphiné's small
towns, 1698–1790', in P. Benedict (ed.), *Cities and social change in early modern France*

were important distinctions in the scale of economic and administrative functions of towns and villages.

Certainly the social make-up of different communities was a crucial element in distinguishing a hierarchy among them; towns contained a range of artisans, merchants and officials not found in villages. In general, the greater the number of these groups in a town, the more urban or higher order the town might be said to be. Towns of any size always contained a number of agricultural labourers, who worked in fields surrounding the town, growing anything from grain to grapes and market gardening. Local agricultural produce was crucial to a town's subsistence and economy, but its role diminished in relative importance as the town grew larger and its economy became more sophisticated. In Burgundian towns at the end of the old regime the percentage of agricultural workers in the *bourgs* and smallest towns with fewer than 2,000 inhabitants was double their prevalence (56 vs. 28 per cent) in the medium-sized towns and small towns with more than 3,200 inhabitants. In a large town the size of Caen (35,000) they made up only 2 per cent. The percentage of those involved in manufacturing was greater in the larger towns than in the smaller (44 vs. 30 per cent) but the real difference was in the service sector, like commerce, transportation and domestic service, which increased from 15 per cent of *bourgs* and towns under 2,000 to 29 per cent of towns over 3,200 and 53 per cent of Caen. The larger towns also had a monopoly on a large number of specialised professions. There was a widespread prevalence of food sellers and preparers, wood- and iron-workers, and makers of clothing, and of men offering basic legal services like notaries and attorneys, but less than half the towns had makers of clocks, cloth, knives, vinegar and woollens, or doctors and schoolteachers, and only a very few claimed a long list of professions dealing with books and bonnets, tapestry, tin, tobacco, tripe, and many other rarefied activities.[6]

A similar hierarchy emerges from the consideration of administrative services located in early modern towns. Large towns could offer a huge range of judicial and financial courts, royal and local governments, and ecclesiastical establishments. Probably half of some 700 towns with at least 2,000 inhabitants in the early nineteenth century had housed a *bailliage* or *sénéchaussée* court that formed the basis of royal justice; certainly most of the 200 cities with more than 5,000 inhabitants had

---

(London, 1989), pp. 224–5; of these 64 towns only 15 had more than 2,000 inhabitants in 1698.

6 C. Lamarre, *Petites villes et fait urbain en France au XVIIIᵉ siècle: le cas bourguignon* (Dijon, 1993), pp. 202–6, 256–7; Perrot, *Genèse*, p. 265. In both cases these refer to percentages of the economically active population.

done so.[7] The geography of such institutions in Burgundy includes
several towns with fewer than 1,000 inhabitants boasting a *bailliage*
court.[8] The growth of royal administration emanated from the towns,
but even very small towns enjoyed a few of these institutions, and
villages had their own communal and seigniorial jurisdictions. A spectrum of goods and services, power and jurisdictions formed a complex
matrix in which towns and villages were not distinguished so much as
bound together.

Urban property in the countryside

One of the most enduring features of the town's interaction with the
countryside was the steady acquisition by townspeople of land in the
countryside around every town. Parisians had been engaged in buying
land for centuries; there was a major push towards the formation of
large estates to the north of Paris as early as the late fifteenth century.[9]
By the seventeenth century they owned half or more of the ploughland
in villages to the south, 30 and 40 km away.[10] Inhabitants of Toulouse
had also been buying rural property since the middle ages and owned at
least three-quarters of the land in the villages within 15 to 20 km by the
late eighteenth century.[11] Even a modest town like Chartres, with a
population of only 13,000 at the end of the old regime, owned a majority
of the land in villages less than 10 km away and as much as a quarter of
the land in villages within 20 km. This property surrounded the town of
Chartres to a distance of some 30 km, with a great many small parcels in
the immediate vicinity of the town owned in large measure by the town's
bourgeois *rentiers*, and a more limited number of larger properties
owned by the nobles or officials of the town at a greater distance.[12] The
bourgeois of a very much smaller town nearby, with barely 1,500
inhabitants, also exercised considerable control over the rural property
in its vicinity, but largely within a radius of 5 km.[13]

[7] The population of these towns, from R. Le Mée, 'Population agglomérée, population
éparse au début du XIXe siècle', *Annales de démographie historique* (1971), 467–94, was
obviously lower in the early modern period.
[8] C. Lamarre, 'Administrations et petites villes en Bourgogne à la fin du XVIIIe siècle', in
J.-P. Poussou and P. Loupes (eds.), *Les Petites Villes du moyen âge à nos jours* (Paris,
1987), pp. 307–21.
[9] J.-M. Moriceau, *Les Fermiers de l'Ile de France* (Paris, 1994), pp. 88–9.
[10] M. Venard, *Bourgeois et paysans au XVIIe siècle* (Paris, 1957), pp. 25–9.
[11] G. Frêche, *Toulouse et la région Midi-Pyrénées au siècle des lumières vers 1670–1789* (Paris,
1974), pp. 465–8.
[12] M. Vovelle, *Ville et campagne au 18e siècle: Chartres et la Beauce* (Paris, 1980),
pp. 85–92, 216–26.
[13] G. Béaur, 'Maintenon et son marché foncier', in Poussou and Loupes, *Petites Villes*,
pp. 335–50.

The income from this rural property played a significant role in the economy of the average town. Philip Benedict has estimated that urban purchases of rural land throughout France in the early modern period directed 10 per cent of land rents to townspeople, though that seems too low.[14] In Chartres, for example, where the merchants dealing in animals, wood, and textiles enjoyed only very modest incomes, 'landed income [was] the most important source of revenue drawn from the rural milieu'. Such landed income produced three times more revenue than did 'movable capital' for the commercial residents and four to five times more for the population as a whole.[15]

One mechanism by which towns acquired rural land was through various forms of debt, which allowed either foreclosure or, at least, a steady stream of income. A quarter of the households in the viticultural village of Verzy in Champagne, for example, owed payments on annuities to a total of 2,000 livres a year on outstanding debts of 40,000 livres, nearly a third of which was owed to people in the region's towns, mostly in Reims.[16] Recent work on credit markets suggests real limits, however, to the impact of urban credit in the countryside. Although Paris mobilised a huge amount of money in long-term loans, little of it went to non-Parisians, and most of the money appears to have ended up in Parisian enterprises.[17] Other studies show that credit was extended over very short distances, usually less than 10 km, because of crucial problems with obtaining adequate information about risk and collateral.[18]

The impact of landowning on towns, particularly on the level and nature of income, was obviously significant; the consequences for the countryside were even greater. Peasants owned little of the land they worked if they lived near a town and the land had value. The peasants around Dijon in the seventeenth and eighteenth centuries owned very little of either the ploughland or the vineyards.[19] Peasants owned only 10 to 20 per cent of the land in villages within 15 km of Toulouse; their portion reached a third or a half only at a greater distance from the city

---

[14] P. Benedict, 'More than market and manufactory: the cities of early modern France', *French Historical Studies* 20 (1997), 523.

[15] Vovelle, *Ville et campagne*, pp. 41–2, 93–101.

[16] Archives Départementales (AD), Marne, C 2347, Verzy, 1770; the average was 28 livres per household.

[17] P. T. Hoffman, G. Postel-Vinay and J.-L. Rosenthal, 'Private credit markets in Paris, 1690–1840', *Journal of Economic History* 52 (1992), 298.

[18] G. Postel-Vinay, *La Terre et l'argent: l'agriculture et le crédit en France du XVIIIᵉ au début du XXᵉ siècle* (Paris, 1998), pp. 60–77.

[19] G. Roupnel, *La Ville et la campagne au XVIIᵉ siècle: étude sur les populations du pays dijonnais* (Paris, 1955), pp. 75–82, has much more impressionistic evidence for his conclusion that there were 'barely fifty peasant proprietors in the 138 villages of the Burgundian plain'.

and, more generally, increased only as their access to important grain markets decreased.[20]

As outsiders bought up the ploughland, they changed the nature of the rural community. In some cases, city people became a regular presence in the village. As an official remarked about the *bourg* of Ay, in Champagne, 'there are also many outsiders who have country houses [*vendangeoirs*] there and come to spend the autumn. It is then that one sees the luxury of the towns contrasted with the simplicity of the natives of this *bourg*.'[21] The contrast rarely pleased the villagers. In many cases outsiders were absentee landlords who created large estates which they leased to *fermiers*, large farmers who gained considerable dominance in the village assembly.[22] With so few landowners of any scale, villages gradually became little more than bedroom communities, places where peasants lived and worked seasonally or as they could scrape by, but where they no longer controlled the principal assets. Artistic depictions of peasants changed through the early modern period in ways that eerily reflect this dispossession. After the vibrant sixteenth-century scenes crowded with robust peasants using sharp tools in the fields, subsequent centuries dealt with the fear of violent, insurrectionary peasant armies and conflicts over landowning by first banishing peasants from paintings of the countryside and then bringing them back only as meek, even effeminate, and isolated figures deprived of their dangerous implements.[23]

Many villages also lost their common lands during years of war and fiscal depredation in the sixteenth and seventeenth centuries. The basic dynamics of the village community was fundamentally disrupted and altered.[24] Nevertheless, Hilton Root has argued that villages in eighteenth-century Burgundy gained a new, if rather artificial, vigour under the state's tutelage.[25] Even though peasants lost their individual lands, the village maintained some of its commons, often meadows, usually forest. These common lands had always given the village a sense collective identity, an administrative responsibility and a source of revenue. Now, in the eighteenth century, as the state took over the financial responsibility of all communities, it worked to defend the

[20] Frêche, *Toulouse*, pp. 150–208.

[21] Paris, Archives Nationales, G^2 26, from the 1780s.

[22] J.-P. Gutton, *La Sociabilité villageoise dans l'ancienne France* (Paris, 1979), pp. 57–93.

[23] L. Vardi, 'Imagining the harvest in early modern Europe', *American Historical Review* 101 (1996), 1357–97.

[24] P. de Saint Jacob, *Les Paysans de la Bourgogne du nord au dernier siècle de l'ancien régime* (Paris, 1960), pp. 83–92, speaks of the 'decadence that slowly led the community to its ruin'. See also Gutton, *La Sociabilité*, pp. 109–18.

[25] H. L. Root, *Peasants and king in Burgundy: agrarian foundations of French absolutism* (Berkeley, 1987).

village as a corporate group in the face of opposition from local seigniors and notables.

In a variety of ways, urban control of rural land had a profound impact on village life. Not only did it constitute a transfer of revenues, but in many cases it brought urban people economically into rural society. The fact that many vine growers sharecropped for urban owners meant that these town-dwellers became intimately involved in selling the wine their lands produced and gradually brought superior sophistication to the development of wines and markets.[26] Urban notables often created large farms of arable land, whose rental helped to create a rural elite of *fermiers*.

Interdependence

Rural immigration

At the same time, the countryside routinely invaded the town and can, indeed, be said to have taken it over. The figures for eighteenth-century cities like Lyons, Caen, Marseilles, Rouen and Bordeaux indicate that roughly a third to a half of their populations were born outside the city.[27] A large majority of immigrants were men, many of whom settled down and married in the city, though there was always a coming and going between town and country. This kind of mobility has been remarked upon for many subsets of the French population – a kind of transhumance affecting certain provinces, like the Auvergne and Limousin, as well as certain social groups, like urban journeymen.[28] Indeed, a recent study of rural populations argues that migration between nearby villages and, occasionally, towns was 'positively endemic in early modern France'.[29] Migrants who returned to the countryside from the city often brought their savings back with them, to reverse at least temporarily the normal flow of wealth.

Although the immigration of peasants to towns was the main source of urban growth, the immigration of the rural elites to towns may have been economically and culturally more significant. The percentage of

[26] Roupnel, *La Ville et la campagne*, pp. 294–7; T. Brennan, *Burgundy to Champagne: the wine trade in early modern France* (Baltimore, 1997), pp. 19–38.
[27] M. Garden, *Lyon et les lyonnais au XVIIIᵉ siècle* (Paris, 1970), p. 100; Perrot, *Genèse*, pp. 156–8; J.-P. Bardet, *Rouen aux XVIIᵉ et XVIIIᵉ siècles: les mutations d'un espace social*, 2 vols. (Paris, 1983), vol. I, p. 211; J.-P. Poussou, *Bordeaux et le sud-ouest au XVIIIᵉ siècle: croissance économique et attraction urbaine* (Paris, 1983), pp. 64–72.
[28] M. Sonenscher, *Work and wages: natural law, politics and the eighteenth-century French trades* (Cambridge, 1989), pp. 117–29.
[29] J. B. Collins, 'Geographic and social mobility in early modern France', *Journal of Social History* 24 (1991), 563–77.

notables living in towns, including royal officials, military officers, nobility, and *rentiers* living off investments, seems to have swelled dramatically in the sixteenth and seventeenth centuries.[30] These people expended substantial amounts of income, in the form of rents from the growing amount of land they owned in the hinterland, revenues from the rapidly increasing royal taxes they collected from rural communities, and fees from the judicial system they imposed on the countryside. Through their hands, in other words, flowed the bulk of the funds transferred from the country to the city. Just as importantly, these groups set the standards of consumption that the rest of the urban population gradually began to emulate.

Studies of some of France's major cities agree that immigration played a large role in urban growth, yet urban growth was very uneven. Whereas the cities on the periphery of the kingdom tended to expand through the seventeenth and eighteenth centuries, those in the interior did less well. Major seaports, like Nantes, Marseilles and Bordeaux, tripled and quadrupled their population in 250 years; smaller ports, like Le Havre, grew as fast. Inland, there was considerable growth in the seventeenth century but less in the eighteenth and, in the north around Paris, none at all. A dozen cities with more than 10,000 inhabitants, forming a band south of Paris from Rennes to Troyes, grew by a third in the seventeenth century and then not at all in the eighteenth.[31] Rouen found itself experiencing both the stagnation of an administrative centre and some of the vigour of a seaport. Its population declined precipitously under Louis XIV, in part because of Huguenot expulsions, and climbed back only partly and slowly through the eighteenth century. A shift in its textile industry to the surrounding countryside helped the city's population very little, although the villages within 10 km grew rapidly.[32]

The comparative fortunes of Bordeaux and Toulouse are instructive. In 1500 Toulouse, with some 50,000 inhabitants, was more than two and a half times bigger than Bordeaux; by 1800, with roughly the same population, it was less than half the size of Bordeaux. Although not really neighbours, they shared much of the south-west region and its economic system. Yet their composition and success as cities were quite

[30] J. Farr, 'Consumers, commerce, and the craftsmen of Dijon: the changing social and economic structure of a provincial capital, 1450–1750', in Benedict, *Cities and social change*, pp. 143–54; Benedict, 'More than market', pp. 511–38; F.-J. Ruggiu, *Les Elites et les villes moyennes en France et en Angleterre (XVIIᵉ–XVIIIᵉ siècles)* (Paris, 1997), pp. 143–74, 195–210.

[31] Based on figures for Rennes, Angers, Tours, Saumur, Poitiers, Blois, Orléans, Bourges, Chartres, Auxerre, Troyes and Dijon, in Benedict, *Cities and social change*, pp. 24–5.

[32] Bardet, *Rouen*, vol. I, pp. 207–13; vol. II, p. 34.

different. Both ultimately drew on a large, and largely the same, hinterland for a variety of mostly agricultural products. But, whereas Bordeaux became a commercial city tied to rapidly growing colonial and
international trade, Toulouse lost control of, and much of the profit
from, its own commercial system. Despite trading substantial amounts
of grain, which travelled by river and canal to major markets, the
merchants of Toulouse failed to develop independent commercial contacts with their more distant markets and yielded economic power to
merchants in other cities.[33] In general, it seems that the cities with a
vibrant commerce, either from sea trade or, like Lyons, Nîmes, Lille,
Amiens and Montauban, from local industries, grew rapidly in both
centuries.[34]

And yet Benedict interprets the overall statistics for urbanisation
rather differently, arguing for a rapid growth in the seventeenth century
but no difference between urban growth and general population growth
in the eighteenth century. From this disparity he suggests that urban
growth was not tied so much to economic growth, which characterised
the eighteenth century, as it was to the administrative growth of the
seventeenth century. To put it crudely, this model sees towns as
consumers rather than producers, growing fat from their ability to
absorb wealth rather than create it.[35]

Markets

It is not hard to see why some historians have characterised urban
society as fundamentally parasitic in its relationship to the countryside.
Towns drew revenues and population from their hinterlands; it can be
difficult to discern what they gave in return. Yet the theme of much
recent work on rural society has been its responsiveness to the market
economy and, in particular, to the commercial opportunities afforded
by towns. We must look to the stimulative effects of urban markets and
merchants on the rural economy.

The most obvious impact of the town's market was on its immediate
hinterland, which was organised to feed the urban population. The list
of goods provided by the countryside for the town was a long one and
growing. Agricultural products had always headed the list, with grain

[33] Frèche, *Toulouse*, pp. 786–95.
[34] The figures in Benedict, *Cities and social change*, pp. 24–5, show the aggregate
populations of Bordeaux, Marseilles, Nantes, Lyons, Lille, Nîmes, Montauban,
Amiens and Montpellier growing by over 60 per cent in both the seventeenth and
eighteenth centuries.
[35] P. Benedict, 'Was the eighteenth century an era of urbanization in France?', *Journal of
Interdisciplinary History* 21 (1990), 179–215.

the most pressing of these commodities, if not necessarily the first in value. Every town had its privileged catchment area that it defended. The Parisian catchment, which extended to a radius of some 100 km in normal circumstances and even more in periods of crisis, was unusual for both the size and the political sensitivity of the capital city. A more representative example is the Norman town of Caen, with a population of over 30,000. A study of Caen's catchment in the eighteenth century indicates its economic dominance throughout a region that more or less matches its administrative region, the *élection*. It drew intensively on its immediate hinterland to a range of some 4 km for fruit and vegetables and weighed heavily on a catchment of some 15 km radius for its grains. It reached more broadly but more intermittently for other commodities: for apple cider, which it consumed at a rate of 200 litres per annum per inhabitant, it reached as far as 25 km away, and for meat it drew on much of the province to some 30–40 km.[36]

The town's effect on its hinterland was rarely left to market forces alone. Municipal regulations enforced the provisioning of the urban population and regulated the dynamics of the markets. Only licensed dealers could buy grain and then only at certain places and times in order to avoid hoarding and reduce the economic power that merchants could gain at the expense of consumers.[37] When they wished to, particularly during times of food shortages, towns could exercise considerable economic and political control over their hinterlands. The rise of the state appears to have encouraged this tendency, while at the same time diminishing the autonomy of the towns. State regulation of the grain trade has provoked controversy since the old regime. In the mid-eighteenth century the royal administration, prodded by the *philosophes*, began to rethink these policies, in the name both of free trade and of rural prosperity. Their arguments are well presented in the work of Hilton Root, who claims that, 'as far as grain policy was concerned, in France, the rise of central authority meant government by the city, from the city, for the city'. He argues that an urban bias in government regulatory policies aided the urban working poor at the expense of poor farmers. Government regulation of the grain market (promoted by fear of urban crowds rioting for bread) protected urban consumers but doomed the free market that could have raised productivity, efficiency and social utility in the countryside.[38] Subsequent research on such

[36] Perrot, *Genèse*, pp. 191–241.
[37] S. L. Kaplan, *Bread, politics and political economy in the reign of Louis XV* (The Hague, 1976), is the most exhaustive of the many books on this subject.
[38] H. L. Root, *The fountain of privilege: political foundations of markets in old regime France and England* (Berkeley, 1994), pp. 106–11.

regulation cautions us, however, against drawing too great a distinction between its effect on town and country.

The work of Judith Miller shows how rarely and reluctantly officials intervened in the grain trade to keep prices down, and Cynthia Bouton reminds us that the thousands of grain markets in bourgs and small towns were also regulated by state authority to protect consumers, peasants as well as city-dwellers. Small farmers, who quickly sold their harvests to pay taxes, and landless rural labourers were grain consumers as well as producers; they too invoked the principles of market regulation and moral economy to protect themselves against scarcity. Indeed, the vast majority of the grain riots during the Flour War of 1775 were 'rural', as rural communities attempted to protect themselves against a liberalised grain trade, rising prices and the pull of Parisian demand on local supplies.[39]

There has not been sufficient study of the agricultural economy to indicate what effect the regulation of the grain trade had on grain prices, but recent studies find the agriculture around Paris to have been as productive as in England and the large *fermiers* around Paris to have been flourishing.[40] Yet the stimulative effects of towns on local agriculture in other parts of the country were quite limited. Philip Hoffman's painstaking study of agricultural productivity in early modern France argues that none of the regions from which he draws his examples show a real link between urban growth and agricultural growth, with the exception of the Paris basin.[41] Paris was apparently unique for several reasons. The grain trade in the Ile de France had long been more complex than in the rest of the country, and by the eighteenth century it was being organised along more efficient lines. Grain from all over the region was now purchased by millers in the city's outskirts, where it was milled before being sent to bakers in Paris.[42] The unrivalled road network around the city reduced transportation costs for this grain, as well as for fodder and manure. Paris had a substantial livestock population, particularly of horses, whose requirements for fodder stimulated the creation of artificial meadows and the commercialisation of straw in much of the Ile de France.[43] The manure produced by this urban

---

[39] C. Bouton, *The flour war: gender, class, and community in late ancien régime French society* (University Park, PA, 1993); J. Miller, *Mastering the market: the state and the grain trade in northern France, 1700–1860* (Cambridge, 1999).

[40] P. T. Hoffman, *Growth in a traditional society: the French countryside 1450–1815* (Princeton, 1996), pp. 145–63; Moriceau, *Fermiers*, pp. 613–62.

[41] Hoffman, *Growth*, pp. 170–84.

[42] S. L. Kaplan, *Provisioning Paris: merchants and millers in the grain and flour trade during the eighteenth century* (Ithaca, 1984), pp. 342–50.

[43] Moriceau, *Fermiers*, pp. 655–7.

livestock, combined with the city's human nightsoil, could make a significant contribution to rural agriculture in return. Hoffman suggests that the trade in manure was not profitable outside towns smaller than Paris, but the town council meetings of Ay in Champagne were roiled for several years by fights over the site used to collect the town's manure, which was then sold to maintain the vines that gave the town its reputation.[44]

A study of the Norman bourg of Pont-St-Pierre illustrates the complexity of most towns' relations with the countryside.[45] Although quite small, the bourg offered a range of services to the villages in its region, including judicial, medical and commercial functions. These last arose from the market and fairs, and the consequent proliferation of merchants, in the bourg. But Pont-St-Pierre's dominance was also the result of geographical advantages and seigniorial privilege, both of which suffered increasing incursions through the early modern period. The general improvement of road networks, as well as an infelicitous shift in the main highway, gradually offered surrounding villages better links to more distant markets. By the eighteenth century, local farmers routinely ignored the market held at Pont-St-Pierre and sold their grain in private arrangements off-market. The bourg and its seignior lacked the clout to enforce the traditional privileges that would have maintained their market's monopoly over the grain trade and could only fume impotently in a variety of official complaints.

Rural manufacture

A more obvious consequence of urban economic stimulus can be found in the growth of rural industry, particularly rural textiles. Not only have historians of France demonstrated that rural industry was indeed significant in many parts of the country, but they emphasise the close relationship between town and country in the organisation of the textile industry. The French textile industry, which produced more than any other country through the early modern period, was primarily urban through most of that period. Although there are no good national statistics until the eighteenth century, there is evidence that many towns, chiefly in the north like Beauvais, Amiens, Rouen, Lille, Reims, and in the south like Carcassonne, Nîmes, Montpellier and Clermont, but also a few on the peripheries like Dijon and Lyons, already had a flourishing textile trade in the sixteenth century. Not surprisingly, these

[44] AD, Marne, C 533.
[45] J. Dewald, *Pont-St-Pierre, 1398–1789: lordship, community and capitalism in early modern France* (Berkeley, 1987), pp. 32–48.

towns had immediate access to international markets; elsewhere in the country textiles were produced on a small scale for local consumption. Around most of these towns, the textile industry gradually infiltrated the countryside.

French historians actually offer several differently nuanced accounts of the development and dynamics of proto-industrialisation. The classic explanation, found more or less clearly in the works of Pierre Deyon on Amiens, Pierre Goubert on Beauvais, and Jean-Pierre Bardet on Rouen, emphasises the restrictions, expense and hostility to innovation common to urban guilds.[46] Entrepreneurs looking to cut costs or corners, trying to produce cheaper goods and greater profits, found more freedom and cheaper labour in the countryside, which had long made cloth for its own consumption. The origins of rural cloth-making are largely speculative, but both Goubert and Deyon propose a, perhaps unduly late, sixteenth-century origin for the widespread rural weaving in the north that aimed at something more than home consumption.

This model tends to emphasise the competition between urban and rural manufacturing, a competition loudly decried in enough guild and municipal memoranda to be undeniable.[47] Rouen complained bitterly as its production of woollen cloth slumped under Louis XIV and after, while production actually increased in smaller towns nearby. At the same time, the city's merchants were putting the new cotton cloth out to be made in the countryside, as far as 20 to 30 km away. A disapproving royal inspector warned that putting-out would 'ruin the city's workers and the country's agriculture' because rural weavers 'who did not gain enough from weaving to stop them from working at planting and harvesting now make so much that they do nothing else'.[48] The tension seems to have been particularly severe in the seventeenth century, when international markets were limited and the government was less liberal about 'unpoliced' manufacturing. Through the seventeenth and into the eighteenth century the authorities sympathised with the complaints of the guilds and attempted to punish rural workers for their regular failures to meet the correct standards, obtain the right seals, and sell through the proper outlets. An improving international market in the late seventeenth century slowly led to a division of labour between town and country and thus a relaxation of the competition. While rural weavers continued to produce cheap, coarse cloth, the towns turned to

[46] Deyon, *Amiens*, pp. 205–15; P. Goubert, *Cent mille provinciaux au XVIIe siècle: Beauvais et le Beauvaisis de 1600 à 1730* (Paris, 1968), pp. 152–5; Bardet, *Rouen*, vol. I, pp. 199–207.

[47] G. Bossenga, *The politics of privilege: old regime and revolution in Lille* (Cambridge, 1991), p. 137.

[48] A report from 1725, cited in Bardet, *Rouen*, vol. I, p. 201.

expensive cloth aimed at foreign markets. Rouen's merchants and brokers also appear to have retained complete control over rural production and its trade through their port.

Recent studies, focusing more on the countryside, find different dynamics and place more emphasis on co-operation between rural and urban industry.[49] J. K. J. Thomson, writing about Languedoc, presents the same competition in cyclical terms, pointing out that urban entrepreneurs gained control of both urban and rural weavers during good times, when their contacts with long-distance markets gave them significant commercial advantages. The relationship in this account is more symbiotic, as entrepreneurs encouraged higher quality production and organised both urban and rural workers into a more rational hierarchy. But during bad times, when prices and long-distance markets declined, the countryside was on its own and competed more directly with urban weavers for a more local market. Like Deyon and Goubert, he identifies the competitive period with the seventeenth century. Thus, the relationship of rural weavers to urban industries could fluctuate between a *Verlagssystem*, in which rural workers were organised by, and dependent upon, the urban merchants, and a *Kaufsystem*, which left them free to produce independently and to compete with the town.[50]

But rural weavers were not any better off with the disappearance of putting-out merchants, whose credit and contacts gave them access to richer, long-distance markets. Gay Gullickson's study of Norman peasants near Rouen in the eighteenth century insists on a complementary relationship, pointing to a division of labour between town and country that harnessed rural spinning to urban weaving. Rural industry was thus the product of urban industry – the result of a town's need for extra manpower and materials, especially yarn, because a single weaver required some eight spinners to keep him supplied with yarn.[51] In the same way, the regulatory attitudes of the urban and royal authorities were quite complex. In late eighteenth-century Lille the attitudes of town elites towards rural weaving were far from uniformly hostile.[52]

Within the general framework of rural industries there has been

---

[49] This is one of the points made by G. Lewis, 'Proto-industrialization in France', *Economic History Review* 47 (1994), 15–64, and P. Deyon, 'Proto-industrialization in France', in S. C. Ogilvie and M. Cerman (eds.), *European proto-industrialization* (Cambridge, 1996), pp. 38–48.

[50] J. K. J. Thomson, 'Variations in industrial structure in pre-industrial Languedoc', in M. Berg, P. Hudson and M. Sonenscher (eds.), *Manufacture in town and country before the factory* (Cambridge, 1983), pp. 61–83.

[51] G. L. Gullickson, *The spinners and weavers of Auffay: rural industry and the sexual division of labour in a French village, 1750–1850* (Cambridge, 1986), pp. 65–70.

[52] Bossenga, *Politics of privilege*, pp. 132–52; J.-P. Hirsch, *Les Deux Rêves du commerce, entreprise et institution dans la région lilloise* (Paris, 1991).

interesting work done on the specific mechanisms by which the countryside responded to the stimulus of urban outlets. The classic account, to
the extent that it considered the problem at all, identified urban
merchants as the initiators and mainsprings of the putting-out system.[53]
After all, they enjoyed nearly sole access to long-distance markets and
possessed the financial resources to carry the inventories of raw and
spun wool that they put out for work. That intermediaries existed,
perhaps even a swarm of them, to connect town and countryside has
been recognised but little studied until recently. But new work has
focused more on the conditions in the countryside, taking rural weavers
as the principal subject and considering their connections to the town in
more detail.

Several studies have emphasised the independence and initiative
shown by peasants in response to the commercialisation of the countryside. Liana Vardi argues for a dynamic response to the town's opportunities, a kind of vent-for-surplus model, in which peasants embraced the
chance to become weavers, and some took the initiative to organise
various aspects of the trade between villages and markets. Her work on
the Cambrésis identifies a significant minority of rural weavers, as many
as a fifth, who bought cloth from other weavers and marketed it along
with their own. Through the eighteenth century, these rural merchants
gained increasing control over the cloth trade in their villages, lending
money and material to other weavers and selling their produce. The
majority of village weavers came to rely on these intermediaries to take
the entrepreneurial risk of selling the cloth, becoming more or less
dependent upon them for credit, marketing, and in some cases even a
wage. Most rural merchants sold their cloth to *négociants* in nearby
towns, but a significant number took it out of the country and sold it as
far away as Silesia.[54] The urban *négociants* emerge from Vardi's study
looking distinctly less important to the process of rural industry than
they did in the classic account, although they provided crucial credit and
outlets to rural merchants.

The studies of rural weaving by Tessie Liu and William Reddy go
even further than Vardi in arguing for the entrepreneurial role of the
peasant weaver. Both insist on the active role of peasant weavers, not
only in producing the cloth but also in marketing it. Liu claims to 'invert
the standard assumptions about the power relations between merchant
and rural small producers' in Anjou by emphasising the peasants' ability
to gain access to markets and raw materials independently of mer-

[53] 'Mais c'est du négociant de la ville que venait l'impulsion' (Deyon, *Amiens*, p. 211).
[54] L. Vardi, *The land and the loom: peasants and profit in northern France, 1680–1800*
(Durham, 1993), pp. 145–57, 165–6, and *passim*.

chants.[55] Both she and Reddy focus on the fights over access to raw materials that slowly led to the merchants' growing economic power, but they largely ignore the complexities involved in marketing the products and simply assert that weavers could sell their goods on their own. Here Vardi shows us that most weavers preferred to let a local merchant-broker handle the marketing and that frequent problems of credit made it difficult for these merchants to keep their place in the market.[56]

Rural brokers stepped forward in the eighteenth-century textile industry around Lille, but the city's merchants worked very hard to restrict their independence. These same merchants, who generally supported a liberalisation of the wool trade when it meant their ability to put cloth-making out to the surrounding countryside, rushed to the defence of the urban guilds when they realised that liberalisation meant that rural merchants were organising the trade and were finding outlets for the cloth that bypassed the city. In the face of much government pressure to free the trade in the surrounding villages and small towns, the city won a victory by forcing rural brokers to send their cloth to city brokers.[57] Attempts by rural entrepreneurs to transcend the local market and insert themselves into the currents of long-distance trade had to overcome the legal limits to their new role, as well as the hurdles of credit and commercial contacts. There is evidence that entrepreneurs were more successful at this in the wine trade.

Viticulture

Another consequence of urban stimulus is the more peculiarly French development of viticulture. The development of vineyards in the Beaujolais whose wine was good enough to be exported out of the region contributed substantially to the rise of the province's agricultural productivity.[58] A similar turn to viticulture could be found in other parts of the country. The economics of viticulture were particularly attractive to the marginal peasant: whereas it required some 10 hectares of plough-land to support a family, it might be possible on less than 2 ha of vineyards.[59] Vineyards required none of the capital equipment necessary

[55] T. Liu, *The weaver's knot: the contradictions of class struggle and family solidarity in western France, 1750–1914* (Ithaca, 1994), p. 46, and *passim*; W. M. Reddy, *The rise of market culture: the textile trade and French society, 1750–1900* (Cambridge, 1984), pp. 19–47.

[56] Vardi, *Land and loom*, pp. 172–202. Her discussion of credit instruments, which included promissory notes and bills of exchange, shows the limits of Postel-Vinay's study of formal loans in *La Terre et l'argent*.

[57] Bossenga, *Politics of privilege*, pp. 137–67.

[58] Hoffman, *Growth*, pp. 108, 128–9.

[59] Brennan, *Burgundy to Champagne*, pp. 6–11, and *passim* for the next three paragraphs.

for grain-growing, such as the ploughteam, or the waste of fallow land, but they needed almost constant, year-round attention. As an occupation requiring intensive labour rather than land or capital, viticulture grew in popularity through the early modern period. Vineyards expanded in the Beaujolais and along the Atlantic and Mediterranean coasts through the seventeenth century, though they retreated from the Channel coast. By the eighteenth century, with roughly 10 per cent of the population producing wine, officials worried that the conversion of ploughland to vineyards threatened a glut of wine and a dearth of grain. The crown issued several laws attempting to slow the spread of vineyards, with no apparent effect. Instead, vine-growers became increasingly sophisticated at finding markets.

Wine has always been a commercial crop and has always connected the countryside to markets. A portion of this wine had always found its way to export or urban markets, which were likely to offer better prices. Thus it is not surprising to find that the provinces (*départements*) with most vineyards show a noticeable correlation with the most urbanised areas. Of course the measure is a rough estimate, since the effect of a large city, like Paris, Bordeaux or Nantes, was felt over several departments, but vineyards correlated fairly well with departments having large populations in towns of more than 10,000 people and very little with departments having large populations in communes of fewer than 10,000.[60] With improvements in transportation and communication and, more importantly, with the growing sophistication of intermediaries like brokers and *négociants*, the effects of urban demand gradually spread to broader areas.

Along with the increasing sophistication of commercial viticulture, the dynamics of the wine trade changed profoundly. With few exceptions, the wine trade was local in the middle ages, but these exceptions made a difference and, as they increased through the early modern period, came to shape a new wine trade. The wine flowing to the rest of Europe through ports at Rouen, Nantes, La Rochelle and, finally, Bordeaux was a small proportion of the total wine traded but a major contribution to France's exports. More important, urban wine consumption in France was a significant 100 to 200 litres per capita through

---

[60] This is based on population data from 1806, by department, in Lepetit, *Pre-industrial urban system*, pp. 453–7; and on data from 1788 about total hectares of vineyards by department, in B. Lachiver, *Vins, vignes et vignerons: histoire du vignoble français* (Paris, 1988), pp. 594–5. The correlation ignored departments where no wine was grown (mostly in the north), and excluded Paris and Corsica. The correlations with population in communes of less than 1,500 inhabitants; 1,500 to 3,000 inhabitants; 3,000 to 5,000; 5,000 to 10,000; and more than 10,000 are respectively 0.166; 0.001; 0.127; 0.125; 0.409.

the early modern period and stimulated the growth of long-distance trade.[61] Until the seventeenth century, these forms of long-distance trade were controlled by merchants in the ports and the big cities. It was their initiative, their credit arrangements and their profits that shaped the inter-regional wine trade. But brokers in the small towns and villages of the wine-producing regions emerged in the late seventeenth century, first to aid the big-city buyers, then to replace them. By the late eighteenth century, improvements in transportation and communication, and in the market facilities of Paris, encouraged modest wine-growers to speculate on shipping their own wine to distant markets quite independently of brokers in big or small towns.

Of course this shifting balance of power was gradual and far from unilinear. Although the countryside, which traditionally provisioned towns in a largely passive manner, did gradually produce brokers and growers who looked actively for markets, the large town continued to enjoy certain advantages and, in some cases, to dominate the trade. An excellent example of this can be found in Reims, which was and still is the capital of an international wine trade even though it produces no wine. Since well before the sixteenth century, the wine merchants of Reims organised the wine trade of the whole northern Champagne region, most of whose vineyards lay 20 to 30 km away. For a brief period in the late seventeenth and early eighteenth centuries, the producers in the vineyards, aided by brokers in local small towns and bourgs like Epernay and Ay, established a flourishing trade with Paris independently of Reims. But this trade foundered by the middle of the century and wine producers looked again to international markets, through Reims. Even more important, however, it was the brokers of Reims who decided in the middle of the century to invest seriously in producing sparkling wine, bottling and storing it in the famous chalk caves under the city. Such an entrepreneurial effort, requiring considerable skill, equipment and risks, was avoided by rural producers if at all possible, but it led rapidly in the nineteenth century to the triumph of a small number of champagne houses and their eventual control of most viticulture in the region.[62]

Networks of trade

In general, however, the stimulus of the city, as both consumption centre and gateway to long-distance trade, encouraged market-oriented

[61] T. Brennan, 'Towards the cultural history of alcohol in France', *Journal of Social History*, 23 (1989), 71–92.
[62] Brennan, *Burgundy to Champagne*, pp. 240–71.

production in the countryside. It also led, more slowly, to the creation of rural agents who began to compete with the city and to look for access to wider markets on their own. In order to understand this process and the effect it had on the organisation of markets, we gain little by looking to central place theory. Central place theory as it was originally formulated identified the urban hierarchy of retail and wholesale networks formed by the dynamics of marketing goods to an essentially uniform sea of consumers.[63] Both its emphasis on retail markets and its static picture of a market hierarchy miss important elements of the early modern urban market. It presupposed, in other words, that towns sold to the countryside and offers little theoretical insight into the process by which the countryside sells to the town. But the flow of goods in pre-modern society was overwhelmingly in the latter direction. The city lived in a sea of producers rather than consumers and offered very little in the way of consumption goods to its hinterland. As these producers gained independent commercial contact with an outside world, and as a small rural elite slowly developed the credit resources and entrepreneurial skills necessary to deal with that world, they began to challenge the hierarchy of old regime markets.

As an alternative to central place theory, one based on the town's essential role as an assembly point for goods originating in the countryside, we might consider the dendritic model that works on the analogy of a root system.[64] Towns were roots that transferred goods from the countryside and, after consuming some of them, sent the rest on to larger conduits in the surplus flow. The key questions to be asked of a system that explains the acquisition, assembling and transference of goods involve the range of a town's reach, the degree and mechanisms of its control over the production of its hinterland, and its connections to other outlets. There are also questions that can be asked from the viewpoint of the countryside, for rural sellers sought the most profitable access to markets, a route that usually took them through the local town but might connect them more directly – and thus more profitably – to a higher order market. Thus there is an element of push–pull in this model, particularly towards the end of the early modern period, as the

---

[63] B. J. L. Berry, *Geography of market centers and retail distribution* (Englewood Cliffs, NJ, 1967), pp. 59–73, offers a useful overview of a theory that 'assume[s] that a large number of goods and services have to be provided for each of the consumers on the plain'.

[64] For examples of this dendritic model, see K. Bonsack Kelley, 'Dendritic central-place systems', in C. A. Smith (ed.), *Regional analysis*, 2 vols. (London, 1976), vol. I, pp. 221–34, and T. Brennan, 'The anatomy of inter-regional markets in the early modern French wine trade', *Journal of European Economic History* 22 (1994), 581–617.

countryside connected itself more aggressively to inter-regional and international markets.

Unlike the regular honeycomb distribution of towns predicted by central place theory, the dendritic model suggests more clustering of sites, particularly along communication routes. There is also a dynamic element inherent in the dendritic model, since it is driven by a struggle for access to market outlets. Whereas much of the traditional communications system, particularly the rivers, was largely unchanging, other elements, like early modern roads and later railroads, might change more quickly. And access was also affected by the availability of credit, information and even personnel, which could all change rapidly. Depending on these conditions, major urban nodes in the dendritic system could actually be quite close to each other, at least for a time, though there was clearly a tendency for individual towns to attempt to control large catchment areas.

The dendritic nature of much of France's trade can be seen by looking at the geographical organisation of its fairs and markets during the Revolution, when it can first be determined on a national scale. With over 2,000 markets and twice as many fairs, there is no simple pattern to their placement or interaction, yet Dominique Margairaz identifies interesting differences between them. Fairs, which generally met once or twice a year, were particularly characteristic of bourgs, even villages: three-quarters of them occurred in centres with fewer than 2,000 people and two-fifths in those under 1,000. Markets, meeting weekly or bi-weekly, took place in small towns – nearly two-thirds of them in towns of 1,000 to 5,000 inhabitants and only a quarter in centres with fewer than 1,000. Markets served an important retail function, principally by organising the regular sale of grain to consumers whose income or storage was too modest to buy in any quantity. Markets conformed to a rough central place model, being fairly evenly distributed around the country and more or less hierarchical in their interactions. However, Bernard Lepetit, using much the same information about markets and fairs as Margairaz, and adding later information about shops and banks, argues that the Paris basin alone shows the kind of marketing order and hierarchy among towns predicted by central place theory.[65] Fairs, in contrast, served overwhelmingly to facilitate the export of agricultural produce, particularly livestock, from its producing areas. The distribution of fairs was much less even through the country, tending to cluster and compete, in a more recognisably dendritic pattern.[66] Only a few of the country's largest markets offered significant amounts of consumer

[65] Lepetit, *Pre-industrial urban system*, pp. 360–96.
[66] D. Margairaz, *Foires et marchés dans la France préindustrielle* (Paris, 1988), pp. 46–69.

goods for sale, although there is evidence of fairs shifting in this direction in the early nineteenth century.

Administration and the law

The shape that trade gave to commercial and urban networks gradually overlaid an earlier structure formed by the town's administrative functions. For, whereas towns cannot be said to have offered much in the way of goods to the surrounding countryside, they provided a range of services that enhanced their influence at the same time as they served the state. These include a variety of administrative offices, particularly fiscal and judicial ones, as well as cultural and charitable functions. This administrative network comes closer to the uniformity predicted by central place theory, although the actual distribution of towns was strongly influenced by historical development of the kingdom and of royal administration.[67] Certainly the most prominent of these administrative roles was the judicial activity of towns.

The monarchy had created a system of royal justice throughout the country during the middle ages, with more than 400 *bailliage* or *sénéchaussée* courts in all the large and medium-sized towns. Over time, these courts competed aggressively with the traditional seigniorial justice of the countryside, rarely replacing it completely but often absorbing the bulk of criminal affairs and leaving the more lucrative civil cases to seigniors. As criminal justice intervened progressively in the countryside, so did the policing arm of the law. The creation of a national police force (*maréchaussée*), in the sixteenth century, put relatively few men into the field and their numbers never grew to anything impressive during the old regime. Nevertheless, the *maréchaussée* was a tangible extension of the royal presence in the countryside. More importantly, it interjected the essentially urban network of law courts into rural society, offering villagers a range of alternatives for dealing with their internal problems. The interests of the royal government and municipal elites clearly coincided here, for the town was the locus of royal law and it 'retailed' this service more effectively than most.

The impact of royal law on the countryside is a subject of continuing research and interpretation. What Roland Mousnier has said about the Grands Jours d'Auvergne in the 1660s, that 'the members of this rural society looked upon urban judges and their agents as strangers to their world and viewed their interference as an intolerable form of aggression and coercion,' may only be true of a particularly remote part of the

---

[67] Lepetit, *Pre-industrial urban system*, pp. 124–75.

country, but recent studies suggest that much of rural society shared a modified version of this attitude.[68] Some studies have presented urban justice as intrusive and heavy-handed, particularly the work that deals with the sixteenth- and seventeenth-century witch craze. Although most of France was visited only lightly by this problem, especially in the jurisdiction of the Parlement of Paris, the eastern frontiers experienced the full horror of judicial inquest, torture and execution. Yet recent work has emphasised the rural, rather than elite, origins of much witch hunting.[69]

At the same time, studies of royal justice and the *maréchaussée*, most of them devoted to the eighteenth century, see the countryside dealing with the courts and the mounted police very much on their own terms. There is general consensus that rural communities enjoyed sophisticated systems for dealing with their internal problems. Village elites, like the priest or the notary, routinely offered arbitration that could be quite formal and explicit in its authority and sanctions. Even the studies of witch trials indicate that formal indictments usually followed years of informal measures for healing breaches of the peace. Rural communities usually turned to the outside for help only after alternatives had failed, or when they confronted an external problem. Villagers were far more likely to invoke or co-operate with the *maréchaussée* to deal with alien vagabonds than one of their own.[70]

In the end, recent work on town and country insists on their interconnection. From every perspective, whether economic, demographic, social, or judicial, the urban and rural worlds impinged on each other. Much of the influence was stimulating, drawing the two worlds closer together and making them more responsive to each other. Rural industries and agriculture produced increasingly for long-distance markets, seeking towns as outlets for their trade. At the same time, the countryside resisted the incursion of urban judges and merchants. But these incursions only increased, and rural societies slowly learned to manipulate them to their own ends.

[68] R. Mousnier, *The institutions of France under the absolute monarchy 1598–1789*, transl. A. Goldhammer, 2 vols. (Chicago, 1984), vol. II, p. 496.
[69] R. Briggs, *Witches and neighbors: the social and cultural context of European witchcraft* (New York, 1996), pp. 319–40.
[70] M. Greenshields, *An economy of violence in early modern France: crime and justice in the Haute Auvergne, 1587–1664* (University Park, PA, 1994); S. G. Reinhardt, *Justice in the Sarladais 1770–1790* (Baton Rouge, 1991); R. M. Schwartz, *Policing the poor in eighteenth-century France* (Chapel Hill, 1988); I. Cameron, *Crime and repression in the Auvergne and the Guyenne, 1720–1790* (Cambridge, 1981).

12　Town and country in Castile, 1400–1650

Pablo Sánchez León

Introduction

The crisis of the seventeenth century has been frequently portrayed as a watershed in the history of early modern Spain which shaped the economic structure of its central region, Castile, until the nineteenth century.[1] Even recent, more optimistic assessments of Spanish economic recovery after 1700 contrast the persistently agrarian features and the slow urban growth of Castile with the increased integration and diversification in peripheral regions like Catalonia and the north Atlantic seaboard.[2] Debates on the seventeenth-century crisis have also cast a deep shadow backwards onto the 'long sixteenth century' between 1450 and 1600. Interpretations of this period focus overwhelmingly on features that allegedly conditioned or directly caused the subsequent economic decline, in particular on the inability of extensive agriculture to meet rising demand in the absence of technological innovation and on the disruption caused by sharply increasing taxation on market structures and manufacture.[3] Paradoxically, however, this pessimism with regard to the period before 1600 contrasts with a diagnosis of seventeenth-century decline in terms of de-urbanisation and market fragmentation, of de-industrialisation and ruralisation,[4] which implies a

---

[1] D. S. Reher, *Town and country in pre-industrial Spain. Cuenca, 1550–1870* (Cambridge, 1990), pp. 15–67; B. Yun, 'Spain and the XVIth-century crisis in Europe: some final considerations', in I. A. A. Thompson and B. Yun (eds.), *The Castilian crisis of the seventeenth century. New perspectives on the economic and social history of seventeenth-century Spain* (Cambridge, 1994), pp. 301–21.

[2] D. Ringrose, *Spain, Europe and the 'Spanish miracle', 1700–1900* (Cambridge, 1996), pp. 249–90.

[3] G. Anes, *Las crisis agrarias en la España moderna* (Madrid, 1970), pp. 87–126; A. García Sanz, *Desarrollo y crisis del Antiguo Régimen en Castilla la Vieja. Economía y sociedad en tierras de Segovia, 1500–1814* (Madrid, 1977), pp. 39–204.

[4] J. E. Gelabert, 'Il declino della rete urbana nella Castiglia dei secoli XVI–XVIII', *Cheiron* 6 (1989–90), 9–46; J. E. Gelabert, 'Urbanisation and de-urbanisation in Castile, 1500–1800', in Thompson and Yun, *The Castilian crisis*, pp. 182–205.

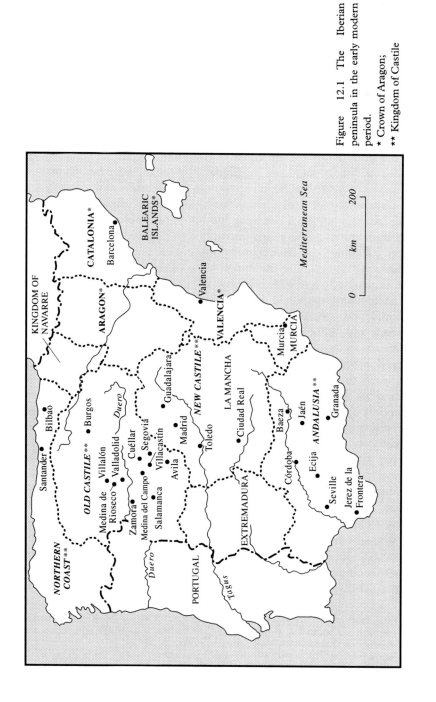

Figure 12.1 The Iberian peninsula in the early modern period.

* Crown of Aragon;
** Kingdom of Castile

far more flattering picture of economic performance and of town–country relations in the preceding centuries.

Despite the merits of a retrogressive approach to the period we are concerned with, the back-projection of seventeenth-century performance to the period between 1400 and 1600 has rather obscured earlier developments. To understand the characteristics of the long economic upswing up to the 1590s on its own terms, we need to push our analysis a step back and consider how the Castilian economy and society emerged from the ravages of the Black Death. Although the region suffered considerably from the epidemics, the late medieval crisis was not felt as badly there as in England, France, or even Catalonia. Recovery in Castile had begun already in the early fifteenth century and was associated with rising population, increasing urbanisation, flourishing markets and fairs servicing the booming wool export trade, and rising agricultural prices that stimulated agrarian and industrial specialisation.[5] Patterns of development were also profoundly shaped by institutional factors. The most significant of these was the growth of a more centralised state with a greater capacity to redistribute resources and co-ordinate economic activity. Its activities altered the prevailing territorial and jurisdictional organisation and modified the system of economic and political constraints and incentives.[6]

Although political reorganisation stimulated the kingdom's economic integration, the consequences of political unification were more ambiguous than is sometimes supposed. Strong institutional differences between the region's various conquered territories persisted throughout the middle ages and the early modern period. These differences essentially reflected the varying degree to which cities could extend their control over, and organise relations with, the countryside, and the capacity of the monarchy to co-ordinate these relations. Christian domination was not expressed uniformly from north to south, nor did royal control and co-ordination increase smoothly and progressively between the high and late middle ages.

Broadly speaking, the different stages of the Reconquista established four areas in pre-plague Castile featuring major differences in urban institutions: the northern coastal area, Old Castile, New Castile and Andalusia. In the mountains and valleys of Navarre, Galicia and the Basque country bordering the Atlantic to the north, the strength of

[5] B. Yun, 'Economic cycles and structural changes', in T. Brady, H. A. Oberman and J. Tracy (eds.), *Handbook of European history, 1400–1600. Late middle ages, Renaissance and Reformation* (Leyden–New York–Cologne, 1994), pp. 377–411.
[6] P. Sánchez León, *Absolutismo y comunidad. Los orígenes sociales de la guerra de los Comuneros de Castilla* (Madrid, 1998), esp. pp. 31–9.

village communities and of feudal authority created a highly atomised institutional landscape that prevented the rise of towns of any significance. The core of medieval Christian urbanisation lay further south, in the area between the Duero and Tagus rivers known as Old Castile, particularly in its southern half, where during the eleventh and twelfth centuries the crown granted town charters to small settlements to attract immigrants and strengthen military efforts, thus establishing the towns pre-eminently as centres of royal power; the more northerly areas of Old Castile tended to share features of the northern valley communities.[7] The conquest and settlement of New Castile, which included La Mancha, Extremadura and Murcia, was directed by the monarchy in alliance with the aristocratic military orders and towns.[8] Together with a rather rapid conquest, the originally low demographic density of these regions prevented the formation of large cities, apart from Toledo in the north. Instead, the jurisdictional landscape featured a leopard-spotting of clearly defined urban jurisdictions scattered across vast and largely empty territories. Lastly, in Muslim Andalusia, which had a long-standing tradition of urbanisation supported by high population density, the Castilian monarchy established and maintained a central co-ordinating role, and many more urban centres had developed in this area already during the fourteenth century.

Urban jurisdictions and markets in the fifteenth century

Political integration and seigniorial jurisdiction

Towards 1350, therefore, the Castilian monarchy's territorial and economic fragmentation reflected its limited abilities to control still quasi-autonomous jurisdictions. During the following century both the economic and political features of Castile became more homogeneous and more sharply defined.

The low rates of urbanisation in the North throughout the medieval and most of the early modern period were a consequence of the weak institutional functions of northern towns compared to their southern peers. In New and Old Castile and Andalusia urban centres took on central administrative, fiscal and distributive functions for the monarchy. Their prerogatives and obligations rested on legal and political

---

[7] F. J. Martínez Llorente, *Régimen jurídico de la Extremadura castellana medieval. Las Comunidades de Villa y Tierra (siglos X–XIV)* (Valladolid, 1990), pp. 118–36, 204–36.

[8] E. Cabrera, 'Del Tajo a Sierra Morena', in J. A. García de Cortázar (ed.), *Organización del espacio en la España medieval. La Corona de Castilla en los siglos XIII al XV* (Barcelona, 1985), pp. 123–61.

arrangements that shaped relations between town and country. Municipal entities or *concejos* had common rights over wood, water and pasture, could both enact and enforce rules over the administration of common lands (such as ensuring that cattle could graze on the open fields after harvest time), and could establish local markets to supply urban consumers and raise taxes.[9] But their most distinctive institutional feature was their power of collective lordship over the surrounding countryside, which meant that although rural villages had a degree of self-government, they depended on the city for criminal and common justice and for political representation.[10] On the other hand, and partly as a consequence of the strong powers of the towns, rural serfdom was very limited and the labour force was highly mobile and could easily migrate to the towns.[11]

These institutional features were generally strengthened during the late medieval economic and social crisis and thereafter. As a result of the crisis the monarchy was able to reinforce its financial and fiscal prerogatives and its role in allocating and redistributing resources. The introduction of a centralised tax, the *alcabala*, initially as an excise on all market exchanges, rationalised royal finances, lowered the costs of exaction, and confirmed the urban sector's function as the linchpin of the royal fisc. The crown also abolished serfdom once and for all. State-led reforms thus stimulated commercialisation and reshaped the sources of feudal wealth, paving the way for a long period of growth. The titled nobility quickly adapted itself to the new conditions. Courtiers were granted rent streams on centralised taxation and the Castilian monarchy began for the first time to compensate aristocratic-military families with urban jurisdictions. In the same years, feudal lineages were defining new, stricter inheritance structures based upon rights of entailment (*mayorazgo*).[12] In the course of the late middle ages aristocratic power, like that of the monarchy, became rooted in the patrimonial ownership of towns.

Interpretations of economic and social developments in the period have centred on the distinction between urban lordship (*señorío*) and

---

[9] J. M. Mangas, *El régimen comunal agrario de los concejos de Castilla* (Madrid, 1981), pp. 95–191.

[10] C. Estepa, 'El realengo y el señorío jurisdiccional concejil en Castilla y León (siglos XII–XV)', in *Concejos y ciudades en la Edad Media Hispánica* (León, 1990), pp. 467–505.

[11] Reher, *Town and country*, pp. 245–98; D. E. Vassberg, *The village and the outside world in Golden Age Castile. Mobility and migration in everyday rural life* (Cambridge, 1996), pp. 67–85, 171–5.

[12] B. Clavero, *Mayorazgo. Propiedad feudal en Castilla. 1369–1836* (Madrid, 1974), pp. 21–50, 102–21; J. Valdeón, *Los conflictos sociales en Castilla en los siglos XIV y XV* (Madrid, 1975), pp. 82–101, 140–53.

royal demesne (*realengo*).[13] Aristocratic entails and feudal territorial control are said to have prevented the development of a truly competitive land market and of an integrated, national state. From an institutional point of view, however, the distinction is scarcely relevant, for from its origins in the early fifteenth century seigniorial jurisdiction was based upon the same kind of urban self-government and rural domination that featured under royal jurisdiction.[14] The characteristic feature of Castilian urban lordship was not its divergence from royal patterns of control, but rather its strong similarities, which were the result of the high degree of institutional homogeneity of the Castilian monarchy and which clearly distinguished town–country relations in Castile from those in the more easterly regions of the peninsula.

Political institutions and markets

In the Iberian lands of the crown of Aragon comprising Aragon, Catalonia, Valencia and the Balearic islands, the development of collective urban lordship along the lines of the *concejo* was restricted to the southern areas of later Christian conquest, where the conquerors could bargain directly with established towns. To the north, the monarchy was forced to rely more on the feudal aristocracy, which drew most of its profits from jurisdictional rights over the peasantry. The crown was thus forced to increase its revenue through the acquisition of foreign territories and the control of Mediterranean inter-regional trade.[15] This policy stimulated the development of commercial metropolises like Valencia and Barcelona, but left the structure of feudal income untouched and restricted the development of autonomous urban settlements with control over the countryside. Not even the disappearance of serfdom after the Remença revolt in late fifteenth-century Catalonia changed the established pattern of urban–rural relations significantly.[16]

In Castile in the early fifteenth century, only Seville, with over 20,000 inhabitants towards 1400, could lay claim to the functions of a metropolis acting on both the international and regional markets. Maritime towns in the north like Bilbao or Santander were far smaller

[13] M. Artola, *Antiguo Régimen y revolución liberal* (Barcelona, 1978), pp. 52–85, 92–112.
[14] A. M. Guilarte, *El régimen señorial en el siglo XVI*, 2nd edn (Valladolid, 1987), pp. 127–60.
[15] J. Vicens Vives, *Manual de historia económica de España* (Barcelona, 1959), pp. 143–53, 215–23.
[16] D. S. Reher, 'Ciudades, procesos de urbanización y sistemas urbanos en la península ibérica, 1550–1991', in *Atlas histórico de ciudades europeas* (Barcelona, 1994), pp. 3–4; on Catalonia, see A. García Espuche, 'Cataluña y Barcelona entre 1462 y 1550', in *Un siglo decisivo. Barcelona y Cataluña, 1550–1640* (Madrid, 1998), pp. 25–33.

and had little institutional and commercial interaction with their hinterlands. The royal towns of Valladolid, Segovia and Toledo, all situated in the border area between Old and New Castile, were growing fast but from a very low base of just over 5,000 inhabitants, a figure that can be considered the minimum size for a town in the region.[17] Already by the late fourteenth century, however, the main difference between Castile and most other west European regions was not demographic but institutional: autonomous urban centres in Castile had strong territorial powers that left virtually no space for competing jurisdictional authorities.

The larger size of the *concejos'* jurisdictions compared to the more fragmented spaces elsewhere in western Europe fostered greater fiscal and commercial integration and co-operation *within* urban territories. On the other hand, the jurisdictional autonomy of individual towns made it hard to establish fruitful commercial linkages *between* towns; co-operation had to be instigated largely by external pressure from the state. Although the development of a more powerful monarchy made such intervention easier, royal authority was deployed more as a source of political than of economic integration. Attempts to improve market integration by lowering domestic barriers to trade had in any case to be negotiated with other political agents, and could not be imposed unilaterally. The limitations to Castilian integration and to the development of market structures promoting growth were the effect of changes in the relative power of the aristocracy, urban elites and the monarchy during the late middle ages that were shaped by local circumstances and differed between regions.

One indication of the growth of more commercially oriented production and of increased commercial competition after 1400 is the development of fairs and markets which connected urban and rural areas and local production with longer distance commodity flows.[18] The creation of a fair was, in principle, an institutional process, since fairs required a legal privilege and detailed regulations to be established and were frequently exempted from trade taxes. Although concessions were a political act by the sovereign, they were not driven solely by political factors. The coming of the Trastamara dynasty (1369–1474) coincided with a long cycle of growth in the number of periodic fairs and tax-exempt weekly markets. In Old Castile, new fairs created during the late fourteenth and early fifteenth centuries doubled the number established

---

[17] M. A. Ladero, *Las ciudades de Corona de Castilla en la Baja Edad Media (siglos XIII al XV)* (Madrid, 1996), pp. 13–15.

[18] S. R. Epstein, 'Regional fairs, institutional innovation, and economic growth in late medieval Europe', *Economic History Review* 47 (1994), 459–82.

during the preceding centuries.[19] Many fairs were granted by way of recompense to the emerging 'new aristocracy' which was extending its powers over the towns in this period, frequently by jurisdictionally segregating villages from pre-existing urban *concejos*.[20] The kings themselves and several members of the royal family also erected new markets in the royal demesne in an attempt to attract trade and population. While the aristocracy established important fairs in Cuéllar, Villalón, Medina de Rioseco and Medina del Campo (although the latter was soon reincorporated under royal authority), royalty also awarded fairs to large demesnial centres like Avila, Segovia and Madrid in response to demands by the urban elites.

In late medieval Old Castile, the original land of the *concejos*, the numerous towns were still in the process of defining their institutional and territorial prerogatives, and the relatively weak nobility adapted rather slowly to the more centralised political framework. This institutional fluidity gave rise to intense competition between urban elites, the aristocracy and members of the royal family for state apanages and politically backed rent streams. Competition for economic privileges led to the establishment of a large number of new fairs and franchised markets, and forced the recipients to offer good commercial conditions to attract trade. More than a third of all fairs established in the kingdom of Castile between 1350 and 1550 were created in the central area between the Duero and Tagus rivers, which ended up having more than 40 per cent of the 150 fairs present in the entire kingdom.[21]

Although further south urban lordships and an urban-based aristocracy were more developed, that did not necessarily make it any easier to modify market institutions for the better. Few new fairs were set up in fifteenth-century La Mancha because most towns had already been granted them during the thirteenth century and because the presence in the region of a small number of powerful and quasi-autonomous military orders made it hard for the crown to co-ordinate and enforce fair requests effectively.[22] The resistance to institutional change in this region revealed by the lack of new fairs is partly responsible for the slow rise in urbanisation during the fifteenth century. In highly urbanised Andalusia, by contrast, the titled nobility had been rewarded with small *concejos* from the early fourteenth century without engendering any conflict with the larger towns in the royal demesne, which gave rise to

---

[19] M. A. Ladero, *Las ferias de Castilla. Siglos XII al XV* (Madrid, 1994), pp. 109–14.

[20] S. de Moxó, 'De nobleza vieja a nobleza nueva. La transformación nobiliaria en la Baja Edad Media', *Cuadernos de Historia* 3 (1969), 1–210.

[21] Ladero, *Las ferias*, pp. 20–43.

[22] E. Rodríguez-Picavea, *La formación del feudalismo en la Meseta meridional castellana. Los señoríos de la Orden de Calatrava en los siglos XII–XIII* (Madrid, 1994), pp. 247–52.

the most competitive and well-developed urban system in fifteenth-century Castile. While the nobility lobbied for fairs for their villages and scattered rural settlements, they were unable to isolate themselves from the larger royal cities.[23]

Fairs and markets granted by the monarchy were among the most effective means of lowering transaction costs and fostering specialisation between different areas. Other, more inclusive attempts to integrate or co-ordinate separate jurisdictions through urban alliances were too episodic or too weak to stimulate the integration of the Castilian market during the fifteenth century. Although the Cortes, a form of parliamentary representation of the seventeen (later eighteen) most important cities of the kingdom set up to negotiate taxation with the crown, established a basic political hierarchy between cities and smaller towns, they were increasingly undermined by political unrest during the late fourteenth and early fifteenth centuries. Consequently the monarchy frequently bypassed them to negotiate fiscal obligations directly with individual towns. In the absence both of stable consultative mechanisms and of political stability at the centre, it was left to the towns to organise and co-operate among themselves; but urban collaboration for joint action arose during only brief periods of extreme political instability and had no durable economic effects.

The only significant pressure towards more effective institutional and economic integration during much of the fifteenth century came from the aristocracy. In order to develop their newly established towns and to gain access to commercial networks, the 'new aristocracy' attempted to establish relations of patronage over larger royal centres. In this period most of the greater aristocracy, the *Grandes*, had influence over a royal city: the Guzmán (dukes of Medina-Sidonia) and Ponce de León in Seville, the Velasco in Burgos, the Sotomayor (counts of Belalcázar) in Córdoba, the Mendoza (marquises of Santillana and later dukes of Infantado) in Guadalajara, and the Alvarez de Toledo (dukes of Alba) in Salamanca.[24] But the strategy was both politically destabilising and economically ineffective. Links between feudal *señorío* and royal *realengo* were maintained by trying to impose the rights of the former over those of the latter, with the result that especially during the second half of the fifteenth century aristocratic power became the main source of unrest in royal towns. In any case, aristocratic control was restricted to individual

---

[23] M. A. Ladero, *Andalucía en torno a 1492. Estructuras. Valores. Sucesos* (Madrid, 1992), pp. 61–5.

[24] L. Suárez, *Nobleza y monarquía. Puntos de vista sobre la historia política de Castilla en el siglo XV,* 2nd edn (Madrid, 1975), pp. 87–97.

royal jurisdictions and could not be extended to include a large number of cities.

Pacification under the Catholic Kings (1474–1504) re-established political co-operation between the court and the aristocracy, but did little to promote institutional reforms conducive to greater institutional and economic integration. The monarchy led the nobility to war against the Muslim kingdom of Granada and confirmed the sources of income the nobles had obtained under the Trastamaras. The new kings drastically reduced aristocratic concessions of urban jurisdictions,[25] reinforced their authority in royal *concejos* against the aristocracy and urban elites, passed general legislation over the import and export trade, and tried to rationalise the market network by turning Medina del Campo, the most international of the Castilian fairs, into a national fair or *feria general*. Since the main rationale for these measures was to increase state revenues rather than to stimulate trade, however, the number of new fairs awarded to the demesne was significantly reduced. Moreover, since the crown was unwilling to attack the prerogatives of the *Grandes*, its activities tended to consolidate the decentralised arrangements that had emerged during the period of civil unrest. Paradoxically, the improvements in market infrastructure reflected in the new fairs were a consequence of a relatively weak state, and as the monarchy strengthened its hold, the margins for institutional change narrowed. Castile ended the fifteenth century without having achieved a significant degree of institutional and economic integration; on the contrary, decades of instability and of *ad hoc* policy-making had reinforced regional differences and established a group of large royal towns as quasi-autonomous centres of economic and jurisdictional power.

Urban networks and urbanisation

By 1500 the urban networks in Castile reflected the two-pronged tendency towards market integration within regions and towards increased differentiation between them. Old Castile was headed by a metropolis of *c.*35,000 inhabitants, Valladolid; beneath it Medina del Campo, Segovia and Salamanca each had more than 10,000 inhabitants. In Andalusia, Seville, with over 35,000 inhabitants, headed a more complex hierarchy of six cities over 10,000: Córdoba, Granada, Jaén, Jerez de la Frontera, Ecija and Baeza. Andalusia was also significantly more urbanised, with a population living in cities above 10,000 of at

---

[25] S. H. Haliczer, *The Comuneros of Castile. The forging of a revolution, 1475–1521* (Madison, WI, 1981), pp. 30–65; S. H. Haliczer, 'The Castilian aristocracy and the *mercedes* reform of 1478–82', *Hispanic American Historical Review* 55 (1975), 449–67.

Table 12.1. *Urbanisation in Castile, 1500–1600 (percentages)*

| | 5,000–10,000 | | 10,000+ | |
	1530	1591	1530	1591
Atlantic coast	0	1	0	0
Old Castile	3	3	6	6
New Castile	7	15	5.5	8
Andalusia	14	22	28	31
Mean	5	10	8	11

Source: J. I. Fortea, 'Las ciudades de la Corona de Castilla en el Antiguo Régimen: una revisión historiográfica', *Boletín de la Asociación de Demografía Histórica* 13 (1995), 3, 51.

least 25 per cent in 1530 compared with only 6 per cent in Old Castile. In New Castile, Toledo with 20,000 inhabitants actually had stronger links with the towns of Old Castile than with its regional hinterland, where Murcia (10,000 inhabitants) in the distant south-east was the only other city of any significance. Lastly, in New Castile the rate of urbanisation was possibly as low as 5 per cent.[26]

Urbanisation increased steadily from the late fifteenth century. As population began to recover, rural migration intensified and consolidated the division of labour between town and country inherited from the late middle ages. Sixteenth-century urbanisation followed a characteristic pattern across Europe. The largest cities attracted the highest numbers of immigrants because of their greater occupational diversity, revealing the development of more hierarchical regional networks and stronger integration between European markets. In Castile, population in the 25 cities with over 10,000 inhabitants nearly doubled to 600,000 during the sixteenth century; by the 1590s the proportion of the population living in these cities had risen from *c*.8 to *c*.11 per cent, significantly higher than the European average but still considerably lower than the Low Countries and Italy.

The sectoral and regional distribution of these gains can be used to assess the degree of integration in Castile as a whole. In the first place, growth was unevenly distributed between towns. Whereas cities with 10,000–25,000 inhabitants grew at the same rate as the total population, the five largest cities with over 25,000 inhabitants grew four times as fast. There was also increased competition for the top slot in the kingdom, especially between Seville in the south and Madrid (which became the capital in 1561), which soared from 10,000 inhabitants in the 1550s to 90,000 by the 1590s. But this apparently straightforward

[26] J. L. Fortea, 'Las ciudades de la Corona de Castilla en el Antiguo Régimen: una revisión historiográfica', *Boletín de la Asociación de Demografía Histórica* 13 (1995), 51.

picture of metropolitan growth, which seems to support the hypothesis of increasing economic integration, needs to be set against the pattern among smaller towns of 5,000–10,000 inhabitants. Elsewhere in sixteenth-century Europe such lower- to middle-ranking towns were generally not very prominent, and their moderate rise seems to confirm the trend towards more sharply defined urban hierarchies in the period. For Castile – where towns in that range had already gained in significance during the fifteenth century – the picture is very different (Table 12.1). Between 1500 and 1600 the number of such centres grew from under 30 to nearly 80 and their inhabitants more than tripled from 160,000 to over half a million; by the 1590s, the total population of these lesser towns was nearly as large as that of the largest cities altogether.[27]

Hegemony of small towns

The importance of lesser towns for Castilian urbanisation was virtually unique in early modern Europe: apart from Sicily and the kingdom of Naples, no other state or major historical region witnessed a similar pattern of growth in the lower urban ranks. The pattern is particularly significant if one considers that such towns already had an unusually high share of the urban population before 1530. In other words, the tendency in sixteenth-century Castile towards more established hierarchies in the upper urban ranks was counterbalanced by an equally strong and opposite process of urban *decentralisation*.[28]

Although the proliferation of small towns in sixteenth-century Castile is well known,[29] its effects on the urban network have been generally ignored. It has been assumed that Castile was already a basically integrated economic region by the beginning of the sixteenth century, and that its towns were functionally specialising in agricultural, manufacturing (textile) and commercial activities in a hierarchical division of labour connecting the upper Meseta to Andalusia and the international markets.[30] This explains why the increasing top-heaviness of Madrid, which reflected the huge political support for flows of capital, labour

[27] Ibid.

[28] P. Sánchez León, 'El campo en la ciudad y la ciudad en el campo: urbanización e instituciones en Castilla durante la Edad Moderna', *Hispania* 58 (1998), 444–51.

[29] J. E. Gelabert, 'Cities, towns and small towns in Castile, 1500–1800', in P. Clark (ed.), *Small towns in early modern Europe* (Cambridge, 1995), pp. 271–94; V. Pérez Moreda and D. S. Reher, 'La población española entre los siglos XVI y XVIII. Una perspectiva demográfica', in J. L Fortea (ed.), *Imágenes de la diversidad. El mundo urbano en la Corona de Castilla (s. XVI–XVIII)* (Santander, 1997), pp. 129–63.

[30] B. Bennassar, *Valladolid au siècle d'or. Une ville de Castille et sa campagne au XVIᵉ siècle* (Paris, 1967), pp. 95–119, 334–56.

and produce to the capital city, is seen as the main cause of market distortion from the end of the sixteenth century onwards.[31] The problem with this view, however, is that at the same time that the court in Madrid was beginning to attract rent-seeking nobles and bureaucrats and to reorient pre-existing commercial networks towards the capital, the lower ranks of the Castilian urban hierarchy were disintegrating.

The growth of small-scale urbanisation suggests that the degree of economic integration in Castile, and thus by implication the effects of the rise of Madrid, was far lower than has been previously assumed. The markedly uneven distribution of small towns among the four constituent regions of Castile also reveals growing differentiation rather than convergence between the territories of the kingdom. On the one hand, the coastal North and Old Castile witnessed no significant increase in the importance of smaller towns. On the other hand, the twenty such towns in Andalusia at the beginning of the sixteenth century saw their share of the population grow 50 per cent in relative terms in 1530–91, whereas by 1591 the core area of La Mancha in New Castile had nearly 130,000 people living in small cities, representing a near quadrupling of their share from 3 per cent in 1530 to 11 per cent of the total population.

This pattern of urbanisation is all the more significant because smaller towns in New Castile had little or no interaction with larger centres. Apart from Toledo, with 40,000 inhabitants in 1591, there was not a single city over 15,000 inhabitants in the broad strip of the lower Meseta stretching between Old Castile and Andalusia. The fact that the growth of small towns in this region was huge and there was no clearly defined urban hierarchy challenges the view that the Castilian economy was becoming increasingly integrated during the sixteenth century. It also seems to cast doubt on the assumption that economic growth was associated with increasingly well-ordered urban hierarchies, since according to another oft-used proxy for economic performance, population growth, New Castile continued to expand even after the period in the late sixteenth century when neighbouring regions were experiencing demographic difficulties.

The case of New Castile suggests an institutional explanation for the development of its unusually amorphous urban system based upon smaller and roughly equal-sized towns with few commercial linkages. Late medieval and early modern urbanisation in this region was shaped by the creation during the high middle ages of jurisdictionally independent urban settlements which could protect their immediate hinterland

---

[31] D. Ringrose, 'The impact of a new capital city: Madrid, Toledo and New Castile, 1560–1660', *Journal of Economic History* 33 (1973), 761–91; D. Ringrose, *Madrid and the Spanish economy, 1560–1850* (Berkeley and Los Angeles, 1983), pp. 88–107.

Table 12.2. *Castilian labour force in manufacture, c.1560–c.1599 (percentages)*

	1560s	1580s	1590s	Population 1591
Avila	61.5	63.2	57.2	11,000
Ciudad Real	40.1	–	34.8	8,000
Salamanca	54.3	48.6	53.5	17,000
Segovia	80	77.4	–	22,000

Sources: S. Tapia, 'Estructura ocupacional de Ávila en el siglo XVI', in *El pasado histórico de Castilla y León* (Valladolid, 1984), p. 223; J. López Salazar, *Estructuras agrarias y sociedad rural en La Mancha (siglos XVI–XVII)* (Ciudad Real, 1986), p. 24; J. Vela, 'Salamanca en la época de Felipe II', in *El pasado histórico*, p. 318; A. García Sanz, 'Segovia y la industria pañera, siglos XVI–XIX', in *Segovia, 1088–1988. Congreso de Historia de la ciudad. Actas* (Segovia, 1991), p. 406. Population figures from J. I. Fortea, 'Las ciudades', pp. 49–50.

from outside competition. Similarly, the limited expansion of towns in Old Castile as opposed to Andalusia shows that the presence of strong rights of urban lordship in the longer run undermined the development of a competitive and integrated urban system. Paradoxically, the strong growth of smaller urban centres during the sixteenth century helped raise rates of urbanisation in Castile to some of the highest in western Europe, but also held back the development of more integrated regional and 'national' urban structures.

We saw that the tendency towards urban decentralisation was counterbalanced by the rapid growth of the largest cities and by the emergence of metropolitan poles acting as major regional trade and manufacturing nodes. However, much of the expansion of metropolitan influence beyond the cities' direct jurisdiction was due to their growing political and administrative functions rather than to strictly commercial factors. Early modern Madrid was only the most extreme example of this phenomenon.[32] The monarchy's policy of encouraging direct relations between individual towns and the court in order to integrate the urban elites into the national political system, exemplified by the increased posting of royal representatives (*corregidores*) in all autonomous *concejos*,[33] also undermined regional linkages between towns and exacerbated conflicts over urban jurisdictional and economic rights, especially after the Revolt of the Comuneros (towns) in 1520 against Charles V. The opportunities for lobbying and rent seeking provided by

[32] Ringrose, *Town and country*, pp. 5–16; J. M López García (ed.), *El impacto de la corte en Castilla. Madrid y su territorio en la época moderna* (Madrid, 1998), pp. 13–20.

[33] M. Lunenfeld, *Keepers of the city. The corregidores of Isabella I of Castile (1474–1504)* (Cambridge, 1987), pp. 1–23.

state centralisation impelled autonomous municipalities to turn their backs on each other.

Manufacture in town and country

An analysis of sectoral employment in some large Castilian towns (Table 12.2) indicates that the share of manufacture remained stable during the second half of the sixteenth century, supporting the hypothesis that wool exports did not rise during most of the period because of strong demand by domestic industry.[34] It is clear, moreover, that industrial specialisation was related to urban size. Although some smaller towns could also specialise, albeit in a narrower range of activities than larger centres,[35] most acted mainly as marketing centres for the agricultural hinterland and were in some sense part of the rural economy themselves.

In spite of the activity of royal *corregidores*, Castilian *concejos* maintained a high degree of self-government. This expressly included the right to promulgate statutes later confirmed by the king.[36] In some ways the sixteenth century saw them increase their autonomy as a result of the monarchy's growing fiscal requirements.[37] Towns therefore could undertake industrial and commercial policies of their own in relation to the strength of local political and economic interests and to their organisational abilities.[38]

Craft guilds

In the industrial sector, Castile suffered from organisational under-development, for guilds were virtually non-existent during the middle ages.[39] Although the Catholic Kings tried to remedy this in the late fifteenth century with protectionist measures against industrial imports and by trying to enforce common rules of industrial organisation,[40] national policies had to overcome long-standing traditions of urban

[34] C. Rahn Phillips, 'The Spanish wool trade, 1500–1700', *Journal of Economic History* 42 (1982), 780.

[35] Pérez Moreda and Reher, 'La población española', pp. 138–44.

[36] Mangas, *El régimen comunal agrario*, pp. 114–25.

[37] J. L. Fortea, *Monarquía y Cortes en la Corona de Castilla. Las ciudades ante la política fiscal de Felipe II* (Salamanca, 1991), pp. 343–414.

[38] D. C. North, *Structure and change in economic history* (Cambridge, MA, 1984), pp. 201–9.

[39] Vicens Vives, *Manual*, pp. 243–53; L. García de Valdeavellano, *Curso de historia de las instituciones españolas* (Madrid, 1968), pp. 284–8.

[40] P. Iradiel, *Evolución de la industria textil castellana en los siglos XIII–XVI. Factores de desarrollo, organización y costes de la producción manufacturera en Cuenca* (Salamanca, 1974), pp. 81–97; M. Asenjo, 'Transformación en la manufactura de paños en Castilla. Las Ordenanzas Generales de 1500', *Historia. Instituciones. Documentos* 18 (1991), 137.

autonomy. Guild regulations began to be established only at the start of the sixteenth century;[41] in many large cities guilds had no recognition at all, while in others, craft ordinances in municipal statutes (*ordenanzas*) were restricted to just a few activities. This pattern applied throughout Castile and stood in no relation to the extent and character of urbanisation or of craft activities; even in the larger Andalusian cities many crafts were not organised in formal guilds.

The main reason for the underdevelopment of craft guilds in Castile was political. When the monarchy reformed local government in the early fourteenth century, it established a system of government that granted sole and undisputed authority over the urban community and its hinterland to a new breed of local officers for life (*regidores*) and expressly banned all kinds of collective representation including popular assemblies and craft associations.[42] Political rights were granted to urban dwellers according to their obligations to the sovereign as tax payers (*pecheros*) or as tax exempt, privileged individuals, but not as producers.[43] Guild functions were consequently restricted to confraternal, social and religious activities, and craftsmen were denied political and economic representation. Craft guilds were not banned outright, but their administration, rules of admission and economic functions were placed under municipal control.

Although the craft guilds' organisational weakness placed them in a position of inferiority in urban government during the fifteenth century and beyond, it is not clear whether this had any negative economic consequences.[44] It may even have made it easier to develop the kind of flexible manufacturing that one observes during the sixteenth century in some important urban centres – the example of Segovia is the best known – which saw guild production, a domestic putting-out system organised by merchants and even large, centralised textile 'factories' operating side by side.[45] By the end of the sixteenth century, artisans and putters-out in the textile industry worked concurrently at different

[41] Iradiel, *Evolución*, pp. 132–43.

[42] B. González Alonso, *Sobre el estado y la administración de la Corona de Castilla en el Antiguo Régimen* (Madrid, 1981), pp. 12–35.

[43] J. M. Monsalvo Antón, 'La sociedad política en los concejos castellanos de la Meseta durante la época del regimiento medieval. La distribución social del poder', in *Concejos y ciudades en la Edad Media Hispánica* (León, 1990), pp. 359–413.

[44] J. M. Monsalvo Antón, 'Solidaridades de oficio y estructuras de poder en las ciudades castellanas de la Meseta durante los siglos XIII al XV (aproximaciones al estudio del papel político del corporativismo medieval)', in *El trabajo en la historia* (Salamanca, 1996), pp. 39–90. See also S. R. Epstein, 'Craft guilds, apprenticeship and technological change in pre-modern Europe', *Journal of Economic History* 53 (1998), 684–713.

[45] F. Ruiz Martín, 'La empresa capitalista en la industria textil castellana durante los siglos XVI y XVII', in *Third international conference of economic history* (Munich, 1969), pp. 267–76; J. P. Le Flem, 'Vrais et fausses splendeurs de l'industrie textile ségovienne

stages of production, and factories run by big entrepreneurs (*hacedores*) played a significant role. Elsewhere also the flexibility of craft-based production was in evidence; in Zamora, for example, urban craftsmanship shifted from clothes and shoemaking to silk weaving within the decade of the 1580s.[46] While the weak institutionalisation of guilds may have made it easier for urban entrepreneurs to recruit women artisans and to decentralise production in the rural hinterland, the causal link between craft guilds and the development of rural industry is far from straightforward. On the one hand, craft guilds began to strengthen their position during the sixteenth century by offering political and financial support to urban elites and the monarchy in exchange for greater administrative and economic independence, and the increasing encroachment of more powerful craft guilds on unregulated urban manufactures has been cited as causing the relocation of industry from Toledo to its hinterland after the mid-sixteenth century.[47] On the other hand, although guilds in the smaller *concejos* never developed very much during the early modern period, rural industry was nevertheless stifled by tax-induced policies that privileged urban manufacture and restricted its development in subject villages after mid-century.

Rural liberties and the absence of manufacture

By contrast with the organisational weakness of manufacturing interests, their agrarian counterparts were generally overrepresented in local institutions. In most towns from the later middle ages landowning oligarchies came to dominate local offices and administration, which resulted in the political marginalisation of other groups, especially industrial entrepreneurs and merchants, and the promotion of policies favourable to landed interests.[48] But although broadly similar interests prevailed in dependent villages, which were of course mostly inhabited by peasants and agriculturalists, this did not result in greater co-operation between town and country, for urban elites used their authority over the hinterland to organise urban food supplies to their advantage. Towns were intent on keeping villagers underrepresented in urban

(vers 1450–vers 1650)', in M. Spallanzani (ed.), *Produzione, commercio e consumo dei panni di lana (nei secoli XII–XVIII)* (Florence, 1976), pp. 525–36.

[46] F. J. Lorenzo Pinar, 'El aprendizaje de los oficios artesanos en la Zamora del siglo XVI', *Studia Historica, Historia Moderna* 6 (1988), 449–64.

[47] F. Ruiz Martín, 'Credit procedures for the collection of taxes in the cities of Castile during the XVIth and XVIIth centuries: the case of Valladolid', in Thompson and Yun, *The Castilian crisis*, pp. 167–81; J. Montemayor, *Tolède au splendeur et déclin, vers 1530–vers 1610* (Limoges, 1996), pp. 228–33.

[48] Monsalvo Antón, 'Sociedad política'; M. A. Ladero, 'Corona y ciudades en la Castilla del siglo XV', *En la España medieval* 8 (1986), 551–74.

government, and rural elites tried to bypass this by transforming their existing freedoms into full-blown territorial jurisdictions.[49] Their resistance was expressed in growing competition for common lands and other resources from the end of the fifteenth century. The monarchy, together with the large cities represented in the Cortes, legislated against the ploughing of waste lands to no avail: land encroachment remained a constant feature of the Castilian countryside during the first half of the sixteenth century. Philip II (1556–98) eventually accepted the *fait accompli* and initiated a massive sell-off of uncultivated land in Old Castile and parts of Andalusia and New Castile.[50] Whereas the urgent financial requirements to meet Philip's busy international agenda found some relief from the measure, its economic impact was probably rather small, benefiting some individual agricultural entrepreneurs but not significantly changing overall patterns of production.

On the contrary, demands for land privatisation were often speculative ventures by urban and rural elites that bore little relation to more general conditions in the land market and may well have diverted resources from industrial investment.

The institutional consequences of land sales for town–country relations were nevertheless profound. Both the smaller *concejos* and the large cities resisted the sales, which they perceived as part of a broader subversion of the monarchy's traditional support of urban interests. From 1530 villages began to acquire from the monarchy privileges of segregation from their urban lords.[51] Charles I granted jurisdictional autonomy and wider self-government to over twenty villages in Old and New Castile, and the number of concessions probably increased under his son Philip II. Once again, this policy served to reinforce direct political ties between local communities and the crown while undermining political and economic links between communities at local and regional levels. The capacity of villages to buy themselves out further complicated the jurisdictional map of town and country and weakened the urban hierarchies established during the late middle ages.

Despite significant regional differences, the overall dominance of agrarian over industrial interests in Castile is indisputable. In New Castile and Andalusia, the system of land distribution after the conquest and settlement had established powerful interest groups of cultivators (*labradores*), mainly in the smaller urban centres but in some cases also

[49] Sánchez León, *Absolutismo y comunidad*, pp. 137–47, 270–89.
[50] D. E. Vassberg, *La venta de tierras baldías. El comunitarismo agrario y la Corona de Castilla durante el siglo XVI* (Madrid, 1983).
[51] H. Nader, *Liberty in absolutist Spain. The Habsburg sale of towns, 1516–1700* (Baltimore and London, 1990), pp. 99–129.

in the larger cities.[52] There, the efforts of rural elites to have more of a
say in urban matters stood a better chance of succeeding and made it
easier to establish economic co-operation between town and country.
However, these centres' rapid growth also reinforced their characteristics as 'agro-towns', possessed of limited abilities to co-ordinate with
neighbouring towns and constrained by strong traditions of land division
(*repartimientos*) along egalitarian lines.

The rise of new rural centres with jurisdictional autonomy challenged
the large cities' hold over their hinterlands and increased inter-urban
competition for capital, labour and trade. However, it did not necessarily enhance economic dynamism, for competition was waged primarily
through jurisdictional rights and monopolies rather than on grounds of
comparative advantage. Although the monarchy did not grant the newly
privileged communities specific fiscal exemptions or periodic fairs that
could compete with those of the neighbouring towns, the latter had to
cope with a shrinking jurisdictional hinterland. Jurisdictional fragmentation did not necessarily benefit the segregated villages either, as the
example of Villacastín – a village under Segovia's jurisdiction that
bought its independence in 1571 – suggests. Whereas prior to the move
Villacastín had specialised in the production of low-quality draperies
complementary to Segovia's higher quality cloths, a few decades later
the new urban centre was losing both population and industrial
impetus.[53] At the least, segregation could not stop a more general
movement towards economic contraction, but it can also be added that,
as everywhere else, jurisdictional autonomy fostered political leverage by
local landed elites as much as it shielded Villacastín from the influence
of neighbouring Segovia, both at the expense of industrial expansion.

Political centralisation, economic fragmentation and the seventeenth-century crisis

By the late sixteenth century the institutional landscape was marked by
a fundamental and unresolved tension between state centralisation and
local autonomy. The growth of the state under the impulse of seemingly
insatiable fiscal requirements took increasing control over relations
between towns and between town and country, creating a web of vertical

---

[52] J. López Salazar, 'El régimen local de los territorios de ordenes militares (ss. XVI y
XVII)', in J. M. de Bernardo Ares and G. Martínez Ruiz (eds.), *El municipio en la
España moderna* (Córdoba, 1996), pp. 249–304; J. Vela, 'Sobre el carácter de la
formación social bética en la segunda mitad del siglo XVI', in *Actas de los II Coloquios de
historia de Andalucía. Andalucía moderna* (Córdoba, 1983), pp. 377–411.
[53] A. García Sanz and V. Pérez Moreda, 'Análisis histórica de una crisis demográfica:
Villacastín de 1466 a 1800', *Estudios Segovianos* 70 (1972), 119–42.

links between court and country and weakening horizontal links between communities. Institutional fragmentation distorted economic incentives and accounts for the nature of seventeenth-century decline. The spectacular growth of Madrid, thanks to vast fiscal and jurisdictional concessions, differed in terms of quantity but not quality from the factors sustaining urban growth elsewhere. The proliferation of fiscal rights and freedoms raised barriers to trade and multiplied the number of equally small-sized and anaemic towns.

Castile's economic growth was abruptly curtailed in the 1590s. A series of epidemics devastated the large cities and birth-rates declined in both town and country. At the same time, the institutional trends established during the preceding period of expansion accelerated, intensifying the emphasis on politically directed redistribution and on jurisdictional isolation. Sales of waste and common land continued in the teeth of strong demographic decline, and sales of segregation rights to villages soared. Landowners and urban rentiers increased their stranglehold over urban government and diverted the tax burden towards a declining number of urban and rural *pecheros*.

The crisis of the seventeenth century was mainly the consequence of an institutionally driven fragmentation of markets. The development of the state gave shape to and ultimately constrained economic growth by impeding regional and national integration. The rise of Madrid as a huge consumption centre during the seventeenth century stimulated integration in the country's core between Old and New Castile,[54] but also made it easier for the peripheral regions of Andalusia and on the northern coasts to tread their own independent paths, the former by shifting its focus from the domestic to the international markets, the latter by increasing economic integration as reflected in rising rates of urbanisation. Paradoxically, the failure of the Spanish state's policy of institutional centralisation may have allowed its regions to follow more sustainable patterns of development.

---

[54] Ringrose, *Madrid*, pp. 278–310. For the limits to this integration, see J. Izquierdo, 'El campesino representado; los fundamentos comunitarios del orden agrario en la Castilla del Antiguo Régimen', unpublished Ph.D. thesis, University of Madrid, 2000.

13   Town and country in central and northern Italy, 1400–1800[1]

Carlo Marco Belfanti

Translated by Lynn Wright and S. R. Epstein

Introduction

The long transition in central and northern Italy from independent city-states to larger territorial states between the fourteenth and sixteenth centuries entrenched major institutional disparities in territorial organisation between regions and within the confines of the same state.[2] A multi-faceted institutional geography was established based upon a variable combination of jurisdictional prerogatives, fiscal policies and commercial and manufacturing regulations. These configurations, whose outlines emerged for the most part during the politically and militarily fraught later middle ages, were frequently renegotiated between the sixteenth and the seventeenth centuries in response to shifts in the balance of power. Demographic change – periods of sustained population increase or, alternatively, a phase of sharp mortality crises – and economic developments – for example, manufacturing success or decline – could give rise to friction within the existing institutional set-up, or, conversely, changes in the institutional status quo could improve conditions for manufacturing activities and demographic growth. Thus, the interplay of political and economic agents and pressure groups, which jostled with each other to defend, extend or challenge the privileges and regulations inherited from the past, introduced an element of institutional dynamism. In some cases the state managed to impose a degree of centralisation and to simplify the institutional infrastructure, even at the cost of inhibiting local dynamism. Elsewhere, a more competitive structure resulted in a more effective balance between the privileged cities (which put up the

[1] I wish to thank S. R. Epstein for comments and suggestions that helped me to clarify my arguments.
[2] G. Chittolini, *La formazione dello stato regionale e le istituzioni del contado* (Turin, 1979), pp. vii–xxxii.

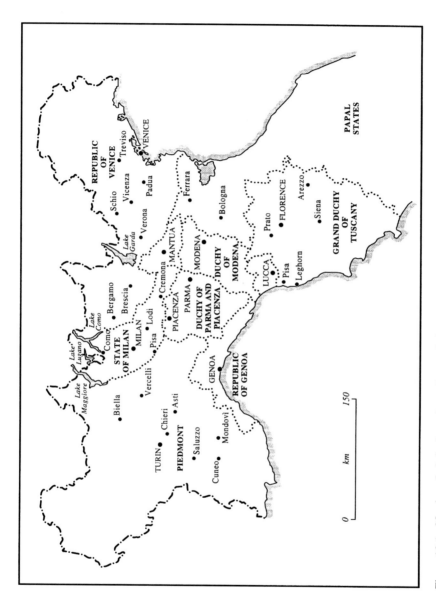

Figure 13.1 Northern Italy in the early modern period

strongest resistance to political centralisation and to the capital city's aspirations to hegemony), the lesser communities that benefited singly or in alliance from special privileges or 'liberties', the rural hinterland – the *contadi* – whose main objective was to reduce traditional urban privileges (principally the inequitable fiscal burden), and the remaining vestiges of feudal jurisdiction.[3]

The variety of institutional arrangements thus established an unequal geography of rights and privileges that could affect economic organisation and the allocation of resources just as much as the pressure of market competition.[4] Economic and institutional relations between town and country must be viewed within such a context, which with few exceptions transcended the territorial structures created by the communal city-states. Our unit of analysis will thus be the state rather than the geographic region, on the understanding that the boundaries between economic regions did not necessarily coincide with political frontiers.[5]

Tuscany

The Tuscan territorial state's most salient feature was the centrality of the capital, Florence, and the subordination of all other cities, towns and territories to it.[6] The subject cities and their *contadi* were absorbed into the Florentine state during the fifteenth century along lines devised by the Florentine government and administered by its representatives. This superseded a balance of power based upon a network of independent city-states which controlled their respective hinterlands, and introduced circumscribed territorial areas which answered directly to central government. The region thus evolved from a characteristically pluralistic and differentiated urban system to a more homogeneous structure,

---

[3] E. Fasano Guarini, 'Centro e periferia, accentramento e particolarismi: dicotomia o sostanza degli Stati in età moderna?', in G. Chittolini, A. Molho and P. Schiera (eds.), *Origini dello stato. Processi di formazione statale in Italia fra medioevo ed età moderna* (Bologna, 1994), pp. 147–76.

[4] D. C. North, *Institutions, institutional change and economic performance* (Cambridge, 1990). See also S. C. Ogilvie, 'Social institutions and proto-industrialization', in S. C. Ogilvie and M. Cerman (eds.), *European proto-industrialization* (Cambridge, 1996), pp. 23–37.

[5] A. Moioli, 'La deindustrializzazione della Lombardia nel secolo XVII', *Archivio storico lombardo* 112 (1986), 174–6; C. M. Belfanti, 'Lo spazio economico lombardo nella transizione del XVII secolo', *Annali di storia moderna e contemporanea* 4 (1998), 445–57.

[6] Chittolini, *Formazione*, pp. 292–326.

[7] P. Malanima, 'Teoria economica regionale e storia: il caso della Toscana (XIII–XIV secolo)', in L. Mocarelli (ed.), *Lo sviluppo economico regionale in prospettiva storica* (Milan, 1996), pp. 133–43. See also Fasano Guarini, 'Centro e periferia', pp. 157–9.

which maintained most local administrative arrangements but had a role subordinate to the dominant city.[7]

The political and institutional supremacy of Florence was backed by its economic hegemony. Supremacy manifested itself first and foremost in the encroachment of Florentine property in the hinterlands of Pistoia, Prato, San Gimignano, Arezzo and, especially, of Pisa, causing the diffusion of Florentine-style sharecropping contracts to those areas.[8] Manufacturing regulations were introduced to protect the interests of the capital's merchant-entrepreneurs. The numerous centres active in the production of woollen cloth since the high middle ages were forbidden to produce the high-quality product that was the speciality of Florence's wool industry. Florence thereby consolidated its monopoly over quality cloth for export, and forced rival manufacturers in the region to convert to low-cost goods for the local market.[9] The Florentine silk industry, which would later become the city's main textile manufacture after the decline of the wool industry between the sixteenth and seventeenth centuries, attracted similar protectionist legislation.[10] The production of high-quality silk cloth was reserved to the capital, while manufacture in Pisa (which would later become Tuscany's second most important producer) was directed towards cloth of inferior quality.

Institutional factors therefore played an important role in allocating resources and directly influenced the shape of the urban network. At the beginning of the fourteenth century, before the rise of the regional state, Tuscany had a relatively balanced urban network in which the great size of Florence – then a major European metropolis with over 100,000 inhabitants – was counteracted by lesser cities like Pisa and Siena (population 50,000) and Lucca (30,000) and by a dense web of towns with populations between 10,000 and 15,000 like Arezzo, Cortona, Pistoia, Prato and Volterra.[11] By the mid-sixteenth century, however, Florentine political and economic centralism had caused the region's

[8] P. Malanima, 'La formazione di una regione economica: la Toscana nei secoli XIII–XV', *Società e storia* 20 (1983), 265. The role and functions of Tuscan sharecropping are discussed in S. R. Epstein, 'Tuscans and their farms', *Rivista di storia economica* 11 (1994), 111–23.

[9] P. Malanima, 'An example of industrial reconversion: Tuscany in the sixteenth and seventeenth centuries', in H. van der Wee (ed.), *The rise and decline of urban industries in Italy and in the Low Countries* (Leuven, 1988), p. 63; P. Malanima, *Il lusso dei contadini. Consumi e industrie nelle campagne toscane del Sei e Settecento* (Bologna, 1990), p. 83; S. R. Epstein, 'Town and country: economy and institutions in late medieval Italy', *Economic History Review*, 2nd ser., 46 (1993), 466–7.

[10] Malanima, 'An example', pp. 68–71.

[11] M. Ginatempo and L. Sandri, *L'Italia delle città. Il popolamento urbano tra Medioevo e Rinascimento (secoli XIII–XVI)* (Florence, 1990), pp. 106–7.

urban network to hollow out. While the capital had suffered a drop in population to 60,000 inhabitants, the second largest city, Pisa, had collapsed to a mere 10,000 residents and Arezzo, Prato, Pistoia and other minor centres had sunk even further; Siena and Lucca, the two competing territorial capitals at the borders of the Florentine state, numbered only 20,000 people.[12] Regional urban patterns did not change significantly thereafter, with the exception of the new port of Livorno created by the Medici, which grew rapidly thanks to tax exemptions offered by the grand duchy.[13]

The Florentine territorial state was therefore organised centrally as a single, integrated province – almost an extended hinterland of the capital – administered as a function of Florence's own economic needs. From this perspective the industrial division of labour between Florence and the other cities appears rather the fruit of a politically driven strategy of monopoly than of a policy of regional economic integration. The latter was certainly not improved by the plethora of customs barriers that persisted up to the late eighteenth century between urban centres and their *contadi* and between *contado* and *contado*.[14] But what may have left the deepest and most long-lasting mark on the region's economy was the diffusion beyond Florence's immediate hinterland of homestead sharecropping (*mezzadria poderale*). It has been suggested that share-cropping inhibited the development of manufacturing in the countryside by stimulating the rise of intensive mixed farming (based upon a combination of cereal, olive and mulberry trees, and vines), which absorbed family labour throughout the year and left no time for seasonal non-agricultural by-employment.[15] But the presence of some manufac-tures in the Tuscan countryside during the late middle ages suggests a different explanation for the weakness of rural industry in the longer term. On this reading, the diffusion of Tuscan sharecropping may have impeded a 'significant redistribution of incomes between land and labour after the Black Death' that elsewhere in Europe had favoured the

[12] Ibid., pp. 113–15. See also Malanima, 'Teoria economica regionale', pp. 136, 144; Epstein, 'Town and country', pp. 459–60; M. Della Pina, 'L'évolution démographique des villes toscanes à l'époque de la naissance e de l'affirmation de l'état régional (XVème–XVIIème siècle)', *Annales de démographie historique* (1982), 43–53.

[13] L. Del Panta, *Una traccia di storia demografica della Toscana nei secoli XVI–XVIII* (Florence, 1974), p. 45; E. Fasano Guarini, 'Esenzioni e immigrazione a Livorno tra sedicesimo e diciassettesimo secolo', in *Livorno e il Mediterraneo nell'età medicea* (Livorno, 1978), pp. 3–23.

[14] Malanima, 'Teoria economica regionale', p. 145; see also Epstein, 'Town and country', p. 460.

[15] P. Malanima, *La decadenza di un'economia cittadina. L'industria di Firenze nei secoli XVI–XVIII* (Bologna, 1982), pp. 64–7; Malanima, 'An example', p. 68; Malanima, *Il lusso*, pp. 104–7.

peasantry and had stimulated demand for cheap textiles produced by domestic rural industry.[16]

The first intimations of structural change in the regional economy can be perceived from the end of the seventeenth century, when the strong demographic recovery in the Tuscan countryside after the severe mortality crisis of 1630 created a pool of cheap labour outside the sharecropping system that could be employed in the rural manufacture of linen, hemp, wool cloth and straw hats. With regard to the woollen industry, rural expansion was stimulated by a provision of 1739 that abolished the Florentine monopoly over higher quality cloth, in response to what by then was the latter industry's irreversible decline.[17] During the period when Florentine wool cloth was exported successfully, the city's comparative advantage over potential domestic competitors – in terms both of product quality and of the market information producers and traders could gain access to – made enforcement of Florence's monopoly very easy; the decline of the Florentine industry made the costs of enforcing the monopoly too high. During the eighteenth century wool production experienced a renaissance in many minor Tuscan centres, which exploited the lower costs of rural weaving. Prato in particular managed to build upon its earlier margins of autonomy from Florentine dominion to become the most important wool-producing area in the region.[18]

Between the seventeenth and eighteenth centuries the combination of rural demographic expansion and Florentine industrial decline reshaped the regional economy. As the seat of the court and government, as well as of Tuscany's main silk-making firms, Florence continued to be the principal urban centre. Nevertheless, although by the end of the eighteenth century the city's population had risen to over 80,000 inhabitants, its relative size was clearly in decline just as its political and industrial hegemony no longer went unchallenged.[19] The regional economy was becoming more diversified, with lesser urban centres gradually establishing a specialised niche (like Livorno in maritime trade and Prato in the woollen industry), while rural areas became increasingly involved in manufacturing activities.

[16] S. R. Epstein, 'Cities, regions and the late medieval crisis: Sicily and Tuscany compared', *Past and Present* 130 (1991), 40–2.

[17] Del Panta, *Una traccia*, pp. 84–6; Malanima, *Il lusso*, pp. 89–107; Malanima, *La decadenza*, pp. 188–90, 289–304.

[18] Epstein, 'Cities, regions', pp. 42–3; Malanima, *Il lusso*, pp. 75–89; Malanima, *La decadenza*, pp. 327–9; C. Maitte, 'Incertitudes et bricolages. L'industrie textile à Prato aux 18e et 19e siècles', *Annales HSS* 52 (1997), 1275–1303.

[19] Del Panta, *Una traccia*, p. 46; L. Del Panta, 'Città e campagna in Toscana nella seconda metà del XVIII secolo: dinamica e distribuzione della popolazione', *Storia urbana* 2 (1978), 62.

Piedmont-Savoy

Tuscany was not the only example of a regional state in which extensive economic and political control by the capital city modified the more complex arrangements inherited from the middle ages. In Piedmont, the rapid expansion of Turin during the sixteenth and seventeenth centuries also caused a certain simplification in the region's urban network, even though the Piedmontese medieval urban system had been far less complex and robust than its Tuscan counterpart.[20] Before the mid-fourteenth-century crisis, the main centres of Asti, Chieri and Vercelli each had a population of about 10,000. During the following two centuries the hierarchy changed but the level of urbanisation did not change significantly. In the sixteenth century only three cities exceeded 10,000 inhabitants, the largest being Mondovì with 26,000, followed by Turin (14,000) and Casale Monferrato (10,000), and by the former leaders, Asti, Chieri and Vercelli, that had sunk to 8,000–9,000.[21] The limited growth of the region's urban backbone was remarked upon by a Piedmontese contemporary, Giovanni Botero, who observed that 'it is not enough to base the greatness of a city upon the fertility of the soil, for we see provinces that are most fertile that nevertheless have no great city, such as Piedmont, which has no equal among other regions of Italy for its abundance of grain, meat and excellent fruits of all sorts'.[22]

The region's urban hierarchy changed once again and more significantly in response to the centralisation of the state initiated by Duke Emanuele Filiberto in the second half of the sixteenth century and prosecuted by his successors into the eighteenth century. Among the most significant effects of this process was the strengthening of the functions of the capital, Turin, and the reduction of the other towns' autonomy. Whereas during the fifteenth century the house of Savoy had simply imposed its rule over local institutions without much affecting pre-existing communal and feudal traditions, the advent of Emanuele Filiberto changed the situation radically. From the 1560s 'the state's presence was increasingly felt at the local level, accentuating the latter's subordination'.[23] Political centralisation continued apace after Emanuele Filiberto and accelerated during the late seventeenth and early

---

[20] Ginatempo and Sandri, *L'Italia delle città*, pp. 98–9.

[21] Ibid., p. 67. However, the population of Mondovì in 1571 is given as either 26,000 inhabitants (ibidem, p. 67) or a more modest 11,000 (G. Levi, 'Come Torino soffocò il Piemonte', in G. Levi, *Centro e periferia di uno stato assoluto* (Turin, 1985), p. 13).

[22] G. Botero, *Della ragion di stato libri dieci con tre libri delle cause della grandezza delle città*, ed. L. Firpo (Turin, 1948), p. 355, cited by Levi, 'Come Torino', pp. 11–12.

[23] P. P. Merlin, 'Il Cinquecento', in P. P. Merlin et al., *Il Piemonte sabaudo* (Turin, 1994), pp. 10–11, 96–105, 120–6.

eighteenth centuries in the reign of Vittorio Amedeo II, whose repression of a rebellion by the ancient towns of Mondovì and Ceva signalled the final defeat of the opponents of ducal policy.[24] Centralisation laid the ground for Turin's primacy as capital of the state and court residence. Its citizens were granted privileges over the rest of the duchy, craft ordinances incorporated manufacturing activities, and the city expanded in response to the immunities and benefits granted to inhabitants of the new quarters.[25]

The rise of Turin and the decay of local urban autonomies initiated changes to the urban network that were already apparent in the first decades of the seventeenth century. By 1614 Turin, with 24,000 inhabitants, was the largest city in the state, followed at a considerable distance by Chieri, Cuneo, Mondovì and Vercelli with populations of approximately 10,000. The most profound changes would, however, occur thereafter in response to a decline in population caused, at least in part, by the epidemic of 1630 and by a spate of rebellions during the last two decades of the seventeenth century. By the early 1700s Turin exceeded 43,000 inhabitants, but population in the former centres of Asti, Chieri and Mondovì was only around the 6,000–8,000 mark. Demographic growth in the first decades of the eighteenth century reinforced Turin's role as the dominant city, so that by 1734 it had doubled its size in 1614, while smaller provincial centres like Asti, Cuneo, Fossano and Savigliano staged a minor recovery to just over 10,000 inhabitants.[26] Perhaps the most dynamic growth outside Turin, however, occurred in the small towns on the plain around Turin itself, which benefited from the commercial and industrial spin-offs from the neighbouring capital.

Whereas in Tuscany the political supremacy of Florence in the territorial state had drawn some legitimacy from its earlier century-long economic primacy, in Piedmont the rise to dominance of Turin was the result of a more strictly political project that aimed to turn the city into the fulcrum of a strongly centralised state and relegated all other centres to subordinate status. Mercantilist policies pursued between the seventeenth and eighteenth centuries consolidated the capital's supremacy by

[24] G. Symcox, 'L'età di Vittorio Amedeo II', in Merlin et al., *Piemonte sabaudo*, pp. 271–438; Levi, 'Come Torino', p. 27. See also S. J. Woolf, 'Sviluppo economico e struttura sociale in Piemonte da Emanuele Filiberto a Carlo Emanuele III', *Nuova rivista storica* 46 (1962), 5.

[25] S. Cerutti, *Mestieri e privilegi. Nascita delle corporazioni a Torino (secoli XVII–XVIII)* (Turin, 1992), pp. 8–20, 109–10, 115–20. See also E. Stumpo, *Finanza e stato moderno nel Piemonte del Seicento* (Rome, 1979), pp. 20, 149, 239–43.

[26] Levi, 'Come Torino', pp. 12–15. Alessandria and Casale Monferrato, with populations of just over 10,000, became part of the state of Savoy during the same century; see K. J. Beloch, *Storia della popolazione d'Italia*, Italian transl. (Florence, 1994), pp. 543, 580.

transforming it into the principal economic centre of the region,[27] as testified by the strengthening of the urban craft guilds and by the strong flows of immigration.[28] Even under the shadow of official policy, however, eighteenth-century demographic growth stimulated manufacturing activities elsewhere also: besides the towns in Turin's hinterland there was the silk-producing area around Racconigi in the province of Saluzzo, the metallurgical and textile area around the garrison town of Cuneo, and the territory of Biella that specialised in woollen cloth.[29] These new growth poles, centred for the most part upon smallish towns, replaced the more traditional towns that had declined during the seventeenth century and formed the basis for a new organisation of regional space under the political and economic centrality of Turin.

The Venetian Republic

The territorial expansion of the Venetian Republic during the fifteenth century led to the formation of a regional state – known as the Terraferma – that included numerous large and wealthy cities, many of which boasted centuries-long communal traditions and institutional domination over the countryside, more along the lines of the highly developed Tuscan situation than of the embryonic urban network in Piedmont. By contrast with Florence, however, the Venetian Republic pursued a pragmatic reconciliation and fusion of institutional diversity within the framework of the regional state, while eschewing a single-minded pursuit of local uniformity.[30]

In the first phase of republican rule, the installation of Venetian representatives in the principal cities was followed by legislative reform and emendation of the urban statutes aimed at erasing all elements that contrasted openly with Venetian sovereignty. Urban control over the

---

27 L. Palmucci Quaglino, 'Gli insediamenti proto-industriali in Piemonte tra Sei e Settecento: aspetti localizzativi e scelte tipologiche', *Storia urbana* 6 (1982), 49–51. For a discussion of 'Savoyard mercantilism' see M. Ambrosoli, 'The market for the textile industry in eighteenth-century Piedmont: quality control and economic policy', paper presented at the 11th International Economic History Congress, Session C 11, Milan, 12–16 September 1994.

28 Cerutti, *Mestieri*, p. 17; Levi, 'Come Torino', pp. 28–69. See also E. Fasano Guarini, 'La politica demografica delle città italiane nell'età moderna', in Società Italiana di Demografia Storica, *La demografia storica delle città italiane* (Bologna, 1982), p. 169.

29 Palmucci Quaglino, 'Gli insediamenti', pp. 47–52; Levi, 'Come Torino', p. 13. On silk production see G. Chicco, *La seta in Piemonte 1650–1800* (Milan, 1995).

30 G. Cozzi, *Repubblica di Venezia e stati italiani. Politica e giustizia dal secolo XVI al secolo XVIII* (Turin, 1982), pp. 262–3. See also the fundamental A. Ventura, *Nobiltà e popolo nella società veneta del '400 e del '500* (Bari, 1964); M. Knapton, 'Tra Dominante e Dominio (1517–1630)', in M. Knapton et al., *La Repubblica di Venezia nell'età moderna* (Turin, 1992), pp. 484–5.

countryside was not generally called into question;[31] however, in some instances – such as the Alpine valleys in the regions of Bergamo and Brescia – strategic considerations led Venice to make significant concessions of autonomy that freed such communities from direct dominion by the cities.[32]

Following the initial phase of territorial expansion, however, between the sixteenth and seventeenth centuries, relations between the capital and subject cities and between these and their *contadi* underwent extensive change. Impulse for change came from the representatives of the rural territories subject to Venetian rule, who asked the Republic to act upon the legally constituted differences in status between town- and country-dwellers. Such differences played a particularly important role in determining the distribution of the fiscal burden, which weighed more heavily on the countryside. The countrymen's requests found a ready hearing in Venice, which was interested in engaging rural communities more actively in its plans for fiscal reform and was also happy to support political forces that could usefully counterbalance the power of the subject cities' patriciates.[33] During the second half of the sixteenth century rural representatives were able to negotiate governmental concessions for tax allocation and collection.[34] While the erosion of ancient urban fiscal privileges did not spell the end of the towns' supremacy over the countryside, the political and institutional recognition of rural representatives by the Venetian state stimulated the rise of dynamic rural elites, who were to play a significant role in the reorganisation of the regional economy during the latter half of the seventeenth century. [35]

Economic relations between Venice and other cities followed the same pragmatic realism that governed political actions. The creation of central offices with economic jurisdiction undoubtedly testify to Venice's

---

[31] Knapton, 'Tra Dominante e Dominio', pp. 484–5; Cozzi, *Repubblica di Venezia*, pp. 262–77; G. Del Torre, *Venezia e la Terraferma dopo la guerra di Cambrai. Fiscalità e amministrazione (1515–1530)* (Milan, 1986), pp. 186, 233–4; C. Povolo, 'Centro e periferia nella Repubblica di Venezia. Un profilo', in Chittolini et al., *Origini dello stato*, pp. 209–10.

[32] Knapton, 'Tra Dominante e Dominio', pp. 485–6; M. Knapton, 'Il sistema fiscale nello Stato di Terraferma, secoli XIV–XVIII. Cenni generali', in M. Knapton et al., *Venezia e la Terraferma. Economia e società* (Bergamo, 1989), p. 14; A. Rossini, *Le campagne bresciane nel Cinquecento. Territorio, fisco, società* (Milan, 1994), pp. 276–7. See also G. Da Lezze, *Descrizione di Bergamo e suo territorio 1596* (Bergamo, 1988), pp. 187–92; *Il catasto bresciano di Giovanni Da Lezze (1609–1610)* (Brescia, 1973), vol. III, pp. 284, 293, 383.

[33] Del Torre, *Venezia*, p. 234; Knapton, 'Tra Dominante e Dominio', pp. 489–90.

[34] Knapton, 'Tra Dominante e Dominio', pp. 484–502; Rossini, *Campagne bresciane*; S. Zamperetti, *I piccoli principi. Signorie locali, feudi e comunità soggette nello stato regionale veneto dall'espansione territoriale ai primi decenni del '600* (Venice 1991).

[35] Knapton, 'Tra Dominante e Dominio', pp. 489–90; Rossini, *Campagne bresciane*, pp. 295–6.

desire to control economic activities within the state, but the plans lacked neither flexibility nor pragmatism.[36] Venetian hegemony was manifested most obviously – analogously to many other early modern capitals – in the priority and exclusivity it assigned to food supply from the output of the Terraferma.[37] The city backed this up with a policy (similar to that pursued by Florence) that favoured the expansion of Venetian landed property in subject *contadi*, specifically to territory east of the river Mincio.[38] By contrast, Venice's commercial supremacy, based upon a secular tradition of trade between Europe and the Levant, would not seem to have had any need of institutional support – which was nevertheless forthcoming.[39] Although by law the merchant-entrepreneurs of subject cities were expected to operate through the Venetian port both for supplies of raw materials and for the sale of finished articles, this did not entirely exclude the use of the most advantageous route instead, as shown by exports of woollen cloth from the Terraferma through the rival port of Genoa recorded in 1541.[40]

In fact, Venetian dominion may have been less rigid than it appears. In sectors like the production of glass, soap, sugar and wax and in ship-building, the city's primacy arose first and foremost from the high technical skills acquired by Venetian manufactures in the centuries preceding the rise of the regional state.[41] Subsequently this industrial supremacy was also sustained by government monopolies, but it is not clear how far these were needed.[42]

Conditions in the textile industry were different. This was a sector in which subject cities could boast of respectable traditions and could pose a dangerous threat. During the fifteenth century the woollen industries of several centres in the Terraferma had achieved notable importance, at times even surpassing that of Venice itself. It might therefore be expected that the spectacular expansion of the Venetian wool industry a

[36] S. Ciriacono, 'Venise et ses villes. Structuration et déstructuration d'un marché regionale (XVIe–XVIIIe siècle)', *Revue historique* 276 (1986), 288–9.

[37] S. Ciriacono, 'L'economia regionale veneta in epoca moderna. Note a margine del caso bergamasco', in Knapton, *Venezia e la Terraferma*, p. 45; Del Torre, *Venezia*, pp. 199–216.

[38] See the fundamental D. Beltrami, *La penetrazione economica dei veneziani in Terraferma* (Venice–Rome, 1961); G. Gullino, 'Quando il mercante costruì la villa: le proprietà dei Veneziani nella Terraferma', in *Storia di Venezia. Dal Rinascimento al Barocco* (Rome, 1994), vol. VI, pp. 875–924.

[39] For a general view see F. C. Lane, *Venice. A maritime republic* (Baltimore, 1973), chs. 3–12. For the sixteenth century, see D. Sella, 'L'economia', in *Storia di Venezia. Dal Rinascimento al Barocco*, pp. 653–75.

[40] Ciriacono, 'Venise', pp. 289–90.

[41] Sella, 'L'economia', pp. 676–9.

[42] B. Caizzi, *Industria e commercio nella Repubblica veneta del XVIII secolo* (Milan, 1965), pp. 24–8, 131–4.

century later would be a major source of friction with the subject cities. In fact, the Venetian government restricted itself to measures forbidding the sale on Venetian territory of cloth that could compete with its own output, but this had no effect on cloth produced on the Terraferma, which was of inferior quality compared with that made in Venice and was therefore aimed at different segments of the market.[43] Regulations over raw materials were a greater source of conflict since Venetian manufacture had privileged access to wool supplies, but they nevertheless did not impede the growth of Bergamo's wool industry despite the fact that it was the most penalised by restrictions on supplies.[44]

Expansion both by Venice and by subject cities in the other major textile manufacture, silk, also presaged potential conflict. In this case also, however, competition resolved itself in a segmentation of the market, with Venice monopolising the production of higher quality material and the cities of the Terraferma, especially Vicenza, specialising in cheaper weaves. In addition, the capital allowed the other cities to produce better kinds of silk cloth that its own industry did not produce, such as black velvet in the Genoese style.[45]

The attainment of a degree of economic and institutional equilibrium in relations between the capital and its subject cities is reflected in the basic stability of the urban network. During the late sixteenth and seventeenth centuries levels of urbanisation comfortably exceeded the levels attained before the crisis of the mid-sixteenth century, while the urban hierarchy did not undergo the kind of radical upheavals caused elsewhere by the advent of the regional state. At the turn of the sixteenth century Venice was easily the largest city with c.150,000 inhabitants, followed by Verona and Brescia with populations of more than 50,000, by Padua (40,000), Vicenza (31,000) and Bergamo (25,000), and lastly by Udine, Crema and Treviso with about 14,000 people.[46]

As in other states examined previously, the demographic crisis of 1630 and the economic problems of the following decades set in motion major transformations in relations between the capital, subject cities and the countryside. The effects of the plague epidemics were felt particularly strongly by urban populations, where numbers fell by 48 per cent compared with losses in the countryside of no more than 30 per cent. Venice in 1633 numbered about 102,000 inhabitants compared

---

[43] Sella, 'L'economia', pp. 681–2; D. Sella, 'The rise and fall of the Venetian woollen industry', in B. Pullan (ed.), *Crisis and change in the Venetian economy* (London, 1968), pp. 106–26; W. Panciera, *L'arte matrice. I lanifici della Repubblica di Venezia nei secoli XVII e XVIII* (Treviso, 1996), pp. 39–66.

[44] Ciriacono, 'Venise', p. 292.

[45] Ibid., p. 293.

[46] Ibid., p. 291; Ginatempo and Sandri, *L'Italia delle città*, pp. 78, 82.

with 150,000 thirty years before. The urban hierarchy, however, did not undergo major changes following the crisis. Of far greater significance was the slow and laborious recovery of urban populations in comparison with the sustained demographic increases in the rural hinterlands. The rate of urbanisation in the Venetian state decreased from 21.2 per cent in 1548 to 15.1 per cent in 1764–6 and declined further to 14.3 per cent by 1790. The relative decline of Venice was even sharper, with its share of the total population decreasing from 9.4 per cent in 1548 to only 5.8 per cent in 1790.[47]

The demographic redistribution sketched by these stark figures is indicative of important changes in the region's economic equilibrium. The first notable feature is the relative decline of Venice, whose manufacturing and commercial activities contracted significantly between the late seventeenth and eighteenth centuries.[48] The capital's increasing economic weakness forced the Venetian government increasingly to abandon remaining restrictions on production on the Terraferma. Thus, for example, limitations on wool supplies were abolished during the eighteenth century and production of a broader range of silk cloth was authorised.[49] On the other hand, among the probable causes of Venetian decline was precisely the growth of several Terraferma industries from the late seventeenth century. Vicenza had become a major centre for finished silk cloth, while Bergamo had taken the lead in the production of silk thread. In the wool industry the organisational reforms initiated in Verona and Padua had produced good results.[50] However, the expansion of non-urban manufactures was both faster and produced the most notable changes to the industrial geography of the Venetian state.

Non-agricultural activities had long been diffused in areas benefiting from the privileges granted by the Republic. By virtue of grants dating back to the early fifteenth century, the Brescian and Bergamascan valleys and the areas on the western shores of Lake Garda had escaped the jurisdiction of the neighbouring city, signifying not only fiscal and commercial advantages but also the faculty to organise production without submitting to the regulations of the urban guilds.[51] Elsewhere

[47] Ciriacono, 'Venise', pp. 294–6, 302–3; R. T. Rapp, *Industry and economic decline in seventeenth-century Venice* (Cambridge, MA–London 1976), pp. 39–41.
[48] D. Sella, *Commerci e industrie a Venezia nel secolo XVII* (Venice–Rome, 1961); Pullan, *Crisis and change*; Caizzi, *Industria*; Rapp, *Industry*.
[49] Ciriacono, 'Venise', pp. 299–302; C. M. Belfanti, 'Le calze a maglia: moda e innovazione alle origini dell'industria della maglieria (secoli XVI–XVII)', *Società e storia* 69 (1995), 495–6.
[50] S. Ciriacono, 'Proto-industria, lavoro a domicilio e sviluppo economico nelle campagne venete in epoca moderna', *Quaderni storici* 18 (1983), 67–70; Panciera, *L'arte matrice*, pp. 115–34; Rapp, *Industry*.
[51] C. M. Belfanti, 'Rural manufactures and rural proto-industries in the "Italy of the

in the state these developments occurred later, during the seventeenth and eighteenth centuries, in reaction to the high costs of production entailed by the urban system of production regulated by guilds. This response occurred in Padua's silk industry and in Friuli for the production of mixed cloths, but it was most notable in the decentralisation of wool manufacture from the towns in the Alpine foothills. During the eighteenth century the woollen industry was precisely the sector in which small towns demonstrated the greatest dynamism. A well-studied example was the small centre of Schio, whose rise was linked to a joint venture between a Venetian patrician and local entrepreneurs.[52]

The rising importance of small towns in this period does not come as a total surprise. It was the outcome of a long evolutionary process that came to maturity in response to the political, economic and demographic decline of the great cities. Thus, the majority of small towns engaged in wool manufacture during the eighteenth century boasted traditions going back at least to the sixteenth century.[53] There is an equally strong correlation between the economic success of these small towns, based at least in part on local entrepreneurship, and the strong presence of their local elites among the rural political representatives that emerged during the second half of the sixteenth century. The extent of these small towns' ambitions to emulate the great cities is testified both by a clear desire to distinguish themselves institutionally from lesser villages (*ville*) and by their efforts to imitate the urban way of life by creating institutions and social arrangements typical of the city.[54]

If the advent of the regional state appeared to establish a form of territorial organisation based, as in Tuscany, upon a balance of power struck between state, capital, and subject cities, the crisis of the 1630s and the consequent demographic and economic difficulties of traditional urban centres accelerated the rise to political and economic significance of the rural areas. Thus a third actor appeared on the stage alongside the capital city and the other subject cities, whose role gained strength from its dynamic industrial apparatus and its recognised political voice. The action of the Venetian government, which was principally orientated towards mediating between the interests of the capital and the demands of the Terraferma (in the first instance those of subject

---

cities"', *Continuity and Change* 8 (1993), 261–4; Ciriacono, 'Proto-industria', pp. 60–3.

[52] Ciriacono, 'Proto-industria', pp. 63–9; Ciriacono, 'Venise', pp. 297–8, 301–2, 326; Panciera, *L'arte matrice*, pp. 177–208.

[53] Panciera, *L'arte matrice*, pp. 23–38.

[54] Knapton, 'Tra Dominante e Dominio', pp. 493–4. See also G. Chittolini, '"Quasi-città". Borghi e terre in area lombarda nel tardo Medioevo', *Società e storia* 47 (1990), 16–17.

cities, followed by those of the countryside) seems to have produced a
less rigid form of dominion compared to Piedmont under the house of
Savoy or to Tuscany under the Medici. On the other hand, one should
not forget that, by virtue of their greater demographic, economic and
political importance, the urban centres that came under Venetian
control were in a far stronger negotiating position than the Piedmontese towns and perhaps also the Tuscan cities had been. Nor should
we underestimate the extent to which a more centralising policy could
have inhibited the commercial and manufacturing activities of the
Terraferma and therefore drastically reduced revenues from the excise
applied to trade within the state.[55] It has been claimed that Venetian
'polycentrism' caused a pronounced fragmentation of 'economic
space', accentuated by the increased attraction exerted by the
Lombard economy on the western provinces of Brescia and Bergamo,
and further enhanced by Venice's inability to create a regional economic organisation. While this interpretation is well grounded, one
may also remark that the proto-industrial centres and activities that
arose during the eighteenth century established a base that was
destined in large part to be industrially consolidated during the nineteenth.[56]

Spanish Lombardy

On the death of its last duke, Francesco II Sforza, in 1535 the state of
Milan was integrated into the Spanish dominions with no significant
changes to existing institutional arrangements.[57] The Visconti and
Sforza rulers had created a state based on a patchwork of quasi-
independent territories, with little attempt to centralise power or to
strengthen the political and economic role of the main city, Milan, at the
expense of the other subject towns.[58] As if to reflect this fact, Milan's
centrality in demographic terms decreased steadily between the fifteenth
and sixteenth centuries. The Lombard state was, if anything, characterised by the largesse with which the lords of Milan granted privileges
and liberties to small towns, Alpine or otherwise peripheral communities, and feudal lordships. Urban authority over the countryside was
somewhat reduced, while the political prestige and negotiating powers

[55] Rapp, *Industry*.
[56] Belfanti, 'Spazio economico'; Belfanti, 'Rural manufactures', pp. 272–4; Ciriacono, 'Venise', pp. 304–7.
[57] G. Vigo, *Uno stato nell'impero. La difficile transizione al moderno nella Milano di età spagnola* (Milan, 1994), pp. 38–9, 47–8, 60–2.
[58] Nevertheless, Milan did try to monopolise silk manufacture; D. Sella, *L'economia lombarda durante la dominazione spagnola* (Bologna, 1982), pp. 66–7 n. 22.

of rural boroughs and communities were enhanced. Consequently, the traditional control exerted by urban guilds over manufacturing activities had come under threat. The significant growth of cloth production in a number of small towns during the fifteenth century occurred as a consequence of the jurisdictional liberties that had released those centres from urban control.[59]

The advent of Spanish domination did not radically alter the internal organisation of the state, whose structure remained 'polycentric and pluralistic' to the point that in the first half of the sixteenth century individual cities and many smaller communities sent their personal representatives to negotiate directly with the regional governor and even with the emperor in Spain.[60] During the middle decades of the same century the conflicts of interest between cities and rural territories, which had already arisen in the fifteenth century over ducal support for the smaller towns and communities, re-emerged over the delicate issue of taxation. In a way similar to contemporary developments in the Venetian Republic, the representatives of Spanish Lombard *contadi* (joined as one into the so-called Contado) mounted a concerted attack against that most consolidated and resented urban privilege, the faculty of allocating tax burdens between town and country. As one of the rural delegates subsequently explained, 'each city ruled and governed its *contado* as it pleased. But, as the *contado* had no other rule than that of the city whose only aim was to free itself of the heavy burdens placed on it, the city found it easy to offload the greater part of them and oppress the poor countryfolk.'[61]

However, the rural communities' success in renegotiating the tax burden should not be exaggerated. Although the representative bodies of the Contado began their fight against the cities in the 1560s, they were only formally recognised by the state of Milan at the turn of the century;[62] nor was this achievement extended to other aspects of town–country relations.[63] Nevertheless, Giovanni Vigo's summing up of the issue is entirely accurate: 'Of one thing there is no doubt: the dominion

[59] Chittolini, *Formazione*, pp. xii–xvi, 76–7; Epstein, 'Town and country', pp. 462, 464–9; Ginatempo and Sandri, *L'Italia delle città*, p. 78.

[60] Epstein, 'Town and country', p. 462 for the quotation. See Vigo, *Uno stato*, pp. 37–62; L. Faccini, *La Lombardia fra '600 e '700. Riconversione economica e mutamenti sociali* (Milan, 1988), pp. 25–9; F. Chabod, *Lo Stato e la vita religiosa a Milano nell'epoca di Carlo V* (Turin, 1971), p. 192.

[61] For parallels between the Venetian Republic and Spanish Lombardy, see G. Chittolini, 'Prefazione', in Rossini, *Campagne bresciane*, pp. 9–24. See also G. Vigo, *Fisco e società nella Lombardia del Cinquecento* (Bologna, 1979), pp. 155–90 (quotation at p. 160); Sella, *Economia lombarda*, pp. 65–70; Faccini, *Lombardia*, pp. 97–106.

[62] Vigo, *Fisco*, pp. 157–90; Vigo, *Uno stato*, pp. 50–1.

[63] Sella, *Economia lombarda*, p. 69.

of city over *contado* had ended forever.'[64] While the larger urban centres continued to play a central role in the Spanish Lombard economy at least up to the 1630s, the bitter conflict over taxation had allowed the *contado*'s political expansion begun under the Sforza to take further hold and had irreversibly weakened the control of town over country. [65]

Despite the fact that the cities maintained their monopoly over most industrial activities and over supplies of raw materials, it is significant that in 1593 the representatives of the Contado managed to have the privileged allocation of raw silk to Milanese manufacture suspended. It is equally significant that between the mid-sixteenth and the early seventeenth century, at a time of great prosperity for the Lombard urban economy, textile production was also active in the countryside. These were generally rural manufactures that produced lower quality cloth for a predominantly regional market, which therefore did not directly compete with urban industries. But there were also instances of higher quality production to which urban guilds objected and which, although still not challenging urban industrial supremacy, portended the new manufacturing structures that emerged after the crisis of the 1630s.[66]

In Spanish Lombardy as elsewhere, during the seventeenth century the combination of high mortality, war and urban industrial decline transformed the demographic and economic balance of the territory.[67] Towards 1600 the urban system was headed by Milan with about 115,000 inhabitants, followed in ranking by Cremona (*c.*40,000), Pavia (18,000), Como (12,000) and Lodi (14,000). By about 1640 Milan had declined to 100,000 inhabitants, but Cremona had collapsed to about 15,000 to match Pavia, Como held less than 10,000 people, and there were no other cities above 10,000. As in the Venetian territories, the few available data suggest that demographic recovery during the second half of the seventeenth century benefited the countryside far more than the cities, particularly the small towns of the Contado.[68]

---

[64] Vigo, *Fisco*, p. 190.

[65] Faccini, *Lombardia*, p. 98.

[66] Sella, *Economia lombarda*, pp. 41–51, 66–70, 236–7; Vigo, *Uno stato*, pp. 63–88, 97–104; V. H. Beonio Brocchieri, 'Artigianati, manifatture e proto-industrie fra città e campagna: la Lombardia del XVI secolo', *Studi di storia medievale e diplomatica* 14 (1992), 193–209.

[67] Vigo, *Uno stato*, pp. 69–78; Sella, *Economia lombarda*, pp. 113–44; Faccini, *Lombardia*, pp. 29–39; Belfanti, 'Spazio economico'.

[68] Data from P. Subacchi, 'Tra carestie ed epidemie: la demografia dell'area lombarda nel "lungo" Seicento', in *La popolazione italiana nel Seicento*, forthcoming. The trend continued in the following century; A. Bellettini, 'L'evoluzione demografica nel Settecento', in A. Bellettini, *La popolazione italiana. Un profilo storico* (Turin, 1987), pp. 115–16.

This trend reflected a process of reorganisation in agriculture, which became more diversified in response to falling demand for basic cereals, and the proliferation of manufacturing activity in the countryside. Successful rural industries included manufactures present already during the sixteenth century such as small-scale metalworks, and fustian, wool and linen industries. However, they also included activities like silk throwing that had previously been restricted to Milan. Between the seventeenth and eighteenth centuries the gradual decline in the number of silk mills in Milan was more than matched by the industrial plant installed in the countryside through the huge expansion of raw silk production.[69]

The diffusion of rural industries for the production of low-cost goods such as linen cloth and fustian was in many ways analogous to the processes of modernisation being experienced by the more dynamic European economies.[70] Moreover, although the proliferation of rural manufacture was due in the first place to entrepreneurial requirements for low-cost production sites, it also occurred in response to rising popular demand for affordable goods. The increase in rural population that had followed the seventeenth-century demographic crisis created a market for cheaper goods, one that could not be satisfied with the traditional luxury goods produced by urban craftsmen.[71]

The sustained demographic recovery and the economic dynamism of the Spanish Lombard countryside from the late seventeenth century are symptomatic of profound changes in town–country relations, above all in terms of the industrial division of labour.[72] Needless to say, however, there was no automatic link between urban demographic decline and industrial contraction, and the spread of rural manufacture. Demographic contraction could equally be a symptom of industrial reconversion, whereby some phases of the production process formerly practised in cities were devolved to the countryside while towns specialised in more sophisticated activities.[73] The fact that processes of rural industrial devolution dated back at least to the second half of the sixteenth century, long before the onset of industrial crisis in the cities, suggests

---

[69] Vigo, *Uno stato*, pp. 104–6; Sella, *Economia lombarda*, pp. 189–210; Faccini, *Lombardia*.

[70] M. Aymard, 'La fragilità di un'economia avanzata: l'Italia e le trasformazioni dell'economia', in R. Romano (ed.), *Storia dell'economia italiana*, 3 vols. (Turin, 1991), vol. II, p. 74; P. Malanima, *La perdita del primato. Crisi e riconversione nell'Italia del Seicento* (Milan, 1998), pp. 102–4.

[71] Moioli, 'Deindustrializzazione', pp. 189–90.

[72] Sella, *Economia lombarda*, pp. 234–45.

[73] E. François, 'Stagnazione, regresso, riconversione: le "città in declino" nell'area tedesca (1600–1800)', *Cheiron* 11 (1990), 111–12.

that the process was at least partly an aspect of a deliberate strategy by urban entrepreneurs.[74]

However, Lombard cities did not so much experience sudden and traumatic phases of 'de-industrialisation' as suffer drawn-out periods of relative decline of different intensity and character from town to town. Against the net decline suffered by centres like Como and Cremona, whose population in the early eighteenth century was still lower than in 1600, other cities held out far better: towards 1720 Milan had over 120,000 inhabitants, compared with the 115,000 recorded in 1600, while Pavia had grown to 24,000 compared with 18,000 in 1600. Milan in particular continued to be a metropolis that attracted the admiration of European travellers.[75] Around the turn of the seventeenth century Milan was still a major centre for the production of luxury goods, as well as a major crossroads for international trade.[76] Milan's cultural activities – an important albeit often neglected indicator of vitality – were also far from moribund at this time. The reopening of the famous Accademia Ambrosiana in 1668 coincided with the formation of the city's great collections of paintings. The Ambrosiana library, holding 40,000 volumes including a Leonardo codex, the large number of colleges for foreign students and the *Wunderkammer* set up by Canon Settala were all features of cultural vitality that aroused the wonder of visitors from across the Alps. Their admiration was even greater regarding Milan's welfare institutions, among which the Ospedale Maggiore – capable of housing up to 4,000 patients – was judged to be one of the most impressive European complexes of its kind in terms of efficiency and size.[77]

Mantua, Parma and Piacenza, Bologna

The lower belt of the Po plain, the area lying between the Po and the Apennines, featured a complex and fragmented political landscape that included city-states of differing size and extension, provinces of the

[74] Sella, *Economia lombarda*, pp. 68–9.
[75] Subacchi, 'Tra carestie ed epidemie'; L. Hollen Lees and P. M. Hohenberg, 'Urban decline and regional economies: Brabant, Castile and Lombardy, 1550–1750', *Comparative Studies in Society and History* 31 (1989), 449–50.
[76] A. Moioli, 'Assetti manifatturieri nella Lombardia politicamente divisa della seconda metà del Settecento', in S. Zaninelli (ed.), *Storia dell'industria lombarda*, 2 vols. (Milan, 1988), vol. I, pp. 50–1; Sella, *Economia lombarda*, pp. 153–5.
[77] G. Bora, 'La pittura del seicento nelle province occidentali lombarde', in *La pittura in Italia. Il Seicento*, 2 vols. (Milan, 1988), vol. I, pp. 95–6; H. Kellenbenz, 'Il volto della Milano secentesca. Guide e consigli per i viaggiatori germanici' and A. Tenenti, 'Lo sguardo francese sulla Milano spagnola', both in *'Millain the great'. Milano nelle brume del Seicento* (Milan, 1989), pp. 285–301, 381–96.

Papal States, and petty lordships and fiefs. Three examples will be examined as representatives of the whole: the duchy of Mantua, the states of Parma and Piacenza under the Farnese, and the legation of Bologna.

The duchy of Mantua was a small state whose territory virtually coincided with the city's medieval *contado*.[78] A seigniorial lordship that had replaced the commune during the thirteenth century without causing any significant change to the character of the city-state stayed in place until the eighteenth century.[79] Relations between town and country therefore continued along the lines established under the communal regime. Urban territorial control followed a familiar pattern: the duke appointed functionaries to administer the communities, citizens enjoyed fiscal privileges, the city's basic food supplies were enforced by law, and urban guilds monopolised manufactures. The city's rigid control made it impossible for rural communities to achieve political representation along the lines of Spanish Lombardy or the Republic of Venice. Indeed, precisely in the mid-sixteenth century around the time when institutional arrangements elsewhere were beginning to loosen up, the duchy of Mantua intensified political centralisation and urban society tightened its grip over the countryside, leading to a chorus of protests among the peasantry.[80]

This state of affairs was reflected in the heavy obstruction posed by urban guilds against attempts to employ rural labour in manufacturing activities. During the latter half of the sixteenth century the Mantuan merchants who organised a putting-out system for the knitting industry resorted to workers residing at the duchy's periphery, in petty feudal states under the cadet branches of the Mantuan Gonzaga family which were not subject to guild control. In the same years Mantua's wool merchants brought a lawsuit before the Senato di Giustizia (the duchy's highest court) against entrepreneurs from a small community in the *contado* that made cheap woollen cloth, accusing them of monopolising the work of local spinners to the detriment of the urban industry. Although the court's final decision is unknown, it is certain that woollen production disappeared from the rural community.

In contrast with the regional states examined previously, moreover,

[78] M. Vaini, *Dal comune alla signoria. Mantova dal 1200 al 1328* (Mantua, 1986), pp. 137–64, 316–22.
[79] During the sixteenth century the marquisate of Monferrato was acquired by the Gonzaga but remained entirely separate from the Mantuan state. See C. M. Belfanti and M. A. Romani, 'Il Monferrato: una frontiera scomoda tra Mantova e Torino (1536–1707)', in C. Ossola, C. Raffestin and M. Ricciardi (eds.), *La frontiera da stato a nazione. Il caso Piemonte* (Rome, 1987), pp. 113–46.
[80] C. Mozzarelli, *Mantova e i Gonzaga dal 1382 al 1707* (Turin, 1987), pp. 53–80.

the depression of the 1630s did not modify the traditional division of labour between town and country. Mantua, besieged, sacked and decimated by epidemics, suffered huge damage, but pestilence and warfare produced equally devastating consequences for the countryside. After the epidemic of 1630 the Mantuan territory was depopulated, the fields abandoned. To cope with the scarcity of agricultural labour the duke banned all non-agricultural activities in the countryside. It was not until the eighteenth century, after the duchy came under Habsburg control and Mantua was turned into a military garrison, that manufacturing activity began to reappear in the *contado*, this time mainly in connection with the manufacture of silk.[81]

Territorial arrangements in the Farnese duchy were far less uniform. The two main urban centres, Parma and Piacenza, had equal ranking within the duchy, which as a result was a state with two competing capitals rather than a hierarchical regional state. The two cities controlled *contadi* of limited size in which land was firmly under urban ownership.[82] Outside this von Thünen band that served to supply the cities with basic foodstuffs, about two-thirds of the territory was subject towards the middle of the sixteenth century to jurisdictions that fell outside the control of the cities and even of the duke. They included feudal investitures, inherited from the late medieval Visconti and Sforza administrations, mountain communities with special liberties, but also fully independent lordships.[83] Although these separate entities were gradually integrated into the duchy, it also meant that a large part of the state territory was irreversibly lost to urban jurisdiction. It is thus no coincidence that silk, hemp and linen manufacture proliferated during the seventeenth and eighteenth centuries precisely in these peripheral areas of the state. Similarly, the development in the former Pallavicino lordship of small towns like Fiorenzuola, Cortemaggiore, Busseto and Borgo San Donnino recalls the rise to prominence of small boroughs in

[81] Ibid., pp. 127–32; C. M. Belfanti, 'Dalla città alla campagna: industrie tessili a Mantova tra carestie ed epidemie (1550–1630)', *Critica storica* 25 (1988), 443–53; C. Vivanti, *Le campagne del Mantovano nell'età delle Riforme* (Milan, 1959), pp. 127–41.
[82] L. Arcangeli, 'Giurisdizioni feudali e organizzazione territoriale nel Ducato di Parma (1545–1587)', in M. A. Romani (ed.), *Le corti farnesiane di Parma e Piacenza, 1543–1622*, 2 vols. (Rome, 1978), vol. I, p. 97; Chittolini, *Formazione*, pp. 261–5.
[83] M. A. Romani, *Nella spirale di una crisi* (Milan, 1975), p. 39 for grain supplies; L. Arcangeli, 'Feudatari e duca negli stati farnesiani (1545–1587)', in *Il Rinascimento nelle corti padane. Società e cultura* (Bari, 1977), pp. 77–80; G. Tocci, *Le terre traverse. Poteri e territori nei Ducati di Parma e Piacenza tra Sei e Settecento* (Bologna, 1985); C. M. Belfanti, 'Territori ed economie nei Ducati di Parma, Piacenza e Guastalla alla fine dell'Antico Regime', in F. Giusberti and A. Guenzi (eds.), *Spazi ed economie. L'assetto di due territori della Padania inferiore* (Bologna, 1986), pp. 30–1.

the Venetian Terraferma, with similar attempts by the aspiring elites to emulate urban social and institutional arrangements.[84]

More than any other city in Emilia, Bologna had managed during its communal phase to establish strong and lasting control over the hinterland. At the beginning of the sixteenth century Bologna and its territory became a 'legation' – a province – within the Papal territories, but the papacy did not attempt to change existing institutional arrangements between town and country. Some small boroughs like Medicina and Castel San Pietro engaged in a long drawn-out legal battle with the city in defence of their ancient privileges, but the Papal government was unable or unwilling to grant the rural communities greater autonomy which would have permanently weakened the Bolognese oligarchy.[85]

Bolognese dominion aimed to satisfy its fundamental needs for foodstuffs and raw materials for urban industry. The economic and social structure of the Bolognese countryside was shaped by the prevalence of sharecropping, which followed the spread of urban property. The contract, which required the sharecroppers to deliver the landlord's share to the city at harvest time, achieved the double objective for the urban oligarchy of guaranteeing an outlet for their produce and of ensuring that the city was well supplied with food. A similar strategy guaranteed a constant flow of raw materials for the most important city manufacture, silk. The silk industry was characterised by exceptionally, indeed uniquely, high levels of concentration of the production process within Bologna itself. Only the production of raw silk – that is, the breeding of silkworms – was allowed outside the city walls, albeit still under a strict ban on exports. The entire output was sold at a specialised market in the city.[86]

The manufacture of hemp saw far greater resistance to urban control. From the late seventeenth century hemp production developed strongly in peripheral mountainous areas and in those small centres (Medicina, Budrio and Castel San Pietro) that had attempted to challenge urban primacy in defence of their ancient privileges. The Bolognese government resolved the resulting controversy between urban guilds and rural craftsmen by incorporating the latter into the former by means of a specially created urban corporation. For the Bolognese oligarchy, the city guilds represented a pre-eminent industrial and political partner

---

[84] Tocci, *Terre traverse*, pp. 47–126; Belfanti, 'Territori', pp. 18, 28, 32, 98–115, 118–21.

[85] Chittolini, *Formazione*, p. 255; A. De Benedictis, *Patrizi e comunità. Il governo del contado bolognese nel '700* (Bologna, 1984), pp. 15–16, 142–56, 231–2.

[86] A. Guenzi, *Pane e fornai a Bologna in età moderna* (Padua, 1982), pp. 9–18; C. Poni, 'Per la storia del distretto industriale serico di Bologna (secoli XVI–XIX)', *Quaderni storici*, 25 (1990), 98–9.

until right to the end of the eighteenth century. In such a context the margins for changes in the consolidated division of labour between town and country were truly exiguous.[87]

Conclusion

The transitional period from city-state to regional state marked a turning-point in relations between town and countryside in central and northern Italy.[88] Cities and their subject territories were brought into a larger and more complex institutional context with a greater number of competing actors – including central state powers, capital cities, other cities with their own *contadi*. Progress in territorial integration was nevertheless made, albeit to differing degrees in different individual cases, up to the demographic crisis of 1630.[89]

The demographic slump and the difficulties experienced by some traditional urban sectors in the following decades marked a new turning-point in town–country relations. The more sustained demographic recovery in the countryside during the second half of the seventeenth century caused a significant redistribution of the population in almost the whole of central and northern Italy. The countryside became a vast reservoir of cheap labour and at the same time a potential market for cheap manufactured goods.[90] On the other hand, a large part of urban manufacture seems to have progressively lost ground to international competition. Consequently, it also became increasingly costly – both economically and politically – to maintain the institutional framework based on guild regulation and urban monopolies.[91]

Between the seventeenth and eighteenth centuries textile manufacture spread almost everywhere in the countryside. Industrial growth was, however, more concentrated within and around communities with semi- or quasi-urban features. Some of these centres emerged after the mid-seventeenth-century crisis, as in Piedmont, but in most instances they were centres that had begun to free themselves from urban dominion

[87] Poni, 'Per la storia', pp. 99–146; C. Poni and S. Fronzoni, 'L'economia di sussistenza della famiglia contadina', in *Cultura popolare in Emilia Romagna. Mestieri della terra e delle acque* (Milan, 1979), pp. 9–10; A. Guenzi, *La fabbrica delle tele fra città e campagna. Gruppi professionali e governo dell'economia a Bologna nel secolo XVIII* (Pesaro, 1987), pp. 12–15, 25, 127; A. Guenzi, 'Governo cittadino e sistema delle arti in una città dello Stato pontificio: Bologna', *Studi storici Luigi Simeoni* 41 (1991), 173–82.

[88] Chittolini, *Formazione*; Epstein, 'Town and country'.

[89] The crisis is discussed in L. Del Panta, *Le epidemie nella storia demografica italiana (secoli XIV–XIX)* (Turin, 1980), pp. 158–78.

[90] Malanima, *Il lusso*.

[91] Sella, *Economia lombarda*, pp. 237–42.

during the fifteenth and sixteenth centuries.[92] Taking advantage of support from the central state, which was not averse to reducing the entrenched powers of urban patriciates, the elites in some of these quasi-cities in Spanish Lombardy and in the Venetian Republic were able to weaken urban control over taxation and manufacturing. Thus, examples of rural or quasi-rural industrial activities were far from unknown even in the fifteenth century.[93] These were generally manufactures that did not directly compete with urban production or segments of the production process that had been decentralised under urban merchant control. The transformations in town–country relations that occurred during the second half of the seventeenth century therefore appear to have been the result of a long-term process that came to fruition after the plague of 1630.

Increased rural involvement in industrial activities did not necessarily imply the irreversible decline of urban manufacture, but was certainly a response to the latter's difficulties.[94] Decline in some traditional urban sectors did not occur suddenly but over a long period of time. Moreover, some urban industries, like silk throwing in Bergamo and Bologna, silk weaving in Vicenza and Florence, and wool-cloth production in Padua, managed to preserve their erstwhile positions for a large part of the eighteenth century without resorting to rural decentralisation.[95] Thus, despite the notable changes that we have documented, the cities did not collapse into de-industrialisation or cease to be the main residential, commercial, administrative, welfare and cultural centres of their regions: the cities, in short, continued to provide the models of social and political organisation that the economically successful small towns tried to imitate.[96]

---

[92] S. R. Epstein, 'Manifatture tessili e strutture politico-istituzionali nella Lombardia tardo medievale: ipotesi di ricerca', *Studi di storia medievale e diplomatica* 14 (1992), 1–32; Belfanti, 'Rural manufactures', pp. 272–3; R. Corritore, 'Il processo di "ruralizzazione" in Italia nei secoli XVII–XVIII. Verso una regionalizzazione', *Rivista di storia economica* 10 (1993), 357–62, 374.

[93] Epstein, 'Manifatture tessili'; Sella, *Economia lombarda*, pp. 189–210; Panciera, *L'arte matrice*, pp. 23–38.

[94] Moioli, 'La deindustrializzazione'.

[95] Moioli, 'Assetti manifatturieri', pp. 11–12; Poni, 'Per la storia'; Ciriacono, 'Proto-industria', pp. 67–8; Malanima, *La decadenza*, pp. 305–20; Panciera, *L'arte matrice*, pp. 209–11.

[96] For the long-standing cultural hegemony of civic life, see R. Putnam, *Making democracy work. Civic traditions in modern Italy* (Princeton, 1993). For small towns see Chittolini, 'Quasi-città', pp. 16–17; Knapton, 'Tra Dominante e Dominio', pp. 493–4; Epstein, 'Town and country', p. 471; Belfanti, 'Territori ed economie', pp. 119–20. On the factors affecting the diffusion of institutional patterns see R. W. Scott, *Institutions and organisations* (Thousand Oaks, CA, 1995).

14   Town and country in the kingdom of Naples, 1500–1800

Brigitte Marin

Translated by S. R. Epstein

The history of early modern southern Italy or Mezzogiorno has been read since the eighteenth century in terms of a contrast between the capital, Naples, the seat of royal authority and of the supreme magistracies, a centre for the development of a powerful bureaucracy, and a cultural pole endowed with a university, museums and libraries, and the provinces, viewed as a vast countryside oppressed by feudal powers. This dualism has been a matter of debate since 1734, when Naples became the residence of an independent monarchy after more than two centuries of foreign domination. The city was praised as the expression of a new reforming central power, but its provincial hegemony was denounced as the cause, together with feudal oppression, of the country's economic retardation. Nineteenth-century historiography tended to continue this polemic, which was further nourished by the way the Neapolitan Republic of 1799 opposed the martyrs of the Revolution, children of the Enlightenment, to the provincial counter-revolutionaries whom it saw as avenging centuries of rural subordination to the capital's interests, exigencies and exploitation.

In the light of this historiographic tradition, relations between town and countryside have attracted little attention and have been largely ignored; discussion tends to focus on Neapolitan domination of a poorly differentiated provincial 'country'.[1] It is significant, for example, that Corrado Vivanti, in a recent essay on town and country in early modern Italy, sees Naples as being the only 'true' city in the kingdom, the other agglomerations appearing to lack the normal characteristics of a city, namely a pronounced division of labour and a degree of political activity expressed in municipal institutions. Vivanti thus accepts a long-standing tradition that opposes the organisation of the central and northern Italian countryside, strictly under urban control, to that in southern

[1] See A. Massafra, *Campagne e terri'torio nel Mezzogiorno fra Settecento e Ottocento* (Bari, 1984), p. 17.

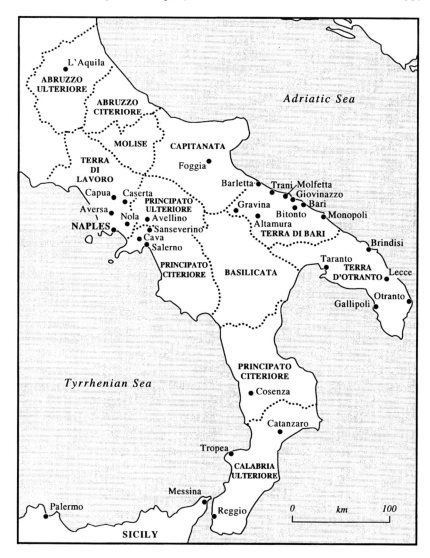

Figure 14.1   The kingdom of Naples in the early modern period

Italy (including Sicily and Sardinia), where the presence of a feudal monarchy posed fundamental constraints to urban autonomy, and where the urban infrastructure was consequently very weak. The monarchy had enfeoffed so many towns that in the kingdom's parliament, which 'even the viceroys had to take some account of', urban representation was largely symbolic.[2]

Thus, as Marino Berengo noted in 1986,

> to talk about town–country relations is to raise a set of questions that are more significant for the history of central and northern Italy than for that of the Mezzogiorno. The feudal structure of the kingdom of Naples, the *Regno*, nipped the communal movement in the bud, and with it, one of the communes' most central features: political and economic control over a rural hinterland (*contado*).[3]

Although urban growth through rural immigration manifested itself precociously in the South, by the twelfth century the Norman rulers had snuffed out all attempts to gain full institutional autonomy.[4] Between the thirteenth and the fifteenth centuries, Angevin and Aragonese rulers enfeoffed a large number of towns, while others that stayed within royal purview came under partial feudal jurisdiction, at the same time as the north Italian communes were extending their rule over feudal lordships in the countryside.

Although not lacking foundation, these arguments have, however, marginalised urban history in the Mezzogiorno while concentrating a disproportionate amount of attention on feudal and seigniorial lordship and on their conflicts with rural communities. Until recently, urban history and urban influence had been removed from historical consciousness,[5] even though the early modern Mezzogiorno did not lack centres of some size, including about forty towns over 10,000 inhabitants; although the proportion of agricultural residents in these towns may have been unusually high by north Italian standards, not all were simply 'agro-towns' or 'rural dormitories'. The building of architecturally well-crafted palaces and churches and the numerous seventeenth-century urban chronicles and descriptions testify to these centres' clear sense of urban identity.[6] This realisation, together with recent interest

[2] C. Vivanti, 'Città e campagne', in R. Romano (ed.), *Storia dell'economia italiana*. vol. II: *L'età moderna: verso la crisi* (Turin, 1991), pp. 267, 270. See also B. Croce, *Storia del Regno di Napoli*, ed. G. Galasso (Milan, 1992), p. 103 (1st edn, 1924).

[3] M. Berengo, 'Città e "contado" in Italia dal XV al XVIII secolo', *Storia della città* 36 (1986), 107.

[4] G. Fasoli, 'Città e campagne nell'Italia meridionale (secc. XII–XIV)', *Storia della città* 36 (1986), 105–6.

[5] See P. Villani, *Numerazioni dei fuochi e problemi demografici del Mezzogiorno in età moderna* (Naples, 1973), p. 23, and the special issue of *Meridiana* 5 (1989), 9.

[6] A. Musi, 'Le piccole e medie città nella storia moderna del Mezzogiorno continentale', *Rassegna storica salernitana* 10 (1994), 149ff., notes the difficulty in identifying

among social and economic historians in the development of integrated
regions, has drawn attention to the urban aspects of the kingdom of
Naples – to the fact, as Maria Antonietta Visceglia has noted with regard
to Terra d'Otranto, that 'the heart of this [and other] provinces is in the
cities: as feudal and oligarchic residences and as centres for the consumption of culture and luxury products, these are entities with municipal roles and therefore also with the functions and offices typical of
true towns'.[7]

Acknowledgement of the important role played by towns in the
Regno, particularly in Puglia,[8] but also in Campania, Calabria and the
Abruzzi, has produced an image of town–country relations that is far
more complex and nuanced than the traditional counterposition of
Naples and the provinces. The southern Italian patriciates, their role in
organising and controlling the economy of the hinterland and their
relations with the feudal classes, are now attracting attention.[9] Work on
the relations between towns and rural agglomerations known as casali is
modifying the traditional image of the southern countryside oppressed
by feudal lords whose powers extended up to the town walls.[10] Although
cities in the Regno did not have a contado of the kind and size controlled
by the cities of north-central Italy, towns in the Abruzzi had jurisdictional rights over the surrounding communities – the sources speak
about 'contado' in the case of L'Aquila, for example – and in other parts
of the Mezzogiorno towns disposed of a hinterland of casali from which
they drew population, food supplies and income from the land. While
these territories cannot be termed contadi in the north Italian sense,
which entails a process of political subordination, the casali nevertheless

specifically urban functions in this literature beyond its rhetorical appeal to the 'city-as-
motherland'.
[7] M. A. Visceglia, Territorio, feudo e potere locale. Terra d'Otranto tra Medioevo ed Età
moderna (Naples, 1988), p. 144.
[8] See F. Tateo (ed.), Storia di Bari nell'antico regime, 2 vols. (Bari, 1991–2); S. Russo
(ed.), Storia di Foggia in età moderna (Bari, 1992); Visceglia, Territorio.
[9] A. Spagnoletti, 'L'incostanza delle umane cose'. Il patriziato di Terra di Bari fra egemonia e
crisi (Bari, 1981); M. A. Visceglia, 'Un groupe social ambigu. Organisation, stratégies
et représentations de la noblesse napolitaine. XVIe–XVIIIe siècles', Annales ESC. 48
(1993), 819–51; G. Delille, 'Migrations internes et mobilité sociale dans le Royaume
de Naples (XVe–XIXe siècles)', in P. Macry and A. Massafra (eds.), Fra storia e
storiografia. Scritti in onore di Pasquale Villani (Bologna, 1994), pp. 559–70.
[10] The casali were villages in a town's vicinity over which it exercised rights of jurisdiction.
See Visceglia, Territorio, esp. ch. 4; C. Massaro, 'La città e i casali', in B. Vetere (ed.),
Storia di Lecce. Dai Bizantini agli Aragonesi (Rome–Bari, 1993), pp. 345–92; S. Russo,
Pellegrini e 'casalini' a Bari in età moderna (Bari, 1996); C. De Seta, I casali di Napoli
(Rome–Bari, 1984); B. Marin, 'Les bourgs ruraux sous juridiction de la ville: les casali',
in C. Vallat, B. Marin and G. Biondi, Naples. Démythifier la ville (Paris, 1998),
pp. 98–104.

reflect the interest 'of all towns, even of southern Italian towns', to exert extensive economic and political control over their hinterland.[11]

Thus, although Naples remains the main urban actor in the South, its long-lasting political and economic primacy no longer overshadows the important roles of a large number of provincial towns.[12] This also makes it easier to compare patterns in the Regno with developments in central and northern Italy, where processes of state formation have been viewed more traditionally in terms of relations between town and country and between dominant and subject towns.[13] While no city, with the exception of Naples, was able to develop as a distinct regional pole under the Spanish and Bourbon regimes, there are still fundamental questions to be answered about institutional, social and economic developments, for example in rural–urban labour mobility, food supplies, and investments in the land, and conflicts between towns and *casali*. A further, interesting focus of recent studies has been the linkages and interactions between centre–periphery and town–country relations and the role of the monarchy in the definition of urban hierarchies.

The urban system and the primacy of the capital

As Jan de Vries has remarked, 'when the urban hierarchies of [early modern] northern and southern Italy are examined separately two distinctive, sharply contrasting patterns emerge'.[14] Whereas northern Italy had a well-articulated urban network in which the largest cities with 100,000 inhabitants or just below controlled regions with large numbers of medium-sized towns, the Italian South matched the exceptional size of Naples with a startling absence of towns of intermediate size. Naples was effectively about fifteen times larger than Lecce at the end of the sixteenth century and twenty times the size of Bari in the eighteenth, both towns being the second largest in the kingdom at these times.

Neapolitan primacy was established between the second half of the fifteenth and the sixteenth century. In the early fourteenth century, Naples, with 50,000 or 60,000 inhabitants, led an urban network with quite a respectable number of medium-sized towns like L'Aquila,

---

[11] G. Muto, 'Pouvoirs et territoires dans l'Italie espagnole', *Revue d'histoire moderne et contemporaine* 45 (1998), 51. See also G. Barone, 'Mezzogiorno ed egemonie urbane', *Meridiana* 5 (1989), 20.

[12] A. Musi, *Mezzogiorno spagnolo. La via napoletana allo stato moderno* (Naples, 1991), p. 81.

[13] See E. Fasano-Guarini, '"Etat moderne" et anciens Etats italiens. Eléments d'histoire comparée', *Revue d'histoire moderne et contemporaine* 45 (1998), 15–41.

[14] J. de Vries, *European urbanization 1500–1800* (Cambridge, MA, 1984), p. 112.

Aversa, Bari, Salerno, Barletta, Brindisi, Lecce, Taranto, Trani, Catanzaro and Cosenza. From the early sixteenth century, the extraordinary growth of the capital, which became the second largest European city after Paris, was accompanied by an increasingly unbalanced urban hierarchy that lasted until the end of the old regime. Whereas no provincial town seemed able to grow above 20,000 inhabitants, by the late fifteenth century Naples had already joined the select group of Italian cities with about 100,000 inhabitants, and by 1630 the population had grown to 300,000. It experienced the fastest growth during the early sixteenth and the seventeenth centuries, when 10 per cent of the kingdom's population lived inside its walls. The plague of 1656 interrupted this formidable expansion and the city only regained its former size in the 1740s; but growth thereafter was again very rapid and by 1798 Naples had over 400,000 inhabitants.[15]

Although Naples had been capital of the kingdom since the second half of the thirteenth century, it was only able to establish its overwhelming lead thanks to a series of fiscal, judicial, economic and supply privileges granted by the Aragonese sovereigns from the 1450s, which included the full exemption of residents from direct taxation and which were later confirmed and expanded by the Spanish monarchy. These rights made the city uniquely attractive to provincial immigrants, all the more because the capital had a well-developed system of welfare provision that included the *annona* or grain supply and a dense network of ecclesiastical support. From the early sixteenth century, political centralisation also drew an increasing proportion of the kingdom's feudal aristocracy, together with their clients and servants, who were attracted by the fact that Naples concentrated to a disproportionate extent the kingdom's main political, administrative, financial, judicial and military resources.[16]

Neapolitan growth has thus been seen as the outcome of the modernisation of the feudal monarchy at the hands of the Spanish, an instance of state formation in the 'French manner' characterised by the preeminence of royal authority and the development of an authoritarian and centralised polity.[17] While political factors may predominate, however, the city's growth was also the effect of economic factors. Naples is situated in Campania, the most fertile region of the contin-

[15] See B. Capasso, 'Sulla circoscrizione civile ed ecclesiastica e sulla popolazione della città di Napoli dalla fine del secolo XIII fino al 1809', *Atti dell'Accademia Pontaniana* 15 (1883), 99–225; C. Petraccone, *Napoli dal Cinquecento all'Ottocento. Problemi di storia demografica e sociale* (Naples, 1974).

[16] G. Galasso, *Alla periferia dell'Impero. Il Regno di Napoli nel periodo spagnolo (secoli XVI–XVII)* (Turin, 1994), p. 336.

[17] G. Galasso, *Napoli spagnola dopo Masaniello*, 2 vols. (Florence, 1982).

ental Mezzogiorno, which ensured a substantial supply of grain, fruit and vegetables and a solid fiscal base. While resorting to more distant grain supplies, most notably from Puglia, its port simply made it easier to ship in outside supplies when local harvests did not suffice.

It has been frequently remarked that from the sixteenth century onwards, Naples blocked the development of urban functions among provincial centres through its dominance of the kingdom's migrants. 'Southern Italian urbanisation was peculiar not so much because of Naples' enormous size but because of the underdevelopment . . . of cities of intermediate rank. In other words, rather than wonder how Naples became so large, historians should wonder why cities of intermediate rank were not larger.'[18] By the late sixteenth century, L'Aquila, Aversa, Bari, Barletta, Brindisi, Salerno and others had seen their populations shrink compared to their previous peaks. Spanish rule and the political dominance attained by Naples – the city acted as sole parliamentary representative for the other towns in the royal demesne – were the major causes driving the redefinition of the urban hierarchy in this period. Thus the Spanish monarchy punished towns that had remained faithful to the 'French party' during the wars of the 1490s and 1500s by depriving them of important economic privileges; L'Aquila, for example, was deprived of its *contado* which was then largely enfeoffed; Lecce's support for Spain was by contrast recompensed with significant privileges, and its population as a result quintupled between the fourteenth and the seventeenth century. The Spanish were, however, generally hostile to expressions of local autonomy and did not hesitate to enfeoff several large towns to curb their pretensions. Naples' economic dominance also distorted the urban hierarchy, its monopoly over silk manufacture leading to the decline of Catanzaro from its previous status as the kingdom's main silk producer. On the other hand, some cities owed their good fortune to the capital city; the growth of the grain port of Foggia in Puglia, for example, was closely linked to Naples' demand for grain from the Tavoliere region of Puglia.

Strong demographic growth during the sixteenth century, gentle decline during the first half of the seventeenth century, the major crisis caused by the epidemic of 1656–7, followed by recovery and renewed expansion of the population in the eighteenth century, did not modify the basic features of the urban structure and caused few changes to urban ranking. Contemporaries were aware of, and concerned by, the fundamental imbalance between an oversized capital and poorly urbanised provinces, and the dangers that the uncontrolled growth of the

---

[18] de Vries, *European urbanization*, p. 112.

capital posed to public order and the state, the difficulties arising from uncontrolled immigration and the organisational complexities of the *annona* system were widely debated within the Neapolitan and Madrid administrations from the latter half of the sixteenth century.

During the last quarter of the eighteenth century the terms of the debate changed. The government launched a series of inquiries on the demographic and economic status of the provincial towns and rural communities, although by then the common view was that the kingdom had been depopulated since Antiquity and that the lack of change thereafter was a sign of the country's backwardness. Some voices were nevertheless raised to defend Naples' growth. For Antonio Genovesi, holder of the chair of political economy at the university of Naples from 1754 to 1768, the size of the capital and its dominance over the rest of the kingdom were not a concern; there was nothing to fear from such a concentration of people and wealth.[19] In the light of neo-mercantilist thought, unbalanced growth and urban primacy were seen as a source of economic dynamism: urban consumption stimulated agriculture, agricultural rents increased, and urban consumption could expand further in a virtuous cycle of growth. Thanks to its political functions, Genovesi argued, Naples attracted the kingdom's elite and concentrated capital resources (including labour) that offered the country a major source of development; the main constraint as he saw it was the misuse of land rent principally to buy expensive luxury imports, which he proposed to solve by convincing urban *rentiers* to invest in the domestic economy. Following a major famine in 1764, however, criticism of Neapolitan growth became unanimous and attempts were made to reduce the city's population and to 'repopulate' the countryside: for Giuseppe Maria Galanti, 'insofar as palaces are built in the capital, the provinces are deserted'.[20] Naples was decried as a parasitical consumer of agricultural rent, the refuge of a slothful and dangerous mass attracted by the city's privileged supply structure and its extensive charitable network.

The themes of the provincial urban system's dependence on the capital and of the stimulating or stunting effects of this vast pool of consumers and investors on the country as a whole have dominated twentieth-century historiography.[21] But although a better understanding

[19] See A. Genovesi, *Lettere accademiche sulla questione se sieno più felici gl'ignoranti che gli scienziati* (Naples, 1764), and his notes on the translation of John Cary, *Storia del Commercio della Gran Brettagna* (Naples, 1757).

[20] G. M. Galanti, *Della descrizione geografica e politica delle Sicilie* (1st edn, 1786–94), ed. F. Assante and D. Demarco, 2 vols. (Naples, 1969), vol. II, p. 160.

[21] For these aspects of the *philosophes'* debates on the capital's role, see B. Marin, 'Naples: capital of Enlightenment', in P. Clark and B. Lepetit (eds.), *Capital cities and their hinterlands in early modern Europe* (London, 1996), pp. 143–67.

of local circumstances is beginning to replace this traditional image of the kingdom with a more nuanced picture – in which, for example, Naples' relative loss of hegemony during the second half of the eighteenth century resulted in the strong growth of Bari – we still lack adequate studies of urban hierarchies, of their structure and their long-run development to challenge the received wisdom in full.[22]

Although the highest urban functions were largely concentrated in Naples, the only large city in the kingdom during the whole early modern period, a high proportion of the Mezzogiorno's population was nevertheless concentrated in settlements of urban dimensions, albeit all with fewer than 20,000 inhabitants. At the end of the eighteenth century, the country had nearly 5 million inhabitants distributed across 2,000 settlements.[23] In 1793, according to d'Angerio Filangieri, 180 centres had over 5,000 inhabitants, 41 of which (excluding Naples) had over 10,000; 24 per cent of the population resided in villages under 2,000, 50 per cent in centres between 2,000 and 7,700, and 26 per cent in centres with more than 7,700 inhabitants (Naples included). The centres, however, were administrative units that could correspond equally to a town and to a group of smaller villages, so the average size of the settlements was smaller than the sources suggest.[24]

During the early modern period there were no significant changes in the ranking of southern towns in the region's urban hierarchy. Shifts in the geographical distribution of the population did, however, have some effects on the network of towns. Thus, demographic recovery during the late seventeenth and eighteenth centuries, which began first in the capital's hinterland, led to a huge concentration of population within a 50–60 km radius around Naples: 43 per cent of the kingdom's population, including 10 per cent in the capital city alone, lived in this territory after 1750. This demographic concentration in the Neapolitan hinterland, which included the provinces of Terra di Lavoro, Principato Citra and Principato Ultra, gave rise to a dense network of small towns within

---

[22] For the many problems with using fiscal sources like the enumerations of hearths to reconstruct population movements in the past, see Villani, *Numerazioni dei fuochi*. From 1765 we dispose of statistical compilations drawn from the 'Stati delle anime', which were based in turn on parish registers; they were utilised by G. M. Alfano in his *Istorica descrizione del Regno di Napoli* (Naples, 1795) and *Compendio portatile di tutte le dodici provincie che compongono il Regno di Napoli* (Naples, 1798), and by L. Giustiniani, *Dizionario geografico ragionato del Regno di Napoli* (Naples, 1797–1805).

[23] G. Galasso, 'Gli insediamenti e il territorio', in G. Galasso, *L'altra Europa. Per un'antropologia storica del Mezzogiorno d'Italia* (Milan, 1982), p. 37, notes how the number of southern Italian settlements was decimated by the fourteenth-century demographic crisis, which transformed the surviving centres into 'peasant dormitories' (*dormitori contadini*).

[24] A. Filangieri, *Territorio e popolazione nell'Italia meridionale. Evoluzione storica* (Milan, 1979), pp. 158, 307ff.

the capital's orbit. Already towards 1595, the region of Principato Citeriore between the peninsula of Amalfi and Sorrento, Vesuvius and the Irno valley, numbered at least two towns of 15,000 inhabitants (Cava and Sanseverino) and a dozen centres over 5,000.[25] By the second half of the eighteenth century this area had fifty or so centres over 5,000 inhabitants with 45 per cent of the local population, and a large number of smaller but still substantial communities. Low birth and death rates point to better living standards than in most other provinces of the kingdom. The region around the capital maintained its primacy despite the fact that population grew faster in some provinces on the eastern, Adriatic side of the country, in part thanks to the commercial stimulus of Naples.[26]

Next to Campania the most urbanised province in the kingdom was Puglia. At the end of the eighteenth century, the region had sixteen towns over 10,000; Terra di Bari alone had a quarter of all the towns of this size in the entire kingdom. Its population had been highly concentrated since the sixteenth century, when 30 per cent of the province's inhabitants lived in only nine coastal towns.[27] Towns in Terra d'Otranto were smaller and more hierarchically ordered. In 1793 35 per cent of the population lived in 11 towns over 5,000 inhabitants; Lecce, with 30,000 inhabitants at the end of the sixteenth century and 14,000 in 1767 dominated the region.[28] Although eighteenth-century economic and demographic expansion helped the rapid growth of Bari, Barletta, Brindisi and Gallipoli, they had never previously challenged Lecce for regional leadership – a sign it has been said of the weakness of their urban functions and of their lack of commercial elites with regional ambitions.[29] Outside Campania and Puglia a few large towns like Reggio, Catanzaro and Cosenza in Calabria, could not make up for generally low rates of urbanisation. Some of these towns were surrounded by a 'Mediterranean garden' (*giardino mediterraneo*) of labour-intensive vineyards, olive groves and fruit trees, but elsewhere, for example around Foggia in Capitanata, extensive grain fields and pastures prevailed.

As we saw, despite the high degree of urban concentration in southern Italy, historians have emphasised the lack of truly urban functions in most centres in contrast with Neapolitan primacy. Terms such as

[25] A. Musi, 'Piccole e medie città', p. 155.
[26] P. Villani, *Mezzogiorno tra riforma e rivoluzione* (Bari, 1977), pp. 4, 96.
[27] A. Massafra, 'Terra di Bari, 1500–1600', in G. Galasso and R. Romeo (eds.), *Storia del Mezzogiorno*, 10 vols. (Rome, 1978–86), vol. VII, p. 520.
[28] M. A. Visceglia, 'Sviluppo e ruolo delle città di Terra d'Otranto tra Medioevo e prima età moderna', in Galasso and Romeo, *Storia del Mezzogiorno*, vol. VII, pp. 368ff.
[29] Galasso, *Alla periferia*, pp. 408ff.

'dormitory' and 'agro-towns' have frequently been used to imply the economic and cultural homogeneity between town and country in the Mezzogiorno in contrast with urban hegemony over the countryside further to the north.[30] While not challenging the importance of the southern countryside and of the social groups which based their leadership on the rural economy, recent studies have begun for the first time to engage directly with local urban societies, and are producing a picture of elite structure and formation, of social organisation and of conflict within local administrations, of economic organisation, patterns of control of and interaction with the countryside, and architectural and building policy that is far more sophisticated and varied than past stereotypes have allowed.

Town and country: contested dominion

One of the grounds for claiming that urban agglomerations in the Mezzogiorno were not 'true' towns has traditionally been the high proportion of agricultural labourers who resided behind town walls: 67.6 per cent in Barletta and up to 80 per cent in Gravina in the mid-eighteenth century, for example.[31] As G. M. Galanti noted in his *Relazione sulla Puglia peucezia* (1791), 'the peasant of Gravina and of Altamura must go up to 15 miles away to work'. The country was ever present in the towns where landlords and merchants gathered and processed agricultural goods: 'numerous peasants reside in every city and the rhythm of urban life is dictated by life in the fields and by the harvests'.[32] But towns also upheld the judicial and administrative framework of the state and had other significant ecclesiastical, economic and cultural functions. The largest centres were often the seat of provincial tribunals (*Udienze*) and of the fiscal administration (*Percettorie*), and some towns derived their main *raison d'être* from their administrative position. Lacking major commercial functions, Salerno, for example, built its urban identity increasingly on its military and administrative role within the Neapolitan state.[33]

Agricultural production was of course shaped and stimulated by urban demand, as a detailed study of the Conca di Bari shows. Bari was, within a radius of 15–20 km of the city, the only marketing centre for

[30] Galasso, 'Insediamenti', p. 58.
[31] B. Salvemini, 'Prima della Puglia. Terra di Bari e il sistema regionale in età moderna', in L. Masella and B. Salvemini (eds.), *Storia d'Italia. Le regioni dall'Unità ad oggi. La Puglia* (Turin, 1989), p. 120.
[32] G. Labrot, 'La città meridionale', in Galasso and Romeo, *Storia del Mezzogiorno*, vol. VIII, p. 221.
[33] A. Musi, 'Piccole e medie città', pp. 156–7.

the fruit, legumes and cheeses produced in its hinterland; olive oil was also exported from other ports, perhaps because it could be stored more easily. The town offered manufactures and services in exchange, which explains why the proportion of peasants living in Bari (44 per cent) was substantially lower than that in the *casali* (over 80 or even 90 per cent), despite the presence even in the latter of school teachers, doctors and notaries. Although patricians and merchants from Bari controlled the credit network, urban property was apparently weak.

Thus not all the kingdom's cities acted as dormitories for the rural hinterland; few rural labourers lived in Reggio Calabria, for example, even though the town was a major collecting and processing centre for rural produce.[34] Avellino, centre of the feudal 'state' of the Caracciolo, drew its wealth from the exploitation of water power and industrial and commercial activities.[35] Strong groups of merchants, shippers and artisans emerged in the eighteenth century in port towns like Monopoli, Bari, Giovinazzo, Molfetta and Bitonto that benefited from the growth of Adriatic trade and from a degree of independence from Naples' *annona*, in contrast with the agricultural centres of Capitanata and Terra d'Otranto, which were linked far more closely to Naples' merchant oligopoly.

Relations between towns and their *casali* were shaped by a range of administrative, judicial and fiscal privileges that the towns defended tooth and nail and which gave them a claim to primacy. Some cities disposed of rights over, and acted as administrative centres for, dozens of villages in their hinterland. Cosenza and its *casali* formed a single administrative unit anxious to protect its exemptions and usage rights in the Sila mountains against feudal hostility. At least eighteen towns had *casali* in Terra di Lavoro (Aversa thirty or so, Capua about forty, Nola twenty), and the same applies to a number of centres in Calabria and Puglia including Bari, Lecce, Tropea, Taranto and Reggio. On the other hand, the jurisdiction of some royal towns did not stretch beyond their walls, and in most feudal lands the baron controlled commercial activities and town–country relations, while urban magistracies had no say over the local market.

In Naples, the population of the *casali* was approximately a quarter of the city's; in Salerno, by contrast, the rural population was twice the size of the town. Although *casali* were defined legally 'members of the town body' (*casalia sunt pars corporis civitatis*) and should thus have enjoyed the latter's immunities and prerogatives, the villages were *de facto*

---

[34] A. Placanica, *La Calabria nell'età moderna*, vol. I: *Uomini, strutture, economie* (Naples, 1985).
[35] F. Barra, *Storia di Avellino* (Avellino, 1992).

subordinate. From 1590 Naples tried to turn might into right, by abolishing the fiscal privileges of its *casali* and levying new excise taxes in response to its financial difficulties, and in L'Aquila also, the town taxed rural produce sold on the town market.

From the early sixteenth century, the Spanish monarchy tried to reduce the towns' jurisdictional powers, which were of little benefit, by splitting up these *contadi* into numerous feudal lordships. This process, which resulted in the dismemberment of the rural hinterland of the largest cities in the kingdom,[36] was intensified by the sale in the seventeenth century of demesnial land, including many *casali* (also at Naples), in response to the poor conditions of royal finance. Towns, however, put up strong resistance to the erosion of their prerogatives. Bari, for example, was engaged in a running conflict with its *casali* and with the neighbouring feudal lords over its jurisdictional and administrative privileges, including the right to tax rural property and to exempt urban landholdings (*bonatenenza*), jurisdiction over two fairs held in the *casali*, and urban claims to a 'great territory' (*gran territorio*). Feudal lords opposed the town's legal jurisdiction over the *casali*, and the latter's inhabitants (*casalini*) tried increasingly to apply the *bonatenenza* to their benefit against urban landlords.[37] During the fifteenth and sixteenth centuries at Lecce, the barons of the *casali* tried to lay claim to the town's criminal jurisdiction, refused to pay the tax on oil and wine sold in the town, and contested the exemptions from the land tax granted to urban landlords.[38] In the same period Taranto lost the grazing rights that had previously underwritten its rural dominance. On the other hand, at L'Aquila in 1670, bearers of feudal rights in the countryside included ten patrician families, although the largest number was owned by the Neapolitan and Roman nobility.[39] Bari patricians and clergy owned a large proportion of the seigniorial rights over the *casali* at the end of the eighteenth century, but the local elites had already been drawing substantial feudal rents from the countryside by the early seventeenth century.[40] Urban landownership and credit seems to have been more common in the countryside around Capua, which may explain why the eighteenth-century Capuan *casali* appear to have been

[36] M. A. Visceglia, 'Dislocazione territoriale e dimensione del possesso feudale nel Regno di Napoli a metà Cinquecento', in M. A. Visceglia (ed.), *Signori, patrizi, cavalieri nell'età moderna* (Rome–Bari, 1992), p. 33.
[37] Russo, *Pellegrini e 'casalini'*.
[38] Visceglia, *Territorio*, p. 211.
[39] G. Sabatini, *Proprietà e proprietari a L'Aquila e nel contado. Le rilevazioni catastali in età spagnola* (Naples, 1995), pp. 84–5.
[40] Russo, *Pellegrini e 'casalini'*, p. 70.

more socially composite and stratified than those near Bari.[41] Relations between towns and their *casali* were thus very intense, notably in the matter of urban food supplies, and in some cases, as at Salerno, there is evidence of a degree of integration between town and *casali* in the manufacturing sector.[42]

Demographic and economic growth in the *casali* themselves gave rise to claims for administrative autonomy. These tensions surfaced more frequently in periods of political crisis, when the crown and the Neapolitan magistracies in Naples reinforced baronial action by supporting the claims of the *casali* against the larger towns. Town–country relations were thus neither purely antagonistic nor strictly bipolar, but were shaped by the state's and the feudal lords' strategy to divide and rule through the judicious use of political privilege.[43] Towns and *casali* appealed to central authority to adjudicate or mediate their claims, and central institutions responded actively to these requests.[44] The state guaranteed the towns' ancient customs and rights and dispensed administrative functions. Town–country relations interacted with, and were strongly conditioned by, monarchical and seigniorial power.[45] At Lecce, town–country relations were the outcome of a complex game that included the great feudal magnates, the lesser aristocracy and the urban patriciate.[46] At Bari, the contrast between feudalised *casali* and the city came to an end during the seventeenth century thanks to emerging relations of patronage between members of the urban patriciate and feudal lineages like the Carafa d'Andria and the Acquaviva of Conversano.[47]

The political reorganisation of the provinces, specifically the administrative functions granted by the Spanish state during the sixteenth and seventeenth centuries, was of crucial demographic and economic importance. In the case of Lecce, rapid growth brought about by its new institutional role also caused its subsequent undoing, because the profits of growth were spent on ostentatious display – most notably, in a rash of prestige secular and ecclesiastical buildings – rather than being reinvested in the local economy.[48] The effect of this was, nevertheless, to maintain Lecce's primacy even after its economic decline during the

---

[41] A. Lepre, *Terra di Lavoro nell'età moderna* (Naples, 1978), p. 70.

[42] A. Musi, 'La città assente: Salerno nella "provincializzazione" del Mezzogiorno spagnolo', *Rassegna storica salernitana* 10 (1988), 63–82.

[43] Visceglia, *Territorio*, pp. 199–200.

[44] See especially A. Spagnoletti, 'Ufficiali, feudatari e notabili. Le forme dell'azione politica nelle università meridionali', *Quaderni storici* 79 (1992), 231–61.

[45] Sabatini, *Proprietà*, p. 12.

[46] Visceglia, *Territorio*, p. 203.

[47] A. Spagnoletti, 'Il patriziato barese nei secoli XVI e XVII. La costruzione di una difficile egemonia', in Visceglia, *Signori, patrizi, cavalieri*, p. 115.

[48] Visceglia, *Territorio*, p. 16.

seventeenth century thanks to the symbolic capital accumulated by the new, Counter-Reformed monastic orders. Culture and religion could be important sources of urban hegemony.

The rediscovery of the city and town in the Mezzogiorno should not make us underestimate the extent to which the vast Neapolitan market conditioned rural development in the kingdom. Naples had a fundamental influence on the extension of cereal cultivation during the sixteenth century and on the levels and volatility of grain prices in the immediate hinterland of Capua, Aversa, Caserta and Nola.[49] In the countryside of Salerno, it has been argued, town–country relations were dominated not by Salerno itself but by Naples. 'The history of the entire region, the Principato Citeriore, can be divided into the history of an area focussed on Naples . . . and that of a different, marginal zone, the Cilento.'[50] As the development in Puglia of large-scale, extensive farms producing wheat for the Neapolitan market demonstrates, the capital's influence could be felt even in the more distant provinces.

Work in the 1970s by Paolo Macry on the grain trade and Patrick Chorley on oil and silk, which analysed the capital's influence on the provinces in the light of the eighteenth-century reformers' criticisms, seemed to offer a clear explanation of the South's economic backwardness. They showed that the contrast between capital and provinces so emphasised by the Neapolitan Enlightenment was not a mere figure of speech. To keep the capital supplied with cheap olive oil, for example, exports abroad were banned – a prohibition that 'would mean the sacrifice of the provinces to the capital'.[51] For Macry, the grain trade between the two was based on a 'colonial' relation, because the Neapolitan *annona* was controlled by a small group of local merchants who benefited from their privileged links with the food administration, the crown and the greater offices of state and were able to impose unfavourable conditions on the producers.[52]

Nevertheless, the capital's influence was not simply that of a parasite; as a center of consumption and a provider of capital it also played a constructive role in the development of certain regions.[53] The claim that the growing subordination of provincial agriculture to the capital's

---

[49] A. Lepre, 'Terra di Lavoro', in Galasso and Romeo, *Storia del Mezzogiorno*, vol. V, p. 190.

[50] A. Musi, ' "Ordini" e rapporti sociali tra XVI e XVII secolo', in A. Leone and G. Vitolo (eds.), *Guida alla storia di Salerno e della sua provincia* (Salerno, 1982), p. 232.

[51] P. Chorley, *Oil, silk and Enlightenment. Economic problems in XVIIIth century Naples* (Naples, 1965), p. 63.

[52] P. Macry, *Mercato e società nel Regno di Napoli. Commercio del grano e politica economica nel Settecento* (Naples, 1974), p. 47.

[53] See Marin, 'Naples'.

needs was a major economic constraint has been questioned for seven-teenth-century Puglia on the basis of trade flows from Barletta, which was the main grain-exporting port in the kingdom.[54] Although trade diversion from the international markets to Naples did occur after the mid-sixteenth century, the Neapolitan market sustained production in Puglia during the first half of the seventeenth century when foreign demand contracted. Yet, although 'dependency' on the capital enabled the region to sustain output and continue growing up to the 1650s, the monopolisation of the grain trade by the great Neapolitan and foreign merchants marginalised local entrepreneurship and nipped in the bud the development of more complex urban functions within the provinces, while the collapse of the Neapolitan market after the epidemic of 1656 caused a parallel crisis of grain production in Puglia. At Foggia, on the other hand, the alleged Neapolitan monopsonists controlled no more than 10 per cent of the traded grain, which left ample margins of manoeuvre for local intermediaries to stockpile local produce.[55]

Conclusion

In an overview of the historiography of the Mezzogiorno, Pasquale Villani remarked some years ago that, since the 1950s, historians had turned their attention away from the capital city to the rural world, from the intellectuals and the political elites to the peasantry and the rural bourgeoisie.[56] Urban history was nevertheless still subordinated to agrarian history; the term 'urban' was used in such a highly restrictive sense that it was considered inapplicable to many large southern Italian settlements during the ancien regime.[57] Since the late 1970s, however, this undifferentiated and monochromatic picture dominated by a single city, Naples, has begun to change, and the extent of the links between the provincial urban systems and the capital has begun to be examined in the light of a more detailed and nuanced understanding of the complex urban pattern of the Mezzogiorno. Southern Italian towns did not dominate their hinterlands, but this made their relations with the countryside more rather than less complex.

[54] E. Papagna, *Grano e mercanti nella Puglia del Seicento* (Bari, 1990).
[55] M. C. Nardella, 'Foggia: la cerealicultura e il rifornimento annonario della capitale in età moderna', in Russo, *Storia di Foggia*, p. 52.
[56] P. Villani, 'Un ventennio di ricerche: dai rapporti di proprietà all'analisi delle aziende e dei cicli produttivi', in A. Massafra (ed.), *Problemi di storia delle campagne meridionali nell'età moderna e contemporanea* (Bari, 1981), pp. 3–15.
[57] E. Di Ciommo, 'Piccole e medie città meridionali tra antico regime e periodo napoleonico', in *Villes et territoire pendant la période napoléonienne (France et Italie)* (Rome, 1987), p. 357.

Index

Lightning Source UK Ltd.
Milton Keynes UK
UKOW03f1811290114

225513UK00001B/57/A